CONSUMER PSYCHOLOGY IN A SOCIAL MEDIA WORLD

Consumer Psychology in a Social Media World seeks to illustrate the relevance of consumer psychology theory and research in understanding the social media world that has rapidly become a key component in the social and economic lives of most individuals. Despite the rapid and widespread adoption of social media by consumers, research focused on individuals' use thereof and its implications for organizations and society has been limited and published in scattered outlets. This has made it difficult for those trying to get either a quick introduction to or an in-depth understanding of the associated issues to locate relevant scientific-based information.

This collection of various streams of academic work on the topic of social and digital media is organized into four broad parts. Part I focuses on social media as a modern form of word of mouth, always considered the most impactful marketing technique on consumers. It also touches upon a motivational explanation for why social media has such a strong and broad appeal. Part II addresses the impact that consumers' switch to social media has had on marketers' branding and promotional efforts, as well as the ways in which consumer involvement can be maintained through this process. Part III takes a methodological perspective on the topic of social media, assessing ways in which big data consumer research is influenced by novel ways of gathering consumer feedback and gauging consumer sentiment. Finally, Part IV considers consumer welfare and public policy implications, including privacy and disadvantaged consumer concerns.

Consumer Psychology in a Social Media World will appeal to those who are involved in creating, managing, and evaluating products used in social media communications. As seen in recent financial and business market successes (e.g., Facebook, Twitter, LinkedIn, Instagram, Pinterest, WhatsApp, etc.), businesses focused on facilitating social media are part of the fastest growing and most valuable sector of today's economy.

Claudiu V. Dimofte is Associate Professor of Marketing at San Diego State University.

Curtis P. Haugtvedt is Associate Professor of Marketing at Ohio State University.

Richard F. Yalch is Professor of Marketing at the University of Washington.

CONSUMER PSYCHOLOGY IN A SOCIAL MEDIA WORLD

Edited by Claudiu V. Dimofte,
Curtis P. Haugtvedt, and
Richard F. Yalch

SCP
SOCIETY FOR CONSUMER PSYCHOLOGY

Routledge
Taylor & Francis Group
NEW YORK AND LONDON

First published 2016
by Routledge
711 Third Avenue, New York, NY 10017

and by Routledge
2 Park Square, Milton Park, Abingdon, Oxon OX14 4RN

Routledge is an imprint of the Taylor & Francis Group, an informa business

Library of Congress Cataloging-in-Publication Data
Consumer psychology in a social media world / edited by Claudiu V. Dimofte, Curtis P. Haugtvedt, and Richard F. Yalch.
pages cm
Includes bibliographical references and index.
1. Consumer behavior. 2. Social media. 3. Marketing—Social aspects. 4. Internet marketing. I. Dimofte, Claudiu V. II. Haugtvedt, Curtis P., 1958– III. Yalch, Richard.
HF5415.32.C65868 2015
658.8′342—dc23
2015015848

ISBN: 978-0-7656-4693-4 (hbk)
ISBN: 978-0-7656-4694-1 (pbk)
ISBN: 978-1-315-71479-0 (ebk)

Typeset in Bembo
by Apex CoVantage, LLC

CONTENTS

FIGURES

TABLES

ABOUT THE EDITORS

Claudiu V. Dimofte is Associate Professor of Marketing at San Diego State University. He researches topics that include implicit consumer cognition (e.g., unconscious processing of brand information), marketing metrics (e.g., scale development and validation), international marketing (e.g., cross-cultural consumer response to global brands), and the interface of marketing with operations and finance (e.g., consumer response to modular products and brand equity effects on stock performance). His research has been published in journals including the *Journal of Consumer Psychology*, the *Journal of Consumer Research*, *Management Science*, and the *International Journal of Research in Marketing*. He serves on the Editorial Board of the *Journal of Consumer Psychology*. Claudiu earned a PhD in marketing from the University of Washington's Foster School of Business.

Curtis P. Haugtvedt is Associate Professor of Marketing at Ohio State University. His primary program of research focuses on the general issue of persuasion and attitude strength. Curt's research has appeared in journals including the *Journal of Personality and Social Psychology*, the *Journal of Consumer Research*, and the *Journal of Consumer Psychology*. He has served as a member of Editorial Boards including those of the *Journal of Consumer Research*, *Journal of Consumer Psychology*, and the *Journal of Advertising*, is a former Associate Editor of the *Journal of Consumer Psychology*, and served as President of the Society for Consumer Psychology. He holds a BA in Sociology/Criminal Justice and a BS in Psychology from North Dakota State University and MA and PhD degrees in Experimental Social Psychology/Marketing from the University of Missouri-Columbia.

Richard F. Yalch is Professor of Marketing at University of Washington. He earned BS and MS degrees from Carnegie-Mellon University and a PhD from Northwestern University. His teaching and research interests are primarily in the area of consumer behavior, with an emphasis on its psychological aspects. Much of the research involves consumer responses to persuasive communications (e.g., verbal versus numerical attribute descriptions, social labeling, jingles, self-referencing, and polysemous slogans). He has served as Associate Editor for the *Journal of Consumer Research* and is currently on the Editorial Review Board of the *Journal of Consumer Psychology*. He co-chaired a Society for Consumer Psychology conference on Online Consumer Psychology in 2001.

CONTRIBUTORS

Jonah Berger, *University of Pennsylvania*

Jonah Berger is an Associate Professor of Marketing at the Wharton School of Business and an expert on word of mouth, social influence, consumer behavior, and how products, ideas, and behaviors catch on. He has published numerous articles in leading academic journals, and popular accounts of his work often appear in places like the *New York Times*, *Wall Street Journal*, and *Harvard Business Review*. Jonah's recent book, *Contagious: Why Things Catch On* is a *New York Times* and *Wall Street Journal* bestseller and hundreds of thousands of copies are in print in over 30 languages. He is a popular speaker at major conferences and events and has consulted for a variety of companies including Google, Coca-Cola, Disney, GE, Vanguard, Unilever, General Motors, 3M, Kaiser Permanente, and the Gates Foundation.

Barbara Bickart, *Boston University*

Barbara Bickart is Associate Professor of Marketing and Department Chair at the School of Management at Boston University. Her research examines how the context of communication influences consumers' inference and judgment processes. Current projects explore how consumers create connections (e.g., emotional, affinity, shared experiences) in the context of both consumer-to-consumer and business-to-consumer communication and how such connections influence the interpretation, perceived value, and persuasive impact of a message. Her work has appeared in journals including the *Journal of Marketing Research*, the *Journal of Consumer Research*, and the *Journal of Consumer Psychology*. She is currently an Associate Editor at the *Journal of Public Policy and Marketing*.

Ryan L. Boyd, *University of Texas*

Ryan L. Boyd is a doctoral candidate in Psychology at the University of Texas. His research interests include language and text analysis across domains, social processes, non-conscious processing of experience, self and self-concept, regulatory processes, psychological disorders, and mental health individual differences, as well as topics related to individuals' motives, values, attitudes, and drives. Ryan has a master's degree in Social and Health Psychology from North Dakota State University and a bachelor's degree in psychology from Indiana University-Purdue University in Fort Wayne, Indiana. His publications include articles in *Psychological Science*, the *Journal of Applied Social Psychology*, and the *Journal of Experimental Social Psychology*.

Frédéric Brunel, *Boston University*

Frédéric Brunel is Associate Professor of Marketing and Dean's Research Fellow at Boston University's School of Management. He is a consumer researcher dedicated to informing two main domains: consumer relationships and product design. His research resides at the intersection of social-psychology and cultural studies and focuses comprehensively on culture, group/community, and personality/gender levels of analyses. He has published in journals such as the *Journal of Consumer Research*, the *Journal of Consumer Psychology*, the *Journal of the Academy of Marketing Science*, and the *Journal of Advertising*. His teaching emphasizes the interdependences and connections between Marketing and other business functions. Frédéric holds a doctoral degree in Marketing from the University of Washington's Foster School of Business.

Eva C. Buechel, *University of South Carolina*

Eva C. Buechel is an Assistant Professor of Marketing at the Darla Moore School of Business, University of South Carolina. She received her doctoral degree from University of Miami, her master's degree from Carnegie Mellon University, and her bachelor's degree from University of Basel in Switzerland. Her research interests focus on the psychological processes that shape consumer judgments, decisions, and behaviors. Specifically, she examines how current experiential states affect cognitions, and how these in turn determine consumers' estimations of utility and value. Her research has appeared in Marketing and Psychology journals that include the *Journal of Consumer Research*, the *Journal of Personality and Social Psychology*, and *Emotion*.

Xi Chen, *Shanghai Normal University*

Xi (Jesse) Chen is currently affiliated with Shanghai Normal University in China. She conducted the research reported in this volume while she was a visiting scholar at the University of Washington in Seattle during the 2012–2013 academic year. During this time, she was completing her doctoral studies in the School of Media & Design at Shanghai Jiao Tong University.

Jenna Clark, *University of North Carolina*

Jenna Clark is a graduate student in Psychology at the University of North Carolina working on topics that include evaluating the outcomes of online social interaction and the impact of evidence type in persuasive communication on person perception.

Jeffrey L. Cohen, *Ball State University*

Jeffrey L. Cohen is a Distinguished Lecturer and Instructor in Marketing Analytics and Social Media in the Miller College of Business at Ball State University and the co-author of *The B2B Social Media Book* (Wiley, 2012). Jeff is also the co-founder and managing editor of SocialMediaB2B.com, the leading online resource for social media's impact on business-to-business Marketing. Jeff led the content Marketing team at salesforce.com, creating and publishing social media content to educate, inform, and entertain customers, prospects, advocates, and influences, all while driving traffic and sales leads. Jeff holds a Bachelor of Science degree in psychology from Duke University and a Master's of Arts degree in radio, television, and motion pictures from the University of North Carolina at Chapel Hill.

Catherine Cole, *University of Iowa*

Catherine Cole is Professor and Department Executive Officer in the Marketing Department at University of Iowa's Tippie College of Business. Her research interests include the effects of couponing on purchase and repeat purchase rates, elderly adults' use of consumer information, as well as measurements and effects of knowledge and experience on consumer behavior. Catherine's articles have appeared in journals including the *Journal of Consumer Psychology*, the *Journal of the Academy of Marketing Science*, and *Marketing Letters*. She holds a doctoral degree from the University of Wisconsin-Madison.

Maria L. Cronley, *Miami University*

Maria Cronley is Senior Associate Dean and Professor in the Marketing Department at the Farmer School of Business. She received a BS in Business from Bowling Green State University and a PhD in Marketing from the University of Cincinnati. Her primary research interests center on consumer judgment and decision processes, with specific emphasis in the areas of consumer inference and biased processing, persuasion, and health Marketing and communication. Maria has published in scholarly journals including the *Journal of Consumer Research*, the *Journal of Consumer Psychology*, the *Journal of Public Policy and Marketing*, the *Journal of Business Research*, and the *Journal of Experimental Psychology: Applied*. She has won more than two dozen awards and grants for her scholarship and teaching and serves on the Editorial Review Board of the *Journal of Consumer Psychology*.

Heather Johnson Dretsch, *NC State University*

Heather Johnson Dretsch is Assistant Professor of Marketing at NC State University' Poole College of Management. Her research interests include the topics of consumer co-creation and innovation, consumer brand relationships, non-conscious priming, and luxury branding. Her research has appeared in the *Journal of Consumer Psychology*. Heather received her doctoral degree in Marketing from the University of Maryland's Smith School of Business.

Susan Fournier, *Boston University*

Susan Fournier is Professor of Marketing, Questrom Professor in Management, and Faculty Director of the MBA Program at Boston University. Susan is credited with founding the brand relationships sub-field in Marketing and claims six best paper awards to her credit, including the Long-Term Contribution Award in Consumer Research and Emerald's Citations of Excellence Award for the top 50 articles in Management. Susan maintains a portfolio of research that explores the creation and capture of value through branding and brand relationships. She is a long-standing member of the Editorial Boards of the *Journal of Consumer Research*, *Journal of Marketing*, *Journal of Relationship Marketing*, *Journal of Business-to-Business Marketing*, and *Marketing Theory*. She serves as Senior Consulting Editor for *Journal of Brand Management* and sits on the Senior Advisory Board of the *Journal of Product and Brand Management*.

Sebastian Fritz, *Leibniz University of Hannover*

Sebastian Fritz is a research associate in the area of Marketing and Management at the Leibniz University of Hannover. He studied Economics at the Leibniz University of Hannover with an emphasis on Marketing, Human Resource Management, and Labor Economics.

Melanie C. Green, *University at Buffalo (SUNY)*

Melanie C. Green is an Assistant Professor in the Department of Communication at the University at Buffalo. Her research examines the power of narrative to change beliefs, including the effects of fictional stories on real-world attitudes. Melanie has examined narrative persuasion in a variety of contexts, from health communication to social issues. She has edited two books on these topics and has published numerous articles in leading psychology, communication, and interdisciplinary journals. Melanie has also investigated the influence of technology (in particular, television and the Internet) on social capital, and the ways in which trust can develop in online relationships. She holds a doctoral degree from the Ohio State University.

Jennifer L. Harris, *Yale University*

Jennifer L. Harris is Director of Marketing Initiatives at the Rudd Center for Food Policy & Obesity. She is responsible for the Rudd Center's research initiatives to understand the extent and impact of children's exposure to food advertising and communicate that information to the health community, parents, and policy makers. Jennifer received an MBA in Marketing from the Wharton School at the University of Pennsylvania and a PhD in Social Psychology at Yale University where she worked with John Bargh. Jennifer's research focuses on marketing and public health, with an emphasis on unconscious effects of food marketing on behaviors, attitudes, and motivation in children and adults. She has written on the psychological effects of food marketing to children and teens and the need to reduce unhealthy food marketing through public policy and advocacy.

Amy Heard, *Loyola University Chicago*

Amy Heard is a doctoral student at Loyola University in Chicago specializing in child and adolescent clinical psychology. She graduated from Washington University in St. Louis with a dual degree in Psychology and Spanish. After working for a year in contracts, Amy decided to pursue her passion for psychology and spent two years as a research assistant at the Rudd Center for Food Policy and Obesity at Yale University. In graduate school she conducts research on childhood obesity prevention and treatment.

Nadine Hennigs, *Leibniz University of Hannover*

Nadine Hennigs is an Assistant Professor at the Institute of Marketing and Management, Leibniz University of Hannover. Nadine completed her studies in economics at the University of Hannover. She focuses on the areas of marketing and management of organizations. She has won several best paper awards at various international conferences.

Heather Honea, *San Diego State University*

Heather Honea completed her doctoral research at the University of California, Berkeley, and she is currently an Associate Professor of Marketing at San Diego State University's College of Business Administration and a Research Fellow at the college's Centre for Integrated Marketing Communications. Heather's background in psychology and economics frame her different research areas and allows her to bring a unique perspective to the digital Marketing process. She also researches the impact of green and decentralized technologies on business, society, and consumer behavior.

Jinfeng (Jenny) Jiao, *University of Iowa*

Jinfeng (Jenny) Jiao is a doctoral candidate in Marketing at University of Iowa. Her areas of expertise include the topics of self and brand relationships, moral judgment and pro-social behaviors, as well as emotion and goal pursuit.

Yogesh Joshi, *University of Maryland*

Yogesh Joshi is an Associate Professor at the Robert H. Smith School of Business at the University of Maryland. He works in the areas of Marketing and innovation and his research focuses on strategic marketing decisions, product differentiation, brand strategy, social influence, the diffusion of innovations, and new product development. His research has been published in journals including *Marketing Science*, *Management Science*, and the *Journal of Marketing Research.* In 2011, he was recognized as a *Marketing Science Institute Young Scholar.* He holds a PhD in Marketing from the Wharton School at the University of Pennsylvania, SM in Engineering from the Massachusetts Institute of Technology, and a B.Tech. in Mechanical Engineering from the Indian Institute of Technology, Bombay.

Frank R. Kardes, *University of Cincinnati*

Frank R. Kardes is the Donald E. Weston Professor of Marketing at the Carl H. Lindner College of Business at the University of Cincinnati. Frank is a recipient of the Distinguished Scientific Achievement Award of the Society for Consumer Psychology and a Fellow of five professional societies. His research focuses on consumer persuasion, judgment, inference, and decision making. He has published in and has served on the Editorial Boards of leading journals including the *International Journal of Research in Marketing*, the *Journal of Consumer Psychology*, the *Journal of Consumer Research*, and the *Journal of Marketing Research.* He holds a doctoral degree in Psychology from Indiana University.

Amna Kirmani, *University of Maryland*

Amna Kirmani is Professor of Marketing at the Robert H. Smith School of Business at the University of Maryland. Her research interests include consumers' inferences of product quality from Marketing signals, consumers' use of persuasion knowledge, and branding. Amna's work has been published in journals including the *Journal of Consumer Research*, the *Journal of Marketing Research*, the *Journal of Marketing*, and the *Journal of Consumer Psychology*. Her articles have won the Paul Green Award in the *Journal of Marketing Research*, the Maynard Award in the *Journal of Marketing*, and the Best Paper Award in the *Journal of Advertising*. Amna serves on the Editorial Boards of the *Journal of Consumer Research*, the *Journal of Marketing Research*, and the *Journal of Marketing*. She is also the current Editor of the *Journal of Consumer Psychology*.

Dale Kunkel, *University of Arizona*

Dale Kunkel is Professor of Communication at the University of Arizona. He studies children and media issues from diverse perspectives, including television effects research as well as assessments of media industry content and practices. He is a former Congressional Science Fellow, and has testified as an expert witness on children's media topics at numerous hearings before the U.S. Senate, the U.S. House of Representatives, and the Federal Communications Commission. Among the topics Dale examines are the effects of television violence, sexual content, and advertising on young people. He holds a PhD degree from the Annenberg School at the University of Southern California.

Sascha Langner, *Leibniz University of Hannover*

Sascha Langner is a research associate in the area of Marketing and Management at the Leibniz University of Hannover. His research focuses on consumer behavior, consumer empowerment, open source marketing, word-of-mouth marketing, customer satisfaction, Internet marketing, and advertising.

Susan Powell Mantel, *Ball State University*

Susan Powell Mantel is the chairperson of the Department of Marketing and a Professor of Marketing at the Miller College of Business, Ball State University. Her research interests include consumer information processing, judgment and inference processes, decision making in a sales setting, and Marketing and sales strategy. She has authored articles in these areas that have been published in business and Marketing journals including the *Journal of Consumer Research*, the *Journal of Consumer Psychology*, the *Journal of Operations Management*, the *Journal of Business Research*, *Psychometric Bulletin and Review*, and *Psychology & Marketing*, as well as national conference proceedings of the Association of Consumer Research, the American Marketing Association, and the Society for Consumer Psychology. Susan received her bachelor's degree in computer science and business from Bowling Green State University and her MBA and doctorate in Marketing from the University of Cincinnati.

Yupin Patarapongsant, *Chulalongkorn University*

Yupin Patarapongsant is a faculty member at Chulalongkorn University's SASIN graduate Institute of Business Administration. Her research interests span the areas of marketing management and social marketing. She has been a visiting assistant professor of Marketing at Rutgers University and the State University of New Jersey and an instructor at the University of Illinois at Urbana Champagne where she received her doctorate degree.

James W. Pennebaker, *University of Texas*

James W. Pennebaker is the Regents Centennial Professor of Liberal Arts and the Departmental Chair in the Psychology Department at the University of Texas. He and his students are exploring natural language use, group dynamics, and personality in educational and other real world settings. His earlier work on expressive writing found that physical health and work performance can improve by simple writing and/or talking exercises. His cross-disciplinary research is related to linguistics, clinical and cognitive psychology, communications, medicine, and computer science. James is the author or editor of nine books and over 250 academic articles and has received numerous awards and honors.

Martin A. Pyle, *Ryerson University*

Martin A. Pyle is an Assistant Professor at the Tod Rogers School of Management at Ryerson University. His research interests primarily lie in the dual domains of self-presentation and social comparison and how these theories apply to consumers' choices regarding the appeal of media depictions of violence. In addition, he is also pursuing a research stream in the area of word-of-mouth (WOM), focusing on how consumers use their WOM to present certain image. His work has been published in the *Journal of Advertising* as well as presented and numerous major conferences.

Steffen Schmidt, *Leibniz University of Hannover*

Steffen Schmidt studied Economics at the University of Hannover. His research interests span the areas of marketing, economics, and computer science. In particular, Steffen is interested in consumer behavior, brand research, customer satisfaction, neuropsychology, and neuroscience.

Tejvir Sekhon, *Boston University*

Tejvir Sekhon is a doctoral candidate in Marketing at Boston University School of Management. He is primarily interested in understanding consumers' use of brands for self-presentation on social media and its downstream consequences for consumers and brands. Theoretically, his research seeks a more nuanced characterization of the word-of-mouth phenomenon beyond the current view focused primarily on recommendations. Tejvir's research encourages marketers to pay attention to not only the frequency of brand mentions but also to the context in which their brands are being mentioned on social media. He holds a bachelor's degree in computer engineering from Delhi University and an MBA from the Indian Institute of Management (IIM), Lucknow.

Andrew N. Smith, *Merrimack College*

Andrew N. Smith is an Assistant Professor of Marketing at the Girard School of Business and International Commerce, Merrimack College. He holds a PhD in business administration (Marketing) from the Schulich School of Business, York University, as well as MSc. (Marketing) and B. Comm. (Commerce) degrees from the Queen's School of Business, Queen's University. Andrew's research broadly focuses on the field of social media and intersects with studies on word-of-mouth, branding, market systems, and consumption communities and culture. He has published his work in venues such as the *Journal of Interactive Marketing* and presented it at a variety of conferences, workshops, and invited talks in North America and Europe. Andrew's research has been supported by competitive external funding grants and awards, including the Association of Consumer Research/Sheth dissertation award for public policy research.

Cansu Sogut, *Boston University*

Cansu Sogut is a doctoral candidate in Marketing at the Boston University School of Management. She holds a BA degree in Business Administration from Koc University in Turkey and a Master of Philosophy (MPhil) degree in Innovation, Strategy, and Organization from the University of Cambridge Judge Business School. Cansu's primary areas of interest are word-of-mouth, social influence, and social media. She is currently investigating the effect of timing of sharing a word-of-mouth message on the audience (e.g., persuasiveness of WOM) and on the affective content. In another project, she examines the effect of simultaneous sharing (e.g., live-tweeting) on consumption enjoyment of the viewed content and how it changes the nature of the experience for the sharer.

Marlene Morris Towns, *Georgetown University*

Marlene Morris Towns is the academic director at the Georgetown Institute for Consumer Research, and a Teaching Professor at Georgetown University's McDonough School of Business. She received a bachelor's degree from the McIntire School of Commerce, University of Virginia, with concentrations in Marketing and Management and a PhD in Marketing from Duke University with a concentration in consumer behavior. Before her current position, Towns was an Assistant Professor of Marketing at Georgetown University and an Assistant Professor of Clinical Marketing at the University of Southern California's Marshall School of Business. Her research has been published in journals including the *Journal of Marketing*, the *Journal of Consumer Affairs*, and *the Journal of Public Policy and Marketing.*

Remi Trudel, *Boston University*

Remi Trudel is an Assistant Professor of Marketing at the Boston University School of Management. His research focuses on consumers' health, financial, and sustainable decision-making. He has published articles in the *Journal of Consumer Research*, *Journal of Marketing Research*, *Journal of Consumer Psychology*, the *International Journal of Research in Marketing*, and *MIT Sloan Management Review*. In 2012, he was awarded the Broderick Prize for excellence in research scholarship at the Boston University School of Management. Trudel joined Boston University in July of 2009 after earning his PhD from the Ivey Business School at the University of Western Ontario.

Klaus-Peter Wiedmann, *Leibniz University of Hannover*

Klaus-Peter Wiedmann is a Chaired Professor of Marketing and Management and the Director of the Institute of Marketing and Management at the Leibniz University Hannover in Germany. He is also Deputy Chair of the Academy of Global Business Advancement (AGBA) and is a Visiting Professor at the Henley Business School at the University of Reading, UK. His main subjects of research include social marketing, international marketing, innovation and technology, brand and reputation management, as well as marketing research and online/mobile marketing. In these areas Klaus-Peter has published over 600 academic publications. He has received awards from the American Marketing Association and has been appointed as Editorial Board Member of five international journals.

Issariya Woraphiphat, *North Bangkok University*

Issariya Woraphiphat has a doctoral marketing degree from the SASIN Business School at Chulalongkorn University and she is currently the Deputy Chief of the Academic Department at the Siam Business Administration College (SBAC), North Bangkok University. Issariya's research interests span topics that include digital marketing, social media marketing, and relationship marketing.

PREFACE

This book illustrates the relevance of consumer psychology theory and research to understanding the social media world that has rapidly become a key component in most individuals' social and economic lives. Despite consumers' rapid and widespread adoption of social media, research focused on individuals' use thereof and its implications for organizations and society has been limited and published in diverse outlets. This has made it difficult for those trying to get either a quick introduction or an in-depth understanding of social media issues to locate relevant scientific-based information. The authors of the chapters gathered in this book are experienced observers of the social media world and present valuable perspectives based on their observations and original research.

This collection of various streams of academic work on the topic of social and digital media is organized into four parts. Part I focuses on social media as a modern form of word of mouth (usually considered the most impactful influence on consumers) and proposes motivational explanations for its strong and broad appeal. Part II addresses the effect that consumers' switching their preferred information channel to social media has had on marketers' branding and promotional efforts. It also explores ways in which marketers can maintain consumer involvement in social media. Part III employs a methodological perspective on social media, assessing ways in which big data and innovative research methods are being used to gather consumer feedback and gauge consumer sentiment, in some cases simultaneously with the consumption or communication event. Finally, Part IV considers consumer welfare and public policy implications, including privacy and disadvantaged consumer concerns.

The topics covered in this book should appeal to those who are involved in creating, managing, and evaluating products using social media communications. The recent financial and business market successes of firms like Facebook,

Twitter, LinkedIn, Instagram, Pinterest, and WhatsApp is evidence of social media's effect on the economy as well as the culture. Facilitating social media is one of the fastest growing and most valuable sectors in today's economy, but its relative newness and dynamic structure suggests that opportunities exist to more effectively employ it to reach consumers. The work presented here should also appeal to those doing research aimed at better understanding social media. These researchers can be found in many university departments including business (especially marketing and organizational behavior), psychology, sociology, economics, anthropology, communications, and education, as well as within business, government, and non-profit organizations. Finally, the book may appeal to those who are actively involved in social media at either end of the communication spectrum (e.g., bloggers, twitter followers, etc.). As research clearly shows, virtually everyone interacts in some way via social media so the issues discussed in this volume will likely resonate with a wide audience. Last, social media's ever increasing integration with traditional communication methods that have moved to the internet such as telephone, television, radio, magazines, and newspaper suggest that these channels for communication may not be studied in the future without considering their related social media. For example, the comments posted in response to newspaper articles are often more informative than the original associated articles and may be more influential in shaping public opinion.

Part I opens with a chapter that nicely summarizes the main motivators that seem to underline consumers' growing engagement with social media. In it, Buechel and Berger (Chapter 1) propose that the need for affiliation, self-expression, identity representation, and information dissemination are the leading drivers of consumers' use of a new type of media defined by virtual interactions wherein users create, share, and exchange user-generated content. Next, Sekhon, Bickart, Trudel, and Fournier (Chapter 2) further argue that consumer self-presentation is a major driver of word-of-mouth (WOM) communication and that in their use of social media, consumers' related use of brand mentions can potentially be seen as bragging. Then, they propose that consumers try to avoid being perceived negatively as braggarts by employing strategically placed brand mention tactics, a proposition whose validity the authors then test empirically. Chapter 3 was written by Powell Mantel, Cronley, Cohen, and Kardes and looks at consumers as receivers of a significant amount of electronic WOM communications that reaches them from various sources and contexts and produces varied responses. The specific relationships that they report should inform marketers of ways to target consumers who are increasingly cynical and resistant to traditional marketing communications. Based on their empirical results, the authors suggest that modern marketers should facilitate consumer conversations and narrate brand stories to engage consumers and motivate them to share their experiences with others. Sogut, Bickart, and Brunel (Chapter 4) then present an intriguing account of the importance that the timing of consumers' sharing of consumption experiences has on the content of their electronic WOM. In short, they find that there is more consumer engagement if sharing occurs during rather than post consumption. Thus, they suggest that astute brand managers should encourage simultaneous rather than retrospective brand-related WOM. Smith and Pyle (Chapter 5) then provide a qualitative analysis of visual electronic WOM to highlight the specific types of consumer value associated with visually oriented WOM. Beyond the value of actually seeing the product and receiving related product usage information, the authors find that opinion seekers also derive social, emotional, and aesthetic value from this type of social media. In Chapter 6, Morris Towns provides a framework for understanding the new consumer-related social and digital media within the 4Ps context of classic marketing and the consumer-marketer and consumer-consumer communication dyads. Importantly, the framework argues that not all social media are created equal when it comes to eliciting consumer interest or engagement. Much like consumers and brands develop, project, and promote specific personalities, the author proposes that media platforms are similarly associated with specific (and different) personalities. To complete the discussion of motivational drivers for consumer social media engagement, Jiao and Cole (Chapter 7) examine consumer goals and, in particular, how goal publicity, perceived controllability, feedback, and goal value affect consumer motivation to engage with social media. Based on their findings, these authors suggest that managers use social media in a manner that encourages consumers to set goals.

Part II places more emphasis on the management side of the social-media-enabled communication process and evaluates strategies that firms should consider in their social media related advertising and branding decisions. In this context, Dretsch and Kirmani (Chapter 8) suggest brand co-creation as a particular strategy that can induce a higher level of consumer engagement. Their empirical results demonstrate that consumers' participation in interactive brand campaigns can lead to desirable pro-brand behaviors, and that such engagement effects can occur even when brand-related social media interactions are brief in duration (on the order of mere minutes). Communicators can glean further guidance from the work of Green and Clark (Chapter 9), who assess some specific variables that may influence the effectiveness of social media communications. In the process, these authors suggest that the choice of which communication medium to employ conveys information in itself to an audience, independent of the content of the persuasive appeal placed therein. Where attempted consumer engagement with social media occurs and audience characteristics matter in terms of the ultimate effectiveness of these attempts. They find that audiences who perceive high reality in social media communications tend to react most favorably to reality-oriented social media messages. In Chapter 10, Yalch and Chen explore the use of social media to disseminate favorable and unfavorable brand information acquired via social media. Their findings show that that high and low brand commitment consumers differ in their forwarding decisions primarily because of their underlying motivations: low commitment consumers seek to provide useful information to others with little consideration of the negative information's effect on a brand, whereas high commitment consumers evidence more concern about the brand. Consequently, when forwarding negative information, they are likely to include disclaimers and counterarguments. Thus, brand managers might consider enlisting committed brand users in their efforts to reduce the effect of negative information being spread via social media. Langner, Schmidt, Fritz, Hennigs, and Wiedmann (Chapter 11) report on their online test of established persuasion techniques in a social media context. For hotels varying in attractiveness, they report that offering social proof (number of customers endorsing the product) was more effective than communicating scarcity (only one room left) in encouraging individuals to recommend the hotel to others. However, the actual quality of the accommodations seemed to matter the most, suggesting a limit to how much consumers could be persuaded to promote an inferior product.

Part III takes an analytical perspective on the social media topic, beginning with a general assessment of the importance of big data in today's marketplace. In her work, Honea (Chapter 12) reiterates how the deluge of data available on consumers and their behaviors often originates with and is analyzed by the consumers themselves. The author discusses the concept of *personal analytics*, which encompasses data provided via people's self-monitoring (e.g., tracking health and wellness, providing social media content, etc.) and suggests several ways in which consumers can be further encouraged to willingly provide such marketer-relevant data. In Chapter 13, Joshi then argues for the need to make appropriate sense of big data in a manner that renders the emerging insights valid and strategically actionable. Importantly, he suggests methods for automating data collection and classifying it into advertising-theory relevant metrics. Developing standardized procedures is an important step in simplifying the study of big data as well as increasing big data's validity. The measurement of verbal consumer information is further discussed by Boyd and Pennebaker in Chapter 14. After briefly reviewing the history of content classification, they present their own methods for analyzing language using dictionary-based and vocabulary-based approaches to assessing language. The goal of their method is to help derive metrics that are psychologically meaningful across domains and research interests.

Part IV offers a note of caution regarding potential downsides to social and digital media usage. In this context, Harris, Heard, and Kunkel (Chapter 15) show how unscrupulous marketers can engage in improper, stealth targeting of underage consumers via social media that results in an excessive desire for unhealthy foods and beverages among young people. In their study, the authors created fictional Facebook accounts for two typical 13-year-old boys and found that over a two-week period each boy received a significant amount of daily marketing messages from brands that were initially provided a simple "like" feedback. Given that children at this age may not be able to appropriately process promotional content that reaches them and correctly perceive it as an attempt to sway their product choices, there is a clear consumer welfare implication associated with brand engagement attempts by marketers of unhealthy foods that is worth careful consideration. By documenting the presence of such activity in the largely unregulated world of social media, the authors demonstrate the need for individuals (e.g., parents, public health officials) to accept responsibility for preventing undesirable responses to social media information. In the second to last chapter (Chapter 16), Patarapongsant and Woraphiphat address the link between the consumption of violent social media and violent behavior. Their study focuses on factors influencing adolescents' preference for violent media consumption and on ways to mitigate the appeal of such media. In employing data from Thailand, this research attests to the global, universal nature of the social and digital media issues discussed in this book and in particular the dangers that younger consumers may be faced with during their interactions across these modern channels. Finally, Chapter 17 by Haugtvedt discusses data collection and data use issues that are central to the social media tools consumers use routinely. In the process, the author highlights relevant privacy issues of which many consumers and marketers appear to be unaware or unconcerned.

In conclusion, the book provides a brief overview of marketing and consumer psychology topics that have been affected by the advent and adoption of social media channels. In it, the chapter authors and book co-editors provide a basic (albeit academic research-based) level of understanding of several important issues such as: why social and digital media have significant appeal for consumers, how marketers can create consumer engagement and obtain actionable big data from it, but also what the perils may be for these social trends among consumers who cannot always detect the marketing element that underlies some of their social media interactions. Given the newness and complexity of the social media issues, we will not be surprised if many readers end up with more questions than answers about the effects of social media after reading various chapters in this book. Beyond merely stimulating psychological research on social media behaviors, we also expect that this book will be a valuable reference for those interested in what may prove to be the most important context for studying consumer behavior in the 21st century.

Claudiu V. Dimofte, Curtis P. Haugtvedt, and Richard F. Yalch

PART I

Consumer Engagement With Social Media

1

MOTIVATIONS FOR CONSUMER ENGAGEMENT WITH SOCIAL MEDIA

Eva C. Buechel and Jonah Berger

Social media is a form of virtual interaction whereby users create, share, and exchange user-generated content (Kaplan and Michael, 2010). Particularly popular examples of social media are online social networks. Online social networks (OSNs) allow users to create profiles and link them with profiles of other users in the network (Boyd and Ellison, 2007). Whereas OSNs differ in the various features they provide or emphasize, they have in common that they allow users to interact with each other, for example by sharing content such as short messages (i.e., microblogs), pictures, videos, and/or private messages to which other users in their network can respond.

Since their inception, OSNs have experienced immense popularity. As of 2010, 75% of American Internet users visited social networks regularly, and an average user spent over three hours a day on these sites. Facebook is the most prominent and popular online social network, with over 200 million users in America and well over a billion users worldwide. Surveys show that over 60% of Facebook users log in to the site daily, 28% of whom report doing so even before getting out of bed in the morning. The second most popular online social network is Twitter, with over 500 million users worldwide. About half of Twitter users log in and tweet daily, resulting in over 500 million tweets per day (Bullas, 2014). These two most popular OSNs are just the top of a long list of other OSNs such as Instagram, Google+, Pinterest, and Tinder, to name a few.

The number of online social networks and the amount of time users spend on these sites demonstrate that networking sites are immensely popular, having become an integrated part of our lives. They have influenced the way we spend time, the way we communicate, and the way we form and cultivate relationships. But why do people in general and consumers in particular use these sites in the first place, and what drives people to use them so often? And how do these sites impact their users?

The present chapter first summarizes and organizes existing literature on the antecedents and consequences of consumer online social network use. We then report on our own research investigating why consumers use a particularly popular feature on online social networks, namely the microblogging feature. The chapter ends with a discussion of the remaining questions pertaining to online social network use, as well as implications and suggestions for future research.

Literature Review: Antecedents and Consequences of Online Social Network Use

With the rise of online social network use, researchers have turned to attempting to understand why online social networks are so popular, what motivates consumers to use them, and how they impact the users of these sites (Wilson et al., 2012). A survey and synthesis of the current literature on social media seems to suggest that consumers engage in online social networking for three key reasons, which we discuss in turn.

Affiliation

Perhaps the most important motivator of online social network use is our desire to socialize and connect with others (Hoffman and Novak, 2012; Wilson et al., 2012). People have a high need to belong, and social relationships are critical for our well-being (Bessière et al., 2008; Bowlby, 1977; Burleson, 1998; Harlow, 1961; Stroebe and Stroebe, 1996). Online social networks cater to this need by allowing users to connect with other users in the network. They allow users to search and befriend new and existing social ties, thus providing a practical and easy way to connect and keep in touch with a broad set of friends, even the ones who are geographically removed.

Accordingly, research has found that the need for affiliation and social interaction is a main driver for ONS use (Ellison et al., 2007; Joinson, 2008). A qualitative survey asking people about the motivations to use Facebook revealed that "keeping in touch," "reconnecting with old friends," and "virtual people-watching" were the most mentioned reasons for Facebook use, and that these activities also yielded the most enjoyment (Joinson, 2008). Furthermore, research has found that the extent of online social network use is driven by an appreciation for social interaction. For example, extroverts, who take pleasure in being social, spend more time and have a greater number of social ties on online social networks (Gosling et al., 2011; Ross et al., 2009; Wilson et al., 2010).

Whereas it is clear that the social aspects of OSNs drive their use, researchers have been interested in how online social networks are impacting users' communication behavior and consumers' well-being. To what extent are online social networks replacing offline interactions and how do interactions on these sites fulfill users' need for affiliation?

Many researchers and philosophers have expressed concerns that the shift to online communication with close friends—as opposed to more traditional forms of offline communication—may have harmful effects on the users and their relationships, leaving them depressed and lonely (Kraut et al., 1998; Tonioni et al., 2012; Yoffe, 2009). The main worry is that the Internet reduces valuable face-to-face interaction with peers and family members, thus detracting from meaningful relationships and diminishing social capital (Green and Brock, 2008; Nie, 2001). Interestingly, initial correlational research investigating the impact of OSN use on social capital suggests that these concerns may not be warranted. Ellison, Steinfield, and Lampe (2007) surveyed undergraduate students about their Facebook usage and their sense of affiliation. They found that higher intensity of Facebook usage was actually associated with higher self-reported social capital and decreased loneliness (Ellison et al., 2007).

Yet, follow-up research points to an important caveat to this finding. Users on OSNs are usually linked to a large group of social connections (the median number of Facebook friends is above 200—Smith, 2014), including strong offline ties with whom they interact directly, as well as weaker ties whom they follow in a more passive manner (Burke et al., 2010; Toubia and Stephen, 2013). Burke and colleagues (2010) found that online interaction with close friends (e.g., direct messaging, commenting, liking) leads to greater social capital and less loneliness, whereas the mere following of online friends did not have the same beneficial effect on users' well-being. The passive consumption of content posted by others actually increased loneliness (Wise et al., 2010; Valkenburg and Peter, 2007). This pattern suggests that the consequences of online social networks depend on how these sites are used. Active online interaction with strong social ties might possibly substitute offline interaction to a certain degree, such that online social networks can promote stronger relationships and well-being. However, this is not true for all online social network use; passive online networking might have negative effects on users.

This finding is important because existing online social networks differ in the type of social ties and interaction they foster. Some online social networks encourage interactions with stronger ties. For instance, Facebook users tend to initiate, maintain, and strengthen friendships with people with whom they also have an offline connection, as opposed to meeting new people (Ellison et al., 2007). Other online social networks (e.g., Twitter, Instragram, Pinterest), on the other hand, encourage connections with weaker ties. These sites encourage users to "follow" other users (friends, public figures, celebrities) without being followed by them in a bidirectional manner (Toubia and Stephen, 2013). If sites such as Facebook encourage active interaction with relatively close ties, whereas other sites (e.g., Twitter) encourage passive online social networking behavior, then the consequences of online social network may not be uniform and likely depend on the platform used. Sites such as Facebook might increase consumer welfare, whereas sites such as Twitter or Instagram may have more detrimental effects on consumer welfare.

To summarize, affiliation is an important, if not the most important motivator for online social network use. Whether users reap the benefits from social interaction on these sites, however, may depend on the nature of the platform, the quality of social ties, and the nature of the interaction with said ties.

Self-Expression and Identity Representation

Another motivator for online social network use that has received attention in the literature is the fact that they allow for self-expression and identity representations (Buffardi and Campbell, 2008; Kraut et al., 1998; Nadkarni and Hoffman, 2012). Online social networks allow users to share content such as biographical information, interests, activities, thoughts, and photos with other users, thus providing an avenue to portray an online version of themselves on these sites.

Users seem to be eager to share information about themselves with other users. The majority of Facebook users disclose their biographical information, their interests and hobbies, as well as their political and dating preference on their Facebook accounts (Gross and Acquisti, 2005). Furthermore, 293,000 statuses and 136,000 photos are uploaded on Facebook per minute (Noyes, 2014), informing social ties about users' current activities, experiences, and thoughts. The amount of self-relevant content and the eagerness with which content is shared on these sites is reflective of the fact that self-representation is a key driver of online social network use.

But how do users represent themselves on these sites? Researchers have wondered whether users on online social networks portray their real identity when they are managing their online social network profiles, or whether they portray an idealized version of themselves.

On the one hand, one could argue that Facebook represents an extension of people's offline environment by mirroring offline interactions in which people can connect and communicate with their social ties. As previously mentioned, extraverts, who enjoy social interaction offline, also spend more time on online social networks (Gosling et al., 2011; Ross et al., 2009; Wilson et al., 2010). Similarly, narcissists have been shown to share more self-indulgent content online (Ryan and Xenos, 2011). It is therefore reasonable to assume that users display their real self (or offline self) on these networks (Gosling et al., 2007).

On the other hand, OSNs allow for deliberate and selective information sharing. Unlike offline representations and interactions, users can choose which parts of their lives to share and selectively post online, or they can delete unflattering contents posted by others (Wilcox and Stephen, 2013). In addition, they have time to construct and refine what to say (Berger and Iyengar, 2012). Some researchers have therefore argued that, as a result, users represent themselves in an idealized and more interesting way, one that is not always reflective of reality (Gonzales and Hancock, 2011; Wilcox and Stephen, 2013).

Back and colleagues (2010) were interested in testing the two competing predictions empirically. To examine whether online representations were extensions of the offline self (extended real-life hypothesis) or whether they represented an idealized version of users (virtual-identity hypothesis), they used a simple but clever set-up. They recruited OSN users, all of whose OSN profiles had been saved before the study. They then asked these target participants to fill out a personality inventory that measured the users' self-reported Big Five personality traits (Extroversion, Openness, Neuroticism, Conscientiousness, and Agreeableness). In addition, they asked four close acquaintances to judge the target's personality using the same personality inventory. The five measures were then aggregated to represent the target participant's "real self." Target participants were asked to fill out the same inventory a second time, this time asking them to describe themselves how they ideally would be. This represented the target's "ideal self." The researchers then asked independent observers to examine the target participant's OSN profile and fill out the personality inventory based on the inferred personality traits, which represented the "observed self." What they found is that the "observed self" more closely resembled users' "real self" than their "ideal self," implying that profiles more closely reflect users' actual self than their ideal self. Supporting these findings, Golbeck and colleagues (2011) were able to predict users' personality profiles from publicly available data on Twitter within a 10% margin.

Whereas these findings suggest that OSN profiles represent relatively accurate impressions of the user's actual personality, there is also some evidence that users do engage in some censoring on online social networks (Das and Kramer, 2013), and that censoring is mainly motivated by positive self-representation. Sleeper and colleagues (2013) followed 18 participants over the course of a week. Participants were asked to send a text message to investigators every time they thought of things that they would like to post on Facebook, but then decided not to. At night, participants filled out a survey containing questions about shared and unshared content (e.g., the reasons the content was not shared). The results of qualitative data analysis revealed that 71% of users engaged in censoring of OSNs, and that the most important determinant of whether they decided for or against posting was how it reflected the way they wanted to represent themselves. The second determinant was whether they perceived the post to be interesting enough to share with the intended audience, suggesting that content posted online may be positively biased. Similarly, Zywica and Danowski (2008) found that individuals with low self-esteem reported managing their profiles in a way to seem more popular and removing unflattering information from their profiles. Together, the results suggest that whereas users seem to have difficulty hiding or changing their personality depicted on online social networks, users are motivated to represent themselves in a way that represents them in a positive light and makes them seem interesting, leading to a certain degree of self-censoring. Perhaps then, whereas it is difficult to hide the real self when online,

online social networks allow users to put forward the best version of themselves, unifying both the "real self" hypothesis and the "ideal self" hypothesis.

Importantly, how and the extent to which users manage impressions of their online persona has important implications for consumer well-being. If users manage to put forward the best version of themselves, this can have positive impact on the user. Indeed, researchers have found that exposure to one's Facebook profile and editing Facebook profiles can enhance self-esteem (Gonzales and Hancock, 2011; Valkenburg et al., 2006). Gonzales and Hancock (2011) demonstrated that spending time on their profile leads to greater increase in participants' self-esteem than simply looking in the mirror. Whereas this temporary increase in self-esteem may be mostly desirable, it is not without potential dangers. Not only can the positive reinforcement of online social networking lead to an increase of use and be potentially addicting (Yoffe, 2009), but recent research suggests exposure to OSNs can actually cause lapses in self-control (Wilcox and Stephen, 2013). Wilcox and Stephen (2013) have shown that spending time on Facebook and the resulting increased self-esteem can make people perform worse on self-control tasks involving health and financial decisions. Given the ample opportunities to make consumption decisions through online stores, self-control lapses caused by exposure to one's online self may be especially consequential as they may lead to impulsive online spending.

The beneficial effect of increased self-esteem due to self-redaction has further limitations. First, the flipside of self-censoring is that other users likely engage in the same favorable redaction practices. Viewing overly positive information about their online friends and the resulting negative social comparisons could have negative consequences for users, again implying that the consequences of online social network use depend on how exactly users spend time on these sites. Indeed, actively viewing other people's updates in the newsfeed seems to counteract the positive effects of users viewing and editing their own profile and, as already mentioned above, increase loneliness (Burke et al., 2010; Gonzales and Hancock, 2011).

Second, the fact that profiles are still very much indicative of a user's real self shows that self-redaction has its limits. This means that enhanced online representation can still result in a negative net-image whereby people do not reap the benefits of online social networking. Research shows that even though low self-esteem individuals are more likely to censor what they share (Zywica and Danowski, 2008), they are still more likely to post negative content on online social networks (Forest and Wood, 2012), which is not well received by the online community. Forest and Wood (2012) show that negative updates posted by low self-esteem individuals receive fewer likes and less feedback than similar posts from high self-esteem individuals. The reason for this, they argue, is that the repeated negative updates are not reflective of an actual issue and are viewed as annoying and tiresome by other users. The relative lack of social rewards from other users may further decrease self-esteem among these individuals, thus aggravating social dynamics and further lowering well-being among these individuals.

To summarize, self-representation is an important driver of online social network use. Whereas the representation is sometimes censored in a way to represent a more desirable self, it seems that the real personality seems to shine through on OSNs. The nature of self-presentation has important implications for users' well-being. How people choose to present themselves and how people spend time on online social networks likely determines the impact of online social networks on the user.

Information Retrieval and Dissemination

The third prominent motivation to engage in online social networking is the ability to access, gather, and spread information in a rapid and convenient way (Valenzuela et al., 2009; Hoffman and Novak, 2012). As previously mentioned, online social networks allow information retrieval and dissemination about users' personal lives. Users can learn about friends' important life events such as engagements or graduations, learn about upcoming events, and be reminded of upcoming birthdays. Whereas certainly informative, this type of information sharing among online friends mostly likely serves the function of a social lubricant, encouraging interactions among social ties by liking or commenting the shared events. In fact, Viswanath et al. (2009) found that 54% of interactions between pairs who interact infrequently were due to Facebook's birthday reminder feature.

Importantly, however, online social networks have also become an important source of timely information outside online friendship circles (Lerman and Ghosh, 2010). The rapid, dynamic, and timely information dissemination has made ONSs a valuable news source. A nationally representative survey of over 5,000 adults revealed that half of Facebook and Twitter users (amounting to 30% and 8% of the U.S. population, respectively) obtain international, national, and local news on the respective sites (Mitchell et al., 2013; Mitchell and Guskin, 2013). The sites, however, differ slightly in their informational function. Facebook is especially critical as a source of news for people who do not follow news on more traditional media and who might otherwise not be exposed to current events (Mitchell et al., 2013). Twitter, on the other hand, is an important news source for the younger and more educated population, and it seems particularly important for passing along new pieces of information of a developing story (Mitchell and Guskin, 2013). The fast spread of information due to retweeting has led some researchers to argue that Twitter has become more of a news source than an online social network (Toubia and Stephen, 2013). Indeed, Kwak and colleagues (2010) classified trending tweets and found that over 85% of topics are related to news headlines, which once retweeted reach an average of 1,000 users independent of the number of followers of the original tweeter.

This rapid and exponential diffusion of information resulting from the snowballing effect of posting and reposting has made online social networks an important crowdsourcing tool. Both Facebook and Twitter have been used to inform users about extreme weather alerts, organize rescue operations, find the owners of lost pets, and even locate bone marrow donors for cancer patients. Recognizing the power of online communities, the National Center for Missing Children now sends Amber alerts to the newsfeed of Facebook users in hopes that the local Facebook community can help locate missing children (Pereira and Sher, 2015).

Thus, OSNs have become a powerful and important information dissemination tool, and these sites can have considerable benefits to users, communities, and the greater society as a whole.

Summary

A review of existing literature shows that ONS simultaneously cater to a variety of social needs (Hoffman and Novak, 2012; Wilson et al., 2012) that can be categorized into three main motivations to engage in online social networking: (1) affiliation (i.e., staying in touch with friends), (2) identity expression (i.e., self-representation), and (3) information dissemination (i.e., the sharing and gathering of personal and public information). Whereas these motivators provide insight into how OSNs yield utility, the reviewed literature also suggests that whether users benefit from OSN use largely depends how they are used. For instance, whereas active participation and communication has positive effects on its users, more passive OSN behavior seems to have negative effect on its users.

The existing literature provides a broad idea of what drives online social networking behavior and how it affects its users. However, it is important to point out that the existing findings are relatively early and rudimentary, and many unanswered questions remain.

First, many of reported findings are exploratory, descriptive, or correlational in nature. Often they rely on qualitative data and on relationships between self-reported survey data, which are subject to biases and alternative interpretations. So, whereas these efforts provide exciting and important initial insights into online social networking behavior, more work is necessary to understand the precise conditions, causal relationships, and mechanisms behind the findings.

Second, the findings do not represent the large and complex world of online social networks. The majority of research reported has only focused on the antecedents and consequences of Facebook use, with few articles focusing on Twitter. Given the long list of different OSNs and the way these differ in the relationships they foster, the existing findings cannot be generalized to any other specific online social network or to the online social networking phenomenon as a whole.

Moreover, the review reveals that past research has treated OSNs as homogenous entities, looking at what drives people to spend time on Facebook or Twitter, for example. In reality, these particular sites differ in their combinations of features and channels of communication (Wilson et al., 2012). Facebook users can spend their time viewing and editing their own profile, they can view other peoples' posts and pictures, or they can use the time to reach out and communicate with others. If they reach out to friends, they can post status updates, share on a friend's wall, or message individual users. Twitter users can send tweets or direct message particular social ties. These features and different subchannels vary in important ways. In order to get a deeper and more differentiated understanding of online social network use, it is important to more systematically investigate and compare specific behaviors or specific features of online social networks.

In the following, we report an initial attempt to understand one of the most popular features and most common behaviors on online social networks. Instead of researching the motivations behind online social network use in general, we narrow our investigation to understanding why people microblog.

Why do People Microblog? The Value of Undirected Communication

Microblogging is a feature that is common to different types of popular online social networks. Although it has different names on different OSNs (i.e., status updates on Facebook, Tweets on Twitter, Yaks on YikYak), the microblogging feature allows users to share information, feelings, actions, and thoughts in brief messages with other users in their network. These users can read them and choose to respond by "liking," "favoriting," "upvoting," "retweeting," or commenting on them. The feature is very popular. Statistics show that 125 million Facebook users update their status at least once a day (Hampton et al., 2011), and Twitter records 250 million tweets every day (Tsotsis, 2011), making microblogging one of the most popular features of Facebook and the hallmark of Twitter.

But why do people use this feature, and what makes this feature so incredibly popular? In our own research we investigate who uses this feature, when they use it, and why. Whereas microblogs certainly provide one way to share information about existing events and one's identity with other users, we argue that microblogs have more subtle and unique properties that might drive their use. Microblogs, we suggest, provide a unique form of communication. Unlike offline communication, they allow for undirected communication with multiple users at the same time. This, we argue, can facilitate social interaction, resulting in a valuable communication channel when communication is desired, but when communication offline is difficult.

Undirected Communication

We know that people have a fundamental need for affiliation and a need to belong (Baumeister and Leary, 1995), and that interpersonal interaction is critical for our well-being (Bowlby, 1977; Harlow, 1961; Stroebe and Stroebe, 1996). Even short and sometimes trivial interactions with others seem to make us feel better. Talking to someone when we feel down, for example, can provide comfort, affection, and social support, which is said to alleviate feelings of despair and loneliness (Rimé, 2009). In line with this, people are especially likely to seek interaction and reach out to others when they experience negative feelings (Derks et al., 2008; Luminet et al., 2000a; Luminet et al., 2000b; Rimé, 2008).

Yet, reaching out for comfort in a directed way is not always easy. Imagine you are having a terrible day and you feel like you want talk to someone. Doing so in the offline environment requires you stop by a friend's house, call someone on the phone, or send a direct message via phone to a particular person. Each of these channels requires you to single out a friend or acquaintance and address that someone in particular, who will be expected to engage in a social interaction. Initiating such interaction can be challenging for some individuals. Some individuals might worry about bothering others with their problems, being unwelcome, or fear being rejected (Forest and Wood, 2012; McCroskey, 1970).

Microblogs, on the other hand, are shared with the entire online social network. Unlike face-to-face interactions (or other types of directed communication, such as text messages or email), microblogging involves non-directed communication with multiple users in a network. Each of these users can then freely decide whether or not they want to respond to the message. This, we argue, makes it easier to reach out to other users, thus facilitating communication (Bargh and McKenna, 2004; Forest and Wood, 2012). If it is true that the undirected nature of microblogs provides value by facilitating sharing, as we suggest, then microblogs should be particularly valuable and useful in situations where interaction is desired (for example, when a person is having a bad day and needs someone to talk to), but when reaching out in a directed manner is difficult.

In the following, we point out circumstances in which reaching out might be desired but difficult to obtain offline, and we test whether this increases the propensity to microblog.

Social Apprehension and the Preference for Microblogging

One factor that increases the difficulty of reaching out to others and might therefore increase the preference for microblogging is the experience of social apprehension. Social apprehension is characterized by fear or anxiety of communication with others (McCroskey, 1970; Schroeder et al., 1992). Individuals who score high on individual difference measures of social apprehension, for example, are particularly likely to feel anxious in situations that require them to communicate (e.g., a social gathering), or when they have the desire to talk and reach out to someone (McCroskey, 1970; Kessler et al., 1998; Wrench et al., 2008). As a result, social apprehension often leads to social avoidance, depriving these individuals of the benefits of communication and social interaction (McCroskey, 1970; Schroeder et al., 1992).

If the undirected nature of microblogs facilitates communication, then they might provide a valuable channel of communications for socially apprehensive individuals. Socially apprehensive individuals would likely prefer microblog over more directed communication channels, offering a way for these individuals to engage in social interaction without the difficulty associated with offline interaction.

Importantly, given our discussion of the beneficial effects of social interaction, socially apprehensive individuals should be particularly likely to use this channel when they experience negative affect. Negative affect activates the desire to share because sharing promises comfort from social interaction (Rimé, 2009; Zech and Rimé, 2005). At the same time, the need for comfort might also make them worried about bothering others with their problems. Microblogs, we believe, can alleviate this problem because they increase opportunities for social interaction while at the same time allowing people not to bother anyone in particular.

We tested this idea in a series of experiments, two of which we report here. In a laboratory study, we induced negative affect in half the participants. The other half served as the control condition. We then asked participants about their likelihood of sharing either via microblog or in a directed manner (i.e., face-to-face). In addition, we measured social apprehension (Wrench et al., 2008), a measure of anxiety (or difficulty) associated with social interaction.

We expected that feeling bad should activate the need to reach out. The undirected nature of microblogs would facilitate reaching out for socially apprehensive individuals, thus leading socially apprehensive individuals to use microblogs. The same pattern would not be observed for more directed communication (i.e., face-to-face) and for individuals who score low on social apprehension.

The results supported our theory. When highly socially apprehensive individuals experienced negative affect, thus eliciting a desire and need to reach out, their willingness to share increased, but only for microblogs. Negative affect increased their likelihood of sharing via microblog compared to the control condition, and they reported being more likely to share via microblog than in person. Individuals who scored low on social apprehension, on the other hand, were less inclined to use microblogs. These individuals preferred more traditional methods of communication across the board; they were more likely to share in person.

The pattern of results (see Figure 1.1) is consistent with our suggestion that the undirected nature of microblogging makes this channel a valuable communication channel when people feel negative and want to reach out (i.e., because they desire comfort and social support), but feel tentative about bothering others.

Importantly, we also wanted to test whether it is indeed the undirected nature of microblogs that increases their likelihood of reaching out to others.

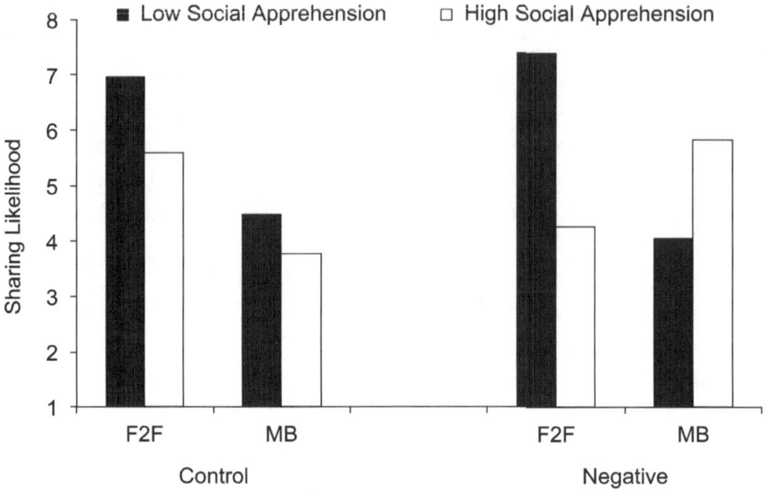

FIGURE 1.1 Social Apprehension and Sharing Across Channels

An additional study was run that included an important channel condition. In addition to asking participants how likely they were to express themselves via microblog or in person, participants were asked about their likelihood of sharing via direct message (i.e., email or text message). The reasoning behind this was that whereas microblogs vary from offline communication in that they are undirected, they also differ in that they do not require face-to-face interaction, and that microblogs are written instead of spoken. This leads to possible alternative explanations for our findings. Perhaps it was not the undirected nature of microblogs that drove the preference for this medium, but the fact that the medium is written and does not involve face-to-face contact. Including the "direct message" condition allowed us to rule out this possibility. Sending a direct message to a particular person by email or text is similar to microblogging in that it is written and not face-to-face, but different in that it is directed at someone specific. Asking participants about direct messaging therefore allowed us to tease apart why people use microblogs and test whether it is indeed the undirected nature that drives its use, as we argue.

In line with our theory that the value stems from the communication's undirected nature, the results from direct messaging approximated the result for face-to-face sharing, but differed from the microblogging condition. In other words, microblogs were the only medium that led socially apprehensive individuals to reach out to others. The fact that the sharing increase was specific to microblogs (and not observed for direct messaging) provides evidence that the appeal of microblogging lies in its undirected nature and not the fact that microblogs are written or non-face-to-face.

Additional Evidence: Neuroticism Predicts Microblogging on Facebook

We have argued that microblogs provide an avenue of sharing when users want to share, but at the same time find it difficult to do so in a more directed manner. In line with this, we have shown that socially apprehensive individuals prefer microblogs, and that they are especially likely to use microblogs when they feel bad, thus desiring social interaction.

But do users actually microblog when they are feeling down and need social interaction, whereas finding it difficult to do so offline? Additional data on Facebook users shows that these factors do indeed drive microblogging behavior, and that they also predict the content of microblogs. In a separate study, we asked participants about their microblogging behavior on Facebook (i.e., how often do you update your Facebook status?). We also asked them to log into their Facebook account and copy their 10 most recent status updates into the survey. We then examined how this behavior related to a personality factor that is marked by both social apprehension and negative affect. Neuroticism is a Big Five personality factor that is marked by experiencing emotions more negatively and more intensely (Barr et al., 2008). In other words, these individuals are more likely to be impacted by negative experiences in their environment. Whereas, as a result, highly neurotic individuals have a heightened need to share emotions (Saxena and Mehrotra, 2010), neuroticism is also associated with social apprehension (Schroeder et al., 1992). Thus, these individuals experience the conditions of negative affect and social apprehension (the conditions that drove microblogging in the previously reported study) more often than individuals who score low on neuroticism.

A regression analysis relating their responses to a Big Five personality inventory revealed that less emotionally stable individuals not only reported microblogging more frequently, but also expressed more emotions in their microblogs. No other personality factors were related to microblogging behavior. This provides additional support for the claim that microblogging's undirected nature provides a valuable outlet when people feel down and want to reach out (i.e., because they desire comfort and social interaction), but feel apprehensive about bothering others.

Summary

We investigated why people microblog (e.g., tweet or share status updates) and demonstrate that part of microblogging's appeal lies in its undirected nature. By allowing users to send undirected communication to multiple other users, people value microblogging when they desire social interaction but feel apprehensive about reaching out in a more directed manner.

In line with this, we find that socially apprehensive individuals who experience negative affect—thus making them want to reach out to others—prefer microblogging over more direct channels of communication. Providing external validity for this claim, we find that these forces lead to increased microblogging behavior on Facebook and to increased emotional content shared in these communications.

The reported work contributes to the understanding of online social networks in critical ways. First, it reaffirms the need for social interaction as a main driver of online social network use and points to the unique and beneficial role that microblogs play in online communication. Some cultural critics have worried that OSNs reduce face-to-face interaction (Kraut et al., 1998; Tonioni et al., 2012; Yoffe, 2009), thus negatively impacting users' well-being and social relationships. However, by outlining how microblogging's undirected nature serves as a valuable communication tool, we discover circumstances in which online social network use can provide benefits precisely *because* it does not involve more personal interaction.

Second, by focusing on the specific microblogging feature, it contributes to prior work investigating personality predictors in the Facebook domain, furthering the understanding of when these predictors diverge from offline behavior. Whereas extroverts may use online social networks to maintain offline social ties (Gosling et al., 2011; Ross et al., 2009), and narcissists may use them to move their tendency to self-promote to the online environment, microblogging seems to cater to people who have difficulty reaching out to others in a more directed, offline environment. As a result, online social networks provide a unique channel of communication, leading to behavior that differs from offline communication.

The reported findings have important implications for consumer welfare. Microblogs might provide valuable benefits, encouraging communication and interpersonal interaction when it is otherwise difficult. Their undirected nature allows consumers to reach out to friends when they might not feel comfortable doing so offline. This begs the question of whether microblogging has beneficial downstream consequences. Could microblogging potentially increase well-being after negative experiences?

Initial evidence from our research suggests that writing to others who might respond—as occurs on OSNs—can increase well-being after negative experiences. In a laboratory study, we induced negative emotions. Participants then completed a "writing study" in which some wrote about a control topic (office products), whereas those in other three conditions wrote about their current emotions, either (1) in private, or (2) to be shared with a known other who they were told would not be able to respond or (3) who might respond.

The results showed that emotional writing to a known other who might respond helped individuals who experienced negative emotions repair their well-being. These benefits did not accrue for participants writing in general (control), writing about emotions (i.e. venting), or sharing emotion with a known other alone. Instead, the notion that a known other would read what they had written and potentially respond (as on OSNs) boosted well-being. This shows that microblogging on OSNs could potentially have beneficial effects, even before actual interaction occurs. The anticipation of a response from online social ties can increase well-being and regulate negative affective experiences. By offering a way to reach out and share while anticipating a response from someone, online social networks thus seem to act as an emotion regulation tool for its users.

Overall then, online social networks seem to act as a unique and valuable communication channel that has the ability to facilitate social interaction, and ultimately potentially increase users' well-being.

Conclusions and Future Directions

Social media, and online social networks in particular, are incredibly popular and shape our everyday lives and our interactions. Given the time people spend on these sites and the role these sites have in our society, it is important to understand how people use them, what drives their use, and how they affect their users. This realization has sparked an initial heave of research on online social networking in various disciplines (Hoffman and Novak, 2012; Wilson et al., 2012).

A review of this existing literature suggests that people seem to engage in online social media for various reasons. A main driver of online social networks, as implied by their name, is the social aspect: OSNs allow people to interact with other users. However, OSNs are also used as a way for users to express and represent themselves to other users, as well as share and consume information posted on these sites.

Although we have a basic understanding of what drives users to engage in online social networking, many questions remain and much more systematic research is necessary. For example, relatively little is known about how OSNs are used across different cultures and demographics, what functions the different types of online social networks serve in different subgroups, what functions the different features of ONSs have, or how these affect consumer welfare. Furthermore, the role of the audience, whether it is clearly defined or whether it is made up of close versus distant ties, has received little attention in the current OSN literature. Even for the already researched questions, further research is necessary to reveal a more fine-grained understanding, such as what the causal relationships are between the investigated phenomena.

In short, much research in the domain needs to be done. Moving forward, we offer the following recommendations for future research on social media.

(1) Studying social media in its entirety: The various social media and online social networks differ in the features they provide and the type of social interaction they encourage. To date, much of the research has been conducted on Facebook, and relatively little research has investigated other popular online social networking sites such as Twitter, Instagram, or Pinterest. In the future,

researchers could extend the investigations to other sites and potentially compare the different platforms, audiences, and different features offered on these sites. For example, Twitter and Pinterest are similar in the ties and behaviors that they foster, but they differ in the type of information they promote (Pinterest focuses on sharing photos, whereas tweeting focuses on text-based microblogs). Examining and directly comparing the motivators and consequences for different platforms may provide insights into what motivates specific features on online social networks and how these features affect the users.

(2) Revealing the uniqueness of online environments: Relatively little is known about how specific the existing findings are to online social networks. Little research has directly compared offline behavior with behavior on online social networks, leaving many questions about the antecedents and consequences of OSN use unanswered. When, why, and how does communication on online social networks differ from offline communication? How does online communication impact well-being and social capital compared to offline communication (i.e., is one more powerful, and if so, are there circumstances in which online communication is superior?). Much work is still needed to understand how social dynamics on online social networks differ from offline environments, which ultimately will help us understand what makes online social networks unique and what role they play in our society.

(3) Using rigorous methodology: Much of the research on social media is either descriptive or correlational, and very little research has investigated online social networks in experimental settings. It is up to future research to more systematically investigate the causal predictors and effects of online social networks use. Unfortunately, however, this is not an easy feat. Experimental control requires the manipulation of isolated variables. Achieving experimental control is difficult when real OSN accounts are used, as users' OSN accounts vary on many dimensions (number of social ties, quality of social ties, the content posted on their own profile, content posted by other users). Furthermore, experimenting with people's real accounts raises ethical concerns. It is difficult to randomly assign students to engage in active online social networking when the consequences of behaviors are not known. At the same time, the complex nature of online social networks makes it nearly impossible to mimic the conditions of OSNs outside of actual OSNs in a way that it would for externally valid inferences. It is also risky to manipulate the online networking environments. In fact, recent attempts to do research on online social networks has suffered backlash by its users (Albergotti, 2014), hindering the possibility to conduct experiments with existing OSNs. To make things more tricky, online social networks are dynamic and change over time, making it difficult to keep up with the most recent developments.

All of this suggests that studying OSNs certainly comes with many challenges. Nevertheless, we hope that researchers rise to the challenge to take the investigations in this area to a new level. After all the existing literature is just the beginning of a new area of research, offering an exciting opportunity for researchers to understand new consumption behaviors and new consumption contexts. We certainly look forward to future contributions on this fascinating topic.

References

Albergotti, Reed. 2014. "Furor Erupts over Facebook Experiment on Users" [online]. *The Wall Street Journal,* [retrieved 30 June 2014 from www.wsj.com/articles/furor-erupts-over-facebook-experiment-on-users-1404085840].

Barr, Leah, Jefferey H. Kahn, and W. Joel Schneider. 2008. "Individual Differences in Emotion Expression: Hierarchical Structure and Relations with Psychological Distress." *Journal of Social and Clinical Psychology* 27 (December): 1045–1077.

Back, Mitja, D., Juliane M. Stopfer, Simine Vazire, Sam Gaddis, Stefan C. Schmukle, Boris Egloff, and Samuel D. Gosling. 2010. "Facebook Profiles Reflect Actual Personality, Not Self-Idealization." *Psychological Science* 21 (3): 372–374.

Bargh, John A., and Katelyn Y.A. McKenna. 2004. "The Internet and Social Life." *Annual Review of Psychology* 55 (February): 573–590.

Baumeister, Roy F., and Mark R. Leary. 1995. "The Need to Belong: Desire for Interpersonal Attachments as a Fundamental Human Motivation." *Psychological Bulletin* 117 (3): 497–529.

Berger, Jonah, and Raghuram Iyengar. 2012. "How Interest Shapes Word-of-Mouth Over Different Channels." Working Paper at the Wharton School of the University of Pennsylvania, Philadelphia, PA.

Bessière, Katherine, Sara Kiesler, Robert Kraut, and Bonka S. Boneva. 2008. "Effects of Internet Use and Social Resources on Changes in Depression." *Information, Community & Society* 11 (1): 47–70.

Bowlby, John. 1977. "The Making and Breaking of Affectional Bonds. II. Some Principles of Psychotherapy. The Fiftieth Maudsley Lecture." *The British Journal of Psychiatry* 130 (5): 421–431.

Boyd, Donah M., and Nicole B. Ellison. 2007. "Social Networking Sites: Definition, History, and Scholarship." *Journal of Computer-Mediated Communication* 13 (1): 210–230.

Buffardi, Laura E., and W. Keith Campbell. 2008. "Narcissism and Social Networking Sites." Personality and Social Psychology Bulletin 34 (10): 1303–1314.

Bullas, Jeff. 2014. "22 Social Media Facts and Statistics You Should Know in 2014." JeffBullas.com, [retrieved 17 January 2014 from www.jeffbullas.com/2014/01/17/20-social-media-facts-and-statistics-you-should-know-in2014/#PKGtikjk8r9x53c8.99].

Burke, Moira, Cameron Marlow, and Thomas Lento. 2010. "Social Network Activity and Social Well-being." In Proceedings of SIGCHI Conference on Human Factors in Computing Systems, New York, NY, April.

Burleson, Brant R. 1998. "Similarities in Social Skills, Interpersonal Attraction, and the Development of Personal Relationships." In *Communication: Views from the Helm for the Twenty-First Century,* ed. J.S. Trent, 77–84. Boston: Allyn & Bacon.

Das, Sauvik, and Adam Kramer. 2013. "Self-censorship on Facebook." Paper presented in the Seventh International AAAI Conference on Weblogs and Social Media, Cambridge, MA, July.

Derks, Daantje, Agneta H. Fischer, and Arjan E.R. Bos. 2008. "The Role of Emotion in Computer-Mediated Communication: A Review." *Computers in Human Behavior* 24 (3): 766–785.

Ellison, Nicole B., Charles Steinfield, and Cliff Lampe. 2007. "The Benefits of Facebook 'Friends:' Social Capital and College Students' Use of Online Social Network Sites." *Journal of Computer-Mediated Communication* 12 (4): 1143–1168.

Forest, Amanda L., and Joanne Wood. 2012. "When Social Networking Is Not Working: Individuals With Low Self-Esteem Recognize but Do Not Reap the Benefits of Self-Disclosure on Facebook." *Psychological Science* 23 (3): 296–305.

Golbeck, J., C. Robles, M. Edmondson, and K. Turner. 2011. "Predicting Personality from Twitter." Paper presented at the IEEE Third International Conference on Social Computing (Socialcom), Vancouver, Canada, October.

Gonzales, Amy L., and Jeffrey T. Hancock. 2011. "Mirror, Mirror on my Facebook Wall: Effects of Exposure to Facebook on Self-Esteem." *Cyberpsychology, Behavior, and Social Networking* 14 (1–2): 79–83.

Gosling, Samuel D., Adam A. Augustine, Simine Vazire, Nicholas S. Holtzman, and Sam Gaddis. 2011. "Manifestations of Personality in Online Social Networks: Self-reported Facebook-related Behaviors and Observable Profile Information." *Cyberpsychology, Behavior, and Social Networking* 14 (9): 438–488.

Gosling, Samuel D., Sam Gaddis, and Simine Vazire. 2007. "Personality Impressions Based on Facebook Profiles." Paper presented at International Conference on Weblogs and Social Media, Boulder, Colorado, March.

Green, M.C., and T.C. Brock. 2008. "Antecedents and Civic Consequences of Choosing Real versus Ersatz Social Activities." *Media Psychology* 11 (4): 566–592.

Gross, Ralph, and Allesandro Acquisti. 2005. "Information Revelation and Privacy in Online Social Networks." Paper presented at ACM workshop on Privacy in the Electronic Society, Alexandria, VA, November.

Hampton, Keith, Lauren S. Goulet, Lee Rainie, and Kristen Purcell. 2011. Social Networking Sites and Our Lives [online]. *Pew Research Internet Project*, [retrieved 16 June 2011 from http://pewinternet.org/Reports/2011/Technology-and-social networks/Summary.aspx].

Harlow, Harry. 1961. "The Development of Affectional Behavior Patterns in Infant Monkeys." In Determinants of Infants' Behaviour: Proceedings of the *Tavistock Seminar on Mother and Infant Interaction*, vol. 1, ed. Brian M. Voss, 75–97. London: Methuen.

Hoffman, Donna L., and Thomas P. Novak. 2012. "Why Do People Use Social Media? Empirical Findings and a New Theoretical Framework for Social Media Goal Pursuit." Working Paper at Sloan Center for Internet Retailing at the University of California Riverside, Riverside, CA.

Joinson, A.N. 2008. "Looking at, Looking Up or Keep Up With People? Motives and Use of Facebook." In Proceedings of the SIGCHI Conference on Human Factors in Computing Systems, pp. 1027–1036.

Kaplan, Andreas M., and Michael Haenlein. 2010. Users of the World, Unite! The Challenges and Opportunities of Social Media. *Business Horizons* 53 (1): 59–68.

Kessler, Ronald C., Murray B. Stein, and Patricia Berglund. 1998. "Social Phobia Subtypes in the National Comorbidity Survey." *American Journal of Psychiatry* 155 (5): 613–619.

Kraut, Robert, Michael Patterson, Vicki Lundmark, Sara Kiesler, Tridas Mukophadhyay, and William Scherlis. 1998. "Internet Paradox: A Social Technology that Reduces Social Involvement and Psychological Well-being?" *American Psychologist* 53 (9): 1017–1031.

Kwak, Haewoon, Changhyun Lee, Hosung Park, and Sue Moon. 2010. "What is Twitter, a Social Network or a News Media?" In Proceedings of the 19th International World Wide Web (WWW) Conference, pp. 591–600.

Lerman, Kristina, and Rumi Ghosh. 2010. "Information Contagion: An Empirical Study of the Spread of News on Digg and Twitter Social Networks." In Proceedings of the Fourth International AAAI Conference on Weblogs and Social Media, pp. 90–97.

Luminet, Oliver, Patrick Bouts, Frederique Delie, Antony S.R. Manstead, and Bernard Rimé. 2000a. "Social Sharing of Emotion Following Exposure to a Negatively Valence Situation." *Cognition and Emotion* 14 (5): 661–688.

Luminet, Oliver, Emanuelle Zech, Bernard Rimé, and Hugh Wagner. 2000b. "Predicting Cognitive and Social Consequences of Emotional Episodes: The Contribution of Emotional Intensity, the Five Factor Model, and Alexithymia." *Journal of Research in Personality* 34 (4): 471–497.

McCroskey, James C. 1970. "Measures of Communication-Bound Anxiety." *Speech Monographs* 37 (4): 269–277.

Mitchell, Amy, and Emily Guskin. 2013. "Twitter News Consumers: Young, Mobile and Educated" [online]. *Pew Research Journalism Project,* [retrieved 4 November 2013 from www.journalism.org/2013/11/04/twitter-news-consumers-young-mobile-and-educated].

Mitchell, Amy, Jocelyn Kiley, Jeffrey Gottfried, and Emily Guskin. 2013. "The Role of News on Facebook" [online]. *Pew Research Journalism Project,* [retrieved 23 October 2013 from www.journalism.org/2013/10/24/the-role-of-news-on-facebook].

Nadkarni, A., and S.G. Hofmann. 2012. "Why do People Use Facebook?" *Personality and Individual Differences* 52 (3): 243–249.

Nie, N.H. 2001. "Sociability, Interpersonal Relations, and the Internet: Reconciling Conflicting Findings." *American Behavioral Scientist* 45 (3): 420–435.

Noyes, Dan. 2014. "The Top 20 Valuable Facebook Statistics" [online]. *Zephoria,* [retrieved 29 October 2014 from https://zephoria.com/social-media/top-15-valuable-facebook-statistics].

Pereira, Jennifer, and Lauren Sher. 2015. "How You Can Help Find a Missing Child on Facebook With New Amber Alert Feature." *Good Morning America,* [retrieved 13 January 2015 from http://abcnews.go.com/Technology/find-missing-child-facebook-amber-alert-feature/story?id=28173570].

Rimé, Bernard. 2009. "Emotion Elicits the Social Sharing of Emotion: Theory and Empirical Review." *Emotion Review* 1 (1): 60–85.

Ross, Craig, Emily S. Orr, Mia Sisic, Jaime M. Arseneault, Mary G. Simmering, and Robert R. Orr. 2009. "Personality and Motivations Associated with Facebook Use." *Computers in Human Behavior* 25 (2): 578–586.

Ryan, Tracii, and Sophia Xenos. 2011. "Who Uses Facebok? An Investigation into the Relationship Between the Big Five, Shyness, Narcissism, Loneliness, and Facebook Usage." *Computers in Human Behavior* 27 (5): 1658–1664.

Saxena, Priya, and Seema Mehrotra. 2010. "Emotional Disclosure in Day-to-Day Living and Subjective Well Being." *Psychological Studies* 55 (3): 208–218.

Schroeder, Marsha L., Janice A. Wormworth, and W. John Livesley. 1992. "Dimensions of Personality Disorder and their Relationships to the Big Five Dimensions of Personality." *Psychological Assessmen*t 4 (1): 47–53.

Sleeper, Manya, Rebecca Balebako, Sauvik Das, Amber Lynn McConahy, Jason Wiese, and Lorrie Faith Cranor. 2013. "The Post that Wasn't: Exploring Self-Censorship on Facebook." In *Proceedings of the 2013 Conference on Computer Supported Cooperative Work*, pp. 793–802.

Smith, Aaron. 2014. "6 New Facts about Facebook." *Pew Research Center,* [retrieved 3 February, 2014 from www.pewresearch.org/fact-tank/2014/02/03/6-new-facts-about-facebook].

Stroebe, Wolfgang, and Margaret Stroebe. 1996. "The Social Psychology of Social Support." In *Social Psychology: Handbook of Basic Principles*, ed. Tory Edward Higgins and Arie W. Kruglanski, 597–621, New York, NY, US: Guilford Press.

Tonioni, Federico, Lucio D'Alessandris, Carlo Lai, David Martinelli, Stefano Corvino, Massimo Vasale, Fabrizio Fanella, Paola Aceto, and Pietro Bria. 2012. "Internet Addiction: Hours Spent Online, Behaviors and Psychological Symptoms." *General Hospital Psychiatry* 34 (1): 80–87.

Toubia, Olivier, and Andrew T. Stephen. 2013. "Intrinsic vs. Image-Related Utility in Social Media: Why Do People Contribute Content to Twitter?" *Marketing Science* 32 (3): 368–392.

Tsotsis, Alexia. 2011. "Twitter Is At 250 Million Tweets Per Day, iOS 5 Integration Made Signups Increase 3x". *TechCrunch*, [retrieved 17 October 2011 from http://techcrunch.com/2011/10/17/twitter-is-at-250-million-tweets-per-day].

Valenzuela, Sebastián, Namsu Park, and Kerk F. Kee. 2009. "Is There Social Capital in a Social Network Site? Facebook Use and College Students' Life Satisfaction, Trust, and Participation." *Journal of Computer-Mediated Communication* 14 (4): 875–901.

Valkenburg, P. M., and J. Peter. 2007. "Internet Communication and Its Relation to Well-Being: Identifying Some Underlying Mechanisms." *Media Psychology* 9 (1): 43–58.

Valkenburg, Patti M., Jochen Peter, and Alexander P. Schouten. 2006. "Friend Networking Sites and Their Relationship to Adolescents' Well-being and Social Self-esteem." *CyberPsychology & Behavior* 9 (5): 584–590.

Viswanath, B., A. Mislove, M. Cha, and K. P. Gummadi 2009, August. "On the Evolution of User Interaction in Facebook." In *Proceedings of the 2nd ACM Workshop on Online Social Networks,* pp. 37–42. ACM.

Wilcox, Keith, and Andrew T. Stephen. 2013. "Are Close Friends the Enemy? Online Social Networks, Narcissism, and Self-Control." *Journal of Consumer Research* 40 (1): 90–103.

Wilson, Kathryn, Stephanie Fornasier, and Katherine M. White. 2010. "Psychological Predictors of Young Adults': Use of Social Networking Sites." *Cyberpsychology, Behavior, and Social Networking* 13 (2): 173–177.

Wilson, Robert E., Samuel D. Gosling, and Lindsay T. Graham. 2012. "A Review of Facebook Research in the Social Sciences." *Perspectives on Psychological Science* 7 (3): 203–220.

Wise, Kevin, Saleem Alhabash, and Hyojung Park. 2010. "Emotional Responses During Social Information Seeking on Facebook." *Cyberpsychology, Behavior, and Social Networking,* 13 (5): 555–562.

Wrench, Jason S., Shannon M. Brogan, James, C. McCroskey, and Doreen Jowi. 2008. "Social Communication Apprehension: The Intersection of Communication Apprehension and Social Phobia." *Human Communication* 11 (4): 409–430.

Yoffe, Emily. 2009. "Seeking: How the Brain Hard-wires Us to Love Google, Twitter, and Texting. And Why that's Dangerous." *Slate* 12 (August): 309–369.

Zech, Emanuelle, and Bernard Rimé. 2005. "Is Talking About an Emotional Experience Helpful? Effects on Emotional Recovery and Perceived Benefits." *Clinical Psychology & Psychotherapy* 12 (4): 260–287.

Zywica, Jolene, and James Danowski. 2008. "The Faces of Facebookers: Investigating Social Enhancement and Social Compensation Hypotheses; Predicting FacebookTM and Offline Popularity from Sociability and Self-Esteem, and Mapping the Meanings of Popularity with Semantic Networks." Journal of Computer-Mediated Communication 14 (1): 1–34.

2

BEING A LIKABLE BRAGGART

How Consumers Use Brand Mentions for Self-Presentation on Social Media

Tejvir Sekhon, Barbara Bickart, Remi Trudel, and Susan Fournier

Introduction

"But Blippy also failed to gain traction outside its early adopter user base because, for some folks, there's something awkward and braggy about sharing lists of things you're buying. Price or no price, it's one thing to Instagram your fabulous new shoes, but posting the purchase on a site dedicated to posting purchases can cross that invisible line between sharing and showing off. Mine will need to tread carefully there"—a quote by Perez (2012) in a TechCrunch article on why purchase sharing social network 'Blippy' (launched in 2009) failed and why its new avatar 'Mine' (launched in 2012, which has also been closed to the public subsequently) needs to tread carefully. This quote illustrates how people are quick to judge others based on their social media posts about brands, which in this case led to the failure of a social media platform. The use of social media to talk about consumption experiences is pervasive (Briggs 2012). People are often confronted by others' mentions of the brands they own or like on social media (Hollenbeck and Kaikati 2012). As the above quote by Perez (2012) suggests, mentioning brands on social media can lead to less than favorable impressions, both for the consumer who posted the information and potentially, for the brand itself (Ferraro, Kirmani, and Matherly 2012).

In this chapter, we propose that the impressions formed based on brand mentions may not just be a matter of *whether* a brand is mentioned but *how* it is mentioned. Specifically, we develop a typology of strategies that consumers use to mention brands for self-presentation on social media. Research on word-of-mouth (WOM) has focused primarily on self-presentation as a *driver of WOM* but has not examined *how* consumers self-present using products and brands (Berger 2012), which is likely to impact the impressions of the communicator and the brand. Therefore, this research aims to develop a more nuanced characterization of the WOM phenomenon by looking at consumer self-presentation strategies in the online medium.

Consumer Self-Presentation Using Brands

It is a common human tendency to try to portray a positive image to others about one's characteristics, achievements, or status (Leary 1995). Any behavior intended to influence the impression of oneself in the minds of others is called self-presentation (Schlenker 2003). A common way to craft a favorable self-presentation is to verbally convey positive self-related information, which has alternatively been labeled as bragging (Berman et al. 2014), self-promotion (Jones and Pittman 1982; Rudman 1998), boasting (Brown and Levinson 1987), self-praise (Dayter 2014), positive self-disclosure (Miller et al. 1992), and positive self-description (Holtgraves and Srull 1989). Mentioning a reputable brand in one's social media communications can be considered a special case of crafting a positive self-presentation in this way (Hollenbeck and Kaikati 2012; Schau and Gilly 2003).

In line with Veblen's (1899) original conceptualization of conspicuous consumption, the consumption literature has mainly focused on self-presentation via conspicuous 'display' of one's possessions to an immediate audience (Berger and Ward 2010; Han, Nunes, and Drèze 2010). Thus, this literature has neglected an increasingly common way of self-presenting with a brand—that of mentioning the brand in linguistic communications. In particular, with the advent of social media, people have an opportunity to craft their self-presentations for a much wider audience via explicit mentions of brands they might or might not own (Schau and Gilly 2003).

On the downside, including positive self-related information in one's own communications is considered bragging (Berman et al. 2014) and can lead to negative evaluations of the communicator (Godfrey, Jones, and Lord 1986). Similarly, we posit that name-dropping reputable brands in one's communications is likely to be considered a form of bragging. Past work has shown that because of inferences of self-presentational motives, conspicuous display of possessions can lead to negative evaluations of consumers and brands (Ferraro et al. 2012). This earlier work has focused primarily on the distinction between conspicuous versus inconspicuous display of a brand. In the social media context, however, linguistic communication gives consumers more latitude than mere display in terms of how to frame brand mentions to signal desirable qualities such as wealth or taste. Moreover, written communication allows for more time to craft brand mentions in subtle ways due to its asynchronous nature (Buffardi and Campbell 2008). Computer-mediated environments also make digital association with brands easier by relaxing the material constraints of ownership (Hollenbeck and Kaikati 2012; Schau and Gilly 2003). All of these affordances of online media can help consumers craft their self-presentations via brand mentions in ways that might minimize negative evaluations by others. As a starting point in understanding the different ways in which consumers mention brands, we develop a typology of brand mentioning strategies in this chapter.

Methodology

Given the exploratory nature of the research objectives, we used content analysis to provide insight into different strategies consumers use while crafting their self-presentations using brands. To examine this phenomenon in naturally occurring statements, we sampled posts from the popular microblogging site Twitter.com, which allows users to post short 140-character updates on a public profile, or 'timeline.' Microblogging updates can be considered parts of an autobiographical narrative and therefore, can achieve the goal of positive self-presentation (Dayter 2014; Leary and Kowalsky 1990; Puschmann 2009). We chose Twitter for sampling the posts as it allowed us to sample public posts from any user that mentioned particular brands.

We sampled posts mentioning luxury brands as they are more likely to be mentioned for self-presentational reasons (Berger 2012). Using NVivo software, we captured tweets with hashtags related to two luxury brands—Mercedes and Louis Vuitton. We captured 1,893 tweets with mentions of Louis Vuitton and 2,398 tweets with mentions of Mercedes posted over a three-day period (4/27/2013–4/30/2013). Then, we used a random number generator to generate a sample of 100 tweets—50 from each brand. We focused on tweets written in English by individuals only (excluding those by organizations). The descriptive information about the tweeters in the final sample of 100 tweets is provided in Table 2.1.

As the purpose of the investigation was exploratory, we allowed categories to emerge from the data. The first author classified these tweets into categories and then followed an iterative process of going back to the literature and identifying patterns to minimize the number of classifications that could account for a broad range of strategies used. This classification scheme was further cross-checked with the co-authors. Our taxonomy represents an extensive—although not exhaustive—list of strategies used to mention brands for self-presentational purposes. Moreover, the categories are not mutually exclusive; that is, one or

TABLE 2.1 Descriptive Information about Tweeters in Sample

	No. of Followers	*No. of Tweets*
Mean	2310	9196
Median	204	2515
Minimum	5	10
Maximum	175445	126312

more strategies may be used within the same communication. Although the small sample size precludes statistical analysis, we will discuss the qualitative findings in detail.

Findings

We found instances of posts claiming ownership of the mentioned brand as well as posts that made no attempt to claim ownership of the mentioned brand. This supports Schau and Gilly's (2003) finding that ownership is not a prerequisite to using the symbolic meanings of brands for self-presentation in the online medium. The brand mentioning strategies conveying ownership can be considered a form of conspicuous consumption behavior signaling wealth. However, signaling wealth by mentioning brands one owns may not encompass all status-seeking practices engaged in by consumers (Chaudhuri, Majumdar, and Ghoshal 2011). Economic capital (wealth) and cultural capital (taste, knowledge, or expertise) are considered two distinct ways to signal status through symbolic consumption (Bourdieu 1984; Chaudhuri and Majumdar 2010; Holt 1998). Therefore, even the strategies that do not convey ownership of the mentioned brands can signal traits such as knowledge or expertise of that particular brand or product category.

We identified four main strategies consumers use to mention brands in their social media communications. These four strategies comprised 90% of the posts in our sample. Table 2.2 summarizes the main strategies. Whereas the four brand mentioning strategies we identified are specific to the consumption domain, we also found evidence of two common tactics that could be used to avoid negative evaluation while bragging in any domain. In the next section, we will describe these strategies and tactics in greater detail.

TABLE 2.2 Typology of Brand Mentioning Strategies

Brand Mentioning Strategy	*Description*	*Conveying Ownership*
Having	When the primary information shared in the post is that one owns a particular brand.	Yes
Doing	When the post mentions or describes an activity one is engaged in and a brand is mentioned as an enabler or a prop in that activity.	Yes
Loving	When the post conveys positive feelings for an owned brand or describes the brand as a loved relationship partner.	Yes
Opinion Sharing	When consumers publicly share their opinion about a brand or a brand action. Posts in this category may also convey desire for a product/brand.	No

Brand Mentioning Strategies

Having

Posts were categorized as using the *having* strategy when the primary information conveyed in the post was that the writer owns the brand. Such posts mention a brand in the context of explicitly announcing to the world that the writer possesses a particular branded product. Use of possessive pronouns (such as my, mine) to convey ownership and linking to a picture of the owned product is common in such posts. Posting a picture with the branded product also authenticates one's claim of ownership of the brand (Dayter 2014). For example, in the following tweet the writer explicitly mentions "MyCar" while linking to a picture of his Mercedes: "#mercedes #classeC #voituredesports #lourd #MyCar #car #iphonephotographie http://t.co/zFw2oFclw6."

Due to the social, environmental, and religious discourses against materialistic and conspicuous consumption behaviors (Belk 1983; Ger and Belk 1999; Mason 1981), posts focused on 'having' material possessions are likely to be considered counter-normative. Seeking happiness through 'having' material things is believed to inhibit self-actualization (Fromm 1976) and is associated with extrinsic goals such as social recognition (Van Boven, Campbell, and Gilovich 2010). Therefore, mentioning owned brands using the 'having' strategy is likely to be categorized as bragging, leading to negative evaluations.

However, we also found examples of tweets in this category where the consumers seemed to be trying to brag 'under the radar.' For example, one can convey *having* in the context of sharing one's recent purchases. Such posts give the writer a chance to show-off branded purchases in the context of sharing excitement about shopping or about a specific purchase. For example: "Vintage shopping! Look what I picked up! #Chanel #LouisVuitton @ LRX Beverly Hills http://t.co/BpOUcDfLsQ." In this post, the writer has conveyed her ownership of Louis Vuitton while framing it as sharing details about an activity (i.e. shopping) she is engaged in.

Tal-Or (2010) showed that observers do not judge the braggarts who create a context for talking about their accomplishments during an interaction. But, how do people create a context for bragging about their consumption experiences in an online scenario? Creating a context for brand mentions on social media is easy because moment-to-moment sharing of what happens in our daily lives is not only acceptable but also encouraged on these media. The central question that Facebook asks its users to answer and share with the world is "what's on your mind?" More than 80% of posts on Twitter consist of announcements about one's immediate experiences (Naaman, Boase, and Lai 2010). Sharing of mundane personal activities, thoughts, and feelings can fulfill a relational maintenance function on social networks (Tong and Walther 2011). Therefore, posts having brand mentions as part of constant, up-to-the-minute updates on what one is doing, feeling, or thinking (as is the case in the next three strategies) can be considered normative in the online medium.

Doing

A post is categorized as using the *doing* strategy when it mentions or describes an activity that the consumer is engaged in and a brand is mentioned as an enabler of the activity or as a prop incidental to the activity. In posts using this strategy, brand mentions pop up as incidental details in the process of cataloging of daily lives on a social network. For example: "#convoi #having #fun #friends #cousin #love #mercedes #flags #ballons http://t.co/I8NzCMbbOJ." Here, the user is tweeting a photograph and sharing information about his fun-filled day with friends and the Mercedes brand just happens to be a part it.

The focus in such updates is on what the brand helps you do or achieve rather than on having the brand as its own reward. For example, in the following tweet, the writer is talking about her walk with 'Sophie,' most likely a dog with a Louis Vuitton collar. "Taking Sophie to the park for an early morning walk . . . I've got my @RachelK_CCcream and she has her #louisvuitton . . . Time to roll!" As the tweet is focused on an activity (walking the dog), the brand mention seems incidental and is less of a central focus in the tweet—the collar or leash simply helps this person attain their goal of walking with the dog.

Using possessions to engage in 'doing' or gaining experiences is often considered more moral and acceptable than just 'having' material possessions (Belk 1985; Van Boven 2005; Weinberger and Wallendorf 2008). Ger and Belk's (1999) informants explicitly mention the use of material goods for "doing more" as a source of true happiness (190). Similarly, Marwick (2010) found that Silicon Valley entrepreneurs use costly sporting equipment as a status symbol but frame it as a means for engaging in self-improvement, making it more acceptable compared to traditional status symbols such as cars. Based on these earlier findings, we suggest that when consumers mention brands using the *doing* strategy, they are framing their communication not as bragging about possessions but as sharing details about activities they are pursuing for self-improvement or intrinsic pleasure.

Loving

A post is categorized as using the *loving* strategy when it mentions a brand in the context of sharing positive feelings (such as love) for the brand or describes the brand as a loved relationship partner. Here is an example: "Is it too weird to say that I missed my baby Louis..? #louisvuitton #attached #mylove #missedyou http://t.co/EH5sdms7eH." Here, the user has anthropomorphized the brand and brought it into the domain of social relationships thus making it more acceptable to mention as part of an update on a social network. Chandler and Schwarz (2010) showed that when people think about objects in anthropomorphic terms, the features relevant to relational partners become applicable to those objects. Therefore, publicly enacting consumer-brand relationships using brand mentions (Fournier 1998; Schau and Gilly 2003) may lead to more positive evaluations of the communicator compared to just talking about 'having' a brand.

Posts in this category also included other features of the brand love prototype such as having a history with the brand and experiencing separation distress (Batra, Ahuvia, and Bagozzi 2012). For example, in the following tweet, the writer is conveying his distress over parting from his Mercedes that he has had for last 2.5 years. "goodbye #Mercedes you served me well over the last 2.5 years, you will be missed."

According to (Ger and Belk 1999), consumers can portray themselves as "passionate connoisseurs" instead of "vulgar materialists" by talking about their passion for a particular possession or consumption experience as passionate consumer relationships are considered praiseworthy (188). Batra, Ahuvia, and Bagozzi (2012) also found that a loved brand for their respondents was more likely to be "connected to something the respondent believed was deeper, such as self-actualization . . ." (4). Therefore, posts using the 'loving' strategy are likely to be categorized not as bragging but as sharing with others the love and enthusiasm for a brand.

Opinion Sharing

The final category focuses on posts that convey opinions about a brand. Although the posts in this category do not signal brand ownership, they can be used as a vehicle to signal the writer's cultural capital (or taste) in a particular consumption domain. Building an audience by displaying one's cultural capital can be an important goal behind using these strategies (McQuarrie, Miller, and Phillips 2013). These strategies also shift the focus of communication from the self to the brand and thus, can be considered as ways of distancing the self from the positive self-presentation.

A common way to implement this strategy is to curate and share with others the images of products that one considers beautiful or extraordinary. In such posts, consumers publicly curate a product that they do not own but find desirable. These posts can also help others discover new products. For example, in the following tweet, the writer shares an image of a new Mercedes model seen on the road. "First I've seen in the wild #Mercedes #sls #amg http://t.co/1FGVJluCSt." Here is another tweet where the consumer is sharing information about discovering a unique Louis Vuitton bag: "One of the most unique #LouisVuitton bags I've seen @Prima Moda http://t.co/YpS3nHl4Po." Although the writers in both the examples above do not own the products they are tweeting about, they clearly have an opinion on and a desire for these products. Moreover, they are also helping their followers discover and appreciate these products. In doing so, they are building their own reputation for being 'in the know.'

Sharing of aesthetic appreciation with others as seen in the above examples can be an important reason people curate on visual social networks such as Pinterest. In her interpretive work contrasting art collectors and museum visitors, Chen (2009) suggested that 'possession' and 'access' are two different expressions of consumer desire. According to the author, possession is about having power and control over an object whereas access is about the desire for sharing the appreciation of the object with others. The responses of the museum visitors in her research highlight "the willingness of sharing the place, moments, feelings and memories and enjoying the magic instance with other people" (Chen 2009, 934). Ger and Belk's (1999) informants also differentiated between buying a painting because "it is the thing to have" versus "enjoying looking at it, being excited by it, moved by looking at it" (189).

In contrast to the previous examples, we also found posts where the writers explicitly conveyed desire to own the mentioned branded product and where the focus is on possession and not access. Here is an example: "I need this car in my life! #Mercedes #sls #amg http://t.co/91rBTFVJcU." Here, the writer seems to be focused on having a Mercedes. Although this post is more likely to signal the writer's taste and not wealth, its explicit focus on having can also be seen as a reflection of the materialistic nature of the writer. Therefore, in contrast to the posts focused on curating, such posts could lead to negative evaluations that people reserve for materialistic people (Van Boven, Campbell, and Gilovich 2010).

In our data there were also instances of mentioning a brand in the context of sharing one's opinion about a brand action or passing along some information about the brand; usually from a company related source (such as a commercial or a website link). For example, in the following tweet, the writer expresses enthusiasm about a new campaign video launched by Louis Vuitton: "Such a great campaign video! #LouisVuitton 'Check In, Check Out!' http://t.co/oWI8ejglau http://t.co/48UGTb3eaW." Here the writer is signaling knowledge and expertise by commenting on and passing along a brand initiated communication. By being an unofficial ambassador for the brand, the writer is conveying an association with the brand.

Although most of the posts in our sample can be seen as vehicles to associate with brands and their symbolic meanings, we also found a few instances of consumers trying to disassociate from brands and brand users through their tweets. For example: "Just because you have #LouisVuitton luggage doesn't mean you have class! #trashyfirstclasspassengers #crewlife."

In this post, the writer is commenting upon people who might want to appropriate Louis Vuitton's association with being classy but whose actions suggest otherwise. Here, the writer is trying to dissociate from such poseurs while at the same time is weakening the association that others might have with being a Louis Vuitton consumer and being classy. However, this post can also be interpreted as the writer trying to dissociate from the brand itself by disapproving the brand users' actions. This is in line with past research showing that digital media has made it easier to enact identities oppositional to brands by using brands as cues for describing to others who one is not (Schau and Gilly 2003).

Likable Bragging Tactics

In addition to the four brand mentioning strategies discussed above, we also found two common tactics that consumers appear to use to manage the tension between bragging and likeability. These tactics could be used with any of the strategies described previously. Specifically, we found evidence that consumers can attempt to impact observers' evaluation of their self-presentation by (a) shifting the focus away from self and/or by (b) tempering the positivity of the presentation by sharing negatives. Table 2.3 below summarizes these tactics.

Shifting the Focus

Shifting the focus of a positive self-presentation away from self can be a way to make the self-presentation more acceptable to the audience (Dayter 2014). Past research has shown that distancing self from one's accomplishments can lead to positive evaluations. For example, Hareli and Weiner (2000) found that accounts ascribing success to external factors such as luck or help from others are seen as modest. Similarly, having another person present the desirable information on one's behalf (Pfeffer et al. 2006) or even restating someone else's positive statements about self can lead to more positive evaluations as compared to self-praising (Speer 2012). We found evidence for two sub-strategies under this category:

Credit Sharing. Consumers use this tactic to communicate possession of a reputable brand but try to come across as modest by attributing it to a person/circumstance external to their selves. Here, one can brag about one's possessions and show gratitude simultaneously by attributing whatever one has to others—a relative, friend, or even God—shifting the focus of communication away from

TABLE 2.3 Likable Bragging Tactics

Tactic	*Sub-strategy*	*Description*
Shifting the Focus	Credit Sharing	When consumers attribute the ownership of a brand to some factor external to themselves such as a close other, luck, or God.
	Basking in Reflected Glory	When the post conveys that a close other (friend or family member) owns a particular branded product.
Sharing Negatives	Self-deprecating	When the consumers mentions an owned brand along with a self-deprecating comment.
	Complaining	When the post mentions an owned brand in the context of sharing some hassle caused by the brand in one's life.

the self. For example: "I love it when Mum hands down her vintage luxury wallets to me. I'm starting to feel pretty lucky. #ChristianDior #LouisVuitton." In this tweet the consumer is attributing ownership of luxury brands to her mother as well as luck. Posts thanking God for one's possessions as well as those commenting on how blessed one feels also fall under this category.

Basking in Reflected Glory. Posts in this category convey that a close other (a friend or a family member) owns a particular branded product. For example: "My moms getting a new car #mercedes." Research on indirect self-presentation has shown that people manage their presentations by associating themselves with successful others, a process called "basking in reflected glory" (Cialdini et al. 1976). Similarly, as in this example, we found evidence of people posting about the luxury brands owned by their family or friends. According to the balance theory (Heider 1958), associated things are generally perceived as similar. Therefore, conveying associations of one's close others with reputable brands can be a way of crafting a positive self-presentation while avoiding direct talk about one's own possessions.

Sharing Negatives

Past research has found that people try to tone down their positive self-presentations on social media by tempering their positive self-related claims (Dayter 2014). For example, people append contextual cues such as emoticons, internet slangs such as "lol" (abbreviation for "laughing out loud") to positive statements about the self in order to convey that they are not taking themselves too seriously (West and Trester 2013). We found evidence for two sub-strategies in this category that tried to downplay the consumer's or the brand's attributes respectively.

Self-deprecating. People using this strategy deprecate themselves on a relatively unimportant dimension while trying to gain the reputational benefits attached with the brand. Including a self-deprecating comment along with a brand mention may also help to reduce the perceived distance between the communicator and the audience and can make the communicator more likable (McQuarrie, Miller, and Phillips 2013). Although we did not find many examples of this strategy in our sample, it appears to be common in the microblogging world (Dayter 2014; Zappavigna 2013) and has been labeled 'humblebragging' in the popular press (Wittels 2012). Here is one example from our sample: "My whip for the day. Oh the places we will go! #Mercedes #benz #notmine #zoom http://t.co/bhbUXB1dy0." In this tweet, the writer conveyed that she is driving a Mercedes. However, she self-deprecates at the same time by implying that the Mercedes is not hers using the hashtag "notmine."

Complaining. Consumers use this tactic to convey association with a reputable brand in the context of sharing some minor hassle caused by the brand in one's life. Any communication showing a downside of one's possessions has a higher chance of being categorized as sharing (one's problems) rather than bragging.

For example: "129.00 for the part & 629.00 for labor to fix a window~ #FML guess I can do the 50 cent piece of plastic #mercedes." In this tweet, the user is complaining about the high cost of getting his Mercedes repaired using the Internet slang "FML" (acronym for Fuck My Life). Past research (Cohen and Olshtain 1993; Vásquez 2011) has shown that complaints often occur as a 'speech act set' (i.e., they co-occur with other speech acts such as warnings, suggestions etc.). Vásquez (2011) showed that a significant proportion of complaints on the review website Tripadvisor.com combined overall negative evaluation with some positive appraisal as the reviewers avoid giving off the impression that they are complaining. Similarly, here we see that self-presentations mentioning one's luxury brands can contain some minor negative information, essentially creating a "speech act set" that combines complaining with bragging.

Conclusion

Consumers use brand mentions to build desirable associations about their wealth, taste, or knowledge. At the same time, mentioning brands can lead to negative evaluations if construed as bragging by others. Our main contribution is to demonstrate how consumers calibrate what they say about brands to avoid negative evaluations. Our findings are in line with past research showing that social media users are aware that overtly positive self-presentations can lead to negative impressions (Barash et al. 2010; Dayter 2014).

We found that although there were a few consumers who were very explicit in conveying their possession of luxury brands, most mentioned luxury brands in the context of what they were doing, feeling, or thinking about the brand. Research has shown that two common motives for engaging in WOM are product/brand involvement and self-presentation (Dichter 1966; Sundaram, Mitra, and Webster 1998). It is likely that by mentioning a brand in the context of doing, loving, or opinion sharing, consumers provide cues to their involvement with the brand making self-expression as a more likely explanation for their behavior as compared to self-presentation.

Moreover, bragging that is relevant to the communication context is less likely to be viewed as a violation of conversational norms, and therefore, is viewed more favorably (Grice 1975; Holtgraves 2002). However, the criteria of relevance are more relaxed in non-directed social media communications such as microblogging updates (whether on a microblogging website such as Twitter or as a 'status update' feature on social networks). As such posts are generally not directed to a particular receiver; they are assumed to be "author-centric" (Kramer and Chung 2011; Puschmann 2009) and the only criteria for relevance seems to be that they contain some information pertaining to what the author is doing, feeling, or thinking at the moment (Bazarova et al. 2012). The brand mentioning strategies of *doing, loving,* and *opinion sharing* seem to be in line with these criteria of relevance for microblogging updates.

In addition to the four brand mentioning strategies, we also found that consumers use the tactics of (a) shifting the focus of the communication away from the self and/or (b) tempering its positivity to impact the evaluations observers make of them. Although there were posts focused only on 'having' the brand, we also found instances of posts focused on others or on the brand itself. Also, although we found that most of the posts were uniformly positive there was some variance in terms of how positive or balanced the posts were. The strategic balancing of valence in posts suggests that consumers recognize (either consciously or unconsciously) the tension between positive self-presentations using brand mentions and likeability.

In sum, in line with the previous research in psychology, communication, and linguistics, our findings suggest that it is possible to avoid negative evaluations while bragging via brand mentions if (1) the brand is mentioned in the context of sharing one's activities, thoughts, or feelings, (2) the focus is shifted away from self and onto others, and/or (3) the positivity of the self-presentation is tempered. Moreover, by mentioning a brand in the context of *doing*, *loving*, or *opinion sharing*, consumers can provide brand attachment cues to observers that make inferences of self-expression more likely than inferences of self-presentation.

Managerial Implications

The brand mentioning strategies we identified also reflect common tactics used by firms to encourage brand mentions on social media. First, some brands encourage consumers to share their purchases with their social networks stimulating posts in the 'having' category. For example, online retailers such as Amazon.com encourage customers to share their purchases (of books, clothes, vacations etc.) with a standard default message such as "I just bought X." Second, firms encourage brand mentioning using the 'doing' strategy by encouraging consumers to share experiences that involve the brand and updates about what they are doing with the brand. For example, with the Nike Fuel band, consumers can easily track and share their daily workout with their friends. Third, firms encourage consumers to publicly enact relationships with brands using the 'loving' strategy. For example, brands ask satisfied consumers to 'like' them on social media or to write supportive testimonials for them or share brand-related stories. Fourth, firms are giving more and more opportunities to consumers to 'share their opinion' publicly. Consumers can curate beautiful images of products they desire on visual social networks such as Pinterest, Instagram, and Tumblr for "serendipitous discovery" by others (Hall and Zarro 2012). Moreover, firms are encouraging consumers to create a wish list of things they want and share with their social networks. For example, Amazon lets consumers share their wish lists with their social networks. Finally, encouraging consumers to share company generated communication or other brand related information has been a primary goal of many social media marketing strategies.

Even though marketers use these tactics, there is no empirical work demonstrating the incidence or effectiveness of these strategies and their downstream consequences for the consumer conveying the information or for the mentioned brands. In fact, when researchers study brands mentions in social media they maintain a gross definition of the construct, noting simply whether a given brand is mentioned or not (Berger 2012). Our research advances this dialogue by qualifying the *types* of brand mentions in social media and exploring their differential effects. This typology can be a first step towards developing a theory that can guide practitioners in the choice of encouraging a particular brand mentioning strategy.

Future Research Directions

The descriptive nature of this research precludes us from making any claims about the success of the strategies and tactics we identified in terms of conveying one's associations with brands while avoiding negative evaluations. Moreover, our small sample size is not conducive to statistical analysis of the frequency of occurrence of particular strategies. However, this typology can help us develop a more nuanced characterization of the word-of-mouth phenomenon and come up with interesting research questions that can be tested empirically.

We propose that the inferences that consumers make based on others' brand mentions and the narrative surrounding those mentions can have important implications for how the brand is perceived. A fruitful step for future research is to examine how the use of these strategies can impact consumer and brand perceptions. Observers' impressions of the communicator and mentioned brands are likely to be influenced by how they interpret the brand mentions in self-presentations (Reis and Shaver 1988). People try to make sense of others' self-presentations by considering their reasons for sharing that information (Miller et al. 1992). Past research has shown that when observers infer a self-presentational motive based on conspicuous brand usage, the attitude towards the consumer is adversely affected (Ferraro et al. 2012; Pancer 2013). Therefore, inferences of self-presentational motives based on the brand mentioning strategy used can lead to negative evaluation of the target consumer.

Moreover, if consumers infer that a brand is mentioned in a positive WOM communication for self-presentational reasons, they are likely to discount that information (Chen and Lurie 2013; Friestad and Wright 1994). Inference of self-presentational motives for brand mentioning can also lead to an inference that the consumer prefers the brand because of its signaling potential and not due to any inherent preference for the brand. Therefore, observers may infer that the brand does not offer any intrinsic value, which might negatively impact the attitude towards the brand.

Moreover, research has shown that consumers' behaviors are dictated by concerns regarding how others might see them (Berger and Heath 2008; Pancer

2013; White and Dahl 2006). As consumers don't like others who are seen as engaging in self-presentation (Ferraro et al. 2012), it is likely that they will try to avoid buying or talking about brands associated with self-presentational motives. Therefore, examining the downstream consequences of the different brand mentioning strategies can be a fruitful topic for future research.

Understanding consumer self-presentation via brand mentions on social media is important for marketers due to its easily observable and highly public nature (Berger 2013). It is almost impossible to visit an online social network without being exposed to others' posts about their consumption experiences (Bernstein 2012). In a world where marketers are creating more and more opportunities for consumers to mention brands (Berger 2013), it is important to understand the impact of exposure to such consumption related bragging on impressions of the brands as well as brand users. By encouraging marketers to pay attention to not only the frequency but also to the context of brand mentions, this research can be helpful in initiating social interactions that will enhance brand value.

References

Barash, Vladimir, Nicolas Ducheneaut, Ellen Isaacs, and Victoria Bellotti. 2010. "Faceplant: Impression (Mis) management in Facebook Status Updates." In Proceedings of 4th International AAAI Conference on Weblogs and Social Media (ICWSM), Washington, DC, May 23–26.

Batra, Rajeev, Aaron Ahuvia, and Richard P. Bagozzi. 2012. "Brand Love." *Journal of Marketing* 76(2): 1–16.

Bazarova, Natalya N., Jessie G. Taft, Yoon Hyung Choi, and Dan Cosley. 2012. "Managing Impressions and Relationships on Facebook: Self-Presentational and Relational Concerns Revealed Through the Analysis of Language Style." *Journal of Language and Social Psychology* 32: 121–141.

Belk, Russell W. 1983. "Worldly Possessions: Issues and Criticisms." *Advances in Consumer Research* 10(1): 514–519.

Belk, Russell W. 1985. "Materialism: Trait Aspects of Living in the Material World." *Journal of Consumer Research* 12(3): 265–280.

Berger, Jonah. 2012. "Word-of-Mouth and Interpersonal Communication: An Organizing Framework and Directions for Future Research." Working paper. Accessed November 4, 2013. https://marketing.wharton.upenn.edu/faculty/berger.

Berger, Jonah. 2013. *Contagious: Why Things Catch on.* New York: Simon and Schuster.

Berger, Jonah, and Chip Heath. 2008. "Who Drives Divergence? Identity Signaling, Outgroup Dissimilarity, and the Abandonment of Cultural Tastes." *Journal of Personality and Social Psychology* 95(3): 593–607.

Berger, Jonah, and Morgan Ward. 2010. "Subtle Signals of Inconspicuous Consumption." *Journal of Consumer Research* 37(4): 555–569.

Berman, Jonathan Z., Emma E. Levine, Alixandra Barasch, and Deborah A. Small. 2014. "The Braggart's Dilemma: On the Social Rewards and Penalties of Advertising Prosocial Behavior." *Journal of Marketing Research*, forthcoming.

Bernstein, Elizabeth. 2012. "Are We All Braggarts Now?" *The Wall Street Journal,* August 14. Accessed August 29, 2013, from http://online.wsj.com.

Bourdieu, Pierre. 1984. *Distinction: A Social Critique of the Judgement of Taste*. Cambridge, MA: Harvard University Press.

Briggs, Zoe. 2012. 'British Holiday-makers Love to Brag When Abroad." *Cosmopolitan*, July 3. Accessed November 4, 2013, from www.cosmopolitan.co.uk/_mobile/lifestyle/british-holiday-makers-brag-abroad-social-newtworks?ignoreCache=1.

Brown, Penelope, and Stephen C. Levinson. 1987. *Politeness: Some Universals in Language Usage*. Cambridge, UK: Cambridge University Press.

Buffardi, Laura E., and W. Keith Campbell. 2008. "Narcissism and Social Networking Websites." *Personality and Social Psychology Bulletin* 34(10): 1303–1314.

Chandler, Jesse, and Norbert Schwarz. 2010. "Use Does Not Wear Ragged the Fabric of Friendship: Thinking of Objects as Alive Makes People Less Willing to Replace Them." *Journal of Consumer Psychology* 20(2): 138–145.

Chaudhuri, Himadri Roy, and Sitanath Majumdar. 2010. "Conspicuous Consumption: Is That All Bad? Investigating the Alternative Paradigm." *Vikalpa* 35(4): 53.

Chaudhuri, Himadri Roy, Sitanath Mazumdar, and A. Ghoshal. 2011. "Conspicuous Consumption Orientation: Conceptualisation, Scale Development and Validation." *Journal of Consumer Behaviour* 10(4): 216–224.

Chen, Yu. 2009. "Possession and Access: Consumer Desires and Value Perceptions Regarding Contemporary Art Collection and Exhibit Visits." *Journal of Consumer Research* 35(6): 925–940.

Chen, Zoey, and Nicholas H. Lurie (2013). "Temporal Contiguity and Negativity Bias in the Impact of Online Word of Mouth." *Journal of Marketing Research* 50(4): 463–476.

Cialdini, Robert B., Richard J. Borden, Avril Thorne, Marcus Randall Walker, Stephen Freeman, and Lloyd Reynolds Sloan. 1976. "Basking in Reflected Glory: Three (Football) Field Studies." *Journal of Personality and Social Psychology* 34(3): 366–375.

Cohen, Andrew D., and Elite Olshtain. 1993. "The Production of Speech Acts by EFL Learners." *Tesol Quarterly* 27(1): 33–56.

Dayter, Daria. 2014. "Self-praise in Microblogging." *Journal of Pragmatics* 61: 91–102.

Dichter, Ernest. 1966. "How Word-Of-Mouth Advertising Works." *Harvard Business Review* 44(6): 147–160.

Ferraro, Rosellina, Amna Kirmani, and Ted Matherly. 2012. "Look at Me! Look at Me! Conspicuous Brand Usage, Self-Brand Connection, and Dilution." *Journal of Marketing Research* 50(4): 477–488.

Fournier, Susan. 1998. "Consumers and Their Brands: Developing Relationship Theory in Consumer Research." *Journal of Consumer Research* 24(4): 343–353.

Friestad, Marian, and Peter Wright. 1994. "The Persuasion Knowledge Model: How People Cope With Persuasion Attempts." *Journal of Consumer Research* 21(1): 1–31.

Fromm, Erich. 1976. "*To Have or to Be*?" New York: Harper & Row.

Ger, Güliz, and Russell W. Belk. 1999. "Accounting for Materialism in Four Cultures." *Journal of Material Culture* 4(2): 183–204.

Godfrey, Debra K., Edward E. Jones, and Charles G. Lord. 1986. "Self-Promotion Is Not Ingratiating." *Journal of Personality and Social Psychology* 50(1): 106–115.

Grice, H. Paul. 1975. "Logic and Conversation." In *Syntax and Semantics, 3: Speech Acts,* edited by Peter Cole and Jerry L. Morgan, 41–58, New York: Academic Press.

Hall, Catherine, and Michael Zarro. 2012. "Social Curation on the Website Pinterest.com." In *Proceedings of the American Society for Information Science and Technology* 49(1): 1–9.

Han, Young Jee, Joseph C. Nunes, and Xavier Drèze. 2010. "Signaling Status with Luxury Goods: The Role of Brand Prominence." *Journal of Marketing* 74(4): 15–30.

Hareli, Shlomo, and Bernard Weiner. 2000. "Accounts for Success as Determinants of Perceived Arrogance and Modesty." *Motivation and Emotion* 24(3): 215–236.

Heider, Fritz. 1958. *The Psychology of Interpersonal Relations.* New York: Wiley.

Hollenbeck, Candice R., and Andrew M. Kaikati. 2012. "Consumers' Use of Brands to Reflect Their Actual and Ideal Selves on Facebook." *International Journal of Research in Marketing* 29(4): 395–405.

Holt, Douglas B. 1998. "Does Cultural Capital Structure American Consumption?" *Journal of Consumer Research* 25(1): 1–25.

Holtgraves, Thomas M. 2002. *Language as Social Action: Social Psychology and Language Use.* Mahwah, NJ: Erlbaum.

Holtgraves, Thomas, and Thomas K. Srull. 1989. "The Effects of Positive Self-Descriptions on Impressions General Principles and Individual Differences." *Personality and Social Psychology Bulletin* 15(3): 452–462.

Jones, Edward E., and Thane S. Pittman. 1982. "Toward a General Theory of Strategic Self-Presentation." *Psychological Perspectives on the Self* 1: 231–262.

Kramer, Adam D. I., and Cindy K. Chung. 2011. "Dimensions of Self-Expression in Facebook Status Updates." In Proceedings of the Fifth International AAAI Conference on Weblogs and Social Media (ICWSM), Palo Alto, CA: 169–176.

Leary, Mark R. 1995. *Self-Presentation: Impression Management and Interpersonal Behavior.* Madison, WI: Brown & Benchmark.

Leary, Mark R., and Robin M. Kowalski. 1990. "Impression Management: A Literature Review and Two-Component Model." *Psychological Bulletin* 107(1): 34–47.

Marwick, Alice E. 2010. "Status Update: Celebrity, Publicity and Self-Branding in Web 2.0." PhD diss., New York University.

Mason, Roger S. 1981. *Conspicuous Consumption: A Study of Exceptional Consumer Behavior.* Farnborough, Hants: Gower.

McQuarrie, Edward F., Jessica Miller, and Barbara J. Phillips. 2013. "The Megaphone Effect: Taste and Audience in Fashion Blogging." *Journal of Consumer Research* 40(1): 136–158.

Miller, Lynn Carol, Linda Cooke, Jennifer Tsang, and Faith Morgan. 1992. "Should I Brag? Nature and Impact of Positive and Boastful Disclosures for Women and Men." *Human Communication Research* 18(3): 364–399.

Naaman, Mor, Jeffrey Boase, and Chih-Hui Lai. 2010. "Is it Really About Me? Message Content in Social Awareness Streams." In *Proceedings of the 2010 ACM Conference On Computer Supported Cooperative Work*, 189–192. New York: ACM Press.

Pancer, Ethan Leigh. 2013. "The Causes and Effects of Inferences of Impression Management in Consumption." PhD diss., Queen's University.

Perez, Sarah. 2012. "Blippy Redux? Mine Launches A Service for Sharing Your Purchases with Friends." Accessed March 7, 2014. http://techcrunch.com/2012/12/10/blippy-redux-mine-launches-a-service-for-sharing-your-purchases-with-friends/

Pfeffer, Jeffrey, Christina T. Fong, Robert B. Cialdini, and Rebecca R. Portnoy. 2006. "Overcoming the Self-Promotion Dilemma: Interpersonal Attraction and Extra Help as a Consequence of Who Sings One's Praises." *Personality and Social Psychology Bulletin* 32(10): 1362–1374.

Puschmann, Cornelius. 2009. "Diary or Megaphone? The Pragmatic Mode of Weblogs." Paper presented at Language in the (New) Media: Technologies and Ideologies, Seattle, WA, September 3–6.

Reis, Harry T., and Phillip Shaver. 1988. "Intimacy as an Interpersonal Process." In *Handbook of Personal Relationships*, edited by Steve Duck, 367–389. Chichester, England: Wiley.

Rudman, Laurie A. 1998. "Self-Promotion as a Risk Factor for Women: The Costs and Benefits of Counter Stereotypical Impression Management." *Journal of Personality and Social Psychology* 74(3): 629–645.

Schau, Hope Jensen, and Mary C. Gilly. 2003. "We Are What We Post? Self-Presentation in Personal Web Space." *Journal of Consumer Research* 30(3): 385–404.

Schlenker, Barry R. 2003. "Self-presentation." In *Handbook of Self and Identity,* edited by Mark R. Leary and June P. Tangney, 492–518. New York: Guilford Press.

Speer, Susan A. 2012. "The Interactional Organization of Self-praise: Epistemics, Preference Organization, and Implications for Identity Research." *Social Psychology Quarterly* 75(1): 52–79.

Sundaram, Dinesh S., Kaushik Mitra, and Cynthia Webster. 1998. "Word-of-Mouth Communications: A Motivational Analysis." *Advances in Consumer Research* 25(1): 527–531.

Tal-Or, Nurit. 2010. "Bragging in the Right Context: Impressions Formed of Self-Promoters Who Create a Context for Their Boasts." *Social Influence* 5(1): 23–39.

Tong, Stephanie, and Joseph B. Walther. 2011. "Relational Maintenance and Computer-Mediated Communication." In *Computer-mediated Communication in Personal Relationships*, edited by Kevin B. Wright and Lynne M. Webb, 98–118. New York: Peter Lang Publishing.

Van Boven, Leaf. 2005. "Experientialism, Materialism, and the Pursuit of Happiness." *Review of General Psychology* 9(2): 132–142.

Van Boven, Leaf, Margaret C. Campbell, and Thomas Gilovich. 2010. "Stigmatizing Materialism: On Stereotypes and Impressions of Materialistic and Experiential Pursuits." *Personality and Social Psychology Bulletin* 36(4): 551–563.

Vásquez, Camilla. 2011. "Complaints Online: The Case of Tripadvisor." *Journal of Pragmatics* 43(6): 1707–1717.

Veblen, Thorstein. 1899. *The Theory of the Leisure Class.* New York: Macmillan.

Weinberger, Michelle F., and Melanie Wallendorf. 2008. "Having vs. Doing: Materialism, Experientialism, and the Experience of Materiality." *Advances in Consumer Research* 35: 257–261.

West, Laura, and Anna Marie Trester. 2013. "Facework on Facebook." In *Discourse 2.0: Language & New Media,* edited by Deborah Tannen and Anna Marie Trester, 133–154. Washington, DC: Georgetown University Press.

White, Katherine, and Darren W. Dahl. 2006. "To Be or Not Be? The Influence of Dissociative Reference Groups on Consumer Preferences." *Journal of Consumer Psychology* 16(4): 404–414.

Wittels, Harris. 2012. *Humblebrag: The Art of False Modesty.* New York: Grand Central Publishing.

Zappavigna, Michele. 2013. "Enacting Identity in Microblogging Through Ambient Affiliation." *Discourse & Communication* 8(2): 209–228.

3

RESISTANCE TO ELECTRONIC WORD OF MOUTH AS A FUNCTION OF THE MESSAGE SOURCE AND CONTEXT

Susan Powell Mantel, Maria L. Cronley, Jeffrey L. Cohen, and Frank R. Kardes

The space within which consumers encounter and process company related information has changed dramatically in recent years. With emerging media such as Twitter, Facebook, blogs, and other avenues for electronic word of mouth (eWOM), consumers are bombarded with company related information, making these media tools relevant to the discussion. Even so, the current state of social media networks is never current for more than a moment. Any discussion of social media that includes current functionality, current advertising opportunities, or specific ways that consumers view or interact with published content within a specific platform must be considered as a snapshot in time.

Even so, companies have, at times, been adept at generating brand presence in social media. When the Super Bowl went dark in January 2013, Oreo quickly took advantage and tweeted, "Power out? No problem" along with a picture of an Oreo cookie spotlighted in a dark space, with the tagline "You can still Dunk in the Dark." (*Huffington Post*, 2013). Conversely, Procter and Gamble is finding social media to be elusive in creating the "reason to buy" because customers compare experiences and share insights without the company in the conversation (Baskin, 2012). How consumers perceive information received via social media is an open question, and there is so much information traveling across social media it can be difficult to sort out the origin of the message. For instance, some Facebook posts are automatically created when a consumer purchases online and then allows a connection to their page; some information comes directly from the company through fan sites and tweets to which the consumer has subscribed; other information comes from seemingly unrelated sources through random posts that mention particular companies; and still other information is encountered through more traditional, paid advertisements that appear around the social networking site. Given these new avenues to reach consumers with company and product related information, it is important for both marketers and researchers to understand the relative effectiveness and impact of the various perceived sources of information and various methods of communication through these emerging interactive technologies.

Understanding how consumers respond to eWOM communications from various sources in different contexts is important because consumers seem to be becoming more and more resistant to traditional marketing communications. Resistance should be lower for eWOM messages than for traditional messages, but even within the eWOM, context resistance may vary across different sources and conditions.

eWOM on Social Media

Interactions and relationships that involve word-of-mouth on social networks, or eWOM, can take many forms, ranging from a relationship that resembles the offline variety to a relationship that is more one-sided. On the one hand, when a person "friends" another person on Facebook, s/he does not see the friend's updates until s/he receives an explicit acceptance of the request. This forms a synchronous relationship, with action required by both parties. These relationships are generally formed between people who know each other in real life and are the most common type of relationship on Facebook. It is also the strongest relationship on Facebook because it exists beyond the platform. In most cases, it was formed through a series of interactions over a period of time and Facebook can now support and continue that connection. In addition, people are most likely interested in the updates, messages, posts, and importantly, recommendations from these friends. Their history offline substantiates their recommendations online. One would suspect that eWOM from this source is strongest on Facebook because it is most reminiscent of the face-to-face WOM. When real friends share updates on Facebook that include product recommendations or they respond to questions like, "who is a reliable local plumber," this can feel as real as a conversation across the fence in the backyard.

Most adults do not have exceptionally large networks of friends on this social media platform. According to a recent survey by the Pew Research Center, adults have an average of 338 friends on Facebook, although the median number of friends is 200 (Smith, 2014). However, these relationships are skewed by age with younger adults (18–29 year olds) having more friends (mean of 300) and older adults (older than 65) having far fewer friends (mean of 30). Certainly, networks of this size are much larger than a small circle of close friends, but familiarity and regular updates keep these friends connected. It is this ongoing connection that drives the continued interaction and the potential authority and power of the eWOM.

Further, the importance of the platform is growing in peoples' lives: Pew reported that 64% of adults visit Facebook daily. What do they do when they are on Facebook? According to the Pew survey, 44% percent of adults "like" content posted by their friends at least once per day, and 29% do so multiple times per day. Although this act may seem like a small, inconsequential "mouse click," this simple act of liking a post can show up as an activity to your friends and thus create a conversation and serve to continue the ongoing relationship.

There is another relational category of Facebook friends that has not been widely adopted, but does exist at the fringes of the social media platform. There are a number of people who use Facebook as their primary social network and connect with everyone they meet online and offline. This creates a large network of friends and less intimate acquaintances that have less influence. This type of Facebook relationship may look and feel more like a broadcast channel. However, the Facebook networker does interact with his network often and this type of eWOM can carry some weight early in the relationship and can grow as the reliability of the updates and posts increases over time.

Finally, a person can set their profile to "public" and allow anyone to follow his/her updates and posts, creating an asynchronous relationship. There is no approval required on the part of the person being followed. In fact, there may be no relationship at all between many of the participants. The public person is acting like a brand or a celebrity, broadcasting and sharing ideas with anyone who follows and happens to be listening.

Whereas the "public" profile category is less common on Facebook, this type of public sharing is at the core of Twitter's functionality. Because Twitter is composed of primarily these asynchronous relationships, it can be more challenging to understand the power of eWOM recommendations or updates in this public forum. We might assume the effect to be similar to a celebrity spokesperson: when it feels forced, insincere, or sponsored, it may carry little weight, but when it seems authentic and natural, people tend to believe it and follow along. On the other hand, the Twitter endorsements are even more enhanced because the person has chosen to follow the tweeting public figure. Thus, it is different than stumbling across a pitch on a late night television infomercial.

Although people also follow companies on Facebook, it is not a prime reason to be on the platform. The Kentico Digital Experience Survey found that 39% of people "liked" only 1–10 companies on Facebook, and 40% did not "like," or "follow," any companies at all (Kentico, 2014). Here again, this online behavior appears to mirror the real world. That is, in the Syncapse survey of 2000 Facebook users, almost half reported that the reason they "like" a company on Facebook is to support a company that they already like in real life. Slightly fewer respondents (42%) reported that they "like" companies on Facebook to get coupons or discounts, and 41% report that they are looking to receive updates from companies they like (as cited in McGee, 2013a). From this data, it can be inferred that people "like" companies with which they have a pre-existing relationship in the real world, and they are now augmenting that relationship through an online connection.

The sheer number of posts generated by friends and "liked" companies has proven to be overwhelming to the Facebook network of users. The programmers at Facebook understand that the flow of content is just too much to show to a user, even one who accesses the site on a daily basis (Facebook, 2013). Thus, they have created an algorithm that takes into account over 100,000 factors to show people the most engaging and interesting content (McGee, 2013b). The algorithm relies heavily on liking, commenting, and sharing as the strongest signals of interest in a particular friend or type of post. This means that a person will be shown more updates from people and companies that they have engaged with in this manner. Thus, many company messages are filtered out to the Facebook user, even though it may not feel that way to the user.

Even while company messages may be filtered out due to lack of engagement, company messages that do get through the clutter may also be ignored. The Kentico survey found that 68% of respondents never, or hardly ever, pay attention to company posts. So whereas Facebook has been successful at injecting advertising into its platform, and getting companies to pay for it, the effectiveness of those messages is still questionable. Because of this, marketers are constantly looking to the next big thing to spread eWOM—as of late 2014, that potential platform might be Instagram.

Instagram is a mobile platform for posting and sharing pictures. It is owned by Facebook, but continues to run separately, and certain companies have grown huge followings on this platform. Style and personality are important factors in creating and sustaining a compelling Instagram presence, but understanding how to tell a visual story is also important on this platform. That doesn't mean every picture has to tell a story, but each picture contributes to the telling the larger story of the individual or company.

In stark contrast to the synchronous relationships so prevalent on Facebook, Instagram users have the ability to "like" and comment on any photo published anywhere on the platform, regardless of whether they follow the user or not. Whereas it is possible to see what photos your friends have liked, the use of comments provides a stronger means of drawing a connection from the picture to friends (both close and casual) thus generating eWOM. When a user tags his/her friends in the comments on a company post, the friends get a notification of that tag on their mobile device and are taken directly to that post. This way they are alerted to a company post that they might otherwise have missed, and can tag other friends to see the post as well. These shared posts might be anything from a lifestyle photo related to a company to a notification or review of a new product release. Communicating with images to mobile device users is a way that companies are more easily getting in front of customers during all times of day across a variety of situations. Further, when they are notified about these posts by their friends, the power of eWOM is leveraged and expanded even more.

Traditional WOM and Consumer Information Processing

Traditionally, word of mouth (WOM) has been considered to be more credible and trustworthy than conventional advertising because it is perceived to be from an altruistic, non-biased source (Brown & Reingen, 1987). However, in today's connected world, given the range of relationships on the various online platforms, information may not be unbiased or independent from company influences. For instance, companies create content and creative messages designed to get people to talk about a new product online in order to generate eWOM and awareness. This "stealth" marketing is an attempt to control the elusive eWOM information flow and gain consumers' attention (Leung, 2004). The current position of most marketers is that they need to have a presence across social media, but how to maximize that investment remains a question to be answered.

The current research into the effectiveness of WOM communications (both traditional forms and online) utilizes observation and self-report data to evaluate the effectiveness of WOM over more traditional marketing tactics. Katz and Lazarsfeld (1955) used self-report and surveys to infer that traditional WOM is between two and seven times more effective than radio ads, personal selling, and print advertisements in generating brand attitudes. More recently, researchers have used self-report to conclude that customers acquired through WOM are two times more important in terms of lifetime customer value, and twice as likely to invite other new customers (Villanueva, Yoo, & Hanssens, 2008). Other researchers have used observation to conclude that WOM leads to higher relative sales (Chevalier & Mayzlin, 2006; Liu, 2006), and higher monetary value for the firm (Trusov, Bucklin, & Pauwels, 2009). However, little is still known about how the various types of eWOM differ in their effectiveness in generating positive attitudes, loyalty, or a long-term relationship with the brand. For example, are differences between types of eWOM driven by message content or message source? Does it matter if the information comes from an actual friend—or does information presented by an unknown other or "public" source on Facebook, Twitter, or Instagram generate equally strong effectiveness?

In order to generate predictions about how the various types of eWOM may differ in effectiveness in generating brand attitudes and behaviors, we can draw from consumer information processing literature. There are many theories that focus on how and when attitudes are formed after exposure to brand information (for a review, see Evans, 2008). Many theories suggest that attitudes are automatic, fast, and efficient, given mere exposure to an object (Fazio et al., 1986), followed by a slow, deliberate evaluation stage to refine the attitude given time and desire to think (e.g., Gilbert, 1991; Kahneman, 2003; Stanovich & West, 2000). More recently, research has suggested that brand attitudes are formed when needed or when the consumer believes the attitude will be needed in the future (Cronley, Mantel, & Kardes, 2010). Thus, consumers will form an attitude "real-time" only if they have the cognitive resources and the motivation to do so; otherwise, they will form the attitude "from memory" at the time that the attitude is required (Tormala & Petty, 2001) and will base that attitude on information that is available at the time of attitude formation (Cronley, Mantel, & Kardes, 2010).

In addition, consumers have a "bounded rationality." This means that, whereas they would like to be rational, they often lack important information or cognitive capacity to fully consider all implications (Bazerman, 2005). Thus, the influence of any information subsequently used in a later decision may be driven by the perceived source of that information and the credibility assigned to that source (Mantel, Tatikonda, & Liao, 2006). Translating these findings to the eWOM domain, the perceived source of eWOM information may determine the effectiveness of that information in influencing attitudes and behaviors.

Resistance to Persuasion

Marketers often talk about consumers' "resistance to persuasion" as a kind of radar that signifies that a source of information may be biased in favor of the company and thus the information should be viewed with suspicion. Historically, researchers have viewed this resistance to persuasion as an outcome-based measure—if the participant shows little or no change to a persuasive message, then they are resistant. However, aspects of the situation and individual differences are very likely to have an effect on the persuasive ability of a message. For example, consumers that believe that they can resist a persuasion attempt are more willing to expose themselves to that stimulus (Wilson, Gilbert, & Wheatly, 1998). Consumers who are trying to resist a persuasive message will generate counterarguments, and by doing so will generate higher confidence in their own position (Petty & Wegener, 1999). Thus, consumers will utilize a number of cues from their own personality and from the situation to respond to persuasive messages.

The flexible correction model (FCM; Petty & Wegener, 1993) suggests that consumers will adjust their analysis to counteract some perceived bias if they are motivated to exert cognitive effort. Thus, if a consumer is presented with product information they perceive to be biased, they will adjust their opinion based on that perceived bias. According to the FCM, an advertisement will have lower persuasive effect compared to an unsolicited statement by a friend (i.e., the WOM effect). By extension, if a person becomes aware that the friend may be motivated by a company to express positive sentiments, their reliance on the friend's opinion should be moderated.

People who perceive themselves to be resistant to persuasion are less likely to change their opinion in the face of a persuasive message (Briñol, Tormala, & Petty 2004). However, the method of resistance may vary based on the source of the message itself. That is, if the source of the message is suspect (i.e., a paid advertisement), then the consumer may use counterarguments to denigrate the source (Zuwerink & Devine, 1996), they may focus on their own ability to resist ("I won't change my opinion"), or they may rely on a selective attention to information available to form their opinion.

The research to date suggests that companies should focus on setting up the company message such that resistance to persuasion is minimized—thus increasing persuasion by reducing resistance. Resistance to persuasion is a robust concept and worthy of study in its own right (Knowles & Linn, 2004). This is important because it is only by understanding resistance to persuasion that a company can create a brand or product message that will be heard, shared, and used as a source of attitude formation or change.

Social Media Communication

To explore these issues, we report a controlled experiment that investigates the relative effectiveness of various communications within the social media environment. The focus of this research is to tease out the effect of perceived information source, the relative influence of a referral from known and unknown others during social media interaction, and the influence of personal (e.g., resistance to persuasion) and situational variables such as awareness of "stealth marketing" (i.e., the use of undisclosed company relationship to promote a product) on the social media information exchange.

In a preliminary review of company content on Facebook (Mantel, Cronley, Schetzsle, & Cohen 2014), several company pages were evaluated to understand how an organization's Facebook page can get "shared" and expand reach beyond first generation Facebook followers. Facebook Insights were collected from several organizations and industries (both for-profit and community not-for-profit) over several weeks. The posts were categorized by format (primarily text/primarily picture), goal (informative/action), and subject matter (upcoming event/sale/point of interest). The results identified the types of post that generated highest reach (numbers of people who see the post), high levels of engagement (number of clicks on the post), high levels of shares (re-posts), and high levels of viral spread (percentage of people who see the post that create a story about the post). "Fans" of the various pages were also interviewed to understand the motivations behind the interaction with the posts. The results generated by this review are useful in understanding the types of posts that generate views among fans and friends of fans, and suggest that organizations can specifically design posts to increase the chances that the message will be picked up and shared.

As companies attempt to understand and use social media to promote their company message, they are looking for an understanding of return on influence. That is, they are trying to find the blogger, tweeters, etc., that carry influence with others and then target those users to share their company content (Schaefer, 2012). For example, Turner Broadcasting was in the midst of introducing a new show called *Falling Skies* that it targeted at a sci-fi audience that is small but passionate. Rather than focusing on traditional program launch that would have entailed press kits and early screenings to traditional critics, Turner Broadcasting turned to a group of social media influencers (i.e., people who had connections that would magnify the message shared) and invited 600 of them to join a 10-week program where they received an "inside experience or secret" about upcoming episodes. The group was offered a chance to have a "walk-on" role at the beginning of season two of the series if they had the most influence as measured by Klout score. Turner Broadcasting perceived the campaign to be a huge success because the well-chosen "insiders" were incented to talk about the show (with free gifts and incentives), they were passionate about the genre, and they had the connections to make a difference (Schaefer, 2012). Not only that, the increase in buzz generated by these "stealth marketers" created a full point increase on the Neilsen Ratings and thus translated into corresponding increases in adverting revenue. This example suggests that these highly connected influencers were effective at generating persuasive conversations among their followers—both close and distant.

To understand how a small group of influencers can generate the kind of response observed by Turner Broadcasting, an experiment was conducted among a national sample (344 participants) using a controlled message scenario (Mantel et al., 2014). It was designed to investigate differences in attitude formation among consumers exposed to new company information via social media. Whereas information content was held constant, the source of the information (friend, friend of a friend, unknown other, or paid advertising) was manipulated in order to ascertain the relative effectiveness of the various eWOM dissemination options. In addition, the credibility of the source via a stealth marketing prime was manipulated and resistance to persuasion was measured.

Given the strong influence of a small group of passionate viewers recruited to spread the word of Turner Broadcasting's new show, it seems likely that consumers perceive these recruited emissaries as unaffiliated, unbiased sources of information rather than an extension of the company itself. As companies try to replicate these results, it is important to understand how consumers react to a persuasive message from various potential sources.

In order to generate reality within the controlled experiment, participants provided the names of the friends and acquaintances that were then used as the identifiers on the fictitious Facebook page stimuli. Awareness of stealth marketing was primed within the Facebook stimuli with a conversation post between two close friends. On a second Facebook page, three of the four fictitious companies were displayed in one of three positions (full factorial design). The company was either discussed by a friend, an acquaintance, or in a display ad located on the right-hand side of the page. The "companies" depicted were fictitious companies selected via a pre-test. The companies presented and source of information were randomly varied across participants and the message content was held constant. The "friends" identified by the participant were assigned to the "Person A" (or "Person B," etc.) to give the page a personal feel (see Figure 3.1).

The results showed main effects for message source, resistance to persuasion, stealth marketing prime, and also showed an interaction in the expected pattern. As predicted, the source of the new company information differed in its effectiveness such that paid company ads were least effective, followed by companies

FIGURE 3.1 Facebook Page Stimulus Example

recommended by acquaintances (i.e., "unknown others"), with recommendations by friends being the most effective. Further, those who saw the prime were less influenced by information presented by the "unknown other," but friends still had a positive influence. Thus, we believe that consumers are naturally wary of information that comes from the company, but are naturally accepting of information that comes from a friend. However, information that is provided by an "unknown other" (i.e., someone who is not really a friend, but who is also not perceived to be an arranged emissary of the brand or company) will be also accepted as credible unless the participant is exposed as not being trustworthy.

The most interesting pattern of results emerged when investigating the interaction between the source message, stealth marketing prime, and reported resistance to persuasion. Results showed that simply making people aware that an information source may be biased is not sufficient to refute an eWOM recommendation, especially among those who report a low resistance to persuasion. This has many important marketing implications. If companies can present their message via stealth marketing so that it is perceived to be recommended by a friend or even from an unknown other, the typical consumer will be likely to adopt that recommendation. It is particularly concerning that those who perceive themselves to be low in resistance to persuasion seem to respond to the stealth marketing prime by lowering their reported attitudes only for company and brand messages that are communicated through traditional marketing channels, not for those that are recommended via stealth marketing channels (see Figure 3.2).

It appears from the various observed behaviors that organizations can design a program to encourage widespread conversations about a brand or company and increase the chances that the conversation will be shared and friends of fans will be exposed to the information. The results of the experiment suggest that if a company can get its fans to share the creative message, then chances are increased that a friend of a friend will see the post and consider it as a recommendation from an acquaintance. This appears to increase the chance that the unrelated viewer will be persuaded by the content of the post.

Given this finding, it is important to view social media as more than just a collection of tools. In fact, leading marketers, such as Procter and Gamble, see digital marketing a part of entire campaign rather than as a goal unto itself. That is, the digital technology is simply a means to reach consumers with a compelling creative message that is worthy of being passed on. Before the digital age, Procter and Gamble focused on creating brands that had distinctive, creative images based on quality products. Today, the focus is the same, create a message that people want to share and then put that message out there on all of the communications tools. In fact, Marc Pritchard, Global Brand Building Officer at Procter and Gamble, noted "you need to inspire creative work that is so brilliant you're willing to bet your career on it" (Neff, 2012). For that reason, the

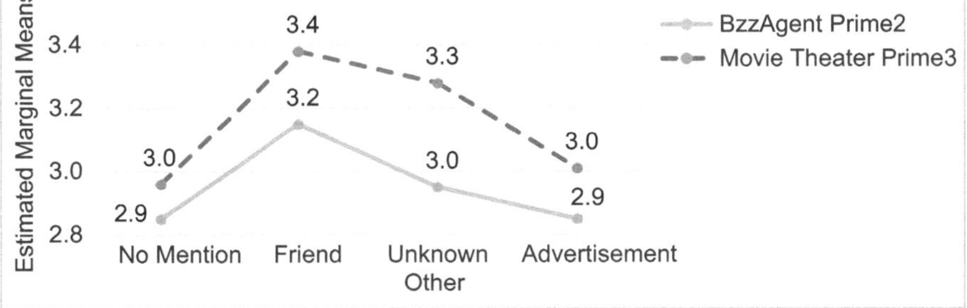

FIGURE 3.2 Brand Ratings

company has reduced the traditionally lengthy creative brief down to a brand concept that is more of a "business challenge." For example, when the company launched Tide Pods, the creative team worked from the simple directive "Make Tide Pods irresistible," and the resulting campaign used pop art and color to make the brand appear fun, cool, and convenient (Neff, 2012).

As more companies follow Procter and Gamble's lead and start to create brand messages with the intent to start and spread a conversation, there will need to be a greater focus on constructing the message with the elements that will encourage the everyday consumer to share the message. One way to think about generating the brand conversation is proposed by Jonah Berger in his book *Contagious: Why Things Catch On* (2009) discussing the science behind social transmission. In Berger's model there are six reasons why people share a message that they encounter. First, they share a message to generate social currency—that is, they want to look "cool" by sharing new or interesting facts that are not widely known. This appears to be the reason that the Turner Broadcasting launch of *Falling Skies* was so successful. By providing the identified "influencers" with valuable information in advance, these selected influencers could share the "inside" information and look "cool" and "smart." That is, they got a lot of social currency by appearing to be in the know.

In addition, if the company can be kept top of mind (Triggers in the environment), it will be more likely to be discussed on social media. For example, consumers often tweet pictures of their food while eating at a restaurant. It is not that the consumer likes the restaurant more while they are sitting at a table (compared to the day before), it is only that the restaurant is on the top of their mind and thus more likely to be shared via social media. In addition, if the product is "public"—that is, people can see others using the product, then they are more likely to share their experiences with the brand.

Similarly, people tend to share issues and messages that they feel emotionally attached to or messages that they feel will help others. Thus, if a company can craft the creative message to generate passion, empathy, or similar strong emotions among the intended audience or create content that seems useful or helpful, then the message is more likely to be passed on to others.

Finally, people like to tell stories. Therefore, if the brand message can be wrapped in a particularly intriguing story, then it is likely to be passed on. It is extremely important that the brand is central to the story, however. Because the story is the element that is passed on, the brand message itself will only be passed on if it is integral to it.

As the world changes, more and more communications pathways are dominated by consumer conversations that are not directly influenced by the company itself. Brand managers must learn to craft their message to encourage sharing between consumers. This can be done by creating content that people want to share because it makes them feel good or it provides some sort of social capital. Once the conversation is started, then the influence can be multiplied as other consumers encounter the message from a friend or a friend of a friend. The primary data suggest that the unknown other is often just as influential as the close friend in generating a persuasive message that is incorporated into the new positive brand attitude.

References

Baskin, Jonathan, S. (2012). "P&G's Social Media Orthodoxy Could Sink Its Innovation Progress." www.forbes.com/sites/jonathansalembaskin/2012/11/17/pgs-social-media-orthodoxy-could-sink-its-innovation-progress/11/17/2012. Accessed 10/2/2014.

Bazerman, Max (2005). "Judgment in Managerial Decision Making," sixth ed. John Wiley and Sons, New York.

Berger, Jonah (2009). *Contagious: Why Things Catch On.* New York: Simon & Schuster.

Briñol, P., D. D. Rucker, Z. L. Tormala, and R. E. Petty (2004). "Individual Differences in Resistance to Persuasion: The role of beliefs and meta-beliefs" in E.S. Knowles and J. A. Linn (eds.) *Resistance and Persuasion* (pp. 83–104), New Jersey: Lawrence Erlbaum Associates.

Brown, Johnson and Peter Reingen (1987). "Social Ties and Word-of-Mouth Referral Behavior," *Journal of Consumer Research,* 14 (December), 350–62.

Chevalier, Judith and Dina Mayzlin (2006). "The Effect of Word of Mouth on Sales: Online Book Reviews," *Journal of Marketing Research,* 43 (August), 345–54.

Cronley, Maria L., Susan Powell Mantel, and Frank R. Kardes (2010). "Online and Memory-Based Attitude Formation: Effects of Accuracy and Need to Evaluate on Mode of Attitude Formation," *Journal of Consumer Psychology,* 20 (3), 274–81.

Evans, J. (2008). "Dual-Processing Accounts of Reasoning, Judgment, and Social Cognition," *Annual Review of Psychology,* 59, 255–78.

Facebook (2013). "NewsFeed FYI: A Window into News Feed," August 6, 2013. www.facebook.com/business/news/News-Feed-FYI-A-Window-Into-News-Feed. Accessed 10/3/14.

Fazio, R. H., Sanbonmatsu, D. M., Powell, M. C., and Kardes, F. R. (1986). "On the Automatic Activation of Attitudes." *Journal of Personality and Social Psychology,* 50 (2), 229–38.

Gilbert, D. T. (1991). "How Mental Systems Believe," *American Psychologist,* 46 (2), 107–119.

Huffington Post (2013). "Oreo's Super Bowl Tweet: 'You Can Still Dunk In The Dark.'" www.huffingtonpost.com/2013/02/04/oreos-super-bowl-tweet-dunk-dark_n_2615333.html. Accessed 10/2/2014.

Kahneman, D. (2003). "A Perspective on Judgment and Choice: Mapping Bounded Rationality," *American Psychologist,* 58, 697–720.

Katz, E., and Lazarsfeld, P. F. (1955). *Personal Influence: The Part Played by People in the Flow of Mass Communications.* Transaction Publishers.

Kentico (2014). "Kentico Digital Experience Survey: 68% Don't Pay Attention to Brands They Like on Facebook," March 3. www.kentico.com/Company/Press-Center/2014/Kentico-Digital-Experience-Survey-68-Don%E2%80%99t-Pay-Att. Accessed 10/2/12014.

Knowles, E. S., and Linn, J. A. (Eds.). (2004). *Resistance and Persuasion.* Psychology Press.

Leung, Rebecca (2004). "Undercover Marketing Uncovered: Hidden Cameras Capture Salespeople Secretly Pitching Products," *60 Minutes,* CBS. www.cbsnews.com/stories/2003/10/23/60minutes/main579657.shtml. Accessed 10/2/2014.

Liu, Y. (2006). Word of Mouth for Movies: Its Dynamics and Impact on Box Office Revenue. *Journal of marketing,* 70 (3), 74–89.

Mantel, S. P., M. Cronley, S. Schetzle, and J. Cohen (2014). "The Effectiveness of Emerging Media in Generating Brand Attitude and Loyalty," *working paper.*

Mantel, Susan Powell, Mohan V. Tatikonda, and Ying Liao (2006). "A Behavioral Study of Supply Manager Decision-Making: Factors Influencing Make versus Buy Evaluation," *Journal of Operations Management,* 24, 822–38.

McGee, Matt (2013a). "Why Do Consumers Become Facebook Fans? Study Says It Depends On the Brand." Marketingland.com. http://marketingland.com/why-do-consumers-become-facebook-fans-49745. Accessed 10/2/2014.

McGee, Matt (2013b). "EdgeRank Is Dead: Facebook's News Feed Algorithm Now Has Close to 100K Weight Factors." Marketingland.com. http://marketingland.com/edgerank-is-dead-facebooks-news-feed-algorithm-now-has-close-to-100k-weight-factors-55908. Accessed 10/2/2014.

Neff, Jack (2012). "P&G's Pritchard Offers Manifesto for the Creative Class: Brand Building Officer Urges Shorter Briefs, Less Slavish Reliance on Copy Tests." *Advertising Age.* http://adage.com/article/special-report-cannes-2012/p-g-s-marc-pritchard-offers-manifesto-creative-class/235548/. Accessed 10/2/2014.

Petty, R. E. and D. T. Wegener (1993). "Flexible Correction Processes in Social Judgment: Correcting for Context Induced Contrast," *Journal of Experimental Social Psychology,* 29, 137–65.

Petty, R. E. and D. T. Wegener (1999). "The Elaboration Likelihood Model: Current Status and Controversies," in S. Chaiken and Trope (eds.), *Dual-Process Theories in Social Psychology* (pp. 41–72), New York: Guilford Press.

Schaefer, Mark W. (2012). *Return on Influence: The Revolutionary Power of KLOUT, Social Scoring and Influence Marketing.* New York: McGraw Hill.

Smith, Aaron (2014). "6 New Facts about Facebook" Pew Research Center. www.pewresearch.org/fact-tank/2014/02/03/6-new-facts-about-facebook/. Accessed 10/2/2014.

Stanovich, K. E. and R. T. West (2000). "Individual Differences in Reasoning: Implications for the Rationality Debate," *Behavioral and Brain Sciences,* 23, 645–65.

Tormala, Z. L. and R. E. Petty (2001). "Online Versus Memory-Based Processing: The Role of 'Need to Evaluate' in Person Perception," *Personality and Social Psychology Bulletin,* 27, 1599–1612.

Trusov, Michael, Randolph E. Bucklin, and Koen Pauwels (2009). "Effects of Word-of-Mouth Versus Traditional Marketing: Findings from an Internet Social Networking Site," *Journal of Marketing,* 73 (September), 90–102.

Villanueva, J., Shijin Yoo, and Dominique M. Hasssens (2008). "The Impact of Marketing-Induced Versus Word-of-Mouth Customer Acquisition on Customer Equity Growth," *Journal of Marketing Research,* 45 (February), 48–59.

Wilson, T. D., D. T. Gilbert, and T. P. Wheatly (1998). "Protecting our Minds: The Role of Lay Beliefs," in V.Y. Yzerbyt and G. Lories (eds.), *Metacognition: Cognitive and Social Dimensions* (pp. 171–201), Thousand Oaks, CA: Sage Publications.

Zuwerink, J. R. and P. G. Devine (1996). "Attitude Importance and Resistance to Persuasion: It's Not Just the Thought That Counts," *Journals of Personality and Social Psychology,* 70, 931–44.

4

NOW OR LATER

Synchrony Effects on Electronic Word-of-Mouth Content

Cansu Sogut, Barbara Bickart, and Frédéric Brunel

> *"Robb is like the dumbest dude ever right now #GameofThrones"*
>
> *"I really love Jaime and Brienne. #gameofthrones"*
>
> *"Oh my god. That was horrible. Oh my god. Tell him, Robb. #gameofthrones"*
>
> *"Oh man. Child murder . . . we had to go there, didn't we. #GameofThrones #Geez"*
>
> *"Why do we see all of Ygritte but we don't get to see all of Jon Snow? Frustrated with #gameofthrones"*

The tweets above occurred during an episode of the television show *Game of Thrones* (04/28/2013; Season 3, Episode 5). They illustrate how consumers now engage in word-of-mouth communication not only after an experience, but also *during* the consumption of the experience. TV viewing is one focal domain in which this type of interaction can often be observed, as reflected in the growth of technologies that enable "social TV" (Proulx and Shepatin 2012). For example, in the United States, 88% of tablet owners and 86% of smartphone owners report that they used their device while watching TV at least once during a 30-day period (Nielsen 2012). Moreover, 41% of U.S. smartphone owners say that they use their phone at least once a day while tuned in to some TV program (Nielsen 2012). These statistics suggest that eWOM is not only spread after an experience, but that people are also increasingly sharing live comments, reaction, or updates at the same time as they engage in an experience. Because past research on WOM and eWOM has usually studied these phenomena as practices taking place after an experience or event, little is known about the nature and dynamics of simultaneous eWOM.

In this chapter, we investigate how the timing of eWOM sharing affects its content and underlying processes. We conceptualize two types of eWOM based on the timing of a communicator's message, (a) *simultaneous sharing* (during consumption), and (b) *retrospective sharing* (after consumption). In two field studies we examine how message content changes with the timing of sharing. Specifically, we focus on two aspects of message content: (i) the communal content, which reflects the self versus communal orientation in the message and (ii) the affective content. Differences in these two aspects of message content may affect the persuasive impact of the message, as well as the likelihood that the message is passed along to others.

The chapter is organized as follows: we first define key constructs, describe a conceptual framework, and derive predictions about the effects of timing of sharing eWOM on the communal and affective content of the message. We then present the findings of two field studies that use Twitter data to test our predictions. Finally, we discuss the implications of our findings for managing eWOM and provide directions for future research.

Conceptual Background

In order to better understand how the timing of sharing affects message content, we draw on social theories of synchrony. Synchrony is defined as "the coordination of movement between individuals in social interactions" (Bernieri, Reznick, and Rosenthal 1988, p. 243). Broadly, it refers to instances where the social interactions become organized in time and space (Bernieri and Rosenthal 1991; Richardson, Marsh, and Schmidt 2005). Literature on synchrony has focused on "muscular bonding" in which people move synchronously with each other (McNeill 1995). For example, when soldiers march together or when worshippers sing together, each member moves/vocalizes synchronously with the other members (McNeill 1995). Anthropologists and sociologists have argued that social activities in which group members "act in synchrony" lead to positive emotions that bring group members psychologically closer to each other (McNeill 1995). For example, research shows that after moving in synchrony with others, people start seeing the other people as more similar to themselves (Valdesolo, Ouyang, and DeSteno 2010; Valdesolo and DeSteno 2011). Furthermore, empirical evidence suggests that because synchronous action is associated with feelings of joint purpose, affiliation, and perceived similarity, synchrony enhances cooperation (Wiltermuth and Heath 2009; Hove and Risen 2009; Valdesolo, Ouyang, and DeSteno 2010).

In the virtual world of social media, participants typically lack the direct physical proximity and the spacial co-location that is generally implied in previous synchrony research. Nonetheless, even in social media worlds (e.g., Twitter, Instagram), social relations cluster and take place in and around shared virtual spaces identified via virtual social markers. These markers can be hashtags (#), which create the bounds and boundaries of the world in which the social agents connect (Zappavigna 2011). As such, they allow online social interactions to be organized in time and virtual space. Building on past research on synchrony, we argue that in social media sites and platforms, socializing around the same experience at the same moment makes the experience more interactive and engenders bonds between communicators. More specifically, with respect to eWOM, we suggest that *simultaneous sharing* of messages with others during a consumption experience (enabled by digital technology) should lead to feelings of shared purpose and perceived similarity, and hence a synchrony both with the experience and with social others. We predict that this synchrony will be reflected in and thus affect the content of message sharing.

Our conceptual framework is summarized in Figure 4.1. In the context of simultaneous eWOM sharing, we conceptualize the synchrony construct as operating via two separate paths: (i) synchrony with social others and (ii) synchrony with the experience. Below, we describe in greater details the processes by which we predict that these two dimensions of synchrony will influence the content of eWOM.

Although there is an increasing interest in understanding the antecedents and consequences of eWOM, the conceptualization of eWOM as a social act is recent. eWOM is not just a one-to-one or one-to-many communication with solely instrumental/information sharing objectives. Instead, as consumers collaborate and co-create online social worlds, eWOM should be seen as a communication form with social goals and serving these social co-creation activities (Toder-Alon and Brunel 2013). As shown on the left path of Figure 4.1, we predict that eWOM shared simultaneously will be more communal, and thus will contain

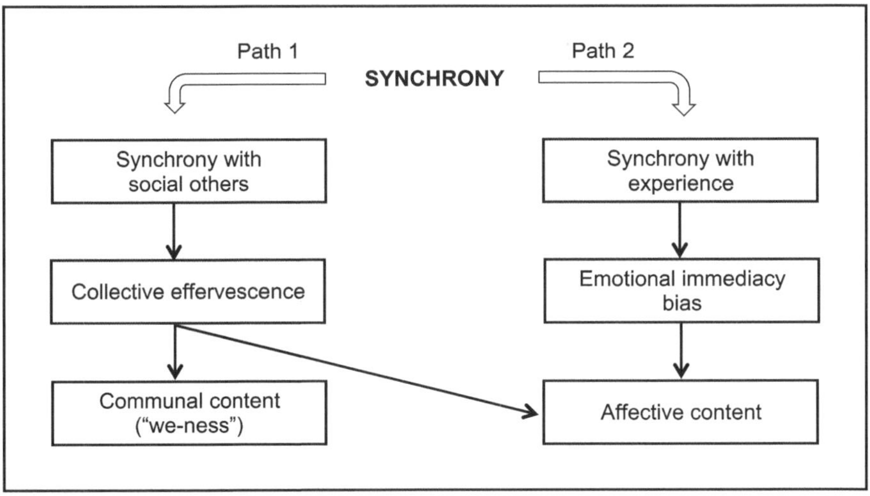

FIGURE 4.1 Conceptual Framework

more words that signal collectiveness. We argue that the act of simultaneous sharing carries characteristics of Durkheim's "collective effervescence" concept, which is defined as the moments when members of a community gather together for shared rituals or events (Durkheim 1912/2012). When these members come together, engage in similar actions, and simultaneously communicate similar thoughts or emotions, feelings of intimacy, intensity, and immediacy are conjured, and these in turn can be energizing and unifying for the group (Durkheim 1912, 2012; Olaveson 2001). One of the most important characteristics of collective effervescence is that in these moments, individuals experience "collective emotional excitement" (Fisher and Chon 1989, p. 2), leading to a sense of empowerment and arousal (Fisher and Chon 1989; Olaveson 2001; Durkheim 1912, 2012). Extending Durkheim's conceptualization and subsequent work on the topic, we expect that the act of simultaneous eWOM sharing can create synchrony with social others that in turn will result in collective effervescence. As an outcome of this enhanced feeling of connection with others, simultaneously shared eWOM messages should reflect a greater collective orientation (e.g., a sense of "we-ness") than messages that are shared retrospectively. Work in social influence and linguistics shows that a sense of "we-ness" is reflected in the occurrence of first person plural pronouns such as "we, us, our, ours." These "we" words indicate "shared identity and affiliative motivation" (Simmons et al. 2005, p. 933; Cialdini et al. 1976). In contrast, an individualistic orientation would lead to a greater occurrence of first person singular pronouns such as "I, me, my, mine" (Buehlman et al. 1992; Simmons et al. 2005; Tausczik and Pennebaker 2010). Hence, when eWOM sharing is simultaneous (versus retrospective), we predict consumers to use more "we" words and fewer "I" words, signaling a sense of shared consumption and communal orientation.

Synchrony with Experience: Affective Content

We predict that because of synchrony with the experience, simultaneous eWOM should have more emotional content than retrospective eWOM. Research has shown that immediate emotions (i.e., those experienced at present) are perceived as being more intense compared to emotions that have been experienced in the past (Van Boven, White, and Huber 2009). People perceive their immediate emotions as more intense because those emotions are more salient, cognitively more available, and generally easier to remember than those for a past consumption experience (Neath 1993, Van Boven et al. 2009). This effect is referred to as the "immediacy bias" in emotional experiences (Van Boven et al. 2009). We expect this effect to hold true in the context of eWOM, and thus, as shown in the right path in Figure 4.1, we predict that during simultaneous sharing, this emotional immediacy bias will increase the affective content in a message, relative to retrospective sharing, as emotional reactions will be more available in memory and easier to recall.

Further, as shown in Figure 4.1 and discussed earlier, collective effervescence may also have an additional direct influence on the affective content of the message. Past research has shown that collective effervescence results in a greater sense of collective excitement and arousal (Fisher and Chon 1989; Olaveson 2001; Durkheim 1912/2012). Therefore, in addition to the direct effect of the emotional immediacy associated with the experience, we expect that the collective effervescence implicated in simultaneous eWOM sharing can also have a positive effect on the affective content of eWOM.

Field Studies

To test our predictions, we conducted two studies using Twitter data. Twitter is a popular social platform and is the dominant medium for exchanging opinions about television, movie, and art content (Proulx and Shepatin 2012). This microblogging platform allows us to naturally observe eWOM content changes based on message timing. In the first study, we examined tweets posted during and after the first showing of an episode of the popular TV show *Game of Thrones*. In the second study, we examined tweets posted during and after the final game of the 2013 Stanley Cup Championship. In both studies we examined how the use of both first person singular (i.e., "I" words) vs. plural (i.e., "we" words) pronouns and the overall affective content of tweets is related to the timing of the message.

Study 1

Method

In Study 1, we collected 6,540 tweets (including retweets) about Episode 5 of the third season of the TV show *Game of Thrones* (#gameofthrones), which originally aired in the United States at 9:00 PM EST on April 28, 2013. We used the NCapture tool of NVivo to capture the tweets and information about the tweeters. We captured tweets (including retweets) with the #gameofthrones hashtag that were posted during a two and a half hour window[1] (i.e., 9:00 PM–11:30 PM EST). Thus, we were able to classify tweets (including retweets) into one of two timing conditions: simultaneous (9:00–10:00 PM, n = 2,598) and retrospective (10:00–11:30 PM, n = 3,942). We excluded retweets (n = 964) and the tweets with GetGlue or ViggleTV hashtags[2] (n = 1,484) from the analysis to prevent duplicate observations, resulting in 4,092 tweets available for further analyses (1,784 in the simultaneous condition and 2,308 in the retrospective condition).

To examine the "we-ness" and the affective content of the tweets, we conducted a content analysis using the linguistic inquiry and word count (LIWC) program (Pennebaker et al. 2007). LIWC software was originally developed to analyze emotional content and its dictionaries have been shown to yield ratings that converge with that of human coders (Pennebaker et al. 2007). LIWC has predefined dictionaries and by using the word counts for a text, it automatically calculates the proportion of words that match the predefined categories. For example, the text "I am happy" consists of three words. The word "happy" is categorized as a positive affect word in the LIWC dictionary. Hence, for this text, LIWC would calculate a positive affect score of 33.33, meaning that 33.33% of this text consists of positive affect. To obtain a count, we multiplied this percentage by the total number of words in a text and divided by 100. For our studies, the content analysis was conducted at the level of the tweet, that is, we examined the number of communal words (i.e., "we" vs. "I" words) and the number of affect words per tweet. Table 4.1 shows some examples of the words used by the LIWC software to calculate our dependent variables. To measure the communal content of a post, we used the number of first person plural pronouns (e.g., we, us, our, ours) as well as the first person singular pronouns (e.g., I, me, my, mine). For affective content, we used the number of affect words (positive and negative).

Results

We predicted that simultaneous tweets would include a higher number of first person plural pronouns. Across all tweets, 29% of the tweets included one or more first-person personal pronouns (both singular and plural). Because a large proportion of the tweets did not contain any "we" or "I" words (i.e., count equals zero for the number of "we" words or "I" words), our data was not normally distributed. Hence, we analyzed the pronoun counts using zero-inflated Poisson (ZIP) regression, with timing (simultaneous vs. retrospective) and total word count (per tweet) being the count model predictors and the total word count (per tweet) being the zero model predictor. As predicted, the number of personal *plural* pronouns (i.e., "we" words) was higher in simultaneous tweets by a count of 0.81 compared to the retrospective tweets, $p < .001$ (see Figure 4.2). Further, the number of first person *singular* pronouns (i.e., "I" words), was higher by 0.12

TABLE 4.1 Word Categories Used to Calculate Affective Content and Sense of Shared Consumption

Personal Pronouns	
1st person singular (I)	*I, Id, I'd, I'll, Im, I'm, Ive, I've, me, mine, my, myself*
1st person plural (We)	*lets, let's, our, ours, ourselves, us, we, we'd, we'll, we're, weve, we've*
Affective Content	
	Examples:
Positive affect	*love, nice, sweet, happy, pretty, wow, benefit, win, enjoy, play*
Negative affect	*hurt, ugly, cry, hate, worthless, enemy, lie, complain, fear, hell*

*Based on LIWC2007 (Pennebaker et al. 2007)

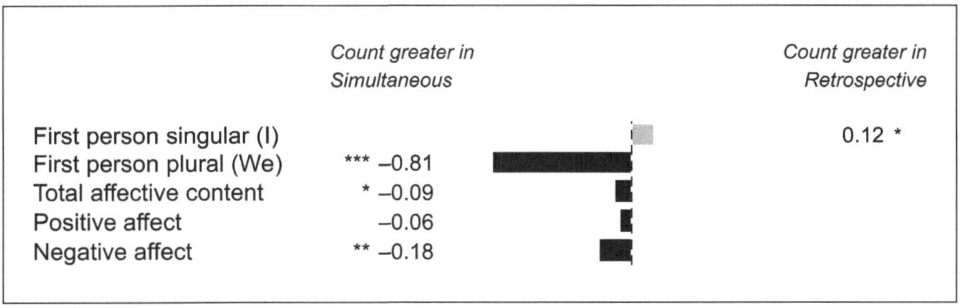

FIGURE 4.2 Study 1—Communal and Affective Content by Timing

when sharing was retrospective, $p < .05$. The higher use of "we" words in simultaneous sharing and "I" words in retrospective sharing suggests an increased communal focus and a decreased individual focus when sharing is simultaneous (versus retrospective).

Across all tweets, the average number of affect words was 0.71, with 50.2% of the tweets not containing any affect words. Again, due to the non-normal distribution of the data points, we analyzed the affect counts with zero-inflated Poisson (ZIP) regression, using timing (simultaneous vs. retrospective) and the total word count (per tweet) as the count model predictors and the total word count (per tweet) as the zero model predictor. The results provide support for our prediction that the affective content is higher for simultaneous tweets (versus retrospective tweets). As expected, simultaneous tweets contained more affect words than retrospective tweets by a count of 0.09, $p < .05$. Overall, these results suggest that when people live-tweet as they watch the show, they share more affective content via a greater use of affect words (both positive and negative) to describe their experiences. We also analyzed the occurrence of positive and negative affective content across the two timing conditions. The counts for positive affective words did not vary by timing condition. Tweets in the simultaneous (versus retrospective) condition, however, included more negative affect words by a count of 0.18, $p < .01$.

Discussion

In this study, our consumption context was entertainment (a TV show) where people shared their opinions and feelings via Twitter during and after an episode of the show. We found that when live-tweeting, consumers used more "we" words (and fewer "I" words), which provides initial support for the prediction that consumers feel more communal (i.e., collective effervescence) when they share eWOM while virtual others are also watching the show. Further, consumers used more "I" words (and fewer "we" words) during retrospective sharing, suggesting a more individualistic focus when looking back on the experience. As predicted, we found that the overall affective content was higher in the simultaneously shared messages compared to the retrospective ones. Further, positive affective content did not differ by timing of sharing, but negative affective content was higher in simultaneous sharing.

One limitation of this study was that the window for the retrospective sharing was so close to the actual experience that emotions were still quite salient, resulting in a more conservative test of our hypothesis. A greater time separation between the experience and the retrospective condition could be helpful in further understanding the phenomenon. In addition, there are likely to be idiosyncratic aspects of the emotions associated with eWOM messages about a specific television show, the moment-by-moment emotions experienced as the plot unfolds on the screen and nature of the show itself. Therefore, replicating this research with a different type of experience would be beneficial. Another limitation is related to the time zones in the United States. The episode of *Game of Thrones* aired twice on that day—once during the 9–10 PM EST slot for Eastern U.S. viewers and the other time during the 9–10 PM PST (which is 12–1 AM EST) slot for Western U.S. viewers—so the show was not on the air between 10:00–11:30 PM EST (i.e., the collection time of the retrospective tweets). This schedule allows us to be confident that we did not capture any simultaneous tweets in the retrospective condition and that we were able to capture tweets in two distinct timing conditions. We cannot, however, eliminate the possibility that some of the tweets (in both the simultaneous and retrospective conditions) were prospective tweets from viewers in the Pacific Time zone who were waiting and anticipating the 9–10 PM PST airing of the show. To address this last issue and the other previously mentioned limitations, we collected data during a second event—the 2013 Stanley Cup Finals. Because the Stanley Cup is aired at the same time in all time zones, we were able to ensure that all tweets were correctly categorized in the appropriate timing condition.

Study 2

Method

The context of the second study is a hockey game, Game 6 of the 2013 Stanley Cup, which was the final game between the Chicago Black Hawks and the Boston Bruins, played on June 24, at 8:00 PM EST. In total, 16,611 tweets (including retweets) with the #stanleycup hashtag were captured using the same tools as in Study 1. We collected 10,219 simultaneous (06/24/2013 Monday, 8:00 PM–10:56 PM EST) and 6,392 retrospective (06/25/2013 Tuesday, 8:00 AM–12:00 PM EST and Tuesday 8:00 PM–12:00 AM EST) tweets (including retweets).[3] In this study, we used a broader time delay for the collection of the retrospective tweets to address some of the limitations of Study 1. As in Study 1, we excluded retweets (n = 5,795) from the analysis. In addition, we excluded the tweets that were posted between 10:55–10:56 PM EST, which was exactly when the game was over (n = 1,844). These moments were characterized by "the thrill of victory and the agony of defeat," thus the tweets were extremely emotional. Because our theory is not about live TV or winning/losing, the tweets that were posted at the ending moment did not reflect the true nature of simultaneous sharing. Among the remaining 8,972 tweets, 58.5% of them had location coordinates attached. The tweets without location coordinates were excluded (n = 3,727). In order to separate the tweets by Chicago and Boston fans and other viewers, we used geographical location as a proxy. We coded the tweets as posted by Boston (Chicago) fans if their location coordinates were no further than approximately ± 100 miles North/South (1.5° latitudes) and approximately ± 100 miles West/East (± 2° longitudes) from Boston (Chicago) city center. The tweets from areas outside of these two areas were categorized as coming from "other viewers." Although it is likely that the Boston Bruins and Chicago Blackhawks have fans outside these boundaries (40,000 square miles respectively), or that some Bruins fans can be found in the Chicago area (and vice versa), we believe that these geographic boundaries allow us to create three distinct groups of respondents and use these three groups to further inform our theory. We observed that the content of tweets is often not enough to identify fan allegiances. For example, a tweet such as "so excited, game 6 is on, gotta love the #stanleycup" cannot be categorized, whereas its GPS coordinates are a reasonable proxy. Based on the location criteria, we were able to classify 2,100 tweets, 1,531 for Chicago and 569 for Boston. The remaining 3,145 tweets were coded as "Other."

Results

As in Study 1, we predicted that simultaneous tweets would include a higher number of "we" words. Thirty-one percent of the tweets included one or more first-person personal pronouns (both singular and plural). Again, due to the non-normal nature of the data, we analyzed the pronoun counts with zero-inflated Poisson (ZIP) regression, using timing (simultaneous vs. retrospective) and the total word count (per tweet) as the count model predictors and the total word count (per tweet) as the zero model predictor. When we compared the frequency of "we" words across conditions, consistent with our predictions, we found that

A. All Fans (N = 5,245; 3,337 in simultaneous, 1,888 in retrospective)

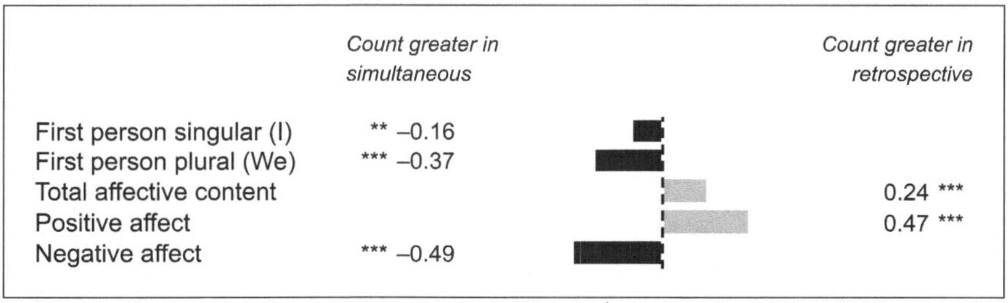

FIGURE 4.3 Study 2—Communal and Affective Content by Timing and Fans

those who posted simultaneously during the hockey game used 0.46 more first person *plural* pronouns compared to those who posted retrospectively, $p < .01$, suggesting more of a social process. In addition, we compared the communal content across three fan groups. For Boston fans, there was not a significant difference in the use of "we" words between the two conditions. For Chicago fans and Other fans, tweets that were posted in the simultaneous condition included a significantly higher number of "we" words, $p < .001$. Specifically, Chicago fans used 0.47 more "we" words and the Other fans used 0.55 more "we" words when they shared messages simultaneously. In addition, we also compared the use of "I" words across timing conditions. Contrary to predictions, across all fans, the use of "I" words was higher by a count of 0.17 in the simultaneous condition compared to the retrospective condition, $p < .01$. Boston and Chicago fans did not use statistically different number of "I" words across the two conditions. Yet, Other fans used 0.20 more "I" words in the simultaneous condition compared to the retrospective condition, $p < .05$.

Across all tweets (n = 5,245), the average number of affect words was 0.81, with 46.5% of the tweets not containing any affect words. To compare the total affect words expressed in the simultaneous and retrospective conditions, we used zero-inflated Poisson (ZIP) regression, with timing (simultaneous vs. retrospective) and total word count (per tweet) as the count model predictors and the total word count (per tweet) as the zero model predictor. Contrary to expectations, the number of total affect words was higher in the retrospective condition than in the simultaneous condition by a count of 0.24, $p < .001$. Again, in order to gain a better understanding, we examined the distribution of the number of tweets across the two fan groups.

As shown in Figure 4.3, the sample includes more tweets by Chicago fans than by Boston fans, probably due to the size of their fan bases and the drop-off of tweets by Boston fans after the game is greater than that for Chicago fans. In order to understand the effect of timing across three groups, we used zero-inflated Poisson (ZIP) regression for each group separately. Boston fans (0.44) and the "Other" fans (0.30) expressed more affect when they tweeted after the game than during the game, $p < .001$. Although the direction was the same, the difference in the number of affect words was not statistically significant across the two conditions for the Chicago fans. The impact of timing on affective content could be contingent on the context (e.g., competitive nature of sports games, the fact that there is a winner and loser etc.) and may also depend on the valence of the affective content, as examined next.

The extent of positive and negative affective content of the different groups' tweets was examined by timing condition. Overall, the tweets in the retrospective condition were significantly more positive than those in the simultaneous condition by a count of 0.47, $p < .001$. Regardless of fan group, people expressed more positive affect when sharing was retrospective (Boston: 0.46; Chicago: 0.46; Other: 0.48). In contrast, the tweets in the simultaneous condition were significantly more negative than those in the retrospective condition by a count of 0.49, $p < .001$. Regardless of fan group, people expressed more negative affect when sharing was simultaneous (Boston: 0.43; Chicago: 1.14; Other: 0.26).

Discussion

The Stanley Cup context differs in several key respects from an episode of a television series. First, this is a live sporting event, so it provides a natural experimental context for simultaneous versus retrospective sharing. Second, two teams are competing, and one side will win and the other will lose. Hence, we expect that fan perspective may affect sharing behavior and message content. Consistent with expectations, we found that simultaneously shared messages had more "we" words than retrospectively shared messages. This provides support for our prediction that simultaneous sharing is associated with a sense of shared consumption. We did not find that simultaneously shared messages had less "I" words. Still, the fact that Other (non-fans) group uses significantly more "we" words in the simultaneous condition provides some evidence for the robustness of the theory. In other words, even for the viewers who may not be supporting any team, simultaneous sharing enhances the sense of community.

In contrast to our predictions, we found that retrospective sharing resulted in more affective content (i.e., total number of positive and negative affect words) than did simultaneous sharing. When we analyzed affective content by valence, we found that retrospectively shared messages expressed more positive affect than simultaneous messages, whereas simultaneously shared messages expressed more negative affect than retrospective messages. This was true for all fan groups. One might have expected that the fans of the losing team would have been more likely to share negative or sad feelings after the loss than during the loss. Interestingly, we have shown that Boston fans were more likely to express positive emotions after the game (compared to during the game). It is somewhat counterintuitive that the fans of a losing team would express relatively more positive emotions retrospectively. As seen by the sharp drop in number of tweets by Boston fans in the retrospective condition (see Figure 4.3), when the team lost the game, the majority of the Boston fans remained silent. Follow-up content analysis of the remaining 77 retrospective tweets showed that these fans were optimistic and respectful, sharing tweets such as "Congratulations to Blackhawks" and "We played well, it is okay, we will win next year" etc. These findings suggest that whereas joy might be shared more collectively, the fans of the losing team grieved more privately.

General Discussion

As marketers increase their efforts and spending on online marketing and seek more control over the eWOM process, a deep understanding about the factors that contribute to the effectiveness of eWOM is important. Mobile communication technologies and multitasking are enabling consumers to share their experiences moment-to-moment, as events unfold. Although it is clear that consumers engage in eWOM during and after consumption, little is known about how the verbatim content of a message might vary with timing. In this chapter, we studied this important issue by proposing a conceptualization of timing of eWOM sharing. Specifically we investigated how the communal nature and the affective content of messages might vary with the timing of the message.

This chapter contributes to the literature on word-of-mouth by providing the first step toward understanding the role of message timing in shaping the message content and ultimately, the persuasive impact of the message itself. First, we examined how the communal nature of messages differs when many consumers communicate about the experience at the same time. Understanding the communal nature of eWOM is important because eWOM is no longer a one-sided communication, hence a deeper understanding of the communal nature of messages can inform strategies for brand engagement. Based on two field studies, we show that messages exhibited a greater sense of communal feeling when they were posted simultaneously. Specifically, we found that consumers used more "we" words when sharing was simultaneous rather than retrospective, presumably due to synchrony with social others. As mentioned earlier, synchrony in motor movement (e.g., marching of soldiers, dancing in rituals) and synchrony in singing (e.g., chanting in rituals) have been studied (e.g., Wiltermuth and Heath 2009). However, what happens when people engage in synchronous activity in a virtual context? We suggest that although people are not physically together, they unite around a common hashtag and this synchrony with social others could contribute to communal feelings. In this chapter, we can only speculate that "virtual synchrony" played an important role in shaping the message content. Examining the effects of virtual synchrony on word-of-mouth content using experimental methods is a fruitful avenue for future research.

Second, we examined how the affective content of eWOM messages differed by timing of sharing. Understanding the affective content of a message is important because emotions differ in the level of activation they evoke (Smith and Ellsworth 1985). For example, anger, anxiety, and sadness are all negative emotions, but whereas anger and anxiety are characterized by states of heightened arousal or activation, sadness is characterized by low arousal or deactivation (Feldman-Barrett and Russell 1998). Therefore, understanding the changes in the affective content of eWOM based on the time of posting would help managers adjust their social media strategies (e.g., promoting simultaneous vs. retrospective sharing) in line with consumer sentiment. In our first study, we found initial evidence to support our prediction that simultaneous eWOM messages contain more affect than retrospective eWOM messages. However, this was not consistently the case in the second study.

These initial studies have several limitations. First, we were restricted by the LIWC software. Although LIWC2007 is a popular, valid, and reliable tool for automated content analysis (Pennebaker et al. 2007; Ludwig et al. 2013), it does not capture sarcasm or negative sentences. For example, a tweet saying, "I am not happy" would get a positive emotion count of one (1) because the software counts it as "happy" rather than "not unhappy." Even given these limitations with the coding scheme, our large sample size and replication across two domains supports the robustness of the finding about the communal nature of content. A second limitation is that the message content is largely dependent on the characteristics of the subject matter being consumed. For example, the Stanley Cup takes place only once a year, the outcome is unknown, and there must be a winner and a loser. In contrast, there are multiple episodes of the *Game of Thrones*, which follow a storyline and characters. Often, episodes end in a surprising cliffhanger with no resolution. We believe that isolating the emotions from the context of consumption (e.g., emotions due to winning the game was prevalent in the retrospective condition) is a challenge for field studies, but could be examined using experimental methods. Thus, understanding how the dimensions of the experience interact with time of sharing to influence message content is an important direction for future research.

When discussing the practical implications of our findings, it is crucial to distinguish eWOM about brand experiences and eWOM in the form of online reviews. In our field studies, consumers were reflecting their thoughts, feelings, and emotions during and after watching TV content. Hence, the content of emotions is not independent of the viewed content. For example, when viewers were talking about the Stanley Cup, they posted tweets such as "I swear the #bruins are trying to kill me . . .," "Holy crap! That was an ugly hit to the face . . .," or "the ice is terrible out there . . ." As these examples show, the content of eWOM reflects reactions to the experience itself (e.g., specific comment about a player's move). The fact that these tweets express negative emotions does not mean that the writer's evaluation of the experience itself is negative. However, interpreting the valence of WOM messages is different when online reviews are considered. For example, negative emotion in an online restaurant review probably indicates that the consumer's dining experience was not positive. For reviews the valence of the message can directly signal the reviewer's evaluation of the experience. However, the fact that people have expressed negative emotions while watching a sports game does not mean that people did not enjoy the experience. This nuance impacts the practical implications of our findings. Although we found that the tweets in the retrospective condition had a lower number of negative affect words relative to the simultaneous condition, we cannot say that those consumers would look back on the experience more favorably than those who tweeted simultaneously. Thus, examining how the effects of message timing on content vary with the communication objective (e.g., sharing versus summarizing) would be an interesting avenue for future research.

Another avenue for future research would be the influence of impression management goals on the likelihood of simultaneous sharing and on the affective content of these simultaneously shared messages. Literature shows that one of the major motivations behind sharing WOM messages is impression management (see Berger 2014 for a recent review). A possible reason for engaging in simultaneous sharing is identity-signaling. People may think that being the first to talk about some consumption experiences (e.g., tweeting about a movie on its first day of release, making a joke about a scene of a TV show before others do) makes them appear cool, in-the-know, or smart. In that vein, people may express more emotions in an effort to grab the readers' attention and get positive feedback (e.g., likes, retweets, and comments). Understanding the underlying motivation for simultaneous sharing could help the marketing managers to tap into these needs and increase the likelihood of simultaneous sharing.

The finding that simultaneous sharing with others is associated with a sense of shared consumption has important practical implications. Brands that want more sentiment and community should encourage customers to share their brand experiences simultaneously. In order to build brand communities, uniting consumers around a common hashtag during consumption is a promising strategy. Currently, the value of live-tweeting is capitalized by televised media. For example, some TV shows integrate TV and Twitter by displaying viewers' live tweets as part of their content. Broadcasters encourage these conversations in order to engage and grow their audiences (Twitter Media 2014). In addition to TV shows (e.g., *The Voice*, *MasterChef*), many product ads (e.g., Dunkin Donuts, ZzzQuil) are promoting their Twitter hashtags on TV to encourage their audiences to mention their brands and create engagement. This practice may be extended to other consumption categories. For example, depending on their brand strategies, service firms (e.g., retailers, restaurants, hotels, movie theaters) should consider allocating resources to encouraging customers to post simultaneous eWOM messages during consumption. Efforts may include enhancing their WiFi structure in order to facilitate simultaneous posting or offering special promotions (e.g., free appetizer, discount) for customers who post simultaneous eWOM messages mentioning the brand name. Further research can examine whether the communal nature of live-tweeting can be generalized to other forms of simultaneous sharing. In our field studies, we have looked at television shows in order to be able to use the proxy of the posting time as an indicator of the timing with respect to consumption. It would be more challenging to determine if sharing was simultaneous on other platforms. In the context of live or premiere TV shows, we know that messages that were shared simultaneously with the consumption (i.e., while watching the show) were also shared at the same time with the other viewers. However, in other consumption contexts, eWOM messages that are shared simultaneously with the experience are not necessarily shared simultaneously with the other consumers. For example, an eWOM message about a special meal is typically not a shared experience with others' in the social media audience, so synchrony is unlikely to occur. Thus, depending on the nature of the experience, simultaneous eWOM messages may vary in their communal content. Understanding the characteristics of the experience that drive communal content would be an important question for future research.

Notes

1. The tweets captured do not cover all the tweets posted, but various intervals. Specifically, for the simultaneous condition, the captured tweets (including retweets) had time stamps that ranged between 9:24 PM–9:28 PM (n = 800) and 9:48PM–9:58 PM (n = 1,798). For the retrospective condition, the captured tweets had time stamps that ranged between 10:14 PM–10:31 PM (n = 1,550) and 10:58 PM–11:26 PM (n = 2,392).
2. GetGlue and ViggleTV are social networking sites offering check-in options for TV fans. These tweets were excluded because they were identical (e.g., "I unlocked the Game of Thrones: Kissed by Fire sticker on #GetGlue! #GameofThrones").
3. The tweets captured do not cover all the tweets posted, but various intervals. Specifically, for the simultaneous condition, the captured tweets (including retweets) had time stamps that ranged between 8:53 PM–9:13 PM (n = 2,297), 9:28 PM–10:24 PM (n = 5,525), and 10:55 PM–10:56 PM (n = 2,397). For the retrospective condition, the captured tweets (including retweets) had time stamps that ranged between 8:53 AM–12:00 PM (n = 5,016) and 8:00 PM–11:59 PM (n = 1,376).

References

Berger, Jonah. 2014. "Word of Mouth and Interpersonal Communication: A Review and Directions for Future Research." *Journal of Consumer Psychology* 24(4): 586–607.

Bernieri, Frank J., J. Stephen Reznick, and Robert Rosenthal. 1988. "Synchrony, Pseudosynchrony, and Dissynchrony: Measuring the Entrainment Process in Mother–Infant Interactions." *Journal of Personality and Social Psychology* 54: 243–253.

Bernieri, Frank J., and Robert Rosenthal. 1991. "Interpersonal Coordination: Behavior Matching and Interactional Synchrony." In *Fundamentals of Nonverbal Behavior: Studies in Emotion and Social Interaction*, edited by Robert S. Feldman and Bernard Rime, 401–432. New York: Cambridge University Press.

Buehlman, Kim Therese, John Mordechai Gottman, and Lynn Fainsilber Katz. 1992. "How a Couple Views Their Past Predicts Their Future: Predicting Divorce from an Oral History Interview." *Journal of Family Psychology* 5(3–4): 295.

Cialdini, Robert B., Richard J. Borden, Avril Thorne, Marcus Rabdall Walker, Stephen Freeman, and Lloyd Reynolds Sloan. 1976. "Basking in Reflected Glory: Three (Football) Field Studies." *Journal of Personality and Social Psychology* 34: 366–375.

Durkheim, Emile. 2012. *The Elementary Forms of the Religious Life.* Translated by Joseph Ward Swain. Mineola: Dover Publications. [Originally published 1912]

Feldman Barrett, Lisa, and James A. Russell. 1998. "Independence and Bipolarity in the Structure of Current Affect." *Journal of Personality and Social Psychology* 74(4): 967–984.

Fisher, Gene A., and Kyum Koo Chon. 1989. "Durkheim and the Social Construction of Emotions." *Social Psychology Quarterly* 52(1): 1–9.

Hove, Michael J., and Jane L. Risen. 2009. "It's All in the Timing: Interpersonal Synchrony Increases Affiliation." *Social Cognition* 27(6): 949–960.

Ludwig, Stephan, Ko de Ruyter, Mike Friedman, Elisabeth C. Brüggen, Martin Wetzels, and Gerard Pfann. 2013. "More Than Words: The Influence of Affective Content and

Linguistic Style Matches in Online Reviews on Conversion Rates." *Journal of Marketing* 77(1): 87–103.

McNeill, William H. 1995. *Keeping Together in Time: Dance and Drill in Human History.* Cambridge, MA: Harvard University Press.

Neath, Ian. 1993. "Contextual and Distinctive Processes and the Serial Position Function." *Journal of Memory and Language* 32(6): 820–840.

Nielsen, 2012. "Global Trends in Tablet and Smartphone Use While Watching TV." Accessed June 10, 2014. www.nielsen.com/us/en/newswire/2012/double-vision-global-trends-in-tablet-and-smartphone-use-while-watching-tv.html.

Olaveson, Tim. 2001. "Collective Effervescence and Communitas: Processual Models of Ritual and Society in Emile Durkheim and Victor Turner." *Dialectical Anthropology* 26(2): 89–124.

Pennebaker, James W., Cindy K. Chung, Molly Ireland, Amy Gonzales, and Roger J. Booth. 2007. "The Development and Psychometric Properties of LIWC2007." Austin, TX: *LIWC. Net.*

Proulx, Mike, and Stacey Shepatin. 2012. *Social TV: How Marketers Can Reach and Engage Audiences by Connecting Television to the Web, Social Media, and Mobile.* New Jersey: John Wiley & Sons.

Richardson, Michael J., Kelly L. Marsh, and R. C. Schmidt. 2005. "Effects of Visual and Verbal Interaction on Unintentional Coordination." *Journal of Experimental Psychology: Human Perception and Performance* 32: 62–79.

Simmons, Rachel A., Peter C. Gordon, and Dianne L. Chambless. 2005. "Pronouns in Marital Interaction What Do 'You' and 'I' Say About Marital Health?" *Psychological Science* 16(12): 932–936.

Smith, Craig A., and Phoebe C. Ellsworth. 1985. "Patterns of Cognitive Appraisal in Emotion." *Journal of Personality and Social Psychology* 48(4): 813.

Tausczik, Yla R., and James W. Pennebaker. 2010. "The Psychological Meaning of Words: LIWC and Computerized Text Analysis Methods." *Journal of Language and Social Psychology* 29(1): 24–54.

Toder-Alon, Anat, and Frederic F. Brunel. 2013. Online Word-of-Moms as Communal Social Acts: Producing Motherhood Culture via Collective and Collaborative Word-of-Mouth Conversations. *Boston U. School of Management Research Paper,* (2012–19).

Twitter Media, 2014. "Live-Tweet During An Award Show." Accessed July 8. https://media.twitter.com/best-practice/live-tweet-a-tv-event.

Valdesolo, Piercarlo, and David DeSteno. 2011. "Synchrony and the Social Tuning of Compassion." *Emotion* 11(2): 262–266.

Valdesolo, Piercarlo, Jennifer Ouyang, and David DeSteno. 2010. "The Rhythm of Joint Action: Synchrony Promotes Cooperative Ability." *Journal of Experimental Social Psychology* 46: 693–695.

Van Boven, Leaf, Katherine White, and Micheala Huber. 2009. "Immediacy Bias in Emotion Perception: Current Emotions Seem More Intense Than Previous Emotions." *Journal of Experimental Psychology: General* 138: 368–382.

Wiltermuth, Scott S., and Chip Heath. 2009. "Synchrony and Cooperation." *Psychological Science* 20(1): 1–5.

Zappavigna, Michele. 2011. "Ambient Affiliation: A Linguistic Perspective on Twitter." *New Media & Society* 13(5): 788–780.

5

A VIDEO IS WORTH 1,000 WORDS

Linking Consumer Value for Opinion Seekers to Visually Oriented eWOM Practices

Andrew N. Smith and Martin A. Pyle

Within word-of-mouth (WOM) research, there is an emphasis on what gets people talking: general motivations behind WOM behavior (e.g., Dichter, 1966; Verlegh, Bujis & Zethof, 2008), aspects of the consumption experience that prompt people to want to share (e.g., Berger & Schwartz, 2011; Brown, Barry, Dacin & Gunst, 2005), and even individual traits that increase or decrease the likelihood of sharing WOM (e.g., Cheema & Kaikati, 2010; Clark & Goldsmith, 2005). Garnering less attention, though, is the phenomenon of consumers' opinion-seeking behavior and in particular, the benefits of getting advice from others, and how various WOM practices might relate to those benefits.

Perhaps this lack of attention stems from the somewhat intuitive explanation for opinion seeking: WOM provides informational value to improve decision making through benefits such as risk reduction, reduced search time, and product usage information (Flynn, Goldsmith & Eastman, 1996; Goldsmith & Horowitz, 2006; Hennig-Thurau & Walsh, 2003–4; Punj & Staelin, 1983), as people perceive WOM to be more trustworthy due to the lack of material benefits associated with sharing such information (Day, 1971; Dichter, 1966; Stephen & Lehmann, 2009). In defining the term *opinion seekers* as "individuals who [seek] information or opinions from interpersonal sources in order to find out about and evaluate products, services, current affairs, or other areas of interest" (p. 302), Feick, Price, and Higie (1986) implicitly assume that rational decision making is the sole need fulfilled from receiving WOM.

This perspective echoes the utility-based conception of consumer value, which argues that value is simply a calculation of the tradeoff between what is given versus what is received (e.g., Zeithaml, 1988). In an opinion-seeking context, this would suggest that consumers perceive the value of WOM as dependent on the balance between the costs involved in the process (i.e., the effort required to find, read, and process the WOM) and the benefits derived from these efforts (i.e., improved decision making). Some findings, however, suggest that opinion-seeking behavior does not directly relate to purchase outcomes, at least in the fashion category (Goldsmith & Flynn, 2005), and that consumers note multiple motivations for opinion seeking (Goldsmith & Horowitz, 2006). Whereas these results do not negate improved decision making as *one* source of value, they demonstrate that opinion seeking may not be as purely rational as intuition indicates, and substantiates the need to explore other potential sources of value that stem from opinion seeking.

Further research sheds light on at least one other source of value derived from opinion seeking, beyond the purely rational approach of information gathering. Seeking the opinions of others also fulfills a social need, confirming a sense of belonging and providing access to socially acceptable practices (Flynn, Goldsmith & Eastman, 1996; Goldsmith & Clark, 2008; Goldsmith & Horowitz, 2006). In other words, people derive value from opinion seeking as a source of social comparison markers. This prompts our first research question: what other sources of value do WOM messages provide to opinion seekers?

Consumer Value and Opinion Seeking

In lieu of the simplistic utility-based view of consumer value, other researchers argue that consumer value is a complex, multidimensional construct that includes experiential aspects to balance the cognitive decision-making element (Batra & Ahtola, 1990; Holbrook & Hirschman, 1982; Sweeney & Soutar, 2001). There is some debate on how many dimensions comprise consumer value, though overlaps in the categories exist across the research. For example, Sheth, Newman, and Gross (1991) offer a five-dimensional model that includes functional, conditional, social, emotional, and epistemic value, whereas Holbrook (1999) posits a typology of eight sources of value (i.e., efficiency, play, excellence, aesthetics, status, ethics, esteem, and spirituality) by crossing three dichotomous dimensions: intrinsic/extrinsic, self-/other-oriented, and active/reactive. Despite the nuanced differences in these varied typologies, the relevant point is that the consumption process offers several benefits to the consumer. This suggests that opinion seeking provides more value than simply the ability to make more efficient decisions. This is particularly likely when we consider novel developments in social media, where electronic word-of-mouth (eWOM) continues to evolve beyond a straight-forward written description of the consumption experience.

Visually Oriented WOM

Within the past decade, consumers using social media have engaged in visual eWOM content generation, adding pictures to, or simply using pictures alone, as a form of communication (e.g., Instagram, Pinterest, Tumblr, etc.), and developing video content (e.g., YouTube, Dailymotion, etc.) to share their consumption experiences. This is a significant departure from the text-based online reviews in forums such as Amazon and ePinions, which typically share a common element: the reviews are pallid descriptions, at least in comparison to face-to-face interactions. In short, whereas some textually oriented eWOM authors wax poetic and offer evocatively phrased messages that paint a picture, the medium is restricted in its capacity. This shift to include visual elements increases the vividness of the shared experience, which can impact message persuasiveness (Herr, Kardes & Kim, 1991), but also potentially enhances existing, and offers additional, sources of value to the opinion seeker.

This visually oriented eWOM provides a rich context for isolating potential sources of value derived from opinion seeking, as it shares common elements with strong-tie face-to-face WOM encounters as well as weak-tie eWOM sharing. Using this media for the purposes of eWOM bridges the gap between face-to-face and text-based eWOM, offering several possibilities for extending our overall understanding of the WOM phenomenon.

As with the prototypical text-based eWOM, there is a certain level of physical and psychological distance between the opinion provider and the opinion seeker. Whereas some content providers become micro-celebrities (c.f., Burgess & Green, 2009; Marwick, 2013), leading to an opinion seeker's sense of *knowing* the person, social media as a medium frequently allows for a degree of anonymity and the ability to construct an online persona that may not tie into the reality of the offline individual (Belk & Costa, 1998; Gibbs, Ellison, & Heino, 2006; Schau & Gilly, 2003). Similar to a face-to-face encounter, though, the inclusion of visual elements into the eWOM communication provides unique additional information beyond the message content, allowing for contextualization and elaboration on the part of the opinion seeker. In essence, it is possible to isolate and differentiate the eWOM content from the contextual information to ascertain how subtle cues apart from the message content affect the message reception and response. Recent research demonstrates the need for exploring WOM at such a nuanced level to better understand the phenomenon.

Meaning-Making and Opinion Seeking

When composing a review, people make choices in the phrasing and content of the message (Pyle, 2013; Ward & Ostrom, 2006). For example, using WOM to project a positive self-image impacts whether people choose to share positive or negative consumption experiences, the level of language complexity, inclusion of self-related content, and the use of personal pronouns (de Angelis, Bonezzi, Peluso, Rucker & Costabile, 2012; Packard & Wooten, 2013; Wojnicki & Godes, 2008). Further research shows how these subtle differences in language and message content impact message persuasiveness and opinion seekers' perceptions of the reviewer (e.g., Hamilton, Vohs & McGill, 2014; Karmarkar & Tormala, 2010).

Whether or not these differences are conscious and intentional on the part of the reviewer, or whether they reflect some socially normative method of communication (Higgins, 1992) is immaterial when focusing on the opinion seeker. Instead, what is important is that nuanced differences in the phrasing of the message act as signaling markers, and can alter the meaning derived by opinion seekers (Bradac, Konsky & Davies, 1976; Higgins, 1981). In other words, certain practices among reviewers directly influence opinion seekers' perceptions. In the context of visually oriented eWOM, a similar signaling effect may occur in addition to the phrasing and content of the message. The extraneous visual information present in this type of eWOM, such as the "set" of a YouTube video or the backdrop and lighting in an Instagram photo, and the way that reviewers *present* the information may impact the types of value derived by opinion seekers as they act as markers signaling additional information. This leads to the second question driving the present research: what is the relationship between specific practices in visually oriented eWOM and the value derived by opinion seekers?

Practice Theory

We use the term *practices* here to suggest routinized types of behavior that are comprised of bodily activities, mental understandings, and the use of 'things' (Reckwitz, 2002). According to practice theory, practices involve a level of common social understanding whereby people engage in a particular practice in relatively similar ways, and that they can convey social competence through their performance of practices.

Consumer researchers leverage practice theory to investigate a variety of phenomena, including digital music consumption (Magaudda, 2011), self-tracking (Pantzar & Ruckenstein, 2014), and eating (Domaneschi, 2012). Prior research also uses this theory as a lens for identifying several brand community practices that create value for consumers (Schau, Muniz & Arnould, 2009,), supporting our use of practice theory as a means to provide useful insights for exploring how opinion seekers derive value from visually oriented eWOM. In this context, presenters craft their performances and communicate their experiences not only through message content, but also by using and/or developing socially recognized visual practices. Thus, our research takes initial steps to identify and link commonly used visual eWOM practices with sources of consumer value.

Method

YouTube is the world's largest video sharing site and community. It hosts a diversity of brand-related user-generated content, from consumer reviews and advertisements to 'unboxing' and 'haul' videos (c.f., Burgess & Green, 2009; Smith, Fischer & Yongjian, 2012), providing an abundance of source material for this study. We specifically study two types of fashion videos, 'haul' and 'outfit' videos, and in doing so, follow the lead of other consumer research that investigates the rich and culturally influential domain that exists at the intersection of fashion and new media (e.g., Goldsmith & Flynn, 2005; McQuarrie, Miller & Phillips, 2013; Scaraboto & Fischer, 2013). In short, in the broad category of visually oriented eWOM (e.g., videos, pictures, etc.), we focus exclusively on video eWOM about fashion for the purposes of this examination.

'Haul' videos are a popular genre of fashion video in which consumers show off and discuss clothing, make-up, and accessories that they recently purchased or acquired. The videos, which frequently run longer than 10 minutes, generally feature a 'haul' of items representing multiple brands from a variety of stores. Some of these YouTube performers develop micro-celebrity status and attract attention from marketers as a result of the 'haul' videos that they produce (Boudreau & Singh, 2011).

'Outfit' videos are another ubiquitous genre of fashion video in which consumers model an outfit or look that they are wearing in preparation for a day or particular event. Presumably, the act of assembling an outfit requires cultural skill and an awareness of current trends and how items pair together. As with 'haul' videos, 'outfit' videos typically feature female consumers; however, they are generally much shorter, rarely running longer than five minutes, unless the presenter models and discusses multiple outfits. Both 'haul' and 'outfit' videos are forms of video eWOM because they feature displays, discussions, and judgments about consumer goods and brands.

Our analysis focuses on 25 'haul' videos and 25 'outfit' videos posted on YouTube as well as the comments associated with each video. The videos allow us to identify common practices whereas the comments provide insight on the opinion seekers' perspectives regarding the value derived from this visually oriented eWOM. The videos run from approximately one minute in length to just over 12 minutes in length. Whereas some videos elicit no more than five comments, others receive hundreds of replies.

We selected our sample of videos at random, according the following protocols. While conducting a separate research project on user-generated content relating to the fashion forward brands American Apparel (AA) and Lululemon (LLL), we downloaded a sample of 200 YouTube videos by conducting a search on the brand name and using every tenth hit. Of the 200 videos, 19 fell into the category of 'haul' videos, and 18 qualified as 'outfit' videos. At a later date, for the purposes of the present research, we added 13 more videos to our sample by specifically searching based on the brand name (AA or LLL) and the type of video (either 'haul' or 'outfit'). In this instance, we randomly selected every fifth result until our sample included 25 'haul' and 25 'outfit' videos, and the associated comments by opinion seekers, for coding and analysis.

We developed our coding protocol for the videos by examining the videos for the presence of explicitly visual eWOM practices and by examining the comments for expressions of derived value. Our coding of both the practices and sources of value emerged inductively, although the literature on consumer value (e.g., Holbrook, 1999; Sheth, Newman & Gross, 1999) informed our coding of the comments. Coding and analysis proceeded iteratively (Miles & Huberman, 1994), as we looked for patterns within the datasets, connecting and comparing emergent findings with prior theory on eWOM, opinion seeking, and consumer practices. Through this process, we identified the types of value and visual eWOM practices associated with both genres of YouTube video; we were also able to glean insights about the relationships between certain practices and the value opinion seekers derive in a video eWOM context.

Findings

Our analysis reveals that opinion seekers regularly derive four types of value—informational, social, emotional, and aesthetic—from video eWOM (Table 5.1), and that presenters employ a variety of visual practices—related to product display, personality and image projection, and audience care—to animate their video eWOM (Table 5.2). Furthermore, our investigation suggests that there are relationships between the presence of particular visual eWOM practices and certain types of consumer value. For many of the identified practices, the relationship with opinion seekers' derived consumer value is one-to-*n*, rather than one-to-one. In other words, consumers can obtain multiple types of consumer value from the presence of a single practice. We discuss each of these findings in turn.

Consumer Value Derived from Video eWOM

One definition of opinion seeking asserts that people engage in such behavior in order to acquire useful information (Feick, Price & Higie, 1986). In other words, they read consumer reviews on Amazon.com, look at accommodation photos on Airbnb, and watch fashion videos on YouTube to gather product-related information from other users in order to improve their decision making. Intuitively, and in accord with this definition, we find that consumers truly derive informational value from watching video eWOM. Opinion seekers say they acquire new ideas, find inspiration, and receive help from watching fashion videos on YouTube. The following comment, written in response to an outfit video, supports this premise:

> . . . i have been trying to figure out how to add a little 'girly' touch to my style because i was told i was dressing too 'boy-ish?' but this reallly really helped me! thank you so much!
>
> *(cristinall5; Outfit Video #6)*

Commenter cristinall5 confesses to having a perceived social problem: pressure related a lack of femininity in her style of dress. The video eWOM endows

TABLE 5.1 Types of Value Derived from Visual eWOM

Types of Value	*Description*	*Illustrative Examples*
Informational Value	Value associated with the acquisition of information that can help a consumer achieve a particular goal (Sheth, Newman & Gross 1991).	• "*The dress is really cute on you. I would have totally over looked it. It seems so plain on the website.*" (Elenluvsmakeup; Outfit Video #19) • "*Love Thursdays outfit! So gonna copy it!*" (Amanda Green; Outfit Video #23) • "*i like the hauls very imformative u should do some watches.*" (Mrsunderstood0321; Haul Video #11) • "*'made in bangladesh' :(i wonder what ethics lulu lemon has . . . after the whole sizing only for thin people, i wouldn't be surprised that the working conditions of the bangladeshi people in their factories were terrible.*" (Méditations Guidées; Haul Video #25)
Social Value	Value related to the perceived association one has with a particular individual or social group (Sheth, Newman & Gross, 1991).	• "*I'm really glad I came across your channel you have awesome style similar to me!*" (angelcreme; Outfit Video #6) • "*We have the same top from topshop. Idk, but I'm feeling special.*" (Stephanie Pink; Haul Video #20) • "*I'm so glad someone else who isn't a little kid wears ivivva! It's so much cheaper for the same thing and they fit me exactly the same.*" (846cookie; Haul Video #23) • "*hey sabrina (: just letting you know, my mum purchased the bio oil, and it really does work, shes been constantly using it for about a year now and it actually has improved the look and feel of her skin. haha just thought i would let you know. :D xoxo.*" (yousafmalik2009; Haul Video #5)
Emotional Value	Value associated with the arousal of positive feelings or affective states (Sheth, Newman & Gross, 1991).	• "*aww your smile at 3:17 was really adorable lol*" (Anna Taylor; Outfit Video #23) • "*awww you're so cute! when you were talking about the skirt saying 'its a lot of money' and when u were talking about your mum giving you the bag. and i love the blooper! aww never ever change- youre just too cute*" (VanillaSecrets; Haul Video #14) • "*'really cute, love it, nice' *throws bag* lol. love the haul*" (cierralovexo; Haul Video #5) • "*oh it was cuute how you filmed yourself while you where moving around at the beginnen xD <3 !*" (jellbb; Outfit Video #16)
Aesthetic Value	Value associated with the appreciation or enjoyment of something that is regarded as beautiful, well designed, or aesthetically pleasing (Holbrook 1998).	• "*Ah love love love your style! I found your channel through the persianbabe and I'm so glad because your style is just perfect! You're like my new favourite haha xx*" (Shanlovestuff; Outfit Video #21) • "*those red shoes are gorgeous !!*" (huddlpj; Haul Video #12) • "*everything is absolutely gorgeous! I especially adore the horse head t-shirt, the sunglasses, and the maxi dress!*" (Hailey5210; Haul Video #16)

TABLE 5.2 Visual eWOM Practices

Visual eWOM Practices	*Description*	*Illustrative Examples*
Modeling (& Pairing)	The practice of showing a product in use. For some product categories, there are more clearly defined understandings with regards to how modeling should occur. For example, in fashion, modeling often entails posing, turning, and walking down a runway in clothes, while channeling appropriately toned emotions and bodily demeanor, to present fashion items or an overall 'look.' Modeling potentially also involves the sub-practice of pairing, in which multiple products are featured together in a constellation to display how they look and function together.	*Modeling* • Wearing a clothing item in a video • Trying on or peeling off a clothing item *Pairing* • Posing in an outfit • Walking toward the camera in an outfit
Product Highlighting (& Romancing)	The practice of visually presenting a product, including many of its various features and details, without actually using the product for its intended purpose. Presenters generally understand that particular conditions, such as brighter lighting and an in-focus camera, are more conducive to showing off the product, as well as that they should focus more attention on particular features and qualities, such as those that are unique or special to product. An exaggerated version of highlighting is product romancing, in which presentation is accompanied by visual expressions of extremely positive judgment or affect.	*Product Highlighting* • Holding up an item to the camera and rotating it • Showing a close-up of, or pointing at, a feature • Pulling at an item or running one's hands over it • Showing product packaging or information tags *Product Romancing* • Hugging or cradling an item • Engaging in an extended inhale of a scented product • Conveying affection for an item through one's facial expressions
Persona Projecting	The practice of visually conveying aspects of one's personality. There is a general understanding that presenters have the potential to become micro-celebrities and develop an audience, and that their personality is part of the image they convey in their performances to help increase their status.	• Dancing • Giving high-fives to the camera • Making amusing facial expressions • Shooting videos in an information rich environment (e.g., whole room is visible vs. only a white wall)

Image Manufacturing	The practice of constructing or performing an idealized cultural image. In the context of fashion, one idealized image is that of the fashion guru. There is a general understanding that the fashion guru is fashion-forward, well put-together, and knowledgeable about trends and 'looks.'	• Featuring unique 'looks' that are complete and exhibited down to the smallest detail • Providing visual tutorials on how to apply make-up or wear an item of clothing • Crafting a context that conveys expertise (e.g., which shows 100 bottles of nail polish in the background)
Audience Appreciating	The practice of visually acknowledging and thanking one's audience. There is a general understanding that presenters perform for an audience in the context of an attention economy, and that such an audience—which helps to establish their status—is potentially fleeting and should be appreciated and cultivated.	• Blowing kisses to audience • Waving 'hi' and 'bye' to audience • Thanking audience on closing slate
Professionalizing	The practice of employing more sophisticated visual techniques that mimic those used in professional publications. There is a general understanding that some visual techniques convey a higher degree of skill and more closely adhere to cultural expectations regarding professional productions than amateur ones.	• Employing animated and aesthetically thoughtful opening and closing slates • Editing in close-up, slow motion, still, and black and white shots into a video • Including video footage from multiple contexts (e.g., inside and outside)

her with ideas and inspiration to help her resolve this issue, and thus provides her with informational value that fulfills a functional purpose and satisfies her desire for knowledge. In this way, it is a hybrid form of value that reflects both of Sheth, Newman, and Gross's (1991) functional value and epistemic value (i.e., her opinion seeking serves both a utilitarian function, as well as stimulates new interests). Arguably, consumers may also derive similar value from watching other types of media as well, including advertisements, news, and 'info-tainment.' Interestingly, though, our results highlight a novel perspective on opinion seeking for informational value. Prototypically, we may think of opinion seeking as a targeted behavior: the consumer has a particular need, such as cristinall5's desire to feminize her wardrobe, and thus actively pursues additional information to fulfill that need. However, our data also indicate that the informational value may be incidental when opinion seekers watch the video eWOM for other reasons or with no particular purchase or need in mind.

Our results align with the extant literature, and offer further evidence relating to video eWOM, that opinion seeking also helps to fulfill social needs, such as achieving a sense of belonging (Goldsmith & Clark, 2008; Goldsmith & Horowitz, 2006). With social value relating to one's perceived association with an individual or social group (Sheth, Newman & Gross, 1991), opinion seekers may feel that they are associated with video eWOM presenters because they share similar lifestyles and tastes. Alternatively, they may feel as if they are in a relationship with the performer because she encourages and engages in interaction with her audience members. The following comment from opinion seeker, Vanessa M, expresses the social value that she derives from watching a particular haul video:

> OMG I SCREAMED WHEN I SAW THE SUNFLOWER ROMPER GURL YOU HAVE THE BEST FASHION SENSE EVER I SWEAR LOOKS LIKE WERE GOING TO BE TWINS
>
> *(Vanessa M; Haul Video #22)*

Vanessa M enthusiastically articulates her affection for the performer's fashion sense, suggesting that it is similar to hers. The fact that they share this similarity helps to validate Vanessa's tastes and form a perceived association with the performer, with whom she will "be twins." Vanessa's use of this term implies social closeness and supports the premise that people derive such social value from watching video eWOM.

In short, our data support and replicate the limited literature in the area by confirming that opinion seekers derive both informational and social value from eWOM, and show that this value also exists in the context of video eWOM. However, our data also extend these findings by identifying two other sources of value generated by video eWOM: emotional and aesthetic value.

Emotional value pertains to the arousal of positive feelings or affective states (Sheth, Newman & Gross, 1991). For example, opinion seekers may enjoy an entertaining eWOM performance, feel comfort from seeing a familiar presenter, or experience the "embodied passion" of desire (Belk, Ger & Askegaard, 2003: 326) after discovering a new product. Opinion seeker, miki2043, expresses the emotional value that she derives from watching a presenter's haul video:

> whenever i get home i come on youtube to watch these videos. i honestly sit here laughing the entire time, you're so funny (:
>
> *(miki2043; Haul Video #8)*

In miki2043's comment, she divulges to the eWOM presenter that entertainment (i.e., emotional) value provides one reason, and perhaps the primary reason, for actively seeking out the latest haul video. Of particular interest, we note that emotional value derived from video eWOM may, at times, be completely disconnected from the focal product or products being discussed, centering more on the presenter and context. This calls into question the persuasive impact of video eWOM when the emotional value supersedes the informational value for the opinion seeker.

We also find evidence of a fourth category of value derived from eWOM: aesthetic value. This type of value relates to the appreciation or enjoyment of something that is regarded as beautiful, well-designed, or aesthetically pleasing (Holbrook, 1998). Whereas some overlap exists between aesthetic and emotional value, in that aesthetics can also be a potential source of positive emotional arousal (e.g., the love of something beautiful), the two categories are conceptually distinct. Aesthetic value extends beyond the emotional; for example, it can encompass an intellectual understanding or appreciation of well executed product design. Thus, we treat the two separately, following Holbrook's (1999) lead.

Opinion seekers who receive aesthetic value might love a product, deem a presenter to be beautiful, or appreciate a unique product design detail. The following comment from opinion seeker beccababyy08 expresses the aesthetic value she derives from watching an outfit video:

> your sooo pretty! i looove your makeup! and your hair! and your outfit you just look stunning all around! <3 p.s. i looove your videos <3
>
> *(beccababyy08; Outfit Video #18)*

In her remark to the presenter, beccababyy08 gushes with enthusiasm. She not only comments on the focal product (i.e., the outfit), she also specifically comments on the presenter's aesthetic beauty, mentioning how "pretty" and "stunning" she is. Her hyperbolic language suggests considerable value that is linked with the aesthetics of the presented visuals. An important aspect of aesthetic value, distinguishing it from social and emotional value, is the appreciation of something beautiful simply because it is visually appealing rather than because it serves as an inspiration for a desired look. Aspirational elements may undergird many aspects of social value, with the opinion seeker hoping to one day acquire the same clothing and accessories to form a similar image. For aesthetic value, this is not a necessary precursor. For instance, someone who prefers a clean and classic look for herself can still appreciate a well-put together hippie image.

We present our analysis as four distinct types of consumer value, but we want to be especially clear on the following point: one type of value does not preclude the existence of other sources of value. To the contrary, we find evidence that indicates a coexistence of several types of value for opinion seekers in single videos. For instance, a commenter might praise the humorous presentation style (emotional value), and mention that she has a similar outfit (social value), and then follow this up with a word of thanks to the presenter for suggesting an inexpensive pair of earrings to complete the whole outfit (informational value). This type of overlap, however, simply reinforces our initial position that opinion seekers gain more than informational value from video eWOM. We turn next to the common practices that seem to enhance these sources of value.

Visual eWOM Practices and Consumer Value

We posit that the practices enacted in video eWOM can affect the types of consumer value stemming from the consumption of particular 'haul' and 'outfit' videos, just as, analogously, the content and language of textually based WOM can impact opinion seekers' meaning-making (e.g., Karmarkar & Tormala, 2010; Kozinets, De Valck, Wojnicki & Wilner, 2010; Packard & Wooten, 2013). Our analysis identifies six practices regularly employed in the animation of video eWOM of this type: modeling, product highlighting, persona projecting, image manufacturing, audience appreciating, and professionalizing. The consistent recurrence of these practices across numerous videos, presenters, and products, implies a level of common social understanding. Given our methodological approach, we do not speculate as to the primacy or strength of these relationships (nor should the reader infer that we are arguing a direct causal link between any practice and consumer value). Rather, our analysis suggests that specific practices may catalyze (i.e. create conditions that increase the likelihood of) one or more types of derived value.

Modeling is a visual eWOM practice in which a presenter shows a product in use. The modeling of fashion items often entails a person posing, turning, and walking down an imaginary runway while wearing clothes. In many instances, modeling entails showing off a constellation of items, which the presenter cobbles together in use: a blazer might be modeled in conjunction with a blouse, slacks, and other items to form a complete outfit. In such situations, pairing may be recognized as being a sub-practice of modeling.

In its most basic form, modeling serves as a demonstration of product usage and can facilitate the decision-making process by reducing risk (e.g., 'I know this top pairs well with those jeans') and providing a source of informational value. But, as Tatiana Christine points out in her comment, modeling also provides aesthetic and social value.

> This helped so much! I'm 5'8" and i was worried they'd be short. They're so adorable. Ordered mine last night!
>
> *(Tatiana Christine; Outfit Video #22)*

From this statement, we can infer that the presenter's modeling facilitated Tatiana's decision ("helped so much," "Ordered mine last night!") by addressing a source of pre-purchase concern ("worried they'd be short"). However, we also note that seeing the product modeled by a similar other can create a bond between the presenter and opinion seeker, providing social value, and enhance aesthetic value by animating the product beyond a static image.

A second, similar, video eWOM practice involves product highlighting: the act of visually presenting a product, including its various features and details without actually using the product for its intended purpose. Both modeling and product highlighting practices emphasize the focal product but in different ways. In a fashion context, for example, modeling involves the presenter actually wearing the product, whereas product highlighting involves showing the product without actually donning the garment. This distinction is relevant because each practice implies different social roles and meanings.

People expect a fashion model to behave differently than a product presenter. Models embody glamour, status, and fame (Parmentier & Fischer, 2011), whereas product presenters generally do not possess the same cultural associations. With the practice of modeling, then, attention is divided more evenly between the model and the product than it would otherwise be with the practice of product highlighting. With less implied attention on the product in modeling, the product focus is generally more holistic. Features and details typically receive greater attention through the practice of product highlighting.

To engage in product highlighting, presenters hold up items to the camera, show close-ups of product details, and display product packaging and information tags. Whereas the presenter might provide informational value while highlighting the product verbally, the practice itself (separate from the verbal message content) involves putting the product 'on a pedestal' and 'under the spotlight,' symbolically elevating the product's importance. In some instances, reviewers amplify the product presentation practice with the addition of visual expressions of judgment and/or affect. For instance, presenters might hug or cradle products and convey affection through facial expressions. In such cases, presenters romance the product, a sub-practice of highlighting. As the comment from VolerVersLeReve demonstrates, the practices of product highlighting and romancing the product seem to enhance the aesthetic and emotional value opinion seekers gain from watching video eWOM.

> i just died when i saw the lace flower jumper sweater!!! its beautiful!!! OH MY GOD i wish i had it i wish i lived in england and i could find it!!!
>
> *(VolerVersLeReve; Haul Video #14)*

In this quotation, we see how VolerVersLeReve expresses the derivation of both aesthetic and emotional value from seeing the highlighted sweater. Even though the garment is unavailable to her (and thus, is not part of her decision set, reducing the informational value of this video), she recognizes its attractiveness from a relatively objective standpoint ("its beautiful"), and expresses an ironic colloquialism ("i just died") that conveys a positive emotional response to the practice of product highlighting. The subtle mannerisms involved in product highlighting and romancing (e.g., facial expressions, treating it with reverence and holding it close to one's body, versus treating it with disdain and holding it at a distance) seem to provide a means for the opinion seeker to vicariously interact with the product, thereby enhancing the potential for deriving emotional value from the video as a whole.

Persona projecting, a third visual eWOM practice, involves actions intended to convey aspects of a desired persona to the audience. Presumably, the assumption that personality helps to comprise a micro-celebrity brand somewhat drives users to adopt these practices. To help convey personality, people engage in acts such as dancing, giving high fives to their camera, making amusing facial expressions, and performing in character-rich spaces (e.g., bedrooms). These practices, from an opinion-seeking perspective, seem to primarily contribute to the social value derived from watching the videos. After one particular video where the presenter danced playfully and made funny facial expressions towards the camera, one opinion seeker responded:

> adorable! but do u ever wear jeans?! i feel like ppl at my school would hate so much if i always wore leggings
>
> *(Sierra Dawn; Outfit Video #23)*

From a social value perspective, we see that persona projection practices seem to bridge the physical and psychological distance between the presenter and the opinion seeker, and help foster an interpersonal closeness. By developing these connections, opinion seekers like Sierra Dawn can feel more comfortable questioning (in a friendly manner) the choices of the presenter, and draw parallels of similarity between her own life and that of the presenter. In short, persona projection practices can convey a range of social information (e.g., introvert/extravert, approachable/haughty, etc.), which seems to directly impact the degree to which opinion seekers feel the development of a social bond.

In a similar vein, presenters also engage in visual eWOM practices relating to image manufacturing. Whereas persona projection focuses on conveying social connection information, image manufacturing practices involve constructing and performing an overall, idealized cultural image. In the context of fashion, presenters frequently seek to create an image of being a fashion guru (a revered expert in the field). Specific practices can include featuring unique 'looks,' providing tutorials, and crafting contexts that convey category expertise (e.g., in large closets or before substantial make-up collections). From an opinion-seeking perspective, these practices seem to provide informational value, in the form of presenter credibility, and thus either provide support for or refutation of the message content. At times, presenters initiate these practices while other times, additional image information requests come from the opinion seekers. Consider the following quotation:

> do a room tour and a makeup tour i love your videos!!! Any video works hahah i love watchin um.
>
> *(Jen Kline; Haul Video #24)*

In this case, commenter Jen Kline explicitly requests further contextual information in the form of a room and makeup tour. This information can be used to established presenter credibility in the field of fashion. In addition, though, image manufacturing practices can also provide social value when the opinion seekers identify similar contextual elements (e.g., a shared poster, matching tastes in bedspreads, etc.) and emotional value, as Jen Kline points out ("i love watchin um").

Those who craft eWOM operate in an attention economy in which audiences must be cultivated. An awareness of this cultural reality encourages many to engage in the visual eWOM practice of audience appreciating. With this practice, performers acknowledge and thank their audiences for their patronage. They do so verbally, but also by blowing them kisses, waving 'hi' and 'bye,' as well as thanking the audience (sometimes even specific commenters by name) in writing on closing slates at the end of videos. As with persona projecting practices, audience appreciation practices not only encourage follower loyalty, but also provide social value by fostering a direct connection, projecting a sense that it is just two friends conversing. For example, following one video in which the presenter starts with greeting the audience and closes with a wave goodbye and a word of thanks on a final slate, yelly201 leaves this comment:

> Those Buxom glosses are fantastic! I have Dani (lol of course :D) What nail polish is that? I love it! BTW . . . 9 for a nail polish being steep? naw! we pay $26 for NARS blushes, what's a $9 np? LOLOL and those American Apparel nail polishes are great! MAKE SURE you wear a base coat under Malibu Green though or it'll STAIN your nails!! be careful!! and please

> please do a review on the foundation! maybe try mixing it wish another foundation like NARS sheer glow or even your new Chanel one?
>
> *(yelly201; Haul Video #10)*

The overall tone of this comment is one of a regular conversation about fashion and beauty that one might expect to hear from two longtime friends. We see that yelly201 asks questions, gives advice, makes requests, and shows concern, manifesting a variety of elements you might see in a conversation between two people who know each other well. In essence, such behavior reflects the opinion seeker's perception that there is a close bond between herself and the presenter, a bond seemingly fostered by the presenter's audience appreciation practices.

Finally, our analysis reveals a sixth common visual eWOM practice: professionalizing. Professionalizing entails the use of more sophisticated visual techniques that mimic those used in professional publications. To engage in professionalizing, presenters must have an awareness of such techniques, the technical skills to pursue them, and access to resources and tools to translate them into action. In contrast to practices such as audience appreciation or product highlighting, there are greater barriers to engaging in the practice of professionalizing (although admittedly, advancing technology and software access continues to lower such barriers). Presenters engage in professionalizing by employing animated and thoughtful opening and closing slates, editing in close-ups and other types of shots and camera angles, and including video footage from multiple contexts. In examining and comparing our data, we find that the degree of professionalization seems to enhance informational, aesthetic, and emotional value. For instance, following a video in which the presenter integrates professional-looking opening and closing slates, splices in still photography shots, and includes footage shot in a different location, AAlexis communicates how she receives multiple types of value from this outfit video, and other video eWOM from the same presenter:

> You always look so sexy!!! I love yours videos!!! And your vlog channel videos are cool too!!! All of the haters are just jealous of you and your style! Keep on doing your thing girl!!! :-)
>
> *(AAlexis; Outfit Video #1)*

First, we see a strong emphasis on the aesthetic value ("You always look so sexy!!!") and emotional value ("I love your videos!!!"). Whereas some of this value certainly stems from the presence of other factors and practices, the use of professionalizing practices presents those other practices, literally, in the best light. Second, we see evidence of how these practices contribute to source credibility and informational value. In defending the presenter ("All of the haters are just jealous of you and your style"), AAlexis demonstrates her staunch support, and thus her belief in the quality of information gathered from the video eWOM. In short, opinion seekers seem to interpret the addition of elements and practices that increase the professional look as more believable and trustworthy.

Discussion and Future Research Directions

Through our analysis, we identify and describe six common visual eWOM practices and speculate about their connection to different types of consumer value derived by opinion seekers. This work sheds new light on WOM phenomena enacted over social media, and challenges the intuitive explanation that informational value provides the sole value of opinion seeking. Although our analysis does replicate past work in identifying information as one source of value for opinion seekers, it goes beyond this starting point to reveal a far more complex array of consumer value relating to visually oriented eWOM. Beyond the value of actually seeing the product and receiving product usage information, we find that opinion seekers derive social, emotional, and aesthetic value as well. Furthermore, the data suggest that six common visual practices present in video eWOM enhance value for the opinion seeker.

We do not presume to argue that textually oriented eWOM cannot provide similar value to the opinion seeker; that is not the purpose of this study. Certainly a well-written review can provide emotional as well as informative value, and consumers can make inferences about the reviewer based on his or her writing that might foster a social connection as well. Instead, we are proposing that the non-message content of these videos—the presenter's visual practices—*facilitate* the derivation of value and, thus, serve an enhancing role.

Furthermore, because not all viewers leave comments (or expressions of value), our coding and analysis likely under-represents the extent of the value these videos provide for opinion seekers. In addition, the comments that one leaves might be in response to something other than a visual eWOM practice featured in a video. For these, and other reasons, the evidence this research offers regarding to the relationship between visual eWOM practices and types of derived value should be considered very preliminary. Rather than providing the definitive piece of research on the topic, we see a key value of this work as being its role as a catalyst, or call-to-arms, for further research in the area.

In identifying these novel sources of value related to opinion seeking, and the common visual eWOM practices that seem to enhance this value, we offer an important first step in further understanding the eWOM process. But, as is often the case in exploratory studies, taking this first step also highlights further unanswered questions. In particular, two areas offer an initial starting point for providing further important theoretical and managerial contributions: (1) establishing a more detailed causal link between the identified practices and consumer value; and (2) exploring the interactive effects of practices and value on persuasive outcomes.

Although qualitative studies such as this offer several benefits for developing new insights, an admitted weakness of this type of work is its inability to conclusively establish causal relationships. Whereas the temporal order of video consumption to opinion seeker comment is clear, and we can observe the presence of practices in conjunction with comments regarding the value derived, this is certainly an area where further controlled experiments might yield fruitful information regarding which practices directly lead to value creation, as well as determining their impact on key outcome variables such as purchase behavior and attitude change. Besides the theoretical extensions such a pursuit offers, it would also serve to inform the growing practice of word-of-mouth marketing.

Word-of-mouth marketing is the process by which companies seek to manage and influence WOM (Kozinets, De Valck, Wojnicki, & Wilner, 2010). The typical approach involves seeding opinion leaders with a product, and then having them report in their medium of choice (e.g., blogs, YouTube©, etc.). Whereas this process is quite similar to the mailing out of free samples, the growth in popularity of social media and the availability of analytics for identifying audience sizes allows for more targeted, and effective, campaigns. By establishing the causal relationships between certain practices and consumer value, marketers can further increase the persuasive power of these efforts. This effect can potentially be refined even more if we can identify how these different sources of value work together, or possibly against one another.

The data show that a single review, and even a particular practice, can provide multiple sources of value. For example, a review might be informative, entertaining, and offer aesthetic value (particularly in the realm of beauty and fashion products). What remains unclear, however, is how these different sources of value work in conjunction with regards to relevant outcome variables such as persuasive impact, and future consumption and opinion seeking from the source. On the one hand, it is possible to argue that value should be additive and thus, increasing the sources value derived from the visually oriented eWOM should also increase the persuasive outcome. In other words, if a visually oriented eWOM message offers two sources of value (e.g., humorous/entertaining and informative), the opinion seeker's attitude towards the recommended brand should be enhanced (Eisend, 2009). Yet, equally plausible is that some sources of value may negate other sources of value, or that the effects may vary depending on differing levels of a certain value. For instance, it is not difficult to imagine watching a haul video where one is so distracted by the aesthetic qualities (e.g., the presenter's beauty) that the information provided is missed completely. In short, this avenue of exploration offers several empirical questions worthy of investigation.

We by no means suggest that the extent of investigation should be limited to these two areas. Several other items of interest came out of our analysis but did not directly relate to the topic at hand. For example, in several videos, the presenters mentioned multiple brand names and concocted multifaceted brand pairings. This suggests a need for further inquiry into how such behavior impacts opinion seekers' attitudes towards the various brands involved, and what happens when some brands in the pairings are available and others are not.

Furthermore, our data source—consumer comments—offers another line of inquiry: how do these forms of 'discursive response' (Smith, 2014) to original eWOM messages offer value and impact consumer attitudes?

We also note that in describing the social value derived from opinion seeking via video eWOM, we focused on social similarity and belonging. In line with identity-building and social comparison research, though, we acknowledge that the inverse process, that of social distancing, is also likely. The anonymity of commenting can lead to derogatory and inflammatory comments as well as positive ones, and merits additional inquiry to understand this aspect of opinion seeking behavior.

In summary, we suggest that visually oriented eWOM, and the practices contained therein, as well as consumer value perspectives on word-of-mouth and opinion seeking, merit further research. Many decades ago, Whyte (1954) reflected that there is something especially powerful about the visual aspect of WOM: seeing a neighborhood full of air conditioners can impact our understandings and choices. Since that time, communications technologies and social media platforms have dramatically expanded our 'neighborhoods' and provided us with means to create and derive value from visual word-of-mouth online. In addition to written product reviews, consumers are now—in great numbers—sharing their product and brand related opinions and insights online through pictures and videos. They are also seeking out this visual eWOM in their pursuit of information, pleasure, and social connectedness. Researchers will gain a better understanding of eWOM as a multifaceted and evolving phenomenon by focusing not only on what is written 'on the page' by consumers, but also by studying the visuals and videos they create and communicate.

References

Batra, R. & Ahtola, O. T. (1990). Measuring the hedonic and utilitarian sources of consumer attitudes. *Marketing Letters*, *2*(2), 159–170.

Belk, R.W. & Costa, J. A. (1998). The mountain man myth: A contemporary consuming fantasy. *Journal of Consumer Research*, *25*(3), 218–240.

Belk, R. W., Ger, G. & Askegaard, S. (2003). The fire of desire: A multisited inquiry into consumer passion. *Journal of Consumer Research*, *30*(3), 326–351.

Berger, J. & Schwartz, E. M. (2011). What drives immediate and ongoing word of mouth? *Journal of Marketing Research*, *48*(5), 869–880.

Boudreau, A. & Singh, N. (2011). Shop-and-tell: 'Haul videos' turn shopping sprees into potential profits. *ABC News* (May 31). URL: http://abcnews.go.com/Business/shop-haul-videos-turn-shopping-sprees-potential-profits/story?id=13694508.

Bradac, J. J., Konsky, C. W. & Davies, R. A. (1976). Two studies of the effects of linguistic diversity upon judgments of communicator attributes and message effectiveness. *Communication Monographs*, *43*(1), 70–79.

Brown, T. J., Barry, T. E., Dacin, P. A. & Gunst, R. F. (2005). Spreading the word: Investigating antecedents of consumers' positive word-of-mouth intentions and behaviors in a retailing context. *Journal of the Academy of Marketing Science*, *33*(2), 123–138.

Burgess, J. & Green, J. (2009). *YouTube: Online video and participatory culture*. Cambridge, UK: Polity Press.

Cheema, A. & Kaikati, A. M. (2010). The effect of need for uniqueness on word of mouth. *Journal of Marketing Research*, *XLVII*(June), 553–563.

Clark, R. A. & Goldsmith, R. E. (2005). Market mavens: Psychological influences. *Psychology and Marketing, 22*(4), 289–312.

Day, G. S. (1971). Attitude change, media and word of mouth. *Journal of Advertising Research, 11*(6), 31–40.

De Angelis, M., Bonezzi, A., Peluso, A. M., Rucker, D. D. & Costabile, M. (2012). On braggarts and gossips: A self-enhancement account of word-of-mouth generation and transmission. *Journal of Marketing Research*: *49*(4), 551–563.

Dichter, E. (1966). How word-of-mouth advertising works. *Harvard Business Review, 44*(6), 147–166.

Domaneschi, L. (2012). Food social practices: Theory of practice and the new battlefield of food quality. *Journal of Consumer Culture, 12*(3), 306–322.

Eisend, M. (2009). A meta-analysis of humor in advertising. *Journal of the Academy of Marketing Science, 37*(2), 191–203.

Feick, L. F., Price, L. L. & Higie, R. A. (1986). People who use people: The other side of opinion leadership. *Advances in Consumer Research, 13*, 301–305.

Flynn, L. R., Goldsmith, R. E. & Eastman, J. K. (1996). Opinion leaders and opinion seekers: Two new measurement scales. *Journal of the Academy of Marketing Science, 24*(2), 137–147.

Gibbs, J. L., Ellison, N. B. & Heino, R. D. (2006). Self-presentation in online personals: The role of anticipated future interaction, self-disclosure, and perceived success in internet dating. *Communication Research, 33*(2), 152–177.

Goldsmith, R. E. & Clark, R. A. (2008). An analysis of factors affecting fashion opinion leadership and fashion opinion seeking. *Journal of Fashion Marketing and Management, 12*(3), 308–322.

Goldsmith, R. E. & Flynn, L. R. (2005). Bricks, clicks, and pix: Apparel buyers' use of stores, internet, and catalogs compared. *International Journal of Retail & Distribution Management, 33*(4), 271–283.

Goldsmith, R. E. & Horowitz, D. (2006). Measuring motivations for online opinion seeking. *Journal of Interactive Advertising, 6*(2), 3–14.

Hamilton, R., Vohs, K. D. & McGill, A. L. (2014).We'll be honest, this won't be the best article you'll ever read: The use of dispreferred markers in word-of-mouth communication. *Journal of Consumer Research, 41*(1), 197–212.

Hennig-Thurau, T. & Walsh, G. (2003–4). Electronic word-of-mouth: Motivates for and consequences of reading customer articulations on the internet. *International Journal of Electronic Commerce, 8*(2), 51–74.

Herr, P. M., Kardes, F. R. & Kim, J. (1991). Effects of word-of-mouth and product-attribute information on persuasion: An accessibility-diagnosticity perspective. *Journal of Consumer Research, 17*(4), 454–462.

Higgins, E. T. (1981). The 'communication game': Implications for social cognition and persuasion. In E. T. Higgins, C. P. Herman and M. P. Zanna (Eds.), *Social cognition: The Ontario Symposium* (343–392). Hillsdale, NJ: Erlbaum.

Higgins, E. T. (1992). Achieving 'shared reality' in the communication game: A social action that creates meaning. *Journal of Language and Social Psychology, 11*(3), 107–131.

Holbrook, M. (1998). Journey to Kroywen: An ethnoscopic auto-auto-auto-driven stereographic photo-essay. In Stern, B. (Ed.), *Representing consumers: Voices, views and visions*. London: Routledge.

Holbrook, M. (1999). Introduction to consumer value. In M. Holbrook (Ed.), *Consumer value: A framework for analysis and research* (1–28). New York: Routledge.

Holbrook, M.B., & Hirschman, E.C. (1982). The experiential aspects of consumption: consumer fantasies, feelings and fun. *Journal of Consumer Research, 9*(2), 132–140.

Karmarkar, U. R. & Tormala, Z. L. (2010). Believe me, I have no idea what I'm talking about: The effects of source certainty on consumer involvement and persuasion. *Journal of Consumer Research, 36*(6), 1033–1049.

Kozinets, R. V., de Valck, K., Wojnicki, A. & Wilner, S. (2010). Networks of narrativity: Understanding word-of-mouth marketing in online communities. *Journal of Marketing, 74*(2), 71–89.

Magaudda, P. (2011). When materiality 'bites back': Digital music consumption practices in the age of dematerialization. *Journal of Consumer Culture, 11*(1), 15–36.

Marwick, A. E. (2013). *Status update: Celebrity, publicity, and branding in the social media age.* New Haven: Yale University Press.

McQuarrie, E. F., Miller, J. & Phillips, B. J. (2013). The megaphone effect: taste and audience in fashion blogging. *Journal of Consumer Research, 40*(1), 136–158.

Miles, M.B. & Huberman, A. M. (1994). Qualitative data analysis. Thousand Oaks, CA: Sage.

Packard, G. & Wooten, D. B. (2013). Compensatory knowledge signaling in consumer word-of-mouth. *Journal of Consumer Psychology, 23*(4), 434–450.

Pantzar, M. & Ruckenstein, M. (2014): The heart of everyday analytics: Emotional, material and practical extensions in self-tracking market. *Consumption Markets & Culture,* DOI: 10.1080/10253866.2014.899213.

Parmentier, M-A. & Fischer, E. (2011). You can't always get what you want: Unsustainable identity projects in the fashion system. *Consumption, Markets & Culture, 14*(1), 7–27.

Punj, G. N. & Staelin, R. (1983). A model of consumer information search behavior for new automobiles. *Journal of Consumer Research, 9*(4), 366–380.

Pyle, M. A. (2013). Using word-of-mouth to portray an image of being knowledgeable about a product category [dissertation]. Kingston, ON: Queen's University.

Reckwitz, A. (2002). Toward a theory of social practices: A development in culturalist theorizing. *European Journal of Social Theory, 5*(2), 243–263.

Scaraboto, D. & Fischer, E. (2013). Frustrated fatshionistas: An institutional theory perspective on consumer quests for greater choice in mainstream markets. *Journal of Consumer Research, 39*(6), 1234–1257.

Schau, H. J., & Gilly, M. C. (2003). We are what we post? Self-presentation in personal web space. *Journal of consumer research, 30*(3), 385–404.

Schau, H. J., Muñiz Jr., A. M., & Arnould, E. J. (2009). How brand community practices create value. *Journal of Marketing, 73*(5), 30–51.

Sheth, J. N., Newman, B. I. & Gross, B. L. (1991). Why we buy what we buy: A theory of consumption values. *Journal of Business Research,* 22, 159–170.

Smith, A. N. (2014). Sensegiving word-of-mouth and collective sensemaking about epistemic objects [dissertation]. Toronto, ON: York University.

Smith, A. N., Fischer, E. & Yongjian, C. (2014). How does brand-related user-generated content differ across YouTube, Facebook, and Twitter? *Journal of Interactive Marketing, 26*(2), 102–113.

Stephen, A.T. & Lehmann, D.R. (2009). Is anyone listening? Modeling the impact of word-of-mouth at the individual level. URL: http://ssrn.com/abstract=1371111.

Sweeney, J. C. & Soutar, G. (2001). Consumer perceived value: The development of a multiple item scale. *Journal of Retailing,* 77(2), 203–220.

Verlegh, P.W.K., Buijs, C. M. & Zethof, A. (2008). Talk, talk, talk: Consumer motives for word-of-mouth referral. *Advances in Consumer Research, 35*, 50–51.

Ward, J. C. & Ostrom, A. L. (2006). Complaining to the masses: The role of protest framing in customer-created complaint web sites. *Journal of Consumer Research, 33*(2), 220–230.

Whyte, W. H. Jr. (1954). The web of word of mouth. *Fortune, 50*(November), 140–143.

Wojnicki, A. C. & Godes, D. (2008). Word-of-mouth as self-enhancement. University of Toronto Working Paper.

Zeithaml, V. A. (1988). Consumer perceptions of price, quality, and value: A means-end model and synthesis of evidence. *Journal of Marketing, 52*(3), 2–22.

6

CONSUMER BEHAVIOR IN THE SOCIAL MEDIA MARKETPLACE

Platform Personality Matters

Marlene Morris Towns

Much like the Internet boom in the early 2000s, there is a rush by marketers to establish and maintain a presence on social media. According to every article, study, talking head and infographic, the social media space is where some of today's most important marketing communication and brand building are taking place and has become an imperative for every brand. But with great opportunity comes great responsibility. Like the Internet boom, many marketers are rushing to the social media space without a strategy for how best to leverage and incorporate it (O'Malley, 2010) and without an understanding of some basic behavioral nuances of the social media marketplace. That makes it both an alluring, economical branding opportunity and a potential field of landmines just waiting to cause major damage to a carefully curated brand image. The reality is that social media is not just another media alternative for broadcasting ad messages, but it is idiosyncratic in terms of market segmentation requirements and capabilities, how, when and why it is used by consumers, and how consumers behave in its environment. Additionally, each social media platform has obvious differences in technological capabilities and function, but they also have very different personalities that should be taken into account when leveraging the platform and its users.

There is a temptation to lump all social media under the same umbrella in terms of how they are used when, in reality, various platforms have different personalities all their own and, as such, are used very differently by consumers. The current chapter describes some of the ways in which social media has changed the marketing landscape and looks more closely at some of the differences between consumer behavior in a social environment and a traditional marketplace. It also examines more closely some of the differences between some of the leading social media platforms—namely Facebook and Twitter—and how they are used by consumers. This leads to a discussion of how marketers can best leverage the different types of platforms to most effectively communicate with different segments of consumers.

The good news for brands still struggling to create or hone their social media strategy is that the more things change, the more they stay the same. Whereas the emergence and prevalence of social media does shake up our trusted 4Ps marketing framework, it does not change the effectiveness of marketing strategy fundamentals. A solid and informed social media strategy is guided by the basic marketing and communication strategies that have been taught in business school classrooms for decades. The technology is constantly changing, but the strategy foundation is timeless. And like all good advertising and promotion, an effective social media strategy is a combination of art and science. Also like all good marketing communication, a solid social media strategy starts with a thorough understanding of the consumer and a well-understood strategy for the brand. That said, the social media space does make things a bit more interesting.

How Social Media Shakes Up the 4Ps of Marketing

One of the mainstays of marketing over the years has been the concept of the 4Ps—Product, Price, Place (distribution) and Promotion. Whereas innovations over the years have had an impact on one or a couple of the Ps at one time—for example, the introduction of e-commerce made Price and Place more dynamic factors by facilitating comparison shopping and creating another channel of distribution via online shopping —none have emerged that affect all 4 of the Ps to the extent that social media does today. They all remain in place and relevant, but social media adds just a bit of complexity to each one.

Place (Distribution Channels)

Whereas e-commerce fundamentally changed the Place, or channel, element of the 4Ps by essentially replacing the catalog business and cutting into retail store visits by allowing customers to shop from their computers (and eventually tablets and phones as well), social media further facilitates the process by serving as the link between the advertisements, blogs and articles on the various platforms and the shopping websites that they link to so that consumers can click right to the brand or product they have seen in their social media content and purchase. In no other setting is the process made so seamless, except perhaps the retail store environment that incorporates mobile technology and apps. Some platforms, like Facebook, are now incorporating shopping into their sites so that brands can set up a store and sell directly through the social media platform. Conversely, some shopping storefront providers like Shopify are built primarily to facilitate commerce but incorporate social elements such as blogs as well as links to the major social media pages.

Price

Like Place, social media facilitates price comparison on the part of consumers, thus making them more aware of online (and in-store) discounts and subsequently encouraging consumer price sensitivity. What makes the social media space even more effective is the fact that not only do marketers have a new medium through which to share pricing and promotion information, but quite often it is one's own friends, family or other connections who are passing along price and promotion information from brands. When deals are activated by a consumer, he/she is given the opportunity to share their deal experience with specific individuals via email or more broadly via social media platforms. Given the influence of word of mouth information, this is even more impactful as a source.

Additionally, the social space has seen the emergence of social sites devoted to price deals. Sites like LivingSocial and Groupon leverage the power of social media to promote price-based deals and discounts that are shared with members who are then encouraged to share further via their own social media circles. Particularly in its early days, Groupon was driven by local communities of members and necessitated those group members working "together" to get a minimum number of subscribers to sign up for a deal before the deal was actually activated, thus making the achievement of the price promotion a truly social effort.

Promotion

E-commerce ushered in the era of somewhat clumsy new advertising outlets in the form of banner and pop-up advertisements, interstitials and the like that peppered and distracted from our online activity, some more obtrusively than others. Social media not only provides a way to reach engaged consumers within a particular platform, but the sites allow for an incredible amount of detailed information about users that can be used to most effectively segment markets and target consumers based not only on demographics but on lifestyle and stated interests as well as on their own search results and posted content. Advertisers and their messages get not only eyeballs, but also engaged and eager consumers who are already in a social platform where they can share the brand information as well as their enthusiasm for it with the click of a button.

Product

One of the more interesting directions that social media has taken of late is the blurring of the line between advertising and content. Much like the blurring of the line between advertising and entertainment that fueled the practice of product placement in the 1990s, which blossomed into branded integration in the early 2000s, the line between advertising content and entertainment content in social media (articles, images etc.) is getting more and more difficult to distinguish. A large part of the appeal of the major social media platforms like Facebook, Twitter and Instagram is the entertaining content in the form of articles, pictures and video, many of which are sponsored by brands. Increasingly, the focus amongst advertisers is on content—making the message the product in many cases. This has led content providers such as Buzzfeed to transition from mere content providers to advertising agencies themselves, using their content to purvey brand messages or influence for their clients.

A recent examination of the increasingly blurry line between advertising and entertainment rates five examples of brands producing advertising as content. It is interesting to note that of the five examples, four are videos produced exclusively for online delivery and consumption with the hope of them going viral, which they did (Thielman, 2014). This speaks to the challenge that brands face in producing (or, as is increasingly the case, outsourcing) engaging content that is to be shared by their online community and beyond. On this topic, it is important to note that although marketers often speak of producing "viral videos," this is not accurate. Marketers do not create viral videos; they produce videos that they *hope* will go viral. Of course they will do what they can in the form of promotion, strategic posting, "public relations" and the like to help it achieve viral status, but it is typically up to the social media marketplace to determine whether a video will actually go viral or be shared and reshared widely. To the extent that brands are successful in providing product in the form of entertainment (articles, pictures, video, games, etc.) they achieve the broader goals of building community around the brand, awareness and equity.

Consumer Behavior in the Social Space

Despite the many changes that social media brings to the marketplace, perhaps the most intriguing aspect of its influence is on consumer behavior itself. Many reasons have been identified as to why users are increasingly participating in social networks. Some of the most common reasons identified by Tuten and Solomon in their textbook on social media (Tuten and Solomon, 2015) include:

- *Affinity impulse*—social networks allow participants to express their affinity, liking and/or relationship with people, products, causes or reference groups.
- *Personal utility impulse*—people are looking to answer the question "what's in it for me?" seeking utility in the form of information, incentive, entertainment, convenience.
- *Contact comfort* and *immediacy impulse*—the relief we feel from knowing that individuals in our network are easily accessible and the relief we feel from knowing that this contact can be immediate.
- *Altruistic impulse*—a way to do something good or pay it forward [as well as a way to publicly pat oneself on the back and/or motivate others to do good by sharing one's own good deeds in a form of self-congratulatory sharing].

- *Curiosity impulse*—satisfy our curiosity about others by following and/or viewing their online social activity.
- *Validation impulse*—also called the ego-defensive function; people seek to eliminate perceived external threats to their beliefs or eliminate potential self-doubt.

In its early days, the Internet was used primarily to maximize marketers' reach and facilitate one-way communication with their customers. It also provided a mechanism for customers to provide feedback, but the primary focus was on outgoing communications. Eventually, the emergence of social media provided consumers with a mechanism for easy and public communication with and about brands as well as with each other. Whereas it is often used to facilitate customer service in place of or in addition to traditional customer service correspondence mechanisms like phone and email, it is increasingly used by consumers to exert voice and power in the customer relationship or for input from the general public. Social media has totally revamped the way that consumers interact with brands as well as how they interact with each other about brands.

The first in the list of reasons why people engage in social media, affinity impulse, speaks to the fact that much of our social media existence involves social relationships with organizations, causes and brands in a somewhat seamless existence with our relationship with human others. This puts the responsibility on brands to be as "likable" and engaging as any other "friend" in one's social media space. As will be discussed later in this chapter, it also necessitates the brand acting "in character" by speaking, writing, posting, sharing and responding as its brand personality would dictate. Social media users want to get something out of their exchanges and they also like to know what to expect from their friends and connections.

Consider one's circle of friends—there is often a role for different individuals based on their personality and the type of friendship you have. Some friends are always good for a laugh, some good confidants, some are the life of the party, some always have wise words of wisdom. We learn these roles after interacting with our friends over time and we value their consistency. In the social media space, this reliability extends to brands as well as friends.

Consumer to Company Communication

Whereas consumers for years were relegated to letting their wallets do the talking, making their feelings known over time through their collective spending or lack thereof, social media has given the general public a direct line to the companies and brands that they wish to reach, and a public forum for doing so. It has provided a somewhat more level playing field where consumers are empowered as never before and everyone with a Twitter account has unprecedented access and voice in the marketplace. Historically, if a company or brand made a decision that consumers felt strongly about, the company would get calls, letters and perhaps eventually see a change in sales as responses to the decision. For example, on April 23, 1985 when Coca Cola changed their beloved formula to a sweeter version and rebranded it as New Coke, fans and loyal consumers were livid. The Coca Cola Company received over 400,000 calls and letters in the following weeks, complaining about the change (Anonymous, 2014). Despite the uproar and vocal demonstrations, it took three months for the Coca Cola Company to bring the old recipe back to the market.

Coke's archrival PepsiCo had its own rebranding debacle, but this time in the era of social media. In January of 2009, PepsiCo changed the packaging of the classic Tropicana brand of orange juice (leaving the actual product unchanged). Underestimating the extent to which consumers felt an attachment to the familiar packaging, they were caught off guard by the instant and powerful backlash, much of which happened on social media. "After a month of being bombarded by e-mails, phone calls, and social media commentary, PepsiCo announced that it would promptly return to the old carton" (Male, 2010). More immediate still was the attempted rebranding by casual clothing retailer the Gap the following year. On October 4, 2010, the Gap announced a totally revamped logo, which was met with a viciously negative social-media-facilitated outcry from advertising industry professionals, Gap loyalists, advertising enthusiasts and pretty much anyone who felt like weighing in. The response was scathing and swift. After scrambling to try to use some of the very social media platforms that were contributing so effectively to its crucifixion to salvage the move, including a Facebook campaign to crowdsource new logo ideas, the Gap promptly scrapped the new logo idea and reverted back to the beloved original. This process, from initial announcement to official recall, took one week (Weiner, 2010).

Consumer to Consumer Communication

In addition to this new era of consumer feedback and corporate responsiveness, companies leverage social media to build community and encourage users to "talk amongst yourselves," with the hopes that their brand will be at the center of that conversation and that the conversation will be positive. Knowing that users in the social media space are not there primarily to communicate with brands (and will become annoyed if brands are too invasive in their social media space), it is the job of marketers not to be in the conversation, necessarily, but to provide the fodder for conversation between friends, family and followers; to guide the conversation directly or indirectly to their product category and brand.

Social media users spend a great deal of time building their social media networks and curating content that is representative of elements of themselves—their families, their friendships, politics, their interests. Facebook estimates that the average American spends 40 minutes a day checking a Facebook feed (Brustein, 2014). Reports estimate that 18-to-34-year-olds spend as much as 3.8 hours per day on social media whereas 35-to-49-year-olds spend an estimated three hours per day on social sites (Bilton, 2014). This results in a massive population of what has been termed Connected Protagonists (Hamm, 2012). These are described by Jon Hamm as a new generation of consumers who are redefining the role that brands can play in their lives. These connected protagonists are constantly connected and use social media to craft carefully constructed images—personal brands, if you will—that represent themselves. In today's environment where brands and marketing are part of our cultural landscape, this presents brands with a particular opportunity and challenge to provide information that these consumers incorporate into their online personas and share with their network of associates. A challenge is that "brands must understand that Connected Protagonists 'own' their own audience and the right to communicate with them. Additionally, the dynamic of 'brand to audience' has shifted to 'brand to Connected Protagonist to audience.'" (Hamm, 2012). In this social media-fueled marketing environment, brands are the purveyors of entertaining content that users can acquire and share, but the consumer is the ultimate gatekeeper of the relationship with his or her extended circle and controls what information that gets filtered through and shared.

Social Media Platform Personality

There has been a great deal of recent discussion about the importance to marketers of the two most well-known and widely used social media sites—Facebook and Twitter—with Twitter being recently recognized by many in industry as the more important social media platform for particular market segments (Edwards, 2013). According to Piper Jaffray's semi-annual teen market research report, whereas teens have historically reported "friends" as the biggest influencer of their purchase decisions, "Internet" is becoming a greater influence. "More than half of teens indicate that social media impacts their purchases with Twitter being the most important, eclipsing Facebook, followed closely by Instagram. But the popularity of Facebook is waning among teens with 23% citing it as the most important, down from 33% six months ago and 42% a year ago" (Piper Jaffray Companies, 2013). Nevertheless, Facebook is hardly suffering from a mass exodus of users and is still the primary outlet for brands. Despite talk of Facebook growing old and suffering from teen flight, it remains the strongest social media platform in the young adult market and incredibly valuable to marketers, with high rates of Internet user penetration (67% of U.S. Internet users are on Facebook and even higher penetration rates in European markets, including 82% in the UK), and the following with the highest income—73% of U.S. Internet users with incomes over $75,000 are on Facebook compared to 17 and 13% in that income bracket who are on Instagram or Pinterest, respectively (Smith, 2013). Facebook also skews only slightly more female in its user base, whereas other sites like Pinterest and Google+ skew heavily female.

Whereas these conclusions are derived primarily from usage numbers and demographic descriptions of users (most notably age, as well as gender and income), our research shows that the two major sites appear to be used in some systematically different ways, an understanding of which could be far more valuable than a demographic breakdown to marketers seeking to segment, target and appeal to users with various campaigns and content on social media.

Platform Personality

Within the topic of consumer behavior, a great deal of attention has been given to the notion of brand personalities, or the set of human characteristics that are attributed to a brand. Previous research has examined the extent to which consumers are able to express his or her own self through the personality of the brand (Belk, 1988). This construct of brand personality was found to have five dimensions (Aaker, 1997): sincerity, excitement, competence, sophistication and ruggedness.

Much like brands have personalities, the retail outlets in which they are sold also have personalities. Sometimes this is the personality of the particular brand of merchandise that they sell (e.g., the Gap) or the retail outlet itself that carries a variety of brands such as a department store (e.g., Bloomingdales). The brand image and the retail image have been found to be inextricably linked, such that the images associated with the brands that a store carries influence perceptions of the store's image (Porter and Claycomb, 1997). Astute marketers match the personality of the brand with that of the retailer so that they will benefit each other in terms of consumer perceptions. They also attempt to match the brand personality of the marketing communication media/vehicle and its audience with the brand and its message. For example, an upscale brand would be sold in high-end retailers and advertise in publications perceived as high-end and exclusive, with readership that is likely to afford the offering and find it appealing. In today's marketplace, the retail setting may also be not just the retailer's physical store, but their online website. Research has also been done that finds that media vehicles also have their own brand personality (Kumar and Kumar, 2014). As an extension of the sponsoring organization's operations and carrier of the brand, a website in particular has personality characteristics that must be matched with the personality characteristics of the brand (Palmer and Griffith, 1998). Much like Aaker's (1997) research found that brand personality has a significant influence on a consumer's brand preference and choice, the personality characteristics of a website influence the preferences and choices of online customers. The scale created by Chen and Rodgers (2006) to measure the brand personality of websites identified five dimensions thereof: Intelligent (proficient, sophisticated, effective and systematic), Fun (engaging, exciting and vital), Organized (confusing and overwhelming), Candid and Sincere.

Like brands, retailers and websites, social media platforms each have distinct personalities and defining characteristics. Tuten and Solomon (2015) find that "social networking sites vary in terms of three important dimensions: (1) Audience and degree of specialization; (2) The social objects that mediate the relationships among members; and (3) Degree of decentralization or openness" (Tuten and Solomon, 2015). Whereas each person's experience on each platform is unique to their own input and to the information that they access and share in curating their own online personas, there is a distinct tenor to each site and a way in which each is used. Some of this is guided by the technical specifications of the site and what it facilitates and allows—for example, Twitter limits posts to 140 characters, thus engendering brevity and directness in its users' posts. Instagram focuses on mobile photos and features a number of stylized photo filters, thus encouraging primarily visual and artistically sophisticated content. Facebook allows for longer posts along with images, links to outside content with images and video, which facilitates more in-depth sharing of a wide variety of content.

Psychologists have also identified specific Twitter and Facebook personality types of users (Hughes et al., 2012). Three hundred people were queried about their social media usage and administered a test of personality. The survey focused on the "Big Five" personality traits: Neuroticism, Extraversion, Openness, Agreeableness, and Conscientiousness and also included some specific personality traits including sociability and Need for Cognition. These researchers found that people who used Facebook mostly to socialize tended to be younger, more social and more neurotic—suggesting that Facebook regulars use the site at least in part as a tool to alleviate loneliness. People who used Twitter to socialize, meanwhile, scored high on openness and sociability but low on conscientiousness. So they would be more likely to use Twitter to procrastinate and to make rash posts and say regrettable things (Baden, 2012). "There were interesting differences, too, when it came to using the two sites to seek or spread information. Twitter users who did this were high on conscientiousness and need for cognition, and low on neuroticism. In short, they were focused, no-nonsense information-gatherers. People who sought information on Facebook, in contrast, were considerably less intellectually curious" (Shea, 2012).

Yet another study sought to find differences in individuals' personalities that were correlated with their choice of social networking platform preference, also using the Big Five personality characteristics. The results indicate that those who have a preference for Facebook see themselves as higher in Sociability, Extraversion, and Neuroticism, but lower in Need for Cognition. The preference for Twitter was significantly correlated with personality traits of Conscientiousness, Openness and Sociability. The authors believe that the lack of association between Neuroticism and Twitter social may suggests that, in contrast to Facebook, users do not see Twitter as a tool to mitigate loneliness, but perhaps as one that serves to facilitate procrastination and decrease time spent on goal-directed behaviors (Hughes et al., 2012).

Aside from technical capabilities, the personality of each platform affects how users interact with the platform and their connections within it. For example, given that Twitter allows for direct contact and/or inclusion of brand users as well as individuals, it serves as a mechanism for a level of direct contact with companies that is unprecedented in the marketplace. Users can also use hashtags to chime in on trending topics with others posting with the same hashtag and topic, so there is a collaborative feel to Twitter. Perhaps because of its fast-moving nature and abbreviated character limitation, it has become a platform of quick, witty and somewhat snarky communiqués. The majority of brand-focused backlash via social media is born and spread on Twitter. Facebook, on the other hand, has a decidedly more friendly feel (as indicated by the word choice for connecting with someone as "friending" as opposed to Twitter's "following") and seems to engender more of a community feel and positive sharing of personal and professional tidbits or major announcements. It is important for marketers to understand these nuanced personalities of each platform in order to craft messages, campaigns and content that is matched with the tenor of each platform in order to get optimal results, at best, and not create disastrous outcomes at worst.

There have been several examples of ill-fated Twitter campaigns that may have gone slightly less poorly had they been conducted on another platform. For example, in April of 2014 the NYPD ran a campaign on Twitter asking New York City residents to post pictures of themselves with their neighborhood NYPD officers using the hashtag #myNYPD. The result was not the feel-good, community-building campaign that they had hoped for; rather, people piled onto the hashtag and campaign with images of police brutality and messages expressing anger and frustration at the NYPD for their treatment of citizens (Oh, 2014).

In November of 2013, JPMorgan, in an attempt to come up with some out-of-the-box ways to use social media, launched a Twitter campaign that featured one of their executives, James Lee, who would answer career questions with a focus on reaching students (De la Merced, 2013). Again, the overall promotion may have been tone-deaf and not taken into account the current climate and the suspicion with which many people still viewed the financial industry and particularly JPMorgan, but it took on an immediate and hostile negative tone fueled by the collaborative and combative nature of Twitter as a platform.

On the other hand, Facebook is seen as more of a platform for sharing good news, positive stories and for seeking encouragement or validation of one's ideas. It is also a more closed and personal platform (although, depending on one's privacy settings, it is possible to post publicly so that even people who are not friends can see one's posts). The fact that Twitter allows direct connection to many brands and to a wide social circle on non-followers through the use of hashtags, also provides the anonymity to make users more likely to post sentiments that are rude, harsh or aggressive as they feel they are less likely to be personally identified.

Different Platform, Different Goals

In many brands' haste to enter the social media space and be on all of the major "it" platforms of the moment, many have succumbed to the temptation to "cut & paste" their content. Because users are on a variety of technologies—computers, tablets, phones and PDAs—and on a number of platforms—Facebook, Twitter, Instagram, Pinterest, Snapchat—many companies took their social media content and replicated it across platforms, formatted for each channel. Whereas this seems like a logical and efficient strategy, the reality is that each of these different platforms has a different style, personality and flow, and people often use them for different things. Thus, a post that is perfectly suited for Facebook might not fit well in a Twitter environment for example.

Despite the recent research results that show that younger consumers are leaving Facebook in droves now that it is overrun with "older" users and taking refuge with platforms like Twitter, this may not be such a cut and dry reality. Perhaps people are just looking to other platforms like Twitter for certain goals and remaining active on Facebook for others. To test this, a sample of 272 millennial consumers, average age 19, received a series of questions about their social media usage. What we found was that these consumers used the different platforms for different purposes. When asked which social media site they would be most likely to use to vent about a bad product, 29% of millennial consumers reported that they would use Facebook whereas 34% said they would use Twitter (30% said they would use none). Similarly, when asked which social media site they would use to vent about a bad service experience, 30% said they would use Facebook and 35% said they would use Twitter (26% said they would use none) (see Figure 6.1).

However, when it came to sharing positive product experiences, the balance shifted, with 36% reporting that they would use Facebook to report a good product experience and 24% reporting that they would use Twitter. Good experiences were also more likely to be shared on visual sites, with 16% saying they would share on Instagram and 4% reporting that they would share on Pinterest (16% said they would use none). Interestingly, subjects were equally likely to share positive experiences on Facebook and Twitter (33%) and only 5% said they

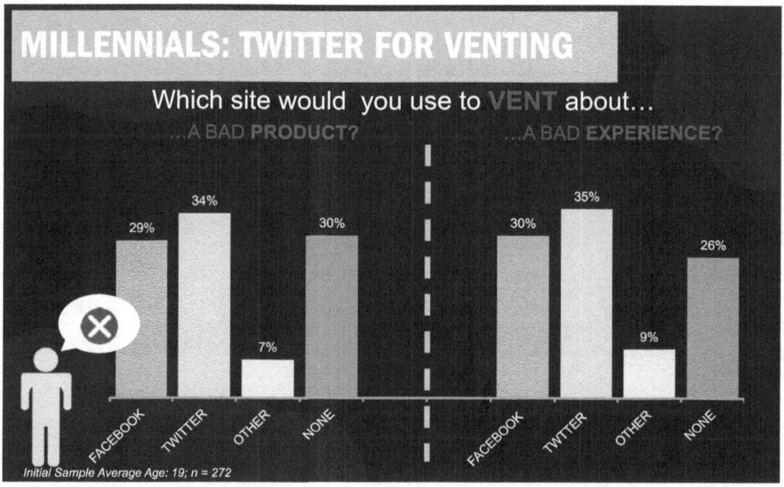

FIGURE 6.1 Motivations for Tweeting Negative Info Among Millenials

would share such experience feedback on Instagram (20% said they would use none) (see Figure 6.2).

Whereas millennials are less likely to share product/service experience in general than their older counterparts, they reported being much more likely to use Facebook to share in a variety of categories, including family-related sharing (Facebook 37%/Twitter 11%), vacations (Facebook 56%/Instagram 18%/Twitter 8%), fashion (Facebook 22%/Pinterest 22%/Instagram 17%/Twitter 9%) and music (Facebook 42%/Twitter 17%/YouTube 15%) (see Figure 6.3).

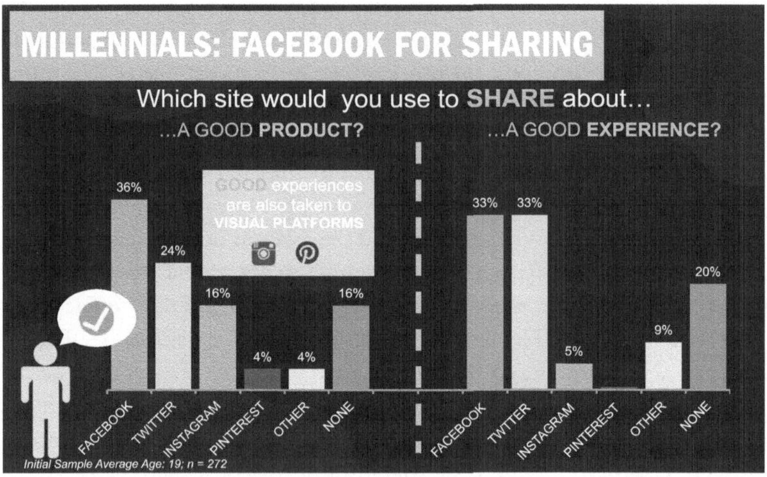

FIGURE 6.2 Motivations for Tweeting Positive Info Among Millenials

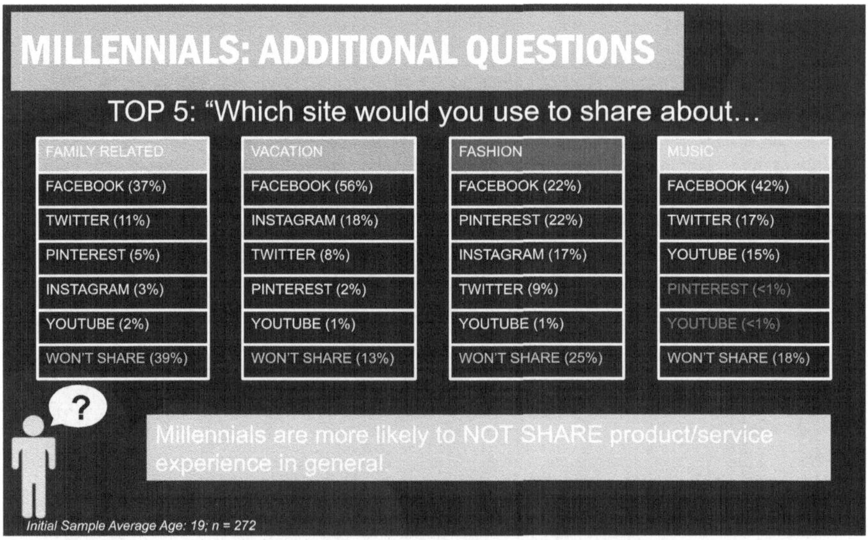

FIGURE 6.3 Platform Choice for Info Sharing Among Millenials

Given all the talk of older users taking over Facebook, and the rapid increase in social media activity amongst Generation X, Boomers and Seniors, it seemed prudent to also survey a group with broader range of ages. It was also suspected that there might be other behavioral motivations aside from just content area for users' decision to share via social media. Particularly when consumers deal with potentially negative product or service experiences, do they attempt to cope with them in different ways and does this lead them to prefer one platform versus another as their preferred method of coping? Folkman and Lazarus (1988) provided the background theory for this line of inquiry with their model of coping mechanisms. They outline four types of coping mechanisms that people utilize (see Figure 6.4):

- Wishful thinking (Ideal Situation Seekers "Daydream a better time or place");
- Seeking Social Support (Ear Seekers "I let my feelings out somehow");
- Problem-Focused Coping (Grounded Sympathizers "Try to analyze . . . to understand");
- Detachment (Situation Separators "Try to forget the whole thing").

The expectation was that people would share based on one of two goals—Seeking Social Support (just wanting a sympathetic ear) or Problem-Focused Coping (wanting to analyze, understand and address the problem). Given the characteristics of the platforms and the personality traits attributed to those who prefer one versus the other, it was hypothesized that these two goals would lead users to two different social media platforms—Facebook for Seeking Social

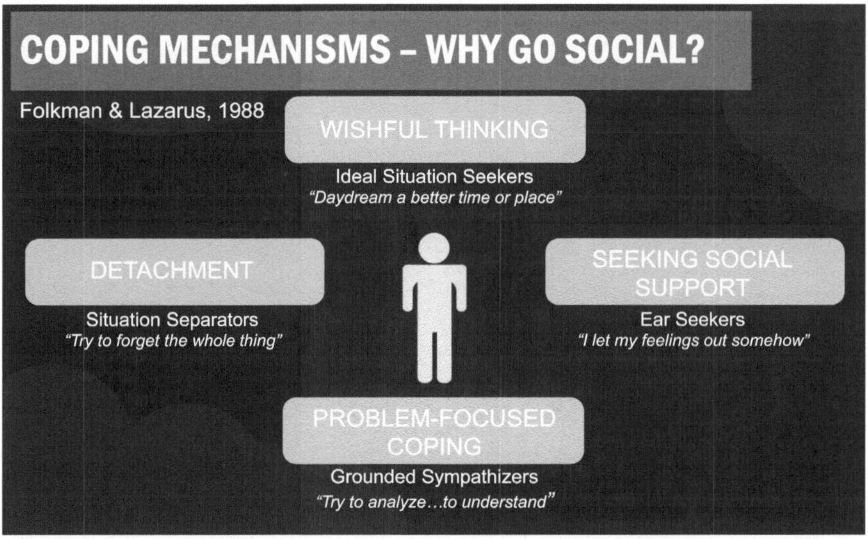

FIGURE 6.4 Coping Mechanisms Associated With Social Media Usage

Support and Twitter for Problem-Focused Coping. These differences were expected primarily in situations where negative experiences were being shared but could also show differences in positive conditions when the focus was on the self versus the product/service. The diagram in Figure 6.5 lays out early expectations and the survey focuses on the right side of the diagram (sharing of negative experience).

The second questionnaire surveyed 307 subjects with an average age of 37 (age range was 18–72, but the majority of subjects fell into the 18–34 and 35–50 categories). What was found was that the overwhelming majority of people shared both positive and negative product experiences via Facebook over any other platform (59% and 56%, respectively). However, subjects were more likely to share on Twitter when sharing negative product experience (16%) than positive (11%). Sharing on YouTube was the same in both positive and negative product experience conditions (4%) but visual platforms Pinterest and Instagram were used by less than 1% in negative product experiences but did register at 4% (Pinterest) and 5% (Instagram) when sharing positive product experience. Results were similar when venting or sharing service experiences. Subjects were more likely to share via Facebook across the board (53% in venting of negative service experience and 60% in sharing of positive) but were a bit more likely to use Twitter when sharing negative experiences (17% versus 14% for positive).

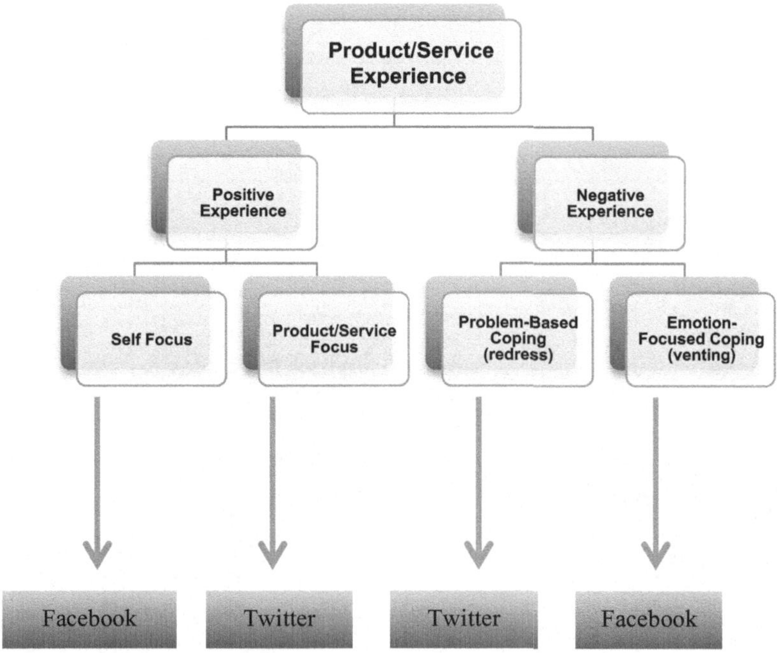

FIGURE 6.5 Conceptual Framework

When the basic demographic measure of age was examined by breaking the age groups into three segments (18–34, 35–50 and 50+), there were some predictable findings, such as the finding that the likelihood of using Twitter decreases as age category increases. But there were a couple of interesting things to note. First, the likelihood of reporting positive or negative product experience via Twitter in the 50+ segment was the same at 5%. The 35–50 year olds were more than twice as likely to report negative product experiences via Twitter at 12% and 18–24 year olds were most likely to use Twitter to share negative product experience at 21%. All groups were more likely to share on Facebook, but the middle segment of 35–50 year olds was most likely at 65%, whereas the 18–34 year olds and 50+ were similar at 53% and 50% respectively. The two oldest age segments were nearly the same on their likelihood of sharing positive product experience via Twitter (at 6% and 5% for 35–50 and 50+) whereas the youngest group of 18–34 year olds were more likely to share positive product experience via Twitter (15%). Subjects were slightly more likely to share positive product experience on Facebook in a pattern similar to negative experience, where 35–50 year olds were the most likely to report using Facebook for such sharing (68%) versus 18–34 year olds (56%) and 50+ (57%) who were very similar to each other (see Figure 6.6). The pattern was the same for service experience as well (see Figure 6.7).

When looking at what personal or psychological characteristics might influence people's choice of platform for sharing product or service information, we looked to the various coping mechanisms referenced earlier for possible explanations. As predicted, Seeking Social Support was a significant deciding factor in individuals' choice of platform, namely what platform they would use to vent about a poor product or service, share about a product that they liked, a great restaurant, family/child related content, a great destination, about fashion, music, television/movies and banking experience.

Whereas Problem-Focused Coping was expected to be a significant predictor of platform choice, given the direct access to companies that Twitter provides as well as the propensity for individuals to use it as a platform for complaining behavior and redress, this construct did not significantly correlate with platform choice in any categories. The factor that was surprisingly correlated with platform choice was Wishful Thinking. Wishful Thinking was significantly correlated to platform choice in conditions of venting about poor products (but not poor service), sharing positive product information (but not great service) and at a marginally significant level, sharing about a great restaurant. The only other factor that was at all influential in choice of social media platform was the Detachment factor, which was a marginally significant predictor of platform choice for sharing banking experience. This factor is characterized by the extent to which consumers "try to forget the whole thing."

Upon reflection and looking at the factors that contribute to each of the four coping mechanisms, these findings make sense, including the lack of results for

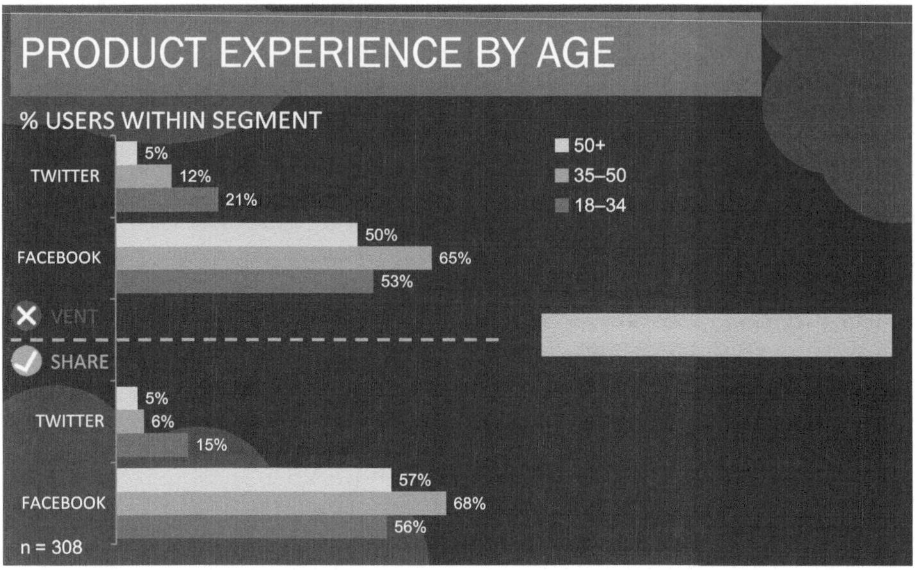

FIGURE 6.6 Product Info Sharing By Age Group

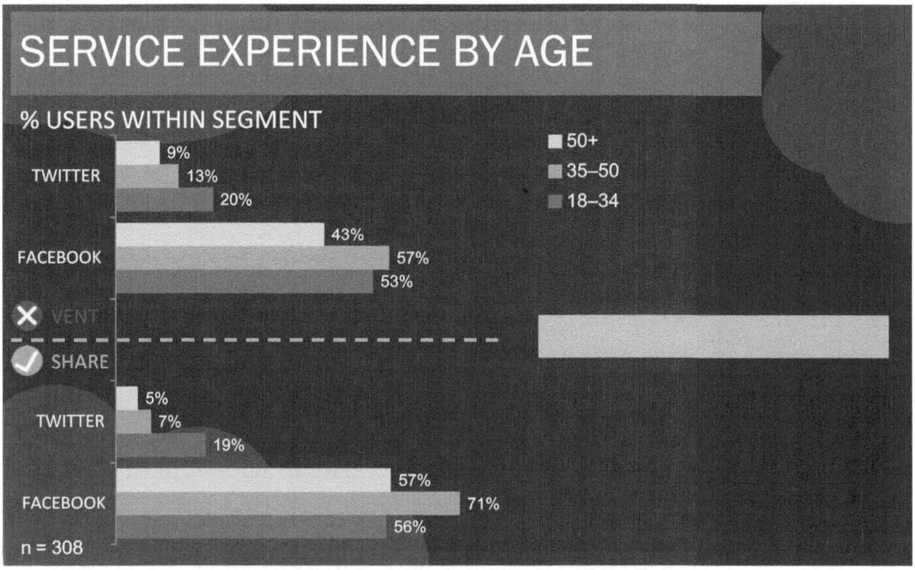

FIGURE 6.7 Service Info Sharing By Age Group

Problem-Focused Coping. The construct of Seeking Social Support is one that would logically lead one to choose one platform over another, namely Facebook. This is where you have a closed circle of friends/family/colleagues/followers that you likely share stories, images, video and more in-depth "status" updates with (at least one is not limited to expressing oneself in 140 characters or less) that you can turn to for validation, consolation and empathy. A look at some of the dimensions of Problem-Focused Coping leads to the conclusion that not only is it not representative of items that would lead one to a platform like Twitter at all. Problem-Focused Coping is comprised of characteristics like thinking deeply about the situation, trying to analyze and understand the problem, developing a thoughtful strategy for addressing the problem, all of which are somewhat the antithesis of how Twitter is used. Twitter is generally a more shoot-from-the-hip, gut reaction, immediate response mechanism. The Twitter world (and feed) moves quickly and topics come and go at a rapid pace, unlike Facebook, where individuals "liking" or commenting on even an old status update can make that post show up again in others' feeds and keep the topic going. This immediacy is part of the Twitter persona and likely contributes to the earlier-cited work that found that Twitter users to be more likely to post rash and regrettable sentiments than on Facebook or other platforms.

Wishful Thinking, on the other hand, is this notion of an ideal situation; wishing the problem was gone, thinking of an ideal situation, daydreaming of a better time or place. This seems like more of a driver of the type of platform would be used, particularly in a positive or negative product experience situation. It does not seem obvious which type of platform would appeal most to individuals using Wishful Thinking as a coping mechanism as arguments could be made for them using either Facebook or Twitter; further analysis of this segment including their preferred platform would be an insightful next step.

Pulling together the theoretical findings and the practical understanding of what these platforms offer and what marketers can do to leverage and maximize their social media content, there are recommendations that can be made. As opposed to using a one-for-all strategy in which marketers use the same content across all social media platforms, there are ways to tailor content to maximize not only the technical capabilities and format of each, but to match the type of consumer using each, their goals in selecting each platform for each occasion and how they are using each platform. So, for the people exhibiting Wishful Thinking coping characteristics, the ideal situation seekers, one thing that marketers could maintain as a goal is to enable bigger dreams by providing striking visual content, narrative, native content, things that help people conjure up their ideal. An example of a marketer that does this well is the Four Seasons Hotel. The travel industry has a wonderful grasp of how to leverage social media to cultivate brand image and build community, but the Four Seasons stands out from their major competition like the Ritz Carlton in that the majority of the images that they share on social media do not focus on their properties or the amenities of each facility. Rather, they focus largely on the lifestyle that they espouse—the luxury in and around the facility in the locale, the local architecture and scenery, lush images and landscapes, exotic cuisine, enchanting nightlife and other elements that help the user complete this picture of what they want to envision as their reality. Another strategy is entrusting the segment to push the brand forward for you online and in their social circles. Give users leeway and incentive to push the brand for you and become your ambassadors. This is done by providing content such as stylized images on Instagram, for example, that entices the user to share the official content as their ideal; content that is so enticing and representative of their desired persona and ideal situation that they incorporate it into the online persona that they are constantly curating as connected protagonists in order to share that persona with others.

To appeal to those Seeking Social Support, users who just want an ear, trust that demographic to actively build these familiar ties and then become part of the conversation not by chiming in but by providing the content around which you and your connections can rally to share or use as representative of or fodder to express your attitudes, concerns, frustrations, pride and the like. A presence here on Facebook, for example can serve as an active reminder of other ways to access the brand, be it in-person, on their website or on other platforms.

This way of thinking brings to the social media space some of the common sense elements of marketing that have so far alluded some in the social media space. Among these is considering not just your audience, but also the time and place that you are reaching them with a particular marketing communication. For example, if you are implementing a feel-good campaign for your state/local/municipal government and you want to query constituents or gather testimonials for a campaign you would consider time and place in soliciting these constituents' input. If you approach citizens at a local park on a lovely weekend afternoon or in a new facility provided by the local government you will likely get just the positive reactions you need for your feel-good campaign. However, if you decide to solicit this feedback mid-afternoon at your local Motor Vehicle Administration office where people have been waiting for hours for their number to be called to receive service, you are likely to get snarky or sarcastic comments (at best) rather than the feel-good testimonials you were looking for. This is much the same as a brand (particularly one that has faced any sort of recent criticism or negative feelings that could be lingering) using an often snarky, sarcastic and fast-moving platform like Twitter to launch a campaign or solicit input. Taking a feel-good campaign to a platform that is viewed and used largely as a complaint or problem-resolution platform creates a mis-match of platform personality and purpose.

It is imperative that brands take into account not just who you are trying to reach or the technological capabilities of each platform, but the platform personality and what people look to that platform for. Whereas it may seem most efficient to use a one-size-fits-all strategy of leveraging social media posts across platforms, it is more effective to manage by platform personality and what users use each platform for. When all of these factors are working in tandem, marketing communications are likely to be better received, more effective and shared more widely.

Acknowledgment

The author thanks Jay Legaspi for assistance with creating the visuals in this chapter.

References

Aaker, Jennifer (1997). "Dimensions of brand personality," *Journal of Consumer Research*, August, 347–56. Anonymous (2014). [available at http://en.wikipedia.org/wiki/New_Coke].

Baden, Trish (2012). "We are social people." [available at http://wearesocialpeople.com/what-is-your-internet-personality-type/].

Belk, Russell (1988). "Possessions and the extended self," *Journal of Consumer Research*, 2, September, 139–68.

Bilton, Nick (2014). "Reclaiming our (real) lives from social media," *New York Times*, July 17, page E2.

Brustein, Joshua (2014). "Americans now spend more time on Facebook than they do on their pets," Businessweek.com, July 23. [available at www.businessweek.com/articles/2014–07–23/heres-how-much-time-people-spend-on-facebook-daily].

Chen Q. and Rodgers S. (2006). "Development of an instrument to measure web site personality," *Journal of Interactive Advertising,* 7, 1.

De La Merced, Michael J. (2013). "After Twitter #Fail, JPMorgan calls off Q. and A," TheNewYorkTimes.com, November 13, [available at http://dealbook.nytimes.com/2013/11/13/after-twitter-fail-jpmorgan-calls-off-q-and-a/?_r=0].

Edwards, Jim (2013). "Facebook is no longer the most popular social network for teens," Slate.com, October 24. [available at www.slate.com/blogs/business_insider/2013/10/24/facebook_and_teen_user_trends.html].

Folkman, S. and R.S. Lazarus (1988). *Manual for the Ways of Coping Questionnaire*, Palo Alto, CA: Consulting Psychologists Press.

Hamm, Jon (2012). "Voice: The Connected Protagonist: To reach the content-hungry consumer, marketers need to shift their own role from star to supporting player," October 15. [available at www.adweek.com/news/advertising-branding/voice-connected-protagonist-144439].

Hughes, David, John, Moss Rowe, Mark Batey, and Andrew Lee (2012). "A tale of two sites: Twitter vs. Facebook and the personality predictors of social media usage," *Computers in Human Behavior*, 28(2), 561–69.

Kumar, Abhishek and Venkatesh R. Kumar (2014). "Brand personality scales for media: A story in the making," *The Business & Management Review*, 5(1), 1–9. London: The Academy of Business and Retail Management (ABRM), June.

Male, Bianca (2010). "10 Major rebranding disasters and what you should learn from them," *Business Insider*, April 7. [available at www.businessinsider.com/rebranding-failures-2010–3?op=1].

O'Malley, Gavin (2010). "Look Ma, no hands: More than half of companies say they are using social media with no strategy." [available at www.mediapost.com/publications/article/130723/look-ma-no-hands-more-than-half-of-companies-say.html?edition].

Oh, Inae (2014). "This NYPD idea backfired horribly on Twitter," *The Huffington Post*, April 22.

Palmer, Jonathan W. and David A. Griffith (1998). "An emerging model of web site design for marketing," *Association for Computing Machinery, Communications of the ACM,* 41(3), 44–51.

Piper Jaffray Companies (2013). "Taking stock with teens" semi-annual survey, October 10. [available at www.piperjaffray.com/2col.aspx?id=287&releaseid=1863548].

Porter, Stephen S and Cidy Claycomb (1997). "The influence of brand recognition on retail store image," *The Journal of Product and Brand Management*, 6(6), 373–87.

Shea, Christopher (2012). "Psychologists identify Twitter and Facebook personality types" Wall Street Journal Blogs, February 10. [available at http://blogs.wsj.com/ideas-market/2012/02/10/psychologists-identify-twitter-and-facebook-personality-types].

Smith, Cooper (2013). "7 statistics about Facebook users that reveal why it's such a powerful marketing platform," Business Insider, October 29. [available at www.slate.com/blogs/business_insider/2013/10/29/a_primer_on_facebook_demographics.html].

Thielman, Sam (2014). "It's getting harder to separate advertising from entertainment: And that's exactly how marketers would have it," March 17. [available at www.adweek.com/news/advertising-branding/it-s-getting-harder-separate-advertising-entertainment-156323].

Tuten, Tracy L. and Michael R. Solomon (2015). *Social media marketing*, 2nd edition, London: Sage Publications.

Weiner, Juli (2010). "New Gap logo, despised symbol of corporate banality, dead at one week," Vanityfair.com, October 12.

7

THE EFFECTS OF GOAL PUBLICITY ON GOAL PERSISTENCE IN THE SOCIAL MEDIA WORLD

Jinfeng (Jenny) Jiao and Catherine Cole

Social media outlets provide novel and interesting ways for marketers to reach consumers. For example, Starbucks reached 25.5 million fans by asking them to click "Like" on the Starbucks Facebook page. Ford Motors used YouTube to help launch its Fiesta model. Instead of choosing a massive ad blitz on TV or in-house promotions at dealers nationwide, Ford tapped 100 top bloggers and gave them a Fiesta for six months. Once a month, they were required to upload a video on YouTube about the car, and were encouraged to talk about the Fiesta on their blogs, Facebook and Twitter (Swartz, 2009).

Advertisers increasingly use social media websites to reach hard-to-target demographic groups, but they struggle to ensure that the target audience spends sufficient time on these social media outlets in order to gain adequate exposure for the paid messages. Each Facebook user spends, on average, 15 hours and 33 minutes a month on the site. Prior research has applied social influence theory, system design theory and personality theory to better understand the factors that influence consumers to remain with and commit to a social media website (Craig et al., 2007; Lin & Lu, 2011; Young & Rogers, 1998). However, despite the growing popularity and increasingly frequent usage of social media, a systematic understanding of why consumers return to social media websites, even if they do not achieve their goals on the first try, is needed. Our research fills this gap in three experiments.

We use goal persistence theory to develop our hypotheses regarding how social media characteristics can increase consumers' motivation to remain engaged with a social media site. Self-regulatory processes guide goal persistence, which is thought to be a multiplicative function of both the goal value and the expectancy or estimated probability of attaining the goal (Karoly, 1993a, 1993b). Existing research suggests that factors, such as the nature of feedback after a goal failure and goal value, influence goal reengagement. However, the goal persistence literature usually studies goal reengagement and persistence in a private context. In a social media setting, consumers often make their goals and goal progress public. As a result, our key research question is whether the factors that increase goal persistence in a private context are the same as those in a public context.

We make contributions to both theory and practice. Whereas much of the goal persistence literature examines self-reported intentions to persist in a goal in a private setting, we compare goal persistence (as measured by the time spent on a task after failure to achieve a goal) between circumstances when goals and outcomes are public and those when goals and outcomes are private. Our studies contribute to the goal pursuit literature by showing that after a goal failure, when goals are private, consumers attend to the social media context (specifically controllability of the outcome, feedback characteristics and goal value) when determining whether to persist in the goal, but when goals are public, consumers make an all-out effort toward the goal regardless of the social media context. We propose a goal publicity that public goals and goal progress increases consumer engagement with the goal pursuit such that consumers in public settings will keep trying after a goal failure no matter what. Based on our findings, we make recommendations for future goal persistence research. Additionally, our results provide a roadmap for brand managers and advertisers to plan their social media strategy.

The remainder of this chapter is organized as follows. First we review the literature that supports our underlying model. Then we test our hypotheses in three studies. We conclude by discussing the implications of our results for understanding consumer goal persistence and for improving social media strategy.

Theoretical Background

From a motivational perspective, people pursue a variety of goals in social media, such as acquiring information about an unfamiliar brand (content) or building social ties with friends (social) (Hoffman & Novak, 1996, 2012; Wilcox & Stephen, 2013). Research suggests that there are many factors influencing goal pursuit; however, little research has been conducted on factors moderating the effect of goal publicity on goal persistence (Fishbach & Dhar, 2005; Fishbach, Shah, & Kruglanski, 2004).

Goal Publicity

Making goals and goal progress public, which is defined as making significant others aware of one's goals, may motivate goal persistence after a failure because it is easy to abandon a goal known only to oneself, but it is hard to abandon a public goal (Pallak & Cummings, 1976; Salancik, 1977; Salancik & Brindle,

1997). Research has shown that public commitment leads to high levels of weight loss motivation (Nyer & Dellande, 2010), as well as increased recycling behaviors and reduced gas and electricity consumption (Burn & Oskamp, 1986; Pallak & Cummings, 1976; Salancik,1977). These effects can be explained both by one's motivation to avoid anticipated personal and social disapproval for failing to follow through with promised actions (Parrott et al., 1998). Furthermore, Bem's (1967) self-perception theory suggests that individuals who make a public commitment to an action may interpret the act of making a public commitment as a signal of their high motivation to engage in the promised action (Bem, 1967).

In the current study, we extend the previous literature on goal publicity by examining how goal publicity influences goal persistence after experiencing a goal failure. In a social media setting, groups (such as those found on Facebook) can be private (only members have access to the group and to what members post) or open (everyone sees everything) (Chu, 2011). For the private setting, we predict that contextual factors will be important in increasing goal persistence.

Contextual Factors

Our research concentrates on three context variables: controllability (H1), feedback characteristics (H2 & H3) and goal value (H4). In each case, we predict that the effects of the contextual factors will be observable in the private condition, but not in the public condition. In general, people perceive a goal as being more attainable when they believe that they can control whether or not they attain it (Bandura, 1997; Fishbach & Dhar, 2005; Huang, Zhang, & Broniarczyk, 2012; Koo & Fishbach, 2008; Weiner, 1986). For example, on its Facebook page, a local restaurant might offer gift cards to contest winners in order to increase consumer engagement with the brand. In a highly controllable outcome contest, a panel of judges might select the best photograph from submissions, whereas in a less controllable contest, a random draw sweepstakes might find the winners. Before reinvesting in a goal, consumers will assess whether they can influence goal achievement or not. As a result we predict an interaction between goal publicity and outcome controllability such that when goals are public, consumers will persist, whether or not they can control the outcome; however, when goals are private, consumers will persist only if they feel control over the outcome (**H1**).

Recent research indicates that the feedback received after a goal failure influences subsequent goal persistence because it provides information about the discrepancy between current goal progress and the destination (Fishbach & Finkelstein, 2011). One factor that could be important is feedback timing. If the feedback is received immediately after a goal failure, it may have a higher impact on consumers' goal persistence than if the feedback is delayed. Past research has suggested that providing negative feedback leads to greater efforts to accelerate the goal pursuit because people are more motivated by the negative affect induced by negative feedback (Carver & Scheier, 2004). As a result, we predict an interaction between goal publicity and feedback timing such that when goals are public, consumers will persist, whatever the timing of the feedback, but when goals are private, consumers will persist more when the failure feedback is immediate (**H2**).

Another factor that could potentially be important is the content of the feedback. Zhang and Huang (2010) show that progress in achieving a goal affects people's motivation for goal persistence. Research suggests that greater perceived progress tends to decrease motivation because people perceive that the goal is attainable when they have made enough progress; therefore, motivation attenuates (Fishbach, Eyal, & Finkelstein, 2010; Fishbach & Finkelstein, 2011). In an online context, a social media website may manipulate perceived progress by using a large or small scale. For example, a website might post the number of points one has earned versus the number one needs for a free ticket (25,000). On the other hand, the site could post the number of points one has earned versus the number of points one needs to achieve elite status (100,000). Again we predict that after a goal failure, if goals are private, consumers will be more sensitive to the social media context than if goals are public. Specifically, when feedback in the private setting indicates that consumers are far from the goal, they will persist more than when feedback indicates that consumers are close to the goal (**H3**).

Prior research suggests that goal value influences goal pursuit, such that consumers work harder for high- versus low-value goals (Zhang et al., 2011). Building upon previous research, we predict that goal value will moderate the relationship between goal publicity and goal pursuit, such that when the goal is private, we will observe an effect of goal value on goal pursuit such that a high goal value increases goal persistence; however, when the goal is public, the goal value will not have a significant effect on goal pursuit (**H4**).

We also tested the mediation role of consumer engagement. The existing literature suggests that contextual effects are strongest when consumers are not engaged with the task (Mao & Oppewal, 2012). We believe that in private settings, controllability, negative feedback, low progress and high goal value can increase consumer engagement, and increased engagement will increase persistence. But in public settings, consumer engagement will be high no matter the contextual variables. Thus, we predict that consumer engagement will mediate the interaction between contextual effects and goal publicity on goal persistence (**H5**).

Overview of Experiments

We test the role of goal publicity in goal persistence across a set of three experiments. In each study we manipulate goal publicity, by either telling participants that their goals and their progress on their goals will be made public (shared by everyone) or will remain private (no one but the individual participant will know them). Study 1, which tests H1 and H2, asks participants to write profile information for a social media website in order to receive enough "Likes" to win a gift card. Participants receive feedback that they didn't receive enough "Likes" to earn a gift card, but are given a second chance to revise their profiles. We measured the time spent and words written as a measure of goal persistence. Study 2 tests H2 and H5 in the same social media context. Study 2 differs from Study 1 because everyone receives immediate feedback, but the content of the feedback differs. We also tested the mediation role of engagement in Study 2. Study 3 extends the previous findings on goal persistence to willingness to recommend the experience to friends. We also add the importance of goal value (H4) as a factor and test how it influences goal publicity on people's willingness to recommend the experience with their friends.

Study 1: Outcome of Controllability

To test our first two hypotheses, we use a 2 (goal publicity: public vs. private) × 2 (outcome controllability: controllable vs. uncontrollable) × 2 (feedback timing: immediate vs. delayed) between-subjects design. During the experiment, participants learned that they would write profiles about themselves for a new social media website (FriendsMatch.com). If they received enough "Likes," they would receive a gift card for a local restaurant of their choice. After they wrote their first profiles, they had another opportunity to revise their profiles, giving us a chance to assess the time spent and the words written on their second try.

Method and Procedure

A total of 292 undergraduate students (163 males, M_{age} = 20.43) from a Midwestern university participated in this study in exchange for partial course credit. Three participants' data were excluded because they failed to complete the survey, which left 288 participants for analysis. Participants completed the study outside of class time at partitioned computers in the behavioral laboratory.

Participants initially learned that they would write a profile for the social network site, FriendsMatch.com. Although they could write anything they wanted, their goal was to attract as many people as possible to read their profile information and click "Like." Participants also learned that the people who received at least 100 "Likes" would receive a $50 gift card for a meal at a local restaurant, but people who did not receive enough "Likes" would receive nothing. Before writing their profiles, participants learned that their profile information and the number of "Likes" they received was either private or public information. Specifically, participants in the private condition learned the following: "Only you can see your profile, how many people have visited your profile and how many people have clicked 'Likes.' No one else can see how you are doing," whereas participants in the public condition learned the following: "Everyone can see your profile, how many people have visited your profile and how many people have clicked 'Likes.' Everyone else can see how you are doing." After writing the profile information, participants waited while the computer calculated the estimated number of "Likes" they would receive. At the time, we also presented information about controllability by indicating the following in the controllable condition: "Our prior research indicates that people can control whether they achieve their goals on websites like this by putting effort into making their profiles unique," while indicating the following in the uncontrollable condition: "Our prior research indicates that people cannot control whether they achieve their goals on websites like this because it is usually just a matter of luck." After receiving the controllability manipulation, participants received either immediate or delayed feedback. In the immediate feedback condition, participants learned, "You did not attract enough visitors to your profile or receive enough 'Likes' to receive the gift." In the delayed feedback condition, participants learned, "We will give you feedback at the end of the study."

Participants then had a second chance to revise their profiles and earn enough "Likes." They could spend as long as they wanted revising their profile information. The time spent and the number of words written when revising their profiles served as dependent variables to measure goal persistence. Finally, participants completed manipulation checks and demographic questions. We then thanked and debriefed the participants.

Results

Manipulation Checks. To check whether we manipulated goal publicity successfully, we asked participants to indicate how much they agreed with the statement that the information on their profiles and the number of "Likes" on their profiles were private information on a 7-point scale anchored with 1 = strongly disagree and 7 = strongly agree. A one-way ANOVA revealed that people who received the private goal manipulation were more likely to agree that the information on their profiles and the number of "Likes" were private information than those who received the public manipulation ($M_{private} = 5.5$ vs. $M_{public} = 3.19$, $F(1, 285) = 135.72$, $p <. 01$). In order to check whether we successfully manipulated controllability perceptions, we asked participants to indicate whether they agreed or disagreed with six statements on a 7-point scale anchored with 1 = strongly agree and 7 = strongly agree (for example: "People can control whether they achieve their goals on a website like FriendsMatch.com by putting effort into making their profiles unique"; "You can control how many people visit your profile and 'Like' your profile"). We averaged the responses to these six statements to form a perceived controllability question (coefficient alpha = .68), with higher means indicating that participants attributed their goal failure to controllable reasons. Consistent with the manipulation, the ANOVA showed that more people in the controllable condition believed that they could control their outcome than those who were in the uncontrollable condition ($M_{control}$ = 4.71 vs. $M_{uncontrol}$ = 4.18, $F(1, 285) = 23.17$, $p < .01$). To measure whether people attended to the feedback, we analyzed responses to a multiple-choice question about the type of feedback received. A logistic model showed that more people who received immediate feedback reported receiving immediate failure feedback vs. immediate success or no feedback (82.88% vs. 2.74% vs. 14.38%, $\chi^2 = 164.24$, $p < .01$). The logistic model also showed that more people who received delayed feedback reported not receiving immediate feedback vs. receiving immediate success or failure feedback (85.43% vs. 9.27% vs. 5.3%, $\chi^2 = 184.78$, $p < .01$).

Goal Persistence. The dependent variables were the words participants wrote and the time they spent on revising their profile information after they received immediate or delayed feedback. We conducted ANCOVAs for the number of words written and the time spent while revising their profile information as a function of goal publicity, feedback and controllability attribution. We used words written (time spent) on writing their first profile information as a covariate. In these analyses, the covariates were significant (Words: $F(1, 276) = 7.00$, $p < .01$; Time: $F(1, 276) = 17.88$, $p < .01$), such that people who put more effort (as measured by words written and time spent) into creating their first entry also put more effort into revising their second entry. In the analyses, there were main effects for the controllability attribution (Words: $F(1,276) = 12.19$, $p < .01$; Time: $F(1, 276) = 6.42$, $p < .01$), such that participants who were in the controllable condition wrote more words and spent more time while revising their profiles than those in the uncontrollable condition. There was also a main effect of feedback on words written ($F(1, 276) = 9.94$, $p < .01$) and time spent ($F(1, 276) = 11.67$, $p < .01$), such that people who received immediate feedback wrote more words and spent more time revising their profile information than people who did not receive feedback.

Most importantly, consistent with H1, as shown in Figures 7.1a and 7.1b, the interactions between controllability and goal publicity on words written and time spent while revising one's profile were significant (Words: $F(1, 276) = 8.01$, $p < .01$; Time: $F(1, 276) = 5.90$, $p < .02$). As expected, when the goal was private, participants wrote more words and spent more time revising their profile information when they were in the controllable condition than those who were in the uncontrollable condition (Words: $M_{control}$ = 98.85 vs. $M_{uncontrol}$ = 48.77, $p < .01$; Time: $M_{control}$ = 3.62 vs. $M_{uncontrol}$ = 2.20, $p < .01$). However, controllability effects disappeared when the goal was public (Words: $M_{control}$ = 88.16. vs. $M_{uncontrol}$ = 82.95, NS; Time: $M_{control}$ = 3.23 vs. $M_{uncontrol}$ = 3.20, $p = .94$, NS). In conclusion, our results showed that participants in the public condition persisted on the task, no matter the level of outcome controllability, whereas participants in the private condition persisted only if they thought they could control the outcome.

The predicted interaction between goal publicity and the timing of the feedback was not significant, contrary to H2. Nor was there a significant three-way

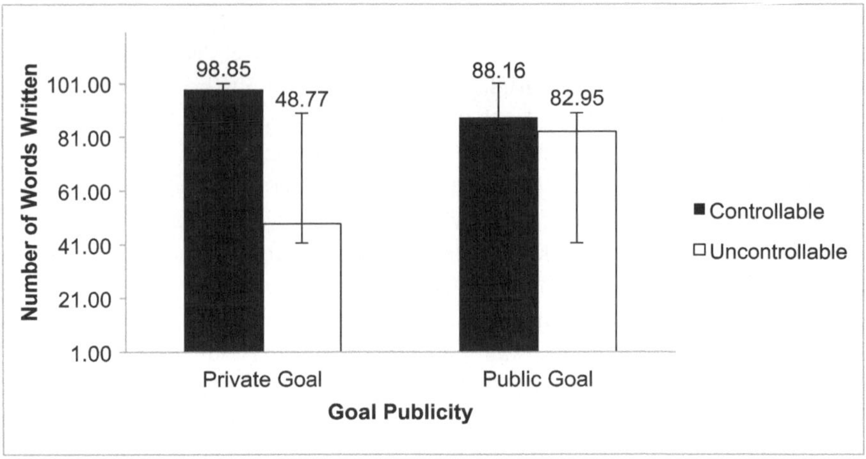

FIGURE 7.1A Goal Persistence (As Measured By Words Written on the Second Essay) As a Function of Goal Publicity and Controllability—Study 1

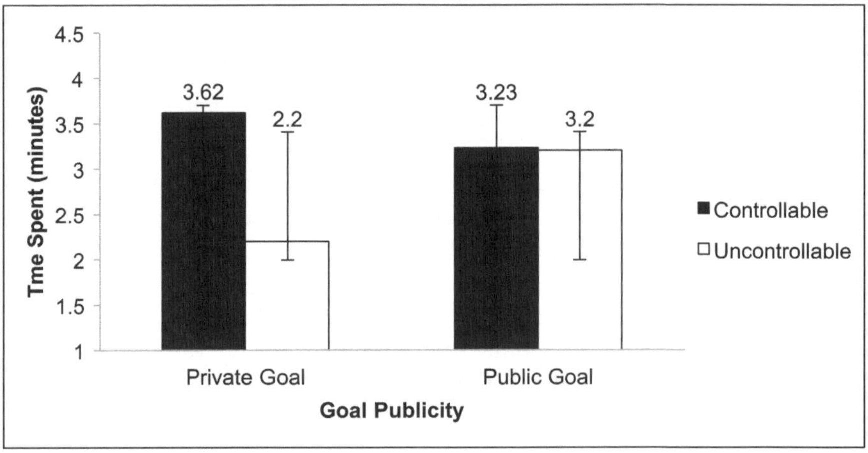

FIGURE 7.1B Goal Persistence (As Measured By Time Spent on the Second Essay) As a Function of Goal Publicity and Controllability—Study 1

interaction involving goal publicity, timing of the feedback and controllability. Interactions between the controllability attribution and feedback on words written and time spent were significant (Words: $F(1, 276) = 6.79$, $p <.01$; Time: $F(1, 276) = 6.40$, $p < .01$). When participants received failure feedback, they wrote more words and spent more time when outcomes were controllable vs. uncontrollable (Words: $M_{\text{control}} = 116.37$ vs. $M_{\text{uncontrol}} = 67.94$, $p < .01$; Time; $M_{\text{control}} = 4.26$ vs. $M_{\text{uncontrol}} = 2.83$, $p < .01$). However, the controllability attribution results disappeared when participants received no feedback (Words: $M_{control}$ = 70.64 vs. $M_{uncontrol}$ = 63.76, NS; Time: $M_{control}$ = 2.58 vs. $M_{uncontrol}$ = 2.56, NS).

Discussion

The results of Study 1 provide the first evidence for our conceptualization that when goals are public, context (in this case controllability) does not matter; however, when goals are private, the opposite result occurs, and context does take on significance. Although the timing of the feedback did not have the expected effect, we designed the second study to determine whether the content of the feedback matters, as predicting in H3.

Study 2: Distance to Goal Success

Study 2 extends Study 1 by again examining whether a different contextual effect (distance to goal success) diminishes in public settings and increases in private settings. The overall design of the study is a 2 (goal publicity: public vs. private) × 2 (controllability attribution: controllable vs. uncontrollable) × 2 (failure feedback: distance to goal: near or far) between-subjects design, with all factors being manipulated. We again use the FriendsMatch.com profile-writing task. Additionally, we test whether consumer engagement mediates the predicted controllability by goal publicity and failure feedback by goal publicity interactions.

Method and Procedure

A total of 281 students (168 males, M_{age} = 20.80) from a large Midwestern university participated in this study in exchange for course credit. We excluded seven participants because they did not finish the study, which left 274 participants. Procedures were almost identical to those of Study 1. One modification was to inform participants that in our prior research, the average number of "Likes" people received was 20. The participants also learned that their goal was to obtain an above average number of "Likes" by writing an appealing personal profile. Also different from Study 1, we did not use gift cards as incentives, making the goal a purely social one.

After writing their profiles, participants waited for the computer to calculate the estimated number of "Likes" they would receive. When receiving feedback, participants read the controllability information (identical to Study 1). Different from Study 1, everyone received immediate failure feedback. In addition, in the near distance to goal condition, participants learned that we estimated they would receive 18 "Likes." In the far distance to goal condition, participants learned that we estimated they would receive three "Likes." Then participants learned that they could spend as long as they wanted writing their profiles on a second try to obtain above average "Likes." Similar to Study 1, we measured the time spent and the words they wrote while revising their profiles as the dependent variables. We also measured engagement by asking respondents to answer three semantic differential scales anchored with 1 = not involved at all, not interested at all, not engaged at all; and 7 = very involved, very interested, very engaged. An engagement scale was calculated by averaging those three items (alpha = .92). Finally, we did manipulation checks, measured demographic questions and debriefed the participants.

Results

Manipulation Checks. In order to check the goal publicity manipulation, we asked participants to indicate whether they agreed that the information on their profiles and the number of "Likes" on their profiles were private (1 = strongly disagree; 7 = strongly agree). An ANOVA on this scale elicited only a main effect of goal publicity ($F(1, 273) = 232.92$, $p < .01$), such that those who received the private goal manipulation believed that the information on their profiles and number of "Likes" were private information vs. those who received the public manipulation ($M_{private} = 5.79$ vs. $M_{public} = 2.71$). No other effects were observed (all *ps* > .10).

In order to check whether we manipulated distance to the goal successfully, we asked participants to recall how many "Likes" they had gotten after receiving feedback regarding their first task. When the distance to the goal was small (18 "Likes"), 95% of the participants successfully recalled that they received 18 "Likes," which was significantly greater than the 5% of the participants who were not able to recall the number of "Likes" they had received (chi-square = 113.40, $p < .001$). When the distance to goal success was large (three "Likes"), 93.88% of the participants successfully recalled that they had received three "Likes," 2.04% participants recalled that they had received more than 20 "Likes," and 7.14 % participants were not able to recall the number of "Likes" they had received (chi-square = 242.57, $p < .001$).

In order to check whether we manipulated controllability successfully, we asked participants to indicate whether they agreed with the six statements used in Study 1. We averaged those six questions into one question to form a controllability question (coefficient alpha = .67), with higher number indicating high perceived controllability. An ANOVA analysis on controllability elicited only a main effect of controllability ($F(1, 271) = 40.17$, $p < .01$), such that more people in the controllable condition believed that they could get more "Likes" if they put more effort into writing than those who were in the uncontrollable condition ($M_{control} = 4.78$ vs. $M_{uncontrol} = 4.06$). No other effects were observed (all $p > .10$).

Goal Persistence. The dependent variables were the words written and the time spent on revising the profile information after participants received feedback. We conducted ANCOVAs for the number of words written and the time spent while revising profile information as a function of goal publicity, distance to goal, controllability and words written (time spent) on writing the first profile, as covariates. The covariates of words written and time spent on the first essay were significant (Words: $F(1,267) = 27.44$, $p < .001$; Time: $F(1,266) = 71.35$, $p < .001$), such that people who put more effort (as measured by words written and time spent) on creating their first entry also put more effort into revising their second entry. The main effect of controllability was significant. Participants who were in the controllable condition wrote more words (and spent more time) than those in the uncontrollable condition (Words: $M_{control} = 128.89$ vs. $M_{uncontrol} = 103.44$, $t = 2.73$, $p = .01$; Time: $M_{control} = 5.95$ vs. $M_{uncontrol} = 5.03$, $t = 2.16$, $p < .05$).

Most importantly, as shown in Figures 7.2a and 7.2b, the interactions between goal publicity and distance to the goal (number of "Likes" received) on words written and time spent were significant (Words: $F(1, 267) = 4.23$, $p < .05$; Time: $F(1, 266) = 8.09$, $p < .01$). Specifically, consistent with H4, when the goal was private, participants wrote more words (and spent more time) revising the profile information when they received three "Likes" instead of 18 (Words: $M_{3likes} = 139.31$ vs. $M_{18likes} = 104.96$, $t = 2.63$, $p < .01$; Time: $M_{3likes} = 6.87$ vs. $M_{18likes} = 4.96$, $t = 3.25$, $p < .01$). However, when the goal was public, participants wrote similar amounts of words (and spent similar amounts of time), regardless of how many "Likes" they received (Words: $M_{3likes} = 108.24$ vs. $M_{18likes} = 112.15$, $t = -.29$, *ns*; Time: $M_{3likes} = 4.83$ vs. $M_{18likes} = 5.32$, $t = -.81$, *ns*). In conclusion, the results showed that when the distance to goal success was far (when participants received three "Likes"), participants in the private goal conditions spent the most amount of time and wrote the most amount of words while revising their profiles than when distance to the goal was close (when participants received 18 "Likes").

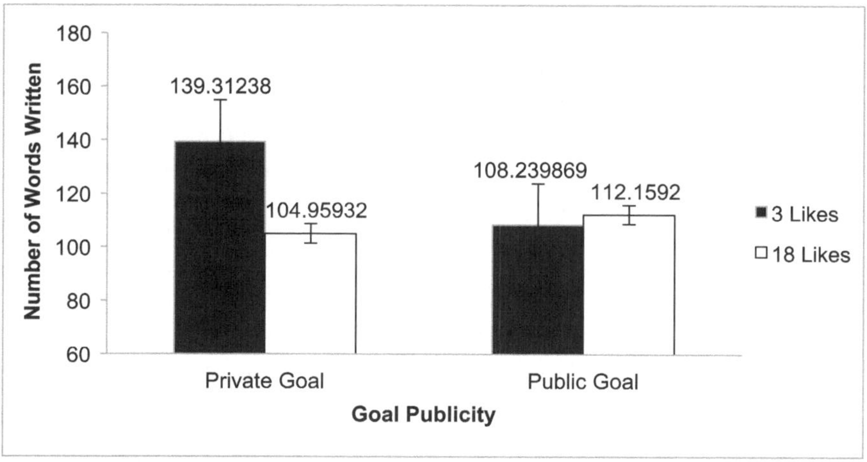

FIGURE 7.2A Goal Persistence (As Measured By Words Written on the Second Essay) As a Function of Goal Publicity and Distance to Goal—Study 2

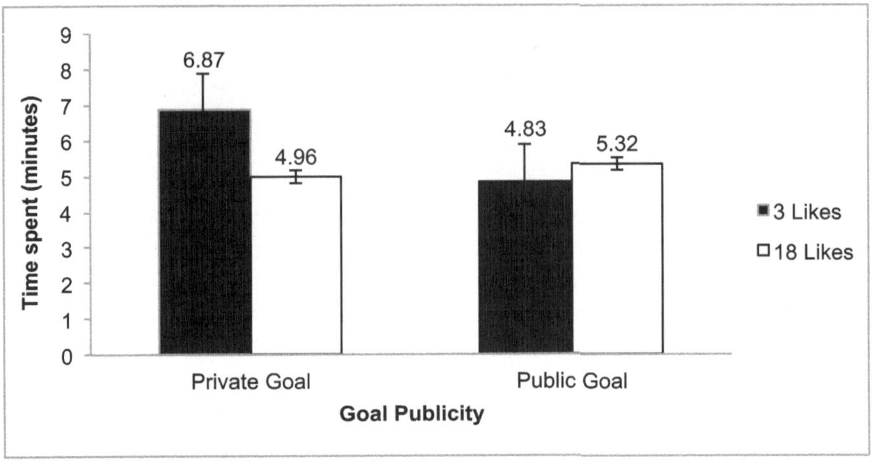

FIGURE 7.2B Goal Persistence (As Measured By Time Spent on the Second Essay) As a Function of Goal Publicity and Distance to Goal—Study 2

Furthermore, as shown in Figures 7.3a and 7.3b, a three-way interaction among goal publicity, distance to goal and controllability was marginally significant for words (Words: $F(1, 267) = 3.19$, $p = .07$; Time: $F(1, 266) = 1.12$, $p = .29$). To further examine the three-way interaction on words, we first selected participants in the controllable condition only and examined the interaction between goal publicity and distance to goal, with words as the dependent variable. The result revealed a significant two-way interaction ($F(1, 131) = 5.14$, $p < .03$). As predicted and shown in Figure 7.3a, when the goal was private, participants wrote more words, revising their profile information when they received three vs. 18 "Likes" (Words: $M_{3likes} = 171.85$ vs. $M_{18likes} = 110.57$, $t = 2.75$, $p = .01$). However, when the goal was public, participants wrote similar amounts of words, regardless of how many "Likes" they received (Words: $M_{3likes} = 116.94$ vs. $M_{18likes} = 124.38$, $t = -.36$, *ns*). Next, we selected participants in the uncontrollable condition only and examined the interaction between goal publicity and distance to goal, with words as the dependent variable. The result revealed a non-significant two-way interaction ($F(1, 131) = .00$, *ns*). As predicted and shown in Figure 7.3b, when the goal was private, participants wrote similar amounts of words when revising their profile information, regardless of how many "Likes" they received (Words: $M_{3likes} = 104.93$ vs. $M_{18likes} = 99.06$, $t = .41$, *ns*). In addition, when the goal was public, participants wrote similar amounts of words, regardless how many "Likes" they received (Words: $M_{3likes} = 103.99$ vs. $M_{18likes} = 97.23$, $t = .42$, *ns*).

Mediating Role of Engagement. We next tested our hypothesis that engagement would mediate the effect of goal publicity and distance to goal interaction on goal persistence in the controllable, but not the uncontrollable condition. We

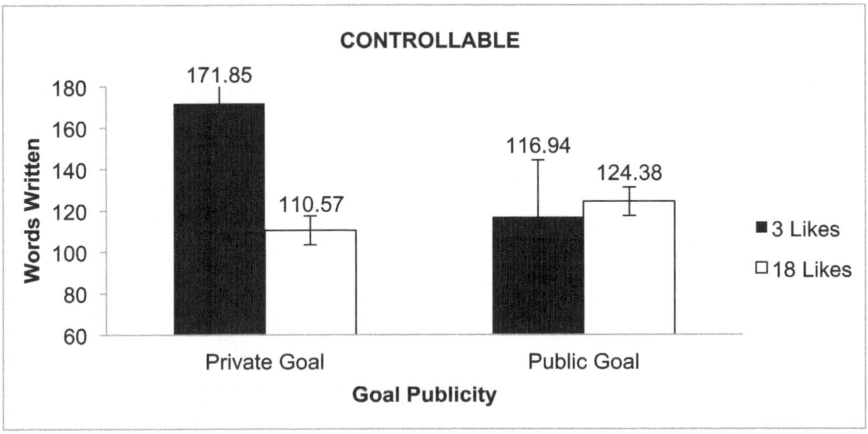

FIGURE 7.3A Goal Persistence (As Measured By Words Written on the Second Essay) As a Function of Goal Publicity and Distance to Goal Controllable—Study 2

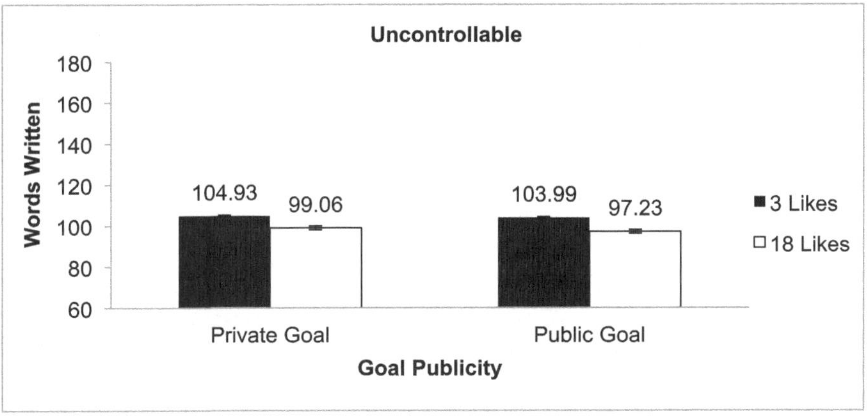

FIGURE 7.3B Goal Persistence (As Measured By Words Written on the Second Essay) As a Function of Goal Publicity and Distance to Goal Uncontrollable—Study 2

first examined the controllable and uncontrollable conditions separately. For the controllable condition, the interaction between goal publicity and distance to goal had a significant effect on engagement (Beta standardized = .40, $t = 2.60$, $p < .01$) and on both measures of persistence (Words: Beta standardized = .30, $t = 2.07$, $p < .05$; Time: Beta standardized = .37, $t = 2.45$, $p < .02$). Additionally, engagement had a significant effect on persistence (Words: Beta standardized: = .31, $t = 3.73$, $p < .01$; Time: Beta standardized = .32, $t = 3.95$, $p < .01$). However, when engagement was controlled for, the interaction between goal publicity and distance to goal on both measures of goal persistence became non-significant (Words: Beta standardized = .18, $t = 1.23$, *ns*; Time: Beta standardized = .24,

$t = 1.63$, *ns*; see Figures 7.4a and 7.4b.). Finally, the results of the 95% confidence intervals from Preachers, Rucker, and Hayes's (2007, model 8) moderated mediation analyses (one for words, one for time) indicated that the interaction indirect effects were significantly different from zero (95% CI: [5.91 to 58.20] for words and [.32 to 3.07] for time). Thus, the moderation was mediated.

The same analysis conducted for uncontrollable conditions found no evidence of mediation. To be specific, the interaction between goal publicity and distance to goal has no significant effect on engagement (Beta standardized = −.01, $t = -.07$, *ns*), no effect on words written, but an effect on time spent (Words: Beta standardized = .08, $t = .54$, *ns*; Time: Beta standardized = .29, $t = 2.02$, $p < .05$). Additionally, engagement had a significant effect on persistence (Words: Beta standardized = .29, $t = 3.82$, $p < .01$; Time: Beta standardized = .30, $t = 3.61$, $p < .01$). Therefore, within the uncontrollable condition, the mediation was not significant.

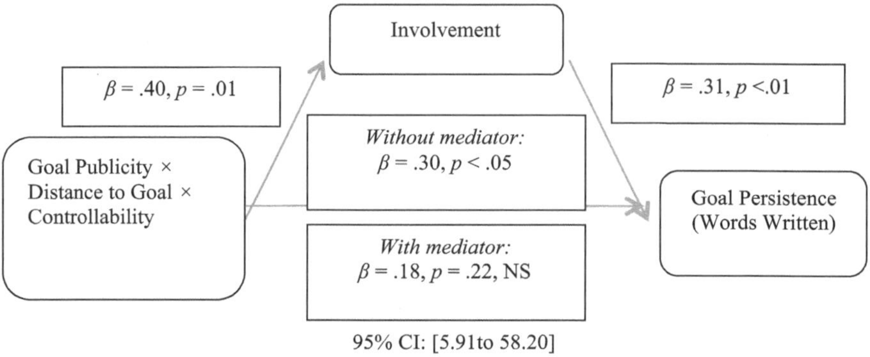

FIGURE 7.4A Moderated Mediation Analysis on Goal Persistence Words_Controllable Condition—Study 2

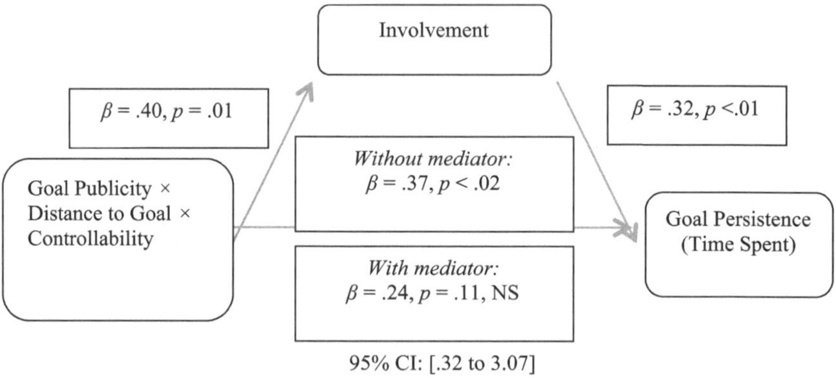

Discussion

FIGURE 7.4B Moderated Mediation Analysis on Goal Persistence Time_Controllable Condition—Study 2

The results of Study 2 provide further evidence for our conceptualization: when goals are public, context does not matter; however, when goals are private, the opposite result occurs, and context takes on significance. This time we used distance to goal success as a contextual factor. In the next study, we introduce a new factor, goal value, and examine whether it moderates the effect of goal publicity on goal persistence.

Study 3: Online Game_Goal Value

The main objective of Study 3 was to assess support for the moderating role of goal value, as stated in H4. Another objective of this study was to replicate the findings from previous studies in a different context (online games). To identify the moderating role of goal value, in Study 3, we used a 2 (goal publicity: public vs. private) × 2 (goal value: high vs. low) between-subjects design with respondents from m-Turk on a hypothetical online game site. The goal was to play games in order to earn a bonus payment. After receiving feedback about their performance on the first game, participants could earn extra points by playing additional games to receive either a high ($1.00) or low ($.10) value bonus payment. As mentioned earlier, we only gave immediate failure and controllable feedback to participants, and we added a new variable: goal value.

Method and Procedure

A total of 121 people were recruited from Amazon m-Turk (109 males, 37.6% are 18–28 years old; 34.4% are 29–39 years old; 17.2% are 40–50 years old and 17.9% are 51–64 years old; Min = 18, Max = 64 years old). We used screening questions to select participants (1) whose first language was English; (2) who lived in the United States; (3) who were between 18 and 64 years old; and (4) who had previously engaged in social media life (such as using Facebook, or playing games online). Four participants' data were excluded because they had either finished the survey within five minutes (the average time to complete the survey was 18.5 minutes), or because the game did not load (e.g., one participant said he used an iPad, but could not play the game with an iPad), which left 117 participants for analysis.

The cover story told participants that we were interested in social media. They had a chance to earn enough points to redeem a bonus award by playing online games. Anyone who earned 2,270 points would be able to get a bonus award. After the introduction, participants were randomly assigned to either the high or low goal value condition. We manipulated goal value by telling participants that they would have a chance to earn bonus points by playing games. If participants earned enough points (2,270 points), they would receive a bonus payment of one dollar (high goal value) or ten cents (low goal value) at the end of the study.

After manipulating the goal value, we manipulated goal publicity. Participants were randomly assigned to either the public or private goal condition. Half of the participants in the public goal condition learned the following: "At the end of the study, we will make the following information public to all participants in this survey in a table with the first names, states of residence and total points earned by all of the people playing these games. We will also indicate whether or not the participants earned the bonus. In other words, we are sharing your performance on the games with others, so that information is public information." The other half of the participants in the private goal condition received the following statement: "At the end of the study, we will keep all of your information confidential. No one else will know whether or not you earned enough points to earn the bonus. In other words, you will be the only one who knows how you are doing on the games. Your information is private information."

After participants read the information, they were asked to play the first game, the "memory matrix." Participants were asked to repeat the pattern of the tiles by clicking on the correct tiles that appeared in the matrix. For each trial, the pattern of tiles appeared for only three seconds, then participants had to use their memory to remember where the tiles were located in the matrix. We chose this game because it was hard for participants to guess how many points they earned, given that the total number of points depended on the number of correct trials, and the number of trials at the maximum level they played, compared to others who were playing at the same time. After they finished playing the first game, participants waited for the computer to calculate the score they received on the game. Everyone received the same immediate feedback: "Based on the analysis of the number of points you earned (calculated from your maximum level, and number of trials at this maximum level when compared with other participants) you have earned 1,146 points. We regret to tell you that you did not earn enough points to receive the award." They learned that in a minute, they could play more games if they wanted. The points they earned on these games would be added to the points they had already earned. Their total points on the games would determine whether they won the bonus award.

Before participants played the subsequent games, they learned that there were several games on the next few screens. All were ways to earn more points. They were also told that we were pretesting these games and that some may take a long time to load correctly if too many people were playing at the same time. If something did not load correctly, they could feel free to move on to the next game by clicking on the red "continue" button at the bottom of the game page. There were a total of five games. After they finished playing the following games, participants were asked to move the slider to indicate their satisfaction with their goal progress on a 0–100 scale: "How satisfied are you with your progress toward earning the bonus award?" In addition, they were asked to move the slider on the gauge to indicate how likely they would recommend the game they played to their friends (1=strongly not recommend to a friend; 100=strongly recommend to a friend). Both satisfaction with goal progress and likelihood of recommending served as the dependent variables.

Results

Manipulation Checks. In order to check the manipulation of goal value, participants were asked to move the slider on the gauge to indicate how valuable the bonus award was (0 = very low; 100 = very high), and how important they thought obtaining the bonus award was (0 = very unimportant; 100 = very important). An index of perceived goal value was calculated by averaging those two items (alpha = .84). Manipulation of the goal value was successful. To assess the manipulation of the goal value, a 2 (goal publicity: public vs. private) × 2 (goal value: high vs. low) ANOVA was conducted, including the perceived goal value as the dependent variable. Results indicated a significant main effect of goal value ($F(1, 114) = 28.80$, $p < .001$), revealing that participants in the high-value ($1.00) condition rated the bonus award as more valuable than those in the low-value ($.10) condition ($M_{high} = 62.43$, SD = 26.19, $M_{low} = 36.38$, SD = 24.01, $t = 5.37$, $p < .001$). No other effects were observed (all *ps* > .70).

In order to check the manipulation of goal publicity, participants were asked to indicate whether the information they provided would be shared with others or not (0 = shared with others; 1 = kept private). A logistic model showed that more people who received the public goal manipulation believed the information was public vs. private (93.85% vs. 6.15%); in addition, more people in the private goal condition believed the information was private vs. public (88.68% vs. 11.32%; $\chi^2(233) = 81.02$, $p < .001$).

Satisfaction with Goal Progress and Recommend to Friends. The dependent variables were satisfaction with goal progress and willingness to recommend the game to one's friends. We conducted a MANOVA for satisfaction with goal progress and recommendation to friends as a function of goal publicity (0 = private; 1 = public) and goal value (0 = low value; 1 = high value) and gender as a covariate. We used gender as a covariate because males tend to like online games more than females. Repeated measure for between-subjects effects showed a marginal significant main effect of gender ($F(1, 113) = 3.33$, $p = .07$) and a significant effect of goal value ($F(1, 113) = 7.85$, $p < .01$). Most importantly, the main effect of goal value was qualified by a significant goal publicity × goal value two-way interaction ($F(1, 113) = 13.37$, $p < .001$).

As predicted and showed in Figures 7.5a and 7.5b, when the goal was private, those in the high goal value condition were more satisfied with their goal progress and were more likely to recommend the game to their friends than those in the low goal value condition (Satisfaction with goal progress: $M_{highvalue} = 45.87$, SD = 29.66 vs. $M_{lowvalue} = 31.37$, SD = 26.34, $t = 2.07$, $p = .04$; Recommendation to friends: $M_{highvalue} = 84.46$, SD = 14.87 vs. $M_{lowvalue} = 54.85$, SD = 33.81, $t = 3.28$, $p = .001$). However, when the goal was public, those in the high goal value condition were equally satisfied with their goal progress and were equally like to recommend the game to their friends, when compared to those in the low goal value condition (Satisfaction with goal progress: $M_{highvalue} = 41.33$, SD = 29.39 vs. $M_{lowvalue} = 42.64$, SD = 15.49, $t = -.39$, *ns*; Recommendation to friends: $M_{highvalue} = 65.80$, SD = 26.99 vs. $M_{lowvalue} = 68.55$, SD = 23.79, $t = .48$, *ns*). No other effects were observed (all *ps* >. 10) (see Figures 7.5a and 7.5b). Repeated measures for within-subjects effects showed only a marginal significant main effect of dv ($F(1, 113) = 3.57$, $p = .06$). No other effects were observed (all $ps > .30$).

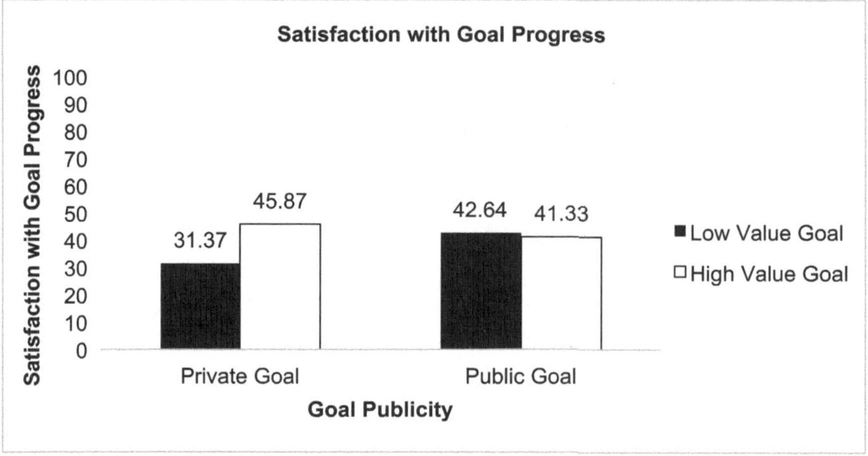

FIGURE 7.5A Satisfaction with Goal Progress as a Function of Goal Publicity and Goal Value—Study 3

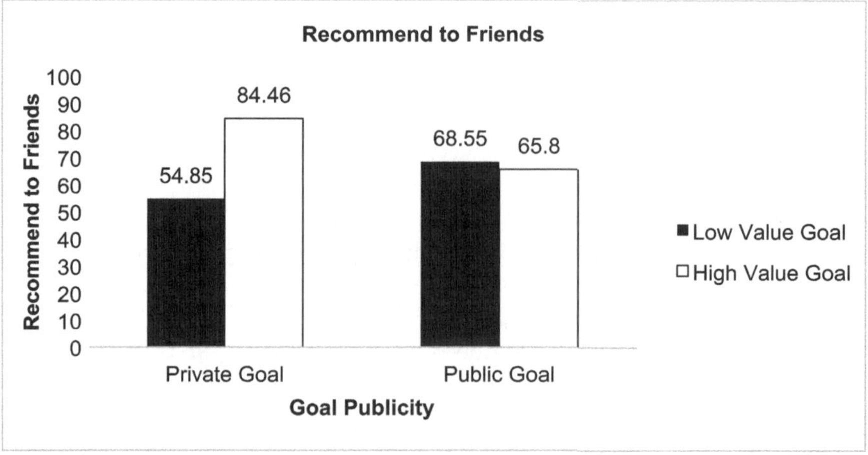

FIGURE 7.5B Recommendation to Friends as a Function of Goal Publicity and Goal Value—Study 3

Discussion

The results of Study 3 provide further evidence for our conceptualization: when goals are public, context does not matter; however, when goals are private, the opposite result occurs, and context, indeed, matters. This time we used goal value as a contextual factor. We also extend the prior findings on goal persistence to satisfaction with goal progress and willingness to make recommendations to friends. In conclusion, the results showed that when a goal is private, participants in the high goal value conditions were more satisfied with their goal progress and were more likely to recommend the game to their friends than when goal value was low. On the other hand, when the goal was public, the goal value did not have a significant effect on participants' satisfaction with their goal progress or their willingness to recommend the game to their friends.

Discussion and Future Directions

In summary, we find that when goals and goal progress are public, consumers are motivated to persist at their goals, no matter the social media context. In contrast when goals and goal progress are private, consumers consider the context when deciding whether to pursue the goals after a failure. In a private setting, whether consumers control the outcome (Study 1), have feedback information about distance to goal (Study 2) and attribute a relatively high value to your goal (Study 3) are important considerations. Specifically, in Study 1, consistent with H1, a significant two-way interaction between goal publicity and controllability on goal persistence shows that when the goal is private, people are more likely to put more efforts toward the goal if they believe they can control the outcome than if they believe they can't control the outcome. However, when the goal is public, people put the same efforts toward the goal, no matter how controllable the outcome is. In Study 2, consistent with H3, we find a significant two-way interaction between goal publicity and distance to goal success on goal persistence, which shows that when the goal is private, people are more likely to put more efforts into achieving a goal if they are far from the goal. However, when the goal is public, people invest the same efforts toward the goal, regardless of the distance from the goal. In Study 3, we find that when the goal and goal progress are private, the value of the goal is important in driving both satisfaction with goal progress and willingness to recommend to a friend, but when goals are public, consumer satisfaction and willingness to recommend the game to a friend are the same no matter the goal value.

The limitations of this research suggest future research directions. We studied relatively minor goals (earning points or likes) in return for a gift card. Future research might investigate the effects of goal publicity on important goals such as maintaining one's health or recycling behavior. Second, our last study uses satisfaction with goal progress and willingness to recommend to a friend as dependent variables. We argue that these are important appraisals which are meaningful to marketers, but don't necessarily correlate with goal persistence. As a result, more research on goal value in a social media context and goal persistence is needed. Finally, our second study shows that engagement mediates goal publicity and distance to goal interaction when outcomes are controllable. Future research, could examine whether different mediators, such as emotions like shame and guilt, underlie goal persistence after a public goal failure.

For a brand manager looking to devise a social media strategy, we can think of several interesting ways in which our research can be informative. For example, some Facebook pages explicitly advise participants to set goals, as when the Weight Watchers Facebook page states "Make small goals—they are easier to reach." We would advise social media websites to configure the page so that information about the consumers, their goals and their goal progress are all public information. Making goals public will motivate consumers to spend time on a website. In contrast, when it is not feasible to make information about consumers, their goals and goal progress public, social media websites need to carefully configure the page so that consumers perceive the outcome as controllable, receive feedback that indicates the distance to goal, and make sure goals are high in value even if they are private. Car Town, for example, could (1) elicit private goals (build your dream garage); (2) provide feedback when goals are not achieved; and (3) emphasize controllable point-earning activities, such as filling out a survey, instead of uncontrollable ones, such as playing casino games.

References

Bandura, A. (1997). *Self-efficacy: The exercise of control.* New York: Freeman.

Bem, D. J. (1967). Self-Perception: An alternative interpretation of cognitive dissonance phenomena. *Psychological Review*, 74 (3), 183.

Burn, S. M. & Oskamp, S. (1986). Increasing community recycling with persuasive communication and public commitmen. *Journal of Applied Social Psychology*, 16 (1), 29–41.

Carver, C. S. & Scheier, M. F. (2004). Self-regulation of action and affect. *Handbook of self-regulation: Research, theory, and applications*, 13–39.

Chu, S-C. (2011). Viral advertising in social media: Participation in facebook groups and responses among college-aged users. *Journal of Interactive Advertising*, 12 (1), 30–43.

Craig, E., Jackson, C., Han, D. Y., & Grimwood, K. (2007). *Monitoring the health of new zealand children and young people: Indicator handbook*. Paediatric Society of New Zealand and New Zealand Child and Youth Epidemiology Service.

Fishbach, A. & Dhar, R. (2005). Goals as excuses or guides: The liberating effect of perceived goal progress on choice. *Journal of Consumer Research*, 32 (3), 370–77.

Fishbach, A., T. Eyal, T., & Finkelstein, S. R. (2010). How positive and negative feedback motivate goal pursuit. *Social and Personality Psychology Compass*, 4 (8), 517–30.

Fishbach, A. & S. R. Finkelstein (2011). "How feedback influences persistence, disengagement, and change in goal pursuit." In J. Forgas & A. Kruglanski (Series Eds.), H. Aarts, & AJ Elliot (Vol. Eds.), *Frontiers of social psychology: Goal-directed behavior*, 203–30. Psychology Press.

Fishbach, A., Shah, J. Y., & Kruglanski, A. W. (2004). Emotional transfer in goal systems. *Journal of Experimental Social Psychology*, 40 (6), 723–38.

Hoffman, D.L. & Novak, T.P. (1996). Marketing in hypermedia computer-mediated environments: Conceptual foundations. *The Journal of Marketing*, 60 (3), 50–68.

——— (2012). Toward a deeper understanding of social media. *Journal of Interactive Marketing*, 26 (2), 69–70.

Huang, S., Zhang, Y., & Broniarczyk, S.M. (2012). So near and yet so far: The mental representation of goal progress. *Journal of Personality and Social Psychology*, 103 (2), 225.

Karoly, P. (1993a). Goal systems: An organizing framework for clinical assessment and treatment planning. *Psychological assessment*, 5 (3), 273.

——— (1993b). Mechanisms of self-regulation: A systems view. *Annual Review of Psychology*, 44 (1), 23–52.

Koo, M. & Fishbach, A. (2008). Dynamics of self-regulation: How (un) accomplished goal actions affect motivation. *Journal of Personality and Social Psychology*, 94 (2), 183.

Lin, K-Y. & Lu, H-P. (2011). Why people use social networking sites: An empirical study integrating network externalities and motivation theory. *Computers in Human Behavior*, 27 (3), 1152–61.

Mao, W. & Oppewal, H. (2012). The attraction effect is more pronounced for consumers who rely on intuitive reasoning. *Marketing Letters*, 23 (1), 339–351.

Nyer, P.U. & Dellande, S. (2010). Public commitment as a motivator for weight loss. *Psychology & Marketing*, 27 (1), 1–12.

Pallak, M.S. & Cummings, W. (1976). Commitment and voluntary energy conservation. *Personality and Social Psychology Bulletin*, 2 (1), 27–30.

Parrott, S., Godfrey, C., Raw, M., Wesr, R., & McNeil, A. (1998). Guidance for commissionees on the cost effectiveness of smoking cessation interventions. *Thorax*, 53 (Supp 5, Part 2), S2–S3.

Preacher, K. J., Rucker, D. D., & Hayes, A. F. (2007). Addressing moderated mediation hypotheses: Theory, methods, and prescriptions. *Multivariate Behavioral Research*, 42 (1), 185–227.

Salancik, G. R. & Brindle, M. C. (1997). The social ideologies of power in organizational decisions. In E. Shapira (Ed.), *Organizational decision-making* (pp. 111–132). New York: Cambridge University Press.

Salancik, Gerald R. (1977). Commitment and the control of organizational behavior and belief. In B. Staw & G. Salancik (Eds.), *New directions in organizational behavior* (pp. 1–54). Oxford: St. Clair Press.

Swartz, J. (2009). More marketers use social networking to reach customers. *USA TODAY*.

Weiner, B. (1986). Attribution, emotion, and action. *Handbook of motivation and cognition: Foundations of social behavior*, 1, 281–312.

Wilcox, K. & Stephen, A. (2013). Are close friends the enemy? Online social networks, self-esteem, and self-control. *Journal of Consumer Research*, 40 (1), 90–103.

Young, K.S. & Rogers, R.C. (1998). The relationship between depression and internet addiction. *Cyberpsychology & Behavior*, 1 (1), 25–28.

Zhang, Y. & Huang, S-C. (2010). How endowed versus earned progress affects consumer goal commitment and motivation. *Journal of Consumer Research*, 37 (4), 641–654.

Zhang, Y., Xu, J., Jiang, Z., & Huang, S-C. (2011). Been there, done that: The impact of effort investment on goal value and consumer motivation. *Journal of Consumer Research*, 38 (1), 78–93.

PART II

Branding and Advertising Issues in Social Media

8

HEARING THEIR VOICE

When Brand Co-creation Leads to Social Brand Engagement

Heather Johnson Dretsch and Amna Kirmani

Social media platforms allow consumers to publicly declare their affinity for brands. Consumers can "Like" a brand on Facebook, share promotions on Pinterest, and spread word-of-mouth about the brand on Twitter. Social media allow interactivity, turning passive watchers of advertising into active brand advocates who engage with the brand. Marketers recognize that today's consumers expect to be involved in the process of creating brand meaning and are investing in multiple pathways to capture consumers' imaginations and transform them into brand fans. On a brand's web page, consumers can play a game, post and rate ideas, create their own ads, tell their brand story, and more. Although these examples are online, such activities exist in retail locations as well.

Many of these activities involve *brand co-creation*, defined as collaboration between the consumer and the marketer to shape brand meaning. For instance, in 2010 Chiquita Banana launched EatAChiquita.com as a platform for brand co-creation, featuring a Sticker Studio application where consumers could create their own iconic blue and yellow sticker for the product. Chiquita had over 500,000 visitors to the site. Creators could download and share their design and even print it on custom merchandise. Consumer voters determined their favorites, and the winning designs appeared on Chiquita® bananas in U.S. stores. Around the same time, Converse featured a Converse Gallery on its web site that asked customers to express what Converse shoes meant to them. Thousands of customers created 24-second films, attesting to the popularity of co-creation activities. In fact, over 85% of marketers consider brand co-creation investments in order to take advantage of social media opportunities (Deloitte, 2012).

According to Prahalad and Ramaswamy (2000), who coined the term "co-creation" through a discussion of COllaborative CREATION, co-creation involves consumers and firms working on product and service ideas together.

The objective of co-creation campaigns such as these is to provide consumers with a means of interacting with the brand, thereby creating brand meaning and encouraging further engagement with the brand. For instance, after participating in a brand co-creation activity, consumers can further engage with the brand on social media. They can seek out the brand's page on Facebook, which signals their relationship with the brand to their social network, or spread positive word-of-mouth about the brand through Google. Thus, co-creation activities are a form of consumer-brand interaction as well as an antecedent to deeper social brand engagement.

Although marketers hope that these co-creation activities will engender deeper social brand engagement, little research examines conditions under which such engagement is likely to occur. Prior research has examined consumer participation in extensive product interactions, such as co-production or brand communities; however, there is little research on *brand* co-creation. Research on co-production examines consumers' involvement in the product design process, either self-designing/customizing a product (e.g., LLBean backpack; Moreau & Herd, 2010) or making the resulting product (e.g., making dinner with a boxed meal; Troye & Supphellen, 2012). In the co-production context, the focus is on the product rather than the brand. Research on brand communities examines the themes that arise from user-managed forums, but the focus is on users rather than a collaboration between marketers and users. For instance, Star Trek lovers bring the brand's values to life through fan clubs (Kozinets, 2001). In these communities, consumers often take control of the brand's meaning away from the marketer (Muniz & Schau, 2005), and the marketer often does not manage the brand interaction. The goal of brand communities is to advance the collective rather than the brand itself (Schau, Muniz, & Arnould, 2009).

In contrast, brand co-creation examines consumers' involvement in the brand development process in a marketer-maintained context that allows for consumer-marketer collaboration. In other words, our research straddles perspectives of consumer and marketer as meaning makers. In this chapter, we examine the effects of different types of brand co-creation activities on deeper engagement with the brand in social media. We suggest that two factors affect the extent to which brand co-creation activities will affect social brand engagement: the consumers' self-brand connection and the strength of voice of the activity. Self-brand connection refers to the fit a consumer perceives between the self and a brand (Escalas & Bettman, 2003). We define strength of voice as the degree of collaboration the consumer feels (s)he has with the marketer in the co-creation process.

We propose that consumers with high self-brand connection are more motivated to participate in a brand co-creation activity than are consumers with low self-brand connection. Moreover, participating in co-creation activities can increase social brand engagement intentions for high self-brand consumers when they have a strong voice to the marketer, but not when voice is weak. When the marketer is emphasized as the audience for the brand co-creation, high self-brand connection consumers can publically declare their attachment and express what the brand means to them. Participating in co-creation activities does not affect social brand engagement intentions for consumers with low self-brand connection because they have little motivation and ability to express brand meaning. Thus, co-creation activities work better with consumers with high self-brand connection, but even for them, only certain types of co-creation activities lead to social brand engagement.

We first describe social brand engagement, followed by what brand co-creation is (and what it is not). We also examine characteristics of the co-creation activity and consumer that may affect response to brand co-creation. Finally, we present some empirical evidence that brand co-creation activities can deepen engagement with the brand on social media for some types of consumers under certain conditions.

Theoretical Framework

Brand Engagement in Social Media

Social brand engagement refers to consumer-driven, brand-related behavior that promotes the brand in an affiliative manner through the consumer's online social network. Examples include seeking out the brand's page on Facebook, Liking the brand's page on Facebook, and sharing brand promotions with friends and family (Dretsch & Kirmani, 2014). Social brand engagement differs from repeat purchase behavior, as it suggests that the brand resonates with the consumer (van Doorn et al., 2010); however, it does not entail actual brand purchase. In essence, the consumer becomes an online brand ambassador who conveys that the brand carries significant meaning to him or her. As such, social brand engagement can signal a consumer's identity to the self, the marketer, or to others within the social network (Kirmani, 2009).

Social brand engagement is an important and under-investigated dependent variable in the context of brand co-creation. Brand co-creation efforts can be an important means of deepening brand engagement via social media. A majority of brand co-creation campaigns offer consumers the option to click through to the brand's Facebook page, Tweet about the brand, or email others a link to the campaign. Marketers hope that consumer participation in brand campaigns will lead to the emergence of social media brand "fans" who can influence others in their social network (FanGager, 2012).

Part of marketers' interest in social brand engagement is due to advances in technology that have made online tracking easy. Toyota seeks to quantify the emotional connection consumers have with the brand (e.g., extent to which the brand is like me), and track how this connection results in the creation of brand advocates (e.g., brand promoters inspired to act on behalf of the brand on or offline; Savary, 2008). Advocates are inspired by their participation with the brand to "do," or act upon their values, experience, and affinity for the brand. Toyota brand advocates exhibit behaviors such as blogging about the brand, as well as using social networks to simply connect with or to evangelize the brand (Savary, 2008). In the academic literature, however, little research examines the effects of brand co-creation activities on social brand engagement. Related research tends to examine consumers' enjoyment (Dahl & Moreau, 2007), willingness to pay (Franke, Schreier, & Kaiser, 2010), or product evaluations (Moreau & Herd, 2010). This chapter focuses on the effects of brand co-creation activities on social brand engagement. In the next section, we describe brand co-creation in greater detail.

Brand Co-creation Activities

Brand co-creation refers to the process by which consumers develop the brand in collaboration with marketers. Brand co-creation activities require the consumer to *do something* with the brand itself, whether it means creating a sticker or an ad, writing a story, or voting on a brand-related idea. Notably, co-creation is not merely surfing a brand's web site, reading others' ideas, or watching ads (i.e., browsing). It is not customizing a product, such as a Nike shoe, or building a product, such as a Chipotle burrito. Such activities are either passive on the part of the consumer or do not involve developing or interpreting brand meaning.

We propose that brand co-creation has the following characteristics: (1) it requires activity involving the brand on the part of the consumer, outside of consuming the branded product; (2) it is willing, purposive, and intentional; (3) the interaction is managed by the marketer, or jointly by the marketer and the consumer; and (4) the output of the interaction results in value for both the marketer and the consumer. We discuss each of these in more detail.

First, brand co-creation focuses on developing the brand rather than branded products or services. This distinguishes brand co-creation from co-production and mass customization. Brand co-creation allows the consumer to shape brand values, characteristics, and attributes. Our conceptualization of brand co-creation is grounded in theorizing on what constitutes brand equity (Keller, 2003). According to Keller (1993, 2003), the brand exists in the minds of consumers, reflecting their brand knowledge, associations, and experiences. In personally reflecting on the brand, consumers process information about experiences with the brand, relationship between brand characteristics and image to the self, and personally referenced opinions and feelings about the brand or brand campaign. This means that there is flexibility to the brand's positioning. Emerging technologies, such as web platforms, enable marketers to solicit consumers to develop the brand, specifically through brand co-creation activities. By designing stickers, creating ads, and telling stories, consumers evolve the brand by expressing what they think the brand means. As the brand changes in real time, both the marketer and consumers alike recognize the evolution of the brand (Merz, He, & Vargo, 2009). In turn, the co-created content becomes a form of positioning in and of itself. For instance, as part of Starbucks' My Starbucks Idea campaign, consumers can post their ideas for how the company can improve the coffee shop experience. In commenting on other consumers' ideas, consumers often echo one another's sentiments while sharing personal anecdotes about brand values, such as warmth and coziness. Thus, the brand can evolve through any number of activities within one brand co-creation campaign.

Second, brand co-creation is a process in which consumers freely elect to participate. When marketers solicit consumer participation in brand campaigns, it is the volition of consumers that dictates whether and to what extent they develop the brand. Some activities, such as writing one's own brand story, allow consumers to put as much or as little as they wish into them. Regardless of length, these activities allow the consumer the opportunity both to develop brand meaning and to provide input to the marketer in the form of content about the brand. Take, for example, Doritos' Crash the Super Bowl contest. Since 2006, PepsiCo has been getting consumers involved in co-creating its Doritos brand of snack foods. The annual "Crash the Super Bowl" contest allows people to create and upload their own Doritos Super Bowl commercial (time-consuming activity) depicting their perspective on what the brand means. The winning commercials, based on the most votes by the public (brief activity), are featured in the Super Bowl. Given that the Super Bowl is the most expensive advertising vehicle, this is a significant commitment on the part of PepsiCo. One of the reasons the company continues to do this is that these ads rank high on the Super Bowl Ad Meter, which measures Liking for ads aired during the Super Bowl. In the process, consumers decide how much to contribute to the development of the brand and its core values.

Third, the marketer provides the context within which brand co-creation happens. The very notion of brand co-creation implies that consumers and marketers share responsibility for creating brand meaning. Similar to theory on the active, constructive consumer who negotiates marketer-imposed meaning in the context of a consumption situation (e.g., Holt, 1997), we suggest that the consumer uses marketer-generated ideas to create his/her own meaning in any given brand co-creation opportunity. The marketer establishes the framework for a virtual dialogue about the brand's meaning, providing a constructive platform upon which consumers can begin expressing themselves. Creativity research shows that providing structure can support ideation (Moreau & Dahl, 2005). In brand co-creation, consumers reflect on the brand and, in doing so, make active contributions to the marketers' given portrayal of brand meaning (e.g., an advertising theme). This is important because these consumer reflections might have otherwise gone unstated. Whereas consumers may be aware of the meaning the marketer suggests for the brand, as well as the brand's meaning to themselves, marketers would not. For example, Jason's Deli, a chain offering healthy sandwiches, soups, and salads, offers consumers the opportunity to vote on ads that communicate what Jason's Deli's offerings mean to them and comment on how the ads resonate with their healthy lifestyle.

Fourth, and similar to the concept of co-creation in the services context (Vargo & Lusch, 2004), we conceptualize brand co-creation as a value generator for both consumer and marketer. Value can be intangible or tangible. Similar to less visible effects observed from customization (Franke, Schreier, & Kaiser, 2010), consumers may experience enjoyment, pride, or satisfaction from co-creating the brand. Research suggests that lead users benefit most from the preference fit achieved in co-production (Franke, Keinz, & Steger, 2009). Whereas marketers value lead users' opinions in brand co-creation, they are also interested in gaining a holistic perspective of the brand from past consumers, employees, and other stakeholders. Thus, brand co-creation campaigns are targeted at a wide range of consumers, and all consumers can derive value from participation. Value can also be visible through brand co-creation activities. For example, in the My Starbucks Idea campaign not only do consumers provide input and see their ideas voted on, but also marketers gain real-time data, review ideas, and implement those with a high number of votes. Finally, value is provided in terms of social brand engagement. Consumers may share the results of co-creation activities with their social networks, thereby becoming brand advocates.

In sum, the marketer is an important—and sometimes unrecognized—partner in the co-creation process. In some brand co-creation campaigns, the marketer acknowledges consumers' co-creations (e.g., by selecting stickers to appear on Chiquita bananas in stores or implementing Starbucks ideas), whereas in others the marketer may remain a silent observer who utilizes information in future advertising. Next, we consider how marketers can design effective brand co-creation activities that lead to social brand engagement. Whereas the nature of the design task (aesthetic versus functional), the product (perishable vs. durable), the intended consumption setting (public vs. private), and the designer (novice vs. expert) are thought to influence the degree to which consumers' involvement in design creates value (Moreau, 2011), we believe brand co-creation activities differ on another dimension: voice. We now discuss voice, as well as the role of self-brand connection, in motivating brand co-creation and determining subsequent social brand engagement.

Strength of Voice of the Brand Co-creation Activity

We propose that brand co-creation activities differ in terms of voice, and that voice affects social brand engagement. Voice in brand co-creation can be considered a positively intentioned expression of personal meaning to the marketer. Literature on voice from organizational behavior and social psychology defines "voice" as intentional expression of ideas, information, and opinions as part of a participatory process (Folger, 1977). Traditional notions of voice imply that expressing ideas enhances a relationship between individual and organization, or in the present context, consumer and brand (Hirschman, 1970). More recent conceptualizations of voice extend the construct from complaining to more proactive, constructively intended speaking up behavior. Speaking up behavior is based on a positive motive of making cooperative contributions to the organization (Van Dyne, Ang, & Botero, 2003).

We define voice as the consumer's ability to express personal brand meaning *to the marketer.* For example, on the Chiquita web site, marketing messages have emphasized either that consumers can share co-creation with Chiquita, with the possibility of having Chiquita select their sticker to appear on bananas in stores (i.e., the audience is the marketer) or that the activity is fun and expresses their identity (i.e., the audience is the self). In the former case, strength of voice is higher because consumers are expressing meaning to the marketer (versus themselves). When the marketer is the implicit (or explicit) audience, the consumer feels that s/he has a say in brand meaning, i.e., that s/he has a role in shaping the brand. Notably, strength of voice in brand co-creation differs from self-involvement in brand co-creation on this dimension. A consumer can involve the self heavily in an activity without sharing brand meaning s/he creates with the marketer. In the latter case, involvement of the self may be higher, but in the former case the consumer is better poised to express meaning to the marketer because s/he believes s/he is sharing the design with Chiquita.

Thus, because marketers can manipulate perceptions that they are listening to the consumer (e.g., seeing their co-creations), not all brand co-creation activities are created equal on the voice dimension. We believe strong voice brand co-creation activities will be systematically more effective at deepening social brand engagement than weak voice activities because they allow the consumer to provide meaningful input to the marketer. In strong voice brand co-creation, the consumer is expressing to the marketer what the brand means, but there is no explicit expectation that the marketer will use the co-creation idea. This notion is consistent with voice literature in social psychology and organizational behavior that suggests that a consumer's idea does not have to be acted on (Van Dyne, Ang, & Botero, 2003). In other words, the consumer's sticker does not have to appear on Chiquita bananas and the story does not have to appear on the brand's web site for her to have a voice.

Activities with strong versus weak voice can be distinguished largely based on the degree to which the consumer feels she has a role in shaping the brand. For this reason, activities that explicitly identify the marketer as audience or that feature the consumer's co-creation as part of the marketer-maintained campaign will have stronger voice than those activities that consumers complete more privately. For example, uploading content (e.g., video, words, pictures) to Coca-Cola's marketing team that expresses what the brand slogan "Open Happiness" means is a stronger voice activity than building a Coke commercial using one's Facebook album content and sharing it with a friend through

Coca-Cola's Share a Coke campaign. Although both activities communicate brand meaning, sharing content directly with the marketer enables the consumer to have a stronger voice.

We next discuss who is likely to engage in brand co-creation and how participation affects social brand engagement.

Self-Brand Connection

Consumers are interested in co-creation because the act allows them to express their identities and derive value (Franke, Schreier, & Kaiser, 2010; Moreau & Herd, 2010). This raises the following question: what is the relationship between a consumer's identity and the brand that might affect outcomes in a brand co-creation context? Broadly speaking, those who are attached to the brand are behaviorally loyal and defend the brand even when presented with negative information (Ferraro, Kirmani, & Matherly, 2013; Swaminathan, Page, & Gürhan-Canli, 2007). More specifically, research on "brand love" suggests that consumers who are attached to the brand are more motivated to engage in behaviors such as spreading positive word-of-mouth about the brand (Batra, Ahuvia, & Bagozzi, 2012). This research suggests that consumers who are attached to the brand may react differently from those who are less attached.

We suggest that this attachment construct is captured through self-brand connection, which refers to the link between the brand and the consumer's values and identity (Escalas, 2004; Escalas & Bettman, 2005; Park et al., 2010). The self-brand connection construct is based on the notion that when the set of brand associations are linked to the self, the associations can help consumers achieve certain goals for themselves, such as what they would like to become (Kruglanski et al., 2002; Escalas, 2004; Kopetz et al., 2012). Self-brand connection is positively correlated with, but differs from, brand attitudes, in that brand attitudes are general affective evaluations and fail to capture the self-relevance of a brand (Fishbein & Ajzen, 1975; Escalas, 2004; Park et al., 2010).

Whereas it behooves marketers to target lead users with co-production and new product development efforts (Franke, Keinz, & Steger, 2009), brand co-creation campaigns tend to cast a wider net. For example, many companies marketing to Millennials target the group as a whole with brand co-creation campaigns, aiming to take advantage of their general proclivity to participate in marketing rather than be marketed to (Fromm & Garton, 2013). We suggest that the likelihood of participating in a co-creation activity will depend on the motivational aspects of self-brand connection, i.e., the extent to which the co-creation activity helps further self-goals. Research suggests that consumers seek out and share branded content that reflects their identity (Kirmani, 2009); these consumers are already connected to the brand and motivated by their self-brand connection. Further, consumers with high self-brand connection have more knowledge about brand meaning and a greater likelihood to self-reference in a brand context (Escalas, 2004; 2007). Literature on voice suggests that individuals who feel personal accountability for expressing opinions become proactively involved in the success of the organization (Fuller, Marler, & Hester, 2006; Liang, Farh, & Farh, 2012). We suggest that because self-brand connection is linked to the self, it fosters an internally motivated reason to co-create the brand (i.e., to further self-goals). Thus, consumers with high (vs. low) self-brand connection are more motivated to co-create because the brand's associated traits and attributes are aligned with their self-goals.

In a brand co-creation context we are interested in determining how self-brand connection might affect social brand engagement. Brand community and story-telling research discuss the participatory process of interpreting brand experience as representative of sophisticated and knowledgeable (e.g., high SBC) consumers (Schau, Muniz, & Arnould, 2009; Thompson, 1997). This tendency for a consumer to espouse brand-related content is echoed by current consumer behavior research philosophies on social media and identity that show "we are what we post" (Schau & Gilly, 2003). Social media platforms such as Facebook provide a way for consumers to complete authenticating acts that allow them to express their identity both to themselves and to friends (Arnould & Price, 1999). In essence, social brand engagement allows people to publically declare their love for the brand. Because consumers with high self-brand connection are those with greater brand love, high SBC consumers are more likely to engage in behaviors such as "Liking" the brand on Facebook.

Hypotheses

Whereas past research has examined the downstream effects of the degree of self-brand connection on response to advertising (Park & Young, 1986), researchers have yet to explore how strength of voice and self-brand connection affect behaviors in a co-creation context. Marketers hope that new customers will be attracted to co-creation activities, such as games or other entertainment applications that allow them to make the brand more fun. In presenting the activity, marketers can choose whether to emphasize collaboration. As an initial step to advancing knowledge in this area, we investigate the effect of co-creating with strong versus weak voice on social brand engagement intentions by level of self-brand connection.

Marketers speculate that social brand engagement stems from a personal experience with the brand that consumers wish to relate to others, or back to the brand itself, rather than from static messages about the brand (e.g., an ad or information on a web site; Savary, 2008). Engagement is based on an experience of meaningfulness of a creative, autonomous task that the individual perceives as a good fit with the self (Kahn, 1990). Extending this theory, strong voice brand co-creation activities should lead to greater social brand engagement for connected consumers than weak voice brand co-creation activities. When consumers have low SBC, they are not affected by voice in brand co-creation activities because they are not motivated to participate in the activity to begin with. Thus, we expect that self-brand connection and strength of voice in brand co-creation interact to affect social brand engagement.

We propose that, for consumers with high self-brand connection, strong voice co-creation (i.e., co-creating for the marketer) increases the intention to engage further with the brand via social media more than does weak voice co-creation. When co-creating for the marketer rather than for entertainment or privately (i.e., for themselves), consumers with high self-brand connection can voice their ideas about what the brand has come to mean to them through experiences and amassed knowledge. To the extent that low self-brand connection consumers are able to generate brand knowledge for the marketer in brand co-creation activities, one might expect that they would be similarly affected. However, for low self-brand connection consumers, strength of voice is irrelevant; the strength of voice of the activity does not affect the intention to engage further with the brand because they are not motivated to participate in the first place. Even the low self-brand connection consumers who do co-create are not likely to increase social brand engagement in the strong voice condition because they do not have the ability to take advantage of the opportunity to express personal brand meaning to the marketer. Thus, we argue that co-creating for the marketer takes loyal (vs. non-loyal) consumers to the next level with the brand.

We report the results of a study designed to test these predictions. The study used a real brand co-creation platform from Chiquita's Sticker Studio. Chiquita bananas are a brand that is familiar and relevant to undergraduate students, who were the participants in the study.

Study: Chiquita's Sticker Studio

One hundred and one undergraduate students (53% female, average age = 20.5 years) completed the study in exchange for course credit. The between subjects design employed one manipulated factor (voice: strong vs. weak) and one measured factor (self-brand connection). Participants were randomly assigned to the voice condition.

Procedure

Participants completed the study on the computer. They came to the research lab in groups of 10–15 as part of a larger research session of various, unrelated studies. Participants first reported their self-brand connection (SBC) to the Chiquita brand, using Escalas and Bettman's (2003) 7-item scale. Items such as "The Chiquita brand reflects who I am," "I can identify with the Chiquita brand," and "The Chiquita brand suits me well," were anchored on a 100-point sliding scale (0 = strongly disagree, 100 = strongly agree; $M = 11.51$, $SD = 16.47$, ranging from 0 to 79.86, $\alpha = .94$). SBC was mean-centered for purposes of analysis.

They then received instructions for interacting with Chiquita's online brand co-creation application for designing their own Chiquita banana sticker. Strength of voice in the brand co-creation activity was manipulated by exposing participants to a common introduction to the Chiquita Sticker Design Studio, "Chiquita recently launched a 'Design Your Own Chiquita Banana Sticker' web application called the Sticker Studio. You can use the Sticker Studio to create your own Chiquita banana sticker. Here is an example of what one person had to say about the sticker they created:" and then a message to design the sticker. Messages were presented as quotations from actual consumers featured on the Chiquita brand campaign web site. Quotations were adapted from real consumer quotations, and care was taken to present quotations that did not differ significantly in word count or form. The strong voice message was designed to emphasize communication of brand meaning to the marketer through the co-creation activity, whereas the weak voice message emphasized communication of meaning to the self through the activity. In the strong voice condition the message read, "Chiquita sticker designs add another dimension to the product and brand itself. Create a sticker! Chiquita can reward you for your design. Chiquita will select stickers to appear on bananas in stores nationwide." In the weak voice condition the message read, "Chiquita sticker designs add another dimension to the product and brand itself. Create your own sticker! It's really fun to design, and you can express what the brand means to you. Mine expresses my identity." As a manipulation check, participants were asked to explain in their own words why they would design a sticker. These responses were coded for mention of self and marketer (coded 1) or only mention of self but no mention of marketer (coded 0).

Participants were next given the opportunity to design their own sticker using Chiquita's Sticker Studio. Choice to design the sticker served as the first dependent variable. Participants who elected to design the sticker were taken to the Sticker Design Studio web page and given instructions to design and save their sticker.

The second and key dependent variable was social brand engagement intentions. Social brand engagement was measured as an average of three items on 7-point scales (alpha = .83): "How much would you like to check out Chiquita's brand page on Facebook" (1 = not at all, 7 = very much); "I would Like Chiquita's brand page on Facebook next time I login to my Facebook account" (1 = definitely would not Like Chiquita, 7 = definitely would Like Chiquita); and "How likely would you be to share a new Chiquita brand promotion with friends or family?" (1 = very unlikely, 7 = very likely). Then, post-activity self-brand connection was measured using the same scale as before ($\alpha = .94$). Finally, enjoyment was measured using one item: how enjoyable was creating your own Chiquita banana sticker? (1 = not at all, 7 = very much).

Results

Manipulation Check. We expected participants exposed to the strong voice message to express greater ability to communicate with the marketer in sticker design than those exposed to the weak voice message. Participants' responses were coded for mention of communicating design to Chiquita (i.e., mention self/"your design" and brand, coded 1) or no communication of meaning to marketer (i.e., no mention of self/"your design" and brand, coded 0). As expected, participants in the strong voice condition were more likely to report that designing a sticker involves sharing it with Chiquita than participants in the weak voice condition (46.5% versus 27%, $\chi^2 = 8.24$, $p < .01$). Thus, our manipulation of the voice variable was successful.

Choice to Co-create. Overall, 54 participants (53.5%) chose to design a sticker (average SBC = 15.90, *SD* = 20.31; average time spent designing = 3 minutes 12 seconds, *SD* = 1 minute 35 seconds; 47 participants (46.5%) choose not to design a sticker (average SBC = 6.47, *SD* = 8.13). A logistic regression with dummy-coded voice (1 = strong, 0 = weak), SBC, and the interaction of SBC and voice on choice revealed a marginally significant effect of mean-centered SBC on choice to design ($\beta = .06$, *Wald* = 3.58, $p = .058$; $\chi^2 = 4.55$, $p < .05$). Consumers with high SBC (+1 *SD*) were more likely to elect to design a sticker than those low in SBC (−1 *SD*) ($M_{\text{high SBC}} = 57.4\%$; $M_{\text{low SBC}} = 42.6\%$). As expected, there were no significant effects of voice ($\beta = -.39$, *Wald* = .77, *ns*) or the interaction of SBC and voice ($\beta = -.02$, *Wald* = .23, *ns*) on choice to design the sticker. This suggests that motivation to participate in a co-creation activity comes from SBC and not from strength of voice of the brand co-creation activity (even when it involves potential reward by the marketer).

Social Brand Engagement Intentions. Ideally, we would like to assess whether brand engagement intentions differ between the consumers who participated in the co-creation activity and those who did not. However, because SBC affected the choice to co-create, we could not run a model with a dummy coded variable for those who chose to co-create. Therefore, to test our hypothesis, we separately examined participants who chose to design a sticker and those who chose not to design a sticker.[1]

A regression on Chiquita social brand engagement intentions revealed significant main effects of SBC ($\beta = .05$, $t(53) = 3.39$, $p < .01$) and voice ($\beta = -.75$, $t(53) = -2.18$, $p < .05$). In addition, the interaction effect was also significant ($\beta = -.04$, $t(53) = -2.29$, $p = .03$). A spotlight analysis (Irwin & McClelland, 2001) showed that consumers with high SBC expressed greater social brand engagement intentions in the strong vs. weak voice condition ($M_{\text{strong}} = 4.32$ vs. $M_{\text{weak}} = 2.72$, $\beta = -1.26$, $t(53) = -2.99$, $p < .01$). In contrast, consumers low in SBC were not affected by voice ($M_{\text{strong}} = 2.21$ vs. $M_{\text{weak}} = 2.31$, $\beta = .14$, $t(53) = .27$, *ns*; Aiken & West, 1991; Fitzsimons, 2008). This supports our hypothesizing.

Regression analysis on social brand engagement intentions for those who chose not to design a sticker revealed a significant effect of SBC ($\beta = .05$,

$t(46) = 3.05$, $p < .01$). Higher SBC led to higher engagement intentions. However, the effect of neither voice ($\beta = -.26$, $t(46) = -1.28$, *ns*) nor the interaction ($\beta = .01$, $t(46) = .50$, *ns*) was significant. This demonstrates that the difference in social brand engagement intentions occurs only for participants who did the co-creation activity.

Post-Activity Self-Brand Connection. We assessed whether the significant interaction effect can be explained by changes in SBC following the co-creation activity. A regression of pre-activity SBC, voice, and their interaction on the post-activity measure of self-brand connection revealed only a significant effect of pre-activity SBC ($\beta = .63$, $t(53) = 4.02$, $p < .01$); voice ($\beta = -.65$, $t(53) = -.61$, $p = .92$) and the interaction term ($\beta = .43$, $t(53) = 1.51$, $p = .14$) were not significant. Thus, changes in the level of self-brand connection cannot account for changes in social brand engagement intentions.

Enjoyment. Finally, we examined whether enjoyment of the brand co-creation experience accounted for the significant interaction effect on social brand engagement intentions. Regression analysis on perceived enjoyment revealed marginal main effects of SBC ($\beta = .03$, $t(53) = 1.85$, $p = .07$) and voice ($\beta = -.74$, $t(53) = -1.78$, $p = .08$). Connected consumers enjoyed co-creating marginally more so than less connected consumers, and the strong voice activity was marginally more enjoyable than the weak voice activity. The interaction effect was not significant ($\beta = -.01$, $t(53) = -.5$, *ns*). Thus, enjoyment does not explain the effects on social brand engagement intentions.

Discussion

Consistent with our hypothesizing, high SBC consumers chose to participate in the co-creation activity more than did low SBC consumers. Interestingly, consumers low in SBC were less likely to co-create—even for fun—and they were unaffected by strength of voice. Of note, there were no significant effects of voice on the choice to co-create. This means that connected consumers' motivation is directed towards the brand itself and not the opportunity to communicate meaning to the marketer. This adds to our understanding of brands as means to self-goal fulfillment (Kirmani, 2009; Kopetz et al., 2012).

Also consistent with our hypothesizing, participation in a strong (versus weak) voice activity led consumers high in self-brand connection to express greater likelihood to engage with the brand on social media. However, consumers with low self-brand connection were unaffected by voice. We ruled out enjoyment and changes in self-brand connection as the underlying mechanism.

Notably, an alternative hypothesis would be that the self instructions in the weak voice manipulation affected intrinsic motivation, whereas the reward aspect of the strong voice condition affected extrinsic motivation. If this were the case, the weak voice condition would have been more effective than the strong voice condition. Given that we find the opposite effect that the strong voice (extrinsic motive) is more effective, this means that the effect must be due to expressing personal brand meaning to the marketer.

Concluding Thoughts and Opportunities for Future Research

Multiple touch points between brands and consumers make consumer-brand connections an increasingly important and complex construct to understand and manage (MacInnis, Park, & Priester, 2009). Companies spend billions of dollars building brand associations and managing the brand. However, fewer brand characteristics are actively created by the firm and more exist in the perceptions and interactions of consumers. Our notion of brand co-creation is grounded in brand equity theory (Keller, 2003) whereby the consumer creates a new idea about the brand (i.e., meaning) through the brand co-creation activity and, importantly, voices it to the marketer. Our conceptualization of voice in the brand co-creation process is based on the management literature, where participation refers to proactive, constructively intended speaking up behavior in the context of organizations (Van Dyne, Ang, & Botero, 2003). We extend this notion to incorporate the consumers' opportunity to share personal brand meaning with the marketer and actively evolve the brand in real-time. Our study shows that consumers high versus low in self-brand connection are more likely to participate in brand co-creation activities regardless of voice (i.e., whether they think they are collaborating with the marketer or simply having fun with the brand). Thus, our findings implicate self-brand connection as precursor to proactive brand development. Knowing that highly connected consumers are those who participate in brand co-creation, marketers could target new brand-related content by using co-creation information as input in the development of more specific brand associations that resonate with connected consumers.

Ideally, brand co-creation activities would attract not only connected consumers but also less connected consumers such as past customers or those who frequent the brand's competition. This would enable marketers to gain a more holistic view of what the brands means and target new brand efforts appropriately. In light of this, marketers make substantial investments in brand campaigns they hope will capture the attention of new consumers, often using an entertainment hook. As our study shows, less-connected consumers are less motivated to participate in a brand co-creation activity, even for fun, and thus are not apt to deepen their brand relationship. Thus, an important avenue for future research becomes investigating conditions under which consumers with low self-brand connection increase social brand engagement.

The study suggests that motives can affect consumers' participation in brand co-creation and social brand engagement. Similar to research on conditions under which motives affect consumer creativity (Dahl & Moreau, 2007), exploring motives in brand co-creation contexts could lead to interesting implications for marketers. Externally induced goals cause individuals to experience their efforts as a loss in autonomy (Ryan & Deci, 2000; Zhang et al., 2011). One exception is a study by Deci (1971), which shows that promise of social reward causes an increase in internal motivation. This finding, coupled with our finding in the study that consumers high in self-brand connection increase brand engagement in the context of the Chiquita promotion over self-involvement in the activity, suggests there may be conditions under which consumers high in self-brand connection experience an increase in internal motivation even when exposed to marketer-related motives. That is, that high self-brand connection consumers attribute the co-creation to themselves versus the marketer, which leads to increased brand-based behavior. Investigation of marketer versus consumer attribution in brand co-creation contexts could provide marketers with clearer guidelines for how to position collaboration with loyal consumers. Relatedly, what other consumer characteristics may affect social brand engagement?

We provide empirical support for advertising and branding models that depict heightened states of the self-brand relationship (i.e., resonance; Keller, 2003) and offer an important measure of brand co-creation value: social brand engagement. This dependent variable bolsters marketers' hope that consumers' participation in interactive brand campaigns will lead to behaviors such as "Liking" the brand on Facebook (FanGager, 2012). Another interesting avenue for research is whether social brand engagement is different on Facebook, Twitter, or other types of social media. Our research suggests that Facebook behavior and sharing promotions are similar. More research is needed on various media in order to understand issues such as boundaries of the consumer-brand relationship, consumer perceptions of affiliation and identity signaling, and scope of the brand. How might voice and self-brand connection differentially affect engagement on specific social platforms?

We show that engagement can occur in brief (i.e., less than five minute) interactions with the brand. Whereas some theoretical conjecture suggests that perceptions of psychological ownership are unlikely to occur in brief experiences (Pierce et al., 2003), recent empirical investigations in mass customization contexts shows that the self can be involved in design and production episodes lasting approximately 25 minutes (Franke, Schreier, & Kaiser, 2010; Moreau & Herd, 2010; Troye & Supphellen, 2012). It is likely that similar effects will result in more extended co-creation contexts as well, such as creating one's own Share a Coke commercial using Facebook album content. Future research may examine boundary conditions for brand co-creation effects, such as how long social brand engagement effects last.

Given the abundance of brand web sites with interactive co-creation activities that allow consumers to upload, email, post, or submit co-creations to marketers, we have discussed the importance of examining how personally reflecting on brand meaning for the marketer can lead to social brand engagement from online campaigns. However, many companies are launching offline interactive campaigns as well. For example, contests, such as Chipotle's Boo-Rito campaign that rewards consumers for dressing like a burrito on Halloween, allow consumers to complete brand-related acts. Whereas most consumers spend minutes wrapping themselves in a sheet of tin foil to make a burrito costume, some could spend hours or more carefully crafting a burrito costume with multiple attributes. Yet, the co-creation is expressed publicly to representatives in stores rather than to Chipotle's corporate marketing team. Another difference could be in how creativity manifests itself offline versus online. Thus, it is unclear whether this form of brand co-creation would also lead to social brand engagement. Further inquiry on consumer-marketer engagement in these contexts can extend the boundaries of brand co-creation research and explore relevant dependent variables beyond social media-based engagement behavior.

Finally, an important avenue for future research involves the benefits and drawbacks of real-time collaboration. Consumers may or may not be aware of the brand's evolution; however in most brand campaigns their identity is acknowledged as part of the posting or submission, so their role in co-creating the brand becomes salient. Brand community research suggests that consumers entrenched in brand development do recognize an evolution taking place as they build upon each other's ideas (Muniz & Schau, 2005). Future research examining the effects of consumer attribution and perceptions of brand ownership would be interesting, as the role of transparency in the co-creation process becomes more of an issue. Consumers benefit from having their voice heard. On the other hand, marketers benefit from the immediate feedback and constant flow of ideas that brand co-creation provides. Future research should address how marketers can optimize the amount of real-time data they gain from co-creation and the appropriate weight of co-creation information in advertising strategy. One drawback is the control that marketers relinquish when offering the brand for co-creation; yet it appears that marketers willingly let go in order to recoup the social brand engagement that co-creation can yield.

Note

1. Results of regression analysis on the entire sample ($n = 101$) reveal the predicted pattern, with a significant effect of SBC ($\beta = .06$, $t(100) = 5.07$, $p < .01$), and voice ($\beta = -.47$, $t(100) = -2.08$, $p < .05$), qualified by the predicted interaction effect (mean-centered SBC × voice: $\beta = -.04$, $t(100) = -2.67$, $p < .01$). Spotlight analysis shows that participants with high SBC (+1 SD) increased brand engagement intentions in the strong (vs. weak) voice condition ($M_{strong} = 3.51$ vs. $M_{weak} = 2.39$, $\beta = -1.12$, $t(100) = -3.32$, $p < .01$; Aiken & West, 1991; Fitzsimons, 2008), whereas those with low SBC (−1 SD) were unaffected by voice ($M_{strong} = 1.50$ vs. $M_{weak} = 1.67$, $\beta = .18$, $t(100) = .54$, *ns*).

References

Aiken, L. S., & West, S. G. (1991). *Multiple regression: Testing and interpreting interactions.* Newbury Park, CA: Sage.

Arnould, E. J., & Price, L. L. (1999). Authenticating acts and authoritative performances: Questing for self and community," In S. Ratneshwar, G. D. Mick, and C. Huffman

(Eds.), *The why of consumption: Contemporary perspectives on consumers motives, goals, and desires* (pp. 140–60). New York: Routledge.

Batra, R., Ahuvia, A., & Bagozzi, R.P. (2012). Brand love. *Journal of Marketing*, 76 (2), 1–16.

Dahl, D.W., & Moreau, C.P. (2007). Thinking inside the box: Why consumers enjoy constrained creative experiences. *Journal of Marketing Research*, 44 (3), 357–69.

Deci, E.L. (1971). The effects of externally mediated rewards on intrinsic motivation. *Journal of Personality and Social Psychology*, 18, 105–15.

Deloitte (2012). Rethink ROI for social media with the engagement curve. www.deloitte.com, accessed February 4, 2013.

Dretsch, H.J., & Kirmani, A. (2014). Designing effective brand co-creation activities. working paper, University of Maryland.

Escalas, J.E. (2004). Narrative processing: Building consumer connections to brands. *Journal of Consumer Psychology*, 14 (1), 168–79.

——— (2007), Self-referencing and persuasion: Narrative transportation versus analytical elaboration. *Journal of Consumer Research*, 33 (4), 421–29.

Escalas, J.E. & Bettman, J.R. (2003). You are what they eat: The influence of reference groups on consumer connection to brands. *Journal of Consumer Psychology*, 13 (3), 339–48.

——— (2005). Self-construal, reference groups, and brand meaning. *Journal of Consumer Research*, 32 (3), 378–89.

FanGager (2012). Fangager case studies. www.fangager.com/site/page/case-study/.

Ferraro, R., Kirmani, A., & Matherly, T. (2013). Look at me! Look at me! Conspicuous brand usage, self-brand connection, and dilution. *Journal of Marketing Research*, 50 (4), 477–88.

Fishbein, M., & Ajzen, I. (1975). *Belief, attitude, intention, and behavior: An introduction to theory and research.* Reading, MA: Addison-Wesley.

Fitzsimons, G.J. (2008). Editorial: Death to dichotomizing. *Journal of Consumer Research*, 35 (1), 5–8.

Folger, R. (1977). Distributive and procedural justice: Combined impact of "voice" and improvement on experienced inequity. *Journal of Personality and Social Psychology*, 35, 108–19.

Franke, N., Keinz, P., & Steger, C.J. (2009). Testing the value of customization: When do customers really prefer products tailored to their preferences? *Journal of Marketing* 73 (5), 103–21.

Franke, N., Schreier, M., & Kaiser, U. (2010). The 'I designed it myself' effect in mass customization. *Management Science*, 56 (January), 125–40.

Fromm, J., & Garton, C. (2103). *Marketing to millennials: Reach the largest and most influential generation of consumers ever.* New York: American Management Association.

Fuller, J.B., Marler, L.E., & Hester, K. (2006). Promoting felt responsibility for constructive change and proactive behavior: Exploring aspects of an elaborated model of work design. *Journal of Organizational Behavior*, 27, 1089–1120.

Hirschman, A.O. (1970). *Exit, voice, and loyalty: Responses to decline in firms, organizations, and states.* Cambridge, MA: Harvard University Press.

Holt, D.B. (1997). Poststructuralist lifestyle analysis: Conceptualizing the social patterning of consumption in postmodernity. *Journal of Consumer Research*, 23, (4), 326–50.

Irwin, J.R., & McClelland, G.H. (2001). Misleading heurisitcs and moderated multiple regression models. *Journal of Marketing Research*, 38 (1), 100–109.

Kahn, W.A. (1990). Psychological conditions of personal engagement and disengagement at work. *Academy of Management Journal*, 33 (4), 692–724.

Keller, K.L. (1993). Conceptualizing, measuring, and managing customer-based brand equity. *Journal of Marketing*, 57 (1), 1–22.

——— (2003). *Strategic brand management: Building, measuring, and managing brand equity*. 2nd ed. Upper Saddle River, NJ: Prentice Hall.

Kirmani, A. (2009). The self and the brand. *Journal of Consumer Psychology*, 19 (3), 271–75.

Kopetz, C.E., Kruglanski, A.W., Arens, Z.G., Etkin, J., & Johnson, H.M. (2012). The dynamics of consumer behavior: A goal systemic perspective. *Journal of Consumer Psychology*, 22, 208–33.

Kozinets, R.V. (2001). Utopian enterprise: Articulating the meanings of Star Trek's culture of consumption. *Journal of Consumer Research*, 28 (1), 67–88.

Kruglanski, A.W., Shah, J.W., Fishbach, A., Friedman, R., Chun, W.Y., & Sleeth-Keppler, D. (2002). A theory of goal systems. In M.P. Zanna (Ed.), *Advances in experimental social psychology*, Vol. 34. (pp. 331–78). San Diego, CA: Academic Press.

Liang, J., Farh, C.I., Farh, J-L. (2012). Psychological antecedents of promotive and prohibitive voice: A two-wave examination," *Academy of Management Journal*, 55 (1), 71–92.

MacInnis, D. J., Park, C. W., & Priester, J. (2009). Why brand relationships. In *Handbook of Brand Relationships* (pp. ix–xx). New York: ME Sharpe.

Merz, M. A., He, Y., & Vargo, S. L. (2009). The evolving brand logic: A service-dominant logic perspective. *Journal of the Academy of Marketing Science*, 37, 328–44.

Moreau, C.P. (2011). Inviting the amateurs into the studio: Understanding how consumer engagement in product design creates value. *Journal of Product Innovation Management*, 28, 409–10.

Moreau, C.P., & Dahl, D. (2005). Designing the solution: The impact of constraints on consumers' creativity. *Journal of Consumer Research*, 32 (1), 13–22.

Moreau, C.P., & Herd, K.B. (2010). To each his own? How comparisons to others influence consumers' evaluations of their self-designed products. *Journal of Consumer Research*, 36 (5), 806–19.

Muñiz, A. M. Jr., & Schau, H.J. (2005). Religiosity in the abandoned Apple Newton brand community. *Journal of Consumer Research*, 31 (4), 737–47.

Park, C. W., MacInnis, D. J., Priester, J., Eisingerich, A. B., & Iacobucci, D. (2010). Brand attachment and brand attitude strength: Conceptual and empirical differentiation of two critical brand equity drivers. *Journal of Marketing*, 74 (6), 1–17.

Park, C. W., & Young, S.M. (1986). Consumer response to television commercials: The impact of self-brand connection and background music on brand attitude formation. *Journal of Marketing Research*, 23 (February), 11–24.

Pierce, J.L., Kostova, T., & Dirks, K.T. (2003). The state of psychological ownership: Integrating and extending a century of research. *Review of General Psych*ology, 7 (1), 84–107.

Prahalad, C. K. & Ramaswamy, V. (2000). Co-opting customer competence. *Harvard Business Review*, 78 (1) 79–90.

Ryan, R.M., & Deci, E.L. (2000). Self-determination theory and the facilitation of intrinsic motivation, social development, and well-being. *American Psychologist*, 55, 68–78.

Savary, J. (2008). Advocacy marketing: Toyota's secrets for partnering with trendsetters to create passionate brand advocates. *Journal of Sponsorship*, 1 (3), 211–24.

Schau, H.J., & Gilly, M.C. (2003). We are what we post? The presentation of self in personal webspace. *Journal of Consumer Research*, 30 (3), 385–404.

Schau, H. J., Muñiz, A. M. Jr., & Arnould, E. J. (2009). How brand community practices create value. *Journal of Marketing*, 73 (5), 30–51.

Swaminathan, V., Page, K. L., & Gürhan-Canli, Z. (2007). "My" brand or "our" brand: The effects of brand relationship dimensions and self-construal on brand evaluations. *Journal of Consumer Research*, 34 (2), 248–59.

Thompson, G. L. (1997). Interpreting consumers: A hermeneutical framework for deriving marketing insights from the texts of consumers' consumption stories. *Journal of Marketing Research*, 34 (4), 438–55.

Troye, S. V., & Supphellen, M. (2012). Consumer participation in coproduction: "I made it myself" effects on consumers' sensory perceptions and evaluations of outcome and input product. *Journal of Marketing*, 76 (2), 33–46.

Van Doorn, J., Lemon, K. N., Mittal, V., Nass, S., Pick, D., Pirner, P., & Verhoef, P. C. (2010). Customer engagement behavior: Theoretical foundations and research directions. *Journal of Service Research*, 13 (3), 253–66.

Van Dyne, Linn, Soon Ang, and Isabel C. Botero (2003). Conceptualizing employee silence and employee voice as multidimensional constructs. *Journal of Management Studies*, 40 (6), 1359–92.

Vargo, S. L., & Lusch, R. F. (2004). Evolving to a new dominant logic for marketing. *Journal of Marketing*, 68, 1, 1–17.

Zhang, Y., Xu, J., Jiang, Z., & Huang, S. C. (2011). Been there, done that: The impact of effort investment on goal value and consumer motivation. *Journal of Consumer Research*, 38 (1), 78–93.

9

CHOOSE WISELY

Individual and Situational Influences on the Effectiveness of Social Media

Melanie C. Green and Jenna Clark

Social media has become an integral part of the communication landscape for both interpersonal and business purposes. Most businesses now feel the need to have at least a minimal social media presence (for example, a Facebook page with basic information about the company), and others devote significant attention to maximizing their social media marketing efforts, including frequent updates across multiple platforms, with creative campaigns designed to engage and attract customers. Social media marketing efforts may support a range of goals, including branding, developing, and maintaining relationships with customers, promoting sales and new products, and providing customer service.

Social media can provide significant benefits to both companies (through increased reputation and profits) and consumers (through rewarding connections with brands or personalized responses to concerns). However, social media may not be the most effective channel for all messages and all consumers. This chapter will focus on two lesser-known factors that may influence the effectiveness of social media. First, some messages may be better conveyed through means other than social media; sometimes more exclusive or private means of communication may be more effective than the potentially broad reach of social media outlets. Second, some individuals may be more open to social media campaigns than others. In particular, some people may have a more positive attitude toward forming connections online, and these people may be more willing to connect with companies and brands online as well. Other consumers may be more skeptical about the utility of online communications, and may be more difficult to reach through these channels.

Features of Communication Media

In modern life, the average person in a developed nation utilizes a range of communication media today that would have baffled the imagination of their great-grandparents. Individuals email their coworkers, text their friends, tweet for an audience that may include strangers from around the world, call their loved ones, and disseminate information to entire social networks over Facebook and other social networking sites. Similarly, companies may reply to customer queries over Twitter, post product updates or promotions on Facebook, or encourage users to share product-related videos on YouTube. Some people rely more heavily on one medium than another, or eschew an entire medium completely, but multiple options are available to communicators in both personal and business settings. Behind these communications lies a decision process that is often overlooked: the choice of communication medium.

When individuals wish to contact someone, the wealth of options available necessitates consideration of which is the most appropriate medium. Many influences factor in to communication media choice, from the content of the message to situational factors and even including the symbolic cues portrayed by the media (Trevino, Webster & Stein, 2000). Management science and communication have studied these influences extensively, primarily through media richness theory (Trevino, Lengel & Daft, 1987), cues-filtered-out theory, and social influence theory (Fulk, Schmitz & Steinfield, 1990; Fulk, 1993).

Channels and Cues in Medium Choice

Media richness theory centers around the idea that certain messages can be equivocal or ambiguous, requiring additional information to clarify their meaning; these messages are considered 'rich.' Communication media can be ranked in richness in terms of the amount of information they are capable of conveying. Media richness theory defines face-to-face communication as the richest medium, as it has the capacity for "immediate feedback, multiple cues, and natural language" (Trevino, Lengel, & Daft, 1987). It is followed by telephone communication and then written documents; the former lacks visual clues, and the latter lacks visual cues and immediate feedback.

Steinfield and Fulk (1987) argued that electronic media was less rich than the telephone but richer than conventional written documents due to the potential for immediate feedback with email. However, in the twenty-five years since, electronic media has broadened into a wide spectrum of options of which email is only one example. These different forms of electronic media may possess very different levels of richness; for example, instant messaging has as much immediacy as a telephone conversation.

The concept of reduced utility in a medium due to reduced cues was not new to media richness theory. Social presence theory (Short, Christie & Williams, 1976) makes a similar argument, suggesting that the fewer communication channels a medium conveys, the less the presence of the user is conveyed, resulting in decreased attention and interest in the interaction. The cues-filtered-out perspective (Culnan & Markus, 1987; Rice, 1993) extended social presence theory by suggesting that online communication tends to lack much of the sensory information we use to understand our conversations. According to the cues-filtered-out perspective, this lack has a deleterious effect on understanding and the quality of communication.

However, social information processing theory (SIPT; Walther 1992) provides a counter-argument. SIPT claims that individuals learn to compensate for the lack of conventional nonverbal cues, substituting in other channels of communication such as chronemic cues (e.g., time delay or time of day for response; Walther & Tidwell, 1995) or typographic cues (e.g., emoticons; Walter & D'Addario, 2001) instead. This would seem to contradict the idea that certain media are inevitably less rich than others, suggesting that richness could depend partially or entirely on one's view of a medium—an idea we will return to later.

Controllability in Medium Choice

Research on specific aspects of communication media has gone beyond simply considering the number and type of channels or cues, however; studies have also focused on other characteristics that may vary between social media and in-person communication. One particularly important aspect beyond channels or cues is the increased level of control over timing and self-presentation that many forms of online communication provide. For example, online communication is asynchronous, allowing for highly precise control over one's self-presentation (Schwaemmlein & Wodzicki, 2012; Walther, 2007). While asynchronicity primarily appears to provide benefits when individuals converse, it also allows for control in multiple other ways—amount of information shared, for example. Indeed, controllability is a highly valued aspect of online social interaction, even among those who do not particularly value online social interaction in general (Peter & Valkenburg, 2006).

Interestingly, Tucker (2014) showed that perceived control over one's personal information increased the effectiveness of personalized ads on websites. Individuals who felt that they could opt out of sharing this information were more likely to click on personalized ads. Currently, individuals have high levels of concern about the privacy of their personal information; making users feel in control of this information (even if the advertisements themselves do not change) can help overcome some of the barriers of distrust in online advertising. Both desires for and perceptions of control may play important roles in medium choice. More generally, Hoffman and Novak (2011) identify control as one of the "four Cs": the defining features of social media as well as the goals that consumers pursue with social media use. (The other three Cs are connect, create, and consume.) In this framework, control includes managing one's own reputation as well as controlling online content such as privacy settings or profile content.

Social Factors in Medium Choice

Thus far, we have discussed largely objective features of communication media: channels, cues, and controllability. However, subjective features are also crucial to considering medium choice. Social influence theory (Fulk, Schmitz & Steinfield, 1990; Fulk, 1993) states that media choice is often driven by perception—the attitudes and behaviors of colleagues in the workplace serve to shape our opinions of different media and their suitability for different tasks. Where media richness theory considers media richness to be unvarying and the most important factor in media choice, social influence theory considers it one of many factors in media choice, most of which are socially constructed. What other factors might explain media choice?

Message Topic and Medium Choice

In addition to the features of the media under consideration, the topic of the message itself can influence medium choice. Studies have shown that people are more likely to choose Internet communications when communicating negative aspects of themselves (Joinson, 2001) or to communicate negative messages such as dislike, anger, or intimidation (Markus, 1994). When it is necessary to communicate negative information, the use of Internet communications may help to buffer both communicators against some of the negativity (O'Sullivan, 2000).

Research in our lab (Crittenden, Green, & Clark, unpublished) examined communication medium preferences for different types of messages or information. In our research, participants responded to a series of hypothetical communication situations that were pretested to vary in importance, self-disclosure, and the level of trust required. For example, a high importance item was "Imagine that your friend tells you that they saw your boyfriend or girlfriend kissing someone else" and a low importance item was, "Imagine that your friend tells you that they saw a famous actor at the mall." Participants rated how appropriate it would be to use in-person communication, email, instant messenger, and telephone for each of the communication situations. Situations requiring a high level of trust between the two people communicating may call for the heightened physical cues (less mediation), which can help enhance credibility (O'Sullivan, 2000).

Our results suggest that individuals prefer to use face-to-face communication over mediated communication when they are discussing topics that are important or that require trust. For low importance topics, communication methods that allowed faster transmission of the message (e.g., phone, instant messenger) were preferred. Utz (2007) found similar results in her study of long-distance friendships. Email was used more often for staying in touch, but friends used the phone to discuss important personal matters.

Although these studies addressed an interpersonal context, there may also be lessons for consumer contexts. For messages that are not highly important or personalized to the individual, social media may be an acceptable way of communicating. For messages that are more important or sensitive, however, more personal means of communicating may be preferred by customers. Elliott (2013a) draws similar distinctions with his distinction between depth, relationship, and reach channels in marketing. Depth channels may involve more personal contact (salespeople or stores), which can provide prospective customers with important details about a product or service, whereas relationship channels such as social media are better used for serving existing customers.

Furthermore, even when businesses do not use in-person channels for some forms of information, it is possible that "richer" communication channels may be beneficial for topics requiring trust. For example, the Webroot Ambassador Program provided online video testimonials from satisfied anti-virus software customers. Pages that included these video testimonials had conversion rates three times higher than those that did not (Elliott, 2013b).

Friendship and Self-Disclosure in Media Choice

Studies of online communication have examined what information people choose to share online and what kinds of reactions others have to the shared information. To explore this question, we conducted a survey with undergraduate and adult Facebook users, and asked them a variety of questions about their expectations and experiences on the site. We were particularly interested in individuals' expectations about the types of information that it was appropriate to share on a relatively public forum such as a social media website, as well as their expectations about whether shared information requires a response.

The ability to share information in such a public arena raises questions about how it affects both the sender and receiver of that information. For the sender: do they expect a response when sharing important information, and what will happen if they don't receive a response? For the receiver: how will they feel about finding out about an important event in a friend's life in this public way, as opposed to more privately? Our results showed that most senders do not expect a response when sharing important information, but that a sizable minority of users do expect a response. This makes it possible that there could be a scenario where someone shares important information and expects responses, but does not get many because his/her friends don't think it necessary to respond. This mismatch between expectations and responses could have negative interpersonal consequences.

Although there may be some ambiguity about whether one should respond to a friend's post, there is likely less social pressure to respond to a post from a company or brand page. However, De Vries, Gensler, and Leeflang (2012) find that more interactive brand posts, such as asking a question, increase the number of comments on that post. Companies that wish to increase customer engagement with their brand "fan" pages can create posts that explicitly invite engagement to increase consumer participation.

On the other side, how do receivers feel when finding out important information about a friend over Facebook? We asked users how they would feel about finding out about a friend's break-up over Facebook. Many users reported that they had been upset in the past when finding out this information publicly over Facebook, in large part because they were hurt that their friend did not tell them personally or privately before posting the information to Facebook. If the information had been disclosed privately first, presumably it would have brought the friends closer together; instead, it pushed them apart by equating a more personal connection with any of the hundreds of Facebook "friendships" a person might have. Finding out personal information about a friend on a social media site appeared to create a perception that the friendship was not as close or important as the individual assumed.

These results make it clear that the channel used in sharing information on Facebook makes a difference in the impact of that information. If it is shared privately, it most likely results in mutual self-disclosure and helps friends feel closer to one another. If instead it is shared publicly first, it could actually hurt the closeness of a relationship by equating close friends with distant acquaintances for self-disclosure purposes.

Public Versus Private Facebook Messages

We tested this comparison between public and private messages more directly in a field study. In this study, undergraduates were randomly assigned to communicate with a small group of their classmates either through private messages or through public postings (status updates) on Facebook. We requested that participants send or post two messages/status updates each week during the study period, but we did not provide any restrictions on the kind of content that should be shared (nor did we track the content of the messages, due to privacy concerns). Beyond these instructions, participants were free to use Facebook as they normally would. Thus, the manipulation was intended to create a minimum baseline of either private or public Facebook communication.

At the end of the study, participants completed measures of liking and interpersonal closeness for each person with whom they had communicated. The experiment found that, as predicted, people who regularly sent private Facebook messages to new acquaintances over a three-month period were then more liked than people who did not. This implies that, in the forming of a new friendship, directed, personal correspondence is a more effective way of using Facebook than entirely public communication.

It is possible that the study conditions created a confound, in that the private messages could have contained more personal information than the public status updates. However, given that the participants were initially sending private messages to near strangers, it is unlikely these messages contained extensive personal information. However, future research is required to examine the possibility that private messages evoked more self-disclosure or otherwise differed in important ways from the status updates.

Although messages from companies do not necessarily attempt to establish an interpersonal relationship, marketers often do hope to create connections between brands and individuals. An interesting question for future research is whether the kind of exclusivity that showed benefits in an interpersonal context would also be beneficial for consumer-oriented communications.

Word of Mouth Communication

Barasch and Berger (2014) have investigated a similar issue in the context of word of mouth communication. They have drawn a distinction between broadcasting, sharing with multiple people at once, and what they term "narrowcasting," or communicating with only a single person. Their results suggest that communicating with a larger audience leads to a focus on self-presentation. In contrast, communicating with a single other person leads to a focus on that individual. Therefore, individuals who are broadcasting information on social media are more likely to select information that shows them in a positive light, whereas individuals who are communicating with just one other individual are more likely to share information that would be useful to the other person.

There are some products and causes that people are proud to support, and organizations can use this positive identification to encourage social media outreach. For example, one of the winners of the Forrester Groundswell Awards (which recognize excellence in social media marketing) in 2013 was the #makebetterhappen City Year campaign. City Year recruits young adults to teach at-risk students. They encouraged their existing members to help spread the word about the program on social networks, which led to substantial activity on Twitter. This campaign nearly doubled awareness of the program among college students, and dramatically increased the number of students who said they had applied or planned to apply (Elliott, 2013b). Furthermore, a product or organization does not have to be explicitly prosocial to gain these benefits. Another Groundswell award-winner, Dr. Pepper's "Pepper lifestyle" Facebook campaign, celebrated the "uniqueness" of Dr. Pepper fans. By highlighting the distinctiveness of Dr. Pepper drinkers, the campaign increased both social media engagement (Facebook fans) and product purchases.

The above examples show the success of broadcasting; however, marketers can also take advantage of narrowcasting. An eMarketer (2012) report found that emails with discounts were shared most often. These kinds of shared emails are potentially valuable to the recipient, which likely increases sharing, and that also helps to increase the reach of the brand.

In addition to the size of the audience, the composition of the audience and the affordances of the particular social network site may also affect what kinds of information people decide to share on social media. For example, most people's Facebook network primarily consists of individuals that they know personally, whereas on Twitter, individuals' messages may go out to a large number of strangers. Research suggests that the type of brand-related user-generated content varies across Twitter, Facebook, and YouTube. For example, YouTube postings tend to focus more on the user than the brand (Smith, Fischer, & Yongjian, 2012). Additional research is needed to determine how people's perception of these different kinds of audiences may affect the information that they feel is appropriate to share or receive over these different forms of social media.

Berger and Iyengar (2013) have also investigated differences between oral and written communication channels. Similar to the processes involved in broadcasting discussed above, written communication also appears to evoke self-presentational concerns. In this research, individuals who used written communication (typing, texting) were more likely that those who used spoken communication to focus on more interesting products and brands. Interesting is defined as novel, exciting, or surprising (e.g., Silvia, 2008), and pretests revealed substantial agreement among consumers about what brands were interesting (e.g., iPhones were considered more interesting than toothpaste). Therefore, some brands may be better positioned for social media success than others. Indeed, research suggests that viral marketing or online social sharing campaigns do not work well for utilitarian products (Schulze, Schöler, & Skiera, 2014).

These results suggest that social media messages about products may be influenced by more than just consumers' opinions about the products. Consumers have different motivations to share product information on social media, and creating products or messages that will make individuals "look good" to their peer group may be an effective way of increasing the reach of a brand's social media message.

Consumers and Social Media

Although the studies discussed above focus primarily on interpersonal uses of social media (communication between friends or acquaintances), some of the same underlying principles likely apply to consumer or business contexts. The choice of communication medium may have implications that go beyond the content of the message itself. In particular, marketing companies may wish to be aware of when it is appropriate to send a message through a mass broadcast channel, and when they may want to enhance the perceived exclusivity of the message. For example, in a fundraising context, it may be appropriate to contact large donors with individual messages or in-person updates about the latest news from the organization; similarly, a company may want to announce particular sales or new products to existing customers before announcing the news more widely through social media. Indeed, an analysis of the strategies used by top social media brands suggested that exclusivity appeals (along with image appeals and incentives) led to greater numbers of Facebook fans (Ashley & Tuten, 2015). Furthermore, one survey suggested that the most frequent motivation for following a brand on Facebook was to be notified of special offers (Lake, 2011).

These findings are consistent with commodity theory and scarcity theory (e.g., Brock, 1968; Lynn, 1991), which states that individuals value opportunities that are scarce or decreasing. Messages that are only available to a select group of consumers may draw more attention and action, in part because they seem more valuable to customers. As Brock (1968) noted, possessing scarce commodities (including information), may create a sense of personal distinctiveness or uniqueness. This exclusivity may also help increase the sense of connection and loyalty between the customer and the brand.

Furthermore, consumers may have different motivations for engaging with a brand's social media presence. Researchers have drawn a distinction between "rational" motivations, such as information seeking, and "emotional" motivations, in which consumers seek to make social connections with others or with the brand (e.g., Krishnamurthy & Dou, 2008). The kinds of processes we are discussing here may be more relevant in situations where consumers have emotional motivations for engaging with corporate social media (for example, cases in which a brand has developed a fan base). If individuals are simply using social media to find out information about a business or product (e.g., checking a Facebook page to find out the opening hours for a restaurant), the psychological processes of relationship valuation and scarcity may not be relevant.

The findings from the Facebook survey about the norms of responsiveness in interpersonal relationships can also apply to business and marketing contexts. If companies have a social media presence, consumers are likely to use that social media site to communicate praise or problems to the company. If the site is not well-monitored, customers are likely to feel that their input is being ignored, which can have even stronger negative consequences for the company or brand. For example, in 2013, both American Airlines and Bank of America came under fire for using an automated service to reply to messages on their Twitter accounts, leading to responses that appeared inappropriate or insensitive.

An additional complexity in the marketing domain is that individuals may see some forms of advertising as inappropriate for social media contexts; if individuals believe that Facebook is for communicating with their friends, they may be annoyed at seeing advertising as part of their newsfeed. The ability to opt in or opt out of seeing such advertisements may play an important role in the acceptance of the ads and products. Furthermore, the presence of these kinds of norms suggests that companies should use caution in choosing which social media platforms are appropriate for different types of communications.

Perceptions of Online Media

We have discussed the possibility of individuals having different reactions to the same approach—some expecting responses on Facebook, while others do not; some viewing Facebook as a platform for personal communication and thus rejecting ads, while others see a wider and different range of uses. Indeed, research examining attitudes toward computer-mediated communication has found varying perceptions of even the most basic qualities of new media. Schriffin, Edelman, Falkenstern, and Stewart (2010) compared computer-mediated communication to face-to-face communication; they found that participants considered computer-mediated communication less useful for exchanging information, less useful for getting work done, less enjoyable, less suitable for building relationships and improving emotional closeness, and less useful for making future plans. On a personal level, computer-mediated communication is still perceived by most individuals as inferior to face-to-face communication (Baym, Zhang & Lin, 2004; Schriffin, Edelman, Falkenstern & Stewart, 2010; Peter & Valkenburg, 2006).

However, Peter and Valkenburg (2006) found that certain young and socially anxious adolescents actually perceived Internet communication as broader, deeper, and more reciprocal than face-to-face communication. Therefore, media choice may not be solely related to concrete features such as number of channels or cues, or even socially constructed factors such as audience or importance of the message; personality factors and demographics may further complicate this picture. Given this potential for variable attitudes toward different media, understanding when and for whom Internet communication can be impactful is an important research question.

Although this question was initially explored in the domain of interpersonal relationships, it is highly relevant for marketing as well. Many social media marketing campaigns rely on user participation: individuals "liking" pages, sharing content, or creating content are an essential part of many brand-promotion efforts. Many marketers emphasize the importance of online word of mouth, and depend on individuals' existing online social networks to spread the word about a product, service, or initiative (Kimmel & Kitchen, 2014). Individual differences in the perception of these online relationships may influence the success of such efforts.

Perceived Reality of Online Interactions

Two basic camps have dominated research on the social effects of the Internet: the idea that the Internet leads to social disconnection, perhaps by displacing in-person ties, and the idea that the Internet is a promising arena for social connection (see Katz, Rice & Aspden, 2001, for an in-depth discussion of both perspectives). The first and earliest approach considered social Internet use as an essentially negative phenomenon, highlighting consequences that seemed to lead to social isolation and unhappiness; the second approach highlighted the Internet's potential to instead bring people closer together and contribute to their well-being.

This dichotomy persists in some fields to this day; however, a growing body of research has already suggested that a more nuanced view of online social interaction better captures reality. Online social interaction can be a force for connection or disconnection, depending on how one uses it. This leads to two further questions: what behaviors or methods of use make the difference, and who is more or less likely to engage in them?

The science of attitudes offers a compelling answer to both questions. Negative attitudes toward online social interactions are widespread (Schriffin, Edelman, Falkenstern & Stewart, 2010). However, online interactions often have the benefits of immediate gratification, reduced effort, and decreased interpersonal risk (Green & Brock, 2008; McKenna & Bargh, 1999, 2000). Given these benefits, it is perhaps unsurprising that some individuals (as discussed earlier) do in fact value online interactions as much or even more so than face-to-face contact. Therefore, we have proposed that there is a continuum of attitudes toward the value of online social contact. We define this concept as 'the perceived reality of online interactions,' or the extent to which an individual believes that online social interactions are suitable for the maintenance and formation of close relationships (Clark & Green, 2013). The term reality is used in this context to map onto a common layperson's definition: online interactions or relationships are often referred to as "not real."

The perceived reality of online interactions is proposed to drive the outcomes of online social interaction. Individuals who are high in perceived reality will approach online social interaction believing that it is possible to create or maintain a relationship via computer-mediated communication. As such, they will engage in relationship-building behaviors, and will reap benefits in closeness and relationship strength from their online interactions. Individuals who are low in perceived reality may avoid online social interaction, or may simply feel that it is best used for more utilitarian sorts of communication. As such, they will not invest effort in relationship-building behaviors, and gain very little from online social interaction.

We tested these ideas in samples of undergraduate students and adults recruited from Amazon's Mechanical Turk. We measured participants' perceived reality with statements such as, "I feel that online relationships can be as meaningful as relationships conducted face-to-face" and "I feel that online relationships can be an important part of someone's social network." We also attempted to manipulate individuals' levels of perceived reality; specifically, we provided individuals with fictitious scientific articles on the positive and negative aspects of online interaction in an effort to shift their views. However, perceived reality appears to be a more stable individual difference that is somewhat difficult to reliably change in experimental contexts.

In a first study, perceived reality was a predictor of social support from online relationships. In a second study, examining the correlations with individuals' self-reported levels of perceived reality, we found that perceived reality has a significant effect on expected positive outcomes of an online interaction, an effect that is mediated through willingness to provide social support and willingness to self-disclose; in other terms, individuals high in perceived reality are indeed more willing to perform affiliative behaviors in an online interaction, which in turn increases their expectations of positive outcomes post-interaction. Moreover, these effects held only for online interactions; perceived reality did not influence affiliative behaviors or expectation of positive outcomes in a face-to-face interaction, further confirming its hypothesized role as an attitude toward online interactions.

Perceived Reality of Online Interactions and Consumer Behavior

Although the current perceived reality studies focus on specifically interpersonal and relationship contexts, it is possible that perceived reality can also play a role in consumer contexts. Individuals high in perceived reality are likely to represent a highly technologically savvy population, one that can be reached more easily by Internet-based advertising and appeals than more conventional media. For example, it may be that individuals higher in perceived reality put more weight on online reviews or testimonials than individuals who are lower in perceived reality.

Additionally, individuals high in perceived reality may draw different signals from medium choice than individuals low in perceived reality; if one believes that online social interaction is no less "real" than other forms of interaction, there may be no perceived slight in communicating through online media. Certain individuals, in fact, may even prefer online social interaction to face-to-face (Caplan, 2003). Reaching out to these individuals through mediated channels may be the most effective method.

It remains an empirical question whether perceived reality can also affect how individuals perceive online messages from businesses (and if so, whether particular types of messages are influenced more than others). However, some highly acclaimed social media marketing campaigns rely on personal engagement with consumers. For example, Proctor and Gamble solicited stories about mothers' roles in the lives of child athletes for their "Thanks, Mom" campaign during the 2012 Olympic Games (Ashley & Tuten, 2015; Berkowitz, 2012). These stories were shared through social networks (as well as through more traditional commercials). This campaign is centered on a human connection; it is possible that individuals high in perceived reality were more likely to feel that connection and thus be influenced by the messages.

Conclusion

The social media landscape is constantly changing, with new services and platforms arising and others fading away (e.g., Hoffman & Novak, 2011). Nonetheless, it appears likely that some form of social media will remain an important part of business and interpersonal communication for the foreseeable future.

Social media provides exciting opportunities for marketers and businesses, but the research reviewed here suggests that these opportunities must be approached with caution. The type of communication medium can send its own message above and beyond the content of a persuasive appeal, and choosing the right medium for a particular message can be an important determinant of effectiveness. Furthermore, there may be important individual differences that affect whether individuals are likely to respond to messages conveyed through social media; for some individuals, other platforms may be a better choice.

References

Ashley, C., & Tuten, T. (2015). Creative strategies in social media marketing: An exploratory study of branded social content and consumer engagement. *Psychology & Marketing, 32*(1), 15–27. doi:10.1002/mar.20761

Barasch, A., & Berger, J. (2014). Broadcasting and narrowcasting: How audience size affects what people share. *Journal of Marketing Research (JMR), 51*(3), 286–299. doi:10.1509/jmr.13.0238

Baym, N.K., Zhang, Y.B., & Lin, M.C. (2004). Social interactions across media interpersonal communication on the Internet, telephone and face-to-face. *New Media & Society, 6*(3), 299–318.

Berger, J., & Iyengar, R. (2013). Communication channels and word of mouth: How the medium shapes the message. *Journal of Consumer Research, 40*(3), 567–579. doi:10.1086/671345

Berkowitz, J. (2012). P&G salutes mothers in 2012 Olympics campaign. Fast Company Co-Create. Retrieved from www.fastcocreate.com/1680577/pg-salutes-mothersin-2012-olympics-campaign.

Brock, T.C. (1968). Implications of commodity theory for value change. In A.G. Greenwald, T.C. Brock, & T.M. Ostrom (Eds.), *Psychological foundations of attitudes* (pp. 243–275). New York: Academic Press.

Caplan, S.E. (2003). Preference for online social interaction a theory of problematic Internet use and psychosocial well-being. *Communication Research, 30*(6), 625–648.

Clark, J. M., & Green, M. C. (2013). Making "real" connections: The perceived reality of online interactions. *International Journal of Interactive Communication Systems and Technologies, 3*(1), 1–19.

Culnan, M., & Markus, M.L. (1987). Information technologies. In F.M. Jablin, L.L. Putnam, K.H. Roberts, & L.W. Porter (Eds.), *Handbook of organizational communication: An interdisciplinary perspective* (pp. 420–444). Newbury Park, CA: Sage.

de Vries, L., Gensler, S., & Leeflang, P.S. (2012). Popularity of brand posts on brand fan pages: An investigation of the effects of social media marketing. *Journal of Interactive Marketing, 26*(2), 83–91.

Elliott, N. (2013a). The funnel we need: Follow customers as they actually behave. *Ad Age,* Retrieved from http://adage.com/article/cmo-strategy/follow-a-customer-s-journey-behaves/239296/

Elliott, N. (2013b). Winners of the 2013 Forrester Groundswell Awards. http://blogs.forrester.com/nate_elliott/13–11–05- winners_of_the_2013_forrester_groundswell_awards

eMarketer (2012). Emails with discounts shared most often. Retrieved from www.emarketer.com/Article.aspx?id=1008868&R=1008868

Fulk, J. (1993). Social construction of communication technology. *Academy of Management Journal, 36*(5), 921–950.

Fulk, J., Schmitz, J., & Steinfield, C. W. (1990). A social influence model of technology use. In J. Fulk & C. Steinfield (Eds.), *Organizations and communication technology* (pp. 117–140). Newbury Park, CA: Sage.

Green, M. C., & Brock, T. (2008). Antecedents and consequences of choosing real versus ersatz social activities. *Media Psychology, 11*(4), 566–592.

Hoffman, D. L., & Novak, T. P (2011). Marketing communication in a digital era. *Marketing Management, 20*(3), 37–42.

Joinson, A. (2001). Self-disclosure in computer-mediated communication: The role of self-awareness and visual anonymity. *European Journal of Social Psychology, 31,* 177–192.

Katz, J. E., Rice, R. E., & Aspden, P. (2001). The Internet, 1995–2000 access, civic involvement, and social interaction. *American Behavioral Scientist, 45*(3), 405–419.

Kimmel, A. J., & Kitchen, P. J. (2014). WOM and social media: Presaging future directions for research and practice. *Journal of Marketing Communications, 20*(1–2), 5–20.

Krishnamurthy, S., & Dou, W. (2008). Advertising with user-generated content: A framework and research agenda. *Journal of Interactive Advertising, 8,* 1–7.

Lake, C. (2011). Why do people follow brands on Facebook? Econsultancy.com. Retrieved from https://econsultancy.com/blog/7136-why-do-people-follow-brands-on-facebook

Lynn, M. (1991). Scarcity effects on value: A quantitative review of the commodity theory literature. *Psychology & Marketing, 8*(1), 43–57.

Markus, M. (1994). Finding a happy medium: Explaining the negative effects of electronic communication on social life at work. *AMC Transactions on Information Systems, 12,* 119–149.

McKenna, K.Y.A., & Bargh, J. A. (1999). Causes and consequences of social interaction on the Internet: A conceptual framework. *Media Psychology, 1,* 249–269.

McKenna, K.Y.A., & Bargh, J. A. (2000). Plan 9 from cyberspace: The implications of the Internet for personality and social psychology. *Personality and Social Psychology Review, 4,* 57–75.

O'Sullivan, P. (2000). What you don't know won't hurt me: Impression management functions of communication channels in relationships. *Human Communication Research, 26,* 403–431.

Peter, J., & Valkenburg, P. M. (2006). Research note: Individual differences in perceptions of Internet communication. *European Journal of Communication, 21*(2), 213–226.

Rice, R. E. (1993). Media appropriateness. *Human Communication Research, 19*(4), 451–484.

Schiffrin, H., Edelman, A., Falkenstern, M., & Stewart, C. (2010). The associations among computer-mediated communication, relationships, and well-being. *Cyberpsychology, Behavior, and Social Networking, 13*(3), 299–306.

Schulze, C., Schöler, L., & Skiera, B. (2014). Not all fun and games: Viral marketing for utilitarian products. *Journal of Marketing, 78*(1), 1–19.

Schwämmlein, E., & Wodzicki, K. (2012). What to tell about me? Self-presentation in online communities. *Journal of Computer-Mediated Communication, 17*(4), 387–407.

Short, J., Williams, E., & Christie, B. (1976). *The social psychology of telecommunications.* London: John Wiley and Sons Ltd.

Silvia, P. J. (2008). Interest—The curious emotion. *Current Directions in Psychological Science, 17*(1), 57–60.

Smith, A. N., Fischer, E., & Yongjian, C. (2012). How does brand-related user-generated content differ across YouTube, Facebook, and Twitter? *Journal of Interactive Marketing, 26*(2), 102–113.

Steinfield, C., & Fulk, J. (1987). On the role of theory in research on information technology in organizations: An introduction to the special issue. *Communication Research, 14*(5), 479–490.

Trevino, L. K., Lengel, R. H., & Daft, R. L. (1987). Media symbolism, media richness, and media choice in organizations: A symbolic interactionist perspective. *Communication Research, 14*(5), 553–574.

Treviño, L. K., Webster, J., & Stein, E. W. (2000). Making connections: Complementary influences on communication media choices, attitudes, and use. *Organization Science, 11*(2), 163–182.

Tucker, C. E. (2014). Social networks, personalized advertising, and privacy controls. *Journal of Marketing Research, 51*(5), 546–562.

Utz, S. (2007). Media use in long-distance friendships. *Information, Communication & Society, 10*(5), 694–713.

Walther, J. B. (1992). Interpersonal effects in computer-mediated interaction a relational perspective. *Communication Research, 19*(1), 52–90.

Walther, J. B. (2007). Selective self-presentation in computer-mediated communication: Hyperpersonal dimensions of technology, language, and cognition. *Computers in Human Behavior, 23*(5), 2538–2557.

Walther, J. B., & D'Addario, K. P. (2001). The impacts of emoticons on message interpretation in computer-mediated communication. *Social Science Computer Review, 19*(3), 324–347.

Walther, J. B., & Tidwell, L. C. (1995). Nonverbal cues in computer-mediated communication, and the effect of chronemics on relational communication. *Journal of Organizational Computing and Electronic Commerce, 5*(4), 355–378.

10

TO FORWARD OR NOT

Consumer Response to Brand Crises in the Context of Micro Blogs

Richard F. Yalch and Xi Chen

Introduction

On March 15, 2013 (International Consumers' Day in China), Apple was accused by CCTV, China's biggest TV network, of having a discriminative customer service policy against China. Soon thereafter, the mainstream Chinese newspaper *People's Daily* blamed Apple for being "dishonest, greedy and arrogant." Although Apple ultimately apologized, many Chinese consumers of Apple products seemed not to agree with the Chinese media's anti-Apple criticisms and posted their disagreeing opinions on *Sina Weibo*, a micro blogging platform much like Twitter. For instance, one "Apple-attack" message that was originally posted on CCTV's official account was forwarded more than 4,650 times with reviews containing a variety of different opinions towards Apple and CCTV. Many of those individuals who supported Apple argued that the media attack was a farce as the problem Apple was being accused of was actually not a big deal, whereas others agreed that Apple should have done better with their after-sale service. The Apple controversy continued as a heated argument on *Sina Weibo* between Apple fans and enemies with neither side able to convince the other of the validity of their viewpoint.

The above Apple case suggested two research questions: (1) In the context of social media such as on micro blogs, what factors motivate consumers to forward or not forward a message critical of popular brand and (2) whether the reluctance of some brand loyal consumers to forward unfavorable information about a brand to which they feel committed might be overcome by information reminding them of a self-enhancing benefit that arises from informing other consumers of the potential harmful consequences they will experience if they consume the brand?

In his recent comprehensive review of word of mouth and interpersonal communication research, Berger (2014) suggests that decisions to engage in such communications are largely driven by self-concerns (p. 588). Specifically he proposes that consumers use social media to manage how others see them, to regulate their own emotions, to acquire information, to enhance social bonding and to persuade others. In some cases, consumers face conflicts between these objectives. In the Apple example described above, a loyal Apple user's decision to inform friends and others of the issue may help these individuals avoid a problem with Apple if the information turns out to be accurate but also suggests that the Apple user's loyalty to Apple was not justified. Thus, the consumers must cope with the dissonance-causing conflict between the desire to maintain a favorable self-impression of being a user of Apple products with an obligation to protect fellow consumers from avoidable problems. As noted by Chung and Darke (2006), a variety of individual and cultural considerations underlie many such social media decisions.

In this chapter, we examine the decision to forward positive and negative brand information using social media. First, we look at effect of the valence of the information in combination with the consumer's expressed commitment to the brand. Although much research suggests that negative information is considered more relevant to decision making than positive information (referred to as a negativity bias, e.g., Fiske, 1980), other research that we review indicates that this effect is moderated by a consumer's brand commitment. Next, we examine how high and low commitment consumers deal with negative information when they are made aware of the importance of sharing information with others. The relevant question is whether making this obligation salient increases the forwarding of all negative information or only negative information that is perceived as highly consequential. The chapter concludes with a discussion of the implications for the dissemination of brand crisis information.

Theoretical Framework

Negative Publicity and Brand Commitment of Consumers

The negativity effect is a robust finding in the impression formation literature and is usually stated as the tendency of individuals to place more weight on negative than positive information in forming overall evaluations of a target (Fiske, 1980; Klein, 1996; Skowronski & Carlston, 1989). This effect has been found in product evaluation contexts as well (e.g., Herr, Kardes, & Kim, 1991; Wright, 1974). Consumer research has extended the initial findings regarding the negativity effect to include the effect of consumers' prior attitudes. Consumers often become attached to various brands and form "relationships" with them (Fournier, 1998), which results in brand equity (e.g., Keller, 1993) and various types of brand loyalty. Consumers can differ in the strength of their attitude toward a brand, with stronger attitudes resulting in greater resistance to negative information (e.g., Petty & Krosnick, 1995). It is also related to one's level of knowledge as those with greater knowledge are likely to have stronger attitudes and be more resistant to change (Wood, Rhodes, & Bick, 1995). One aspect of attitude strength is brand commitment (Krosnick et al., 1993; Pomerantz, Chaiken, & Tordesillas, 1995), which has been found to play a significant moderating role in the negative publicity effect (Ahluwalia, Burnkrant, & Unnava, 2000). Commitment is generally defined as an emotional or psychological attachment to a brand within a product class (Lastovicka & Gardener, 1978).

Brand commitment has been found to have a moderating role on the negativity effect. Ahluwalia, et al.'s (2000) research indicated that low-commitment consumers exhibit a greater amount of attitude change in response to negative than positive information, whereas high-commitment consumers do not; in other words, the negativity effect only emerged when consumers' commitment toward the brand was low. The authors attributed this effect to low-commitment consumers processing negative information more objectively, whereas high-commitment consumers engaged in biased information processing.

We propose a similar difference between high and low brand commitment consumers when it comes to their forwarding behavior in the context of social media information that they might share in micro blogs. Forwarding allows consumers to express their opinions or attitudes towards the brand publicly much as they do when posting their thoughts or reviewing products based on their experiences. A difference, however, is that forwarding a message maintains the original source of the information as well as a link to themselves. When people simply forward a message without adding their own thoughts, the forwarding behavior might be seen as a passive agreement with or even an endorsement of the views expressed in the original message. However, forwarding without comment remains ambiguous as it implies only a vague expression of consumers' attitude (an act of omission) as opposed to an expressed comment of agreement (an act of commission). Reactions vary between acts of omission and commission depending on perceptions of individual and group behavior regarding actions and inactions (Baron & Ritov, 2004).

When negative messages are forwarded through the social networks of forwarders on micro blogs, the crisis-related information can diffuse widely in a short time period and cause much damage to a brand. For those consumers with a high level of commitment toward a brand, their forwarding of negative information is likely to suggest that their commitment was unwise, potentially causing others to question their judgment. On the other hand, forwarding favorable brand information is likely to enhance their standing among their social contacts by making them aware of the consumer's smart buying decisions. For example, Wojnicki and Godes (2011) found that restaurant reviewers tended to report positive experiences to reinforce the impression that they were knowledgeable about finding good places to eat. Consequently, high-commitment consumers should be reluctant to forward negative information but anxious to forward favorable information about their brand.

Conversely, low-commitment consumers may not have such ego-related considerations and be more objective in processing and circulating brand-related information on social media. Assuming their desire is to inform and persuade their fellow consumers about good and bad products in order to be viewed as a reliable source of information, we expect to find low brand commitment consumers to exhibit a negativity bias. For example, Amabile (1983) reported that negative book reviewers were viewed as more intelligent, competent and expert than positive reviewers. Similarly, Schlosser (2005) reported that individuals who posted information on message boards adjusted their public attitudes downwards to present themselves as more discriminating. Because low-commitment individuals are unlikely to take ownership for the brand (as would high-commitment consumers), we expect them to be more likely to forward negative information than positive information because it will have a greater effect on the receiver of the information and may create a more favorable impression of them.

Attitudinal Effects and Hypotheses

In addition to examining forwarding decisions, we were also interested in how brand commitment affects reactions to positive and negative brand information. Based on Ahluwalia et al.'s (2000) findings, we proposed that consumers' attitudes would be affected by their brand commitment. When exposed to either positive or negative brand information, low-commitment consumers should change their attitude toward the target brand consistent with the valence of the information. On the other hand, high-commitment consumers' attitudes were expected to be affected only by the positive information. High-commitment individuals resist change in response to negative information and can evoke several strategies for resisting efforts to undermine their brand commitment (Ahluwalia, 2000). Our formal hypotheses were thus:

H1: Brand commitment will moderate the willingness to forward positive and negative brand information such that:

H1a: Low-commitment consumers will be more willingly to forward a message with negative information than positive information (i.e. the negativity effect).

H1b: High-commitment consumers are more likely to forward a message with positive information than negative information.

H2: Consumer's attitude change will vary with their brand commitment, such that:

H2a: Low brand commitment consumers' attitudes will change in a direction consistent with whether the message contains positive or negative brand information.

H2b: High brand commitment individuals' attitudes will change only when the information is positive toward their brand.

Experiment 1

Method

Participants and Experimental Design. Eighty Chinese undergraduate and graduate students who identified themselves as a micro blog user were recruited to participate in the study. The experiment used a 2 (consumer commitment toward the target brand: high and low) × 2 (valence of brand message: positive and negative) between-subjects design with commitment as a measured variable and message valence as a manipulated variable. A fast food brand, *Little Sheep Hot Pot*, was selected as the target brand because participants in the subject pool were quite familiar with the brand and its product category. Given the many brands of fast food in China, we expected that these consumers would vary meaningfully in their level of commitment toward this brand.

Independent Variables and Stimuli. Brand commitment was measured with the three-item brand commitment scale ($\alpha = .88$) proposed and tested by Beatty, Kahle and Holmes (1988). In addition, a closely associated variable—involvement—was also tested by a three-item scale ($\alpha = .89$) (Betty et al., 1988) and used a control for the potential influence of differences in category involvement.

Negative and positive messages were carefully developed in several pretests. Both versions of messages described food safety issues at the target brand. The negative message argued that *Little Sheep Hot Pot* was exposed as having a food safety problem—using dirty rat meat instead of mutton, which is a main ingredient of their food. The positive message praised the brand for maintaining a high level of food safety throughout its operations. In a pretest, 160 subjects were recruited and randomly assigned to read either the positive or negative message about an unidentified brand and then asked to respond to the question: "Is the presented message favorable or unfavorable toward the target brand?" Of those who read the negative message, 93.8% considered it to be unfavorable toward the brand, whereas 96.2% of those who read the positive message considered it to be favorable toward the brand. These results support the conclusion that a meaningful difference existed in the valence of the two messages.

Dependent Variables. Attitude toward the target brand was measured twice using four nine-point semantic differential scales (good/bad, beneficial/harmful, desirable/undesirable, and nice/awful), once before and once again after reading the message to assess the extent to which each message changed the subject's attitude. Using these measures ($\alpha_{previous} = .92$; $\alpha_{post} = .96$), a before message mean attitude score and a post one were computed. In both cases, higher numbers reflected a more favorable attitude toward the target brand.

In order to measure willingness to forward the message, subjects were asked to respond to three items using a 9-point scale ($\alpha = .94$). The items included "how much are you willing to forward the target message publicly?" "how much would you like to forward the target message in a public way?" and "how much are you unwilling to forward the target message in a public way?" The latter item was reversed scored.

Procedure. All 80 subjects responded to an online questionnaire that included among other questions measures of their commitment, involvement and previous attitude toward the target brand or product category before reading one of the test messages. Then, subjects were randomly presented with either the negative message or positive message. Their post attitude toward the target brand was measured after they read the messages as well as their willingness to forward the message, and why they would or would not forward it.

Results

Consumers' forwarding willingness. A regression analysis with willingness to forward the message as the dependent variable and the valence of the message (negative = 0 and positive = 1), the continuous measure of consumer's brand commitment and their interaction as independent variables, and the product involvement measure as a control variable revealed a significant main effect for valence (*std* $\beta = -1.29$; $t = -2.83$; $p < .01$), qualified by a significant two-way interaction between the valence and the brand commitment (*std* $\beta = 1.42$; $t = 3.12$; $p < .01$). Their willingness to forward was also analyzed using a mean split (mean = 5.38) to create a 2 (commitment: high vs. low) × 2 (valence: negative vs. positive) ANCOVA while controlling for involvement. A significant commitment × valence interaction emerged ($F(1, 34) = 12.12$, $p = .001$). As shown in Figure 10.1, consistent with Hypothesis 1a, low-commitment consumers were significantly more willing to

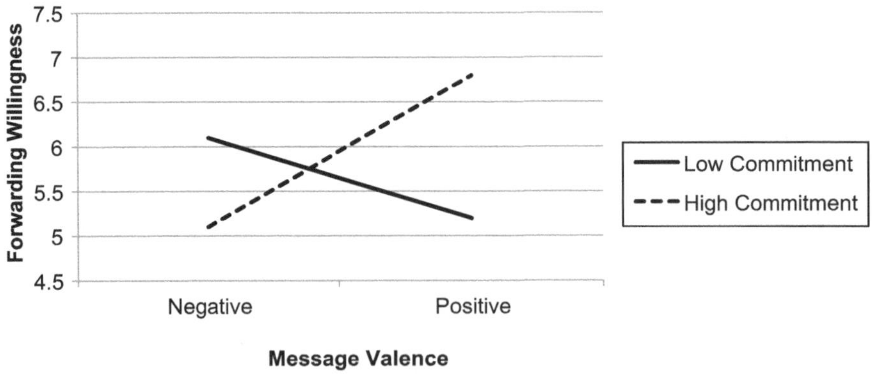

FIGURE 10.1 Interaction of Valence and Commitment on Forwarding Willingness

forward the negative message rather than the positive one toward the target brand, which implies the existence of a negativity effect ($M_{negative} = 6.10$, $M_{positive} = 5.07$; $t = 2.16$, $p < .05$). Also as predicted in Hypothesis 1b, high-commitment consumers did not exhibit greater willingness to forward the negative message. In fact, the negativity effect was reversed for the high-commitment group of consumers. They were significantly more willing to forward the positive message rather than the negative one ($M_{negative} = 5.23$, $M_{positive} = 6.80$; $t = -2.73$, $p = .01$). These results suggest that any negativity effect for the high-commitment group was more than countered by other considerations.

Consumers' attitude change. The analysis used to evaluate the effect of the messages on attitudes employed a procedure commonly used in the persuasion literature (e.g., Tormala, Clarkson, & Petty, 2006; Duhachek, Zhang, & Krishnan, 2007). In this procedure, the post attitude measure is treated as the dependent variable and the pre-exposure measure is used as a control variable or covariate. In the regression analysis, valence of message, brand commitment and their interaction were the independent variables. In contrast to the results for willingness to forward the message, the regression results showed there was a significant main effect for message valence (*std* $\beta = 1.10$; $t = 3.70$; $p < .001$), but no significant interaction between the valence and commitment (*std* $\beta = -.44$; $t = -1.48$; *ns*). No significant interaction was found also when analyzing the post attitude using a mean split of commitment (mean = 5.38) to create a 2 (commitment: high vs. low) × 2 (valence: negative vs. positive) ANCOVA with the pre-exposure attitude measure as the covariate ($F(1, 75) = .16$, *ns*). These results indicate that consumers' attitude change was only affected by the valence of message ($F(1, 75) = 85.46$, $p < .001$), but not the commitment ($F(1, 75) = .003$, *ns*). These results support Hypothesis 2a, predicting an attitude change consistent with message valence for low-commitment consumers but do not support Hypothesis 2 predicting a moderating effect of brand commitment. Further the results do not support Hypothesis 2b predicting that high-commitment individuals would resist changing their attitudes in response to the negative message and do not indicate that low-commitment consumers would be more influenced by the negative message than the positive message.

Discussion

The results of Experiment 1 demonstrate a negativity effect for in the forwarding behavior of low-commitment consumers but not high-commitment consumer. In other words, low-commitment consumers were more willing to forward the negative rather than positive message, whereas high-commitment consumers resisted forwarding a message questioning the safety of a favored brand but were willing to forward the positive message promoting the brand safety reputation.

To explore motivations for these behaviors, the reasons provided by the subjects for their decision to forward or not forward the message were examined.

This somewhat qualitative analysis revealed that 68.33% of those who were willing to forward the message (n = 60) indicated personal reasons for forwarding the original message and with most of these individuals stating that they agreed with the author (*n* = 41). A sizable number (26.7%) gave no reason but just would forward it to someone (*n* = 16). Interestingly, only 5% of the participants indicated that they would forward the message because they did not agree with the author (*n* = 3). This analysis of the forwarding reasons revealed that most people forward messages when they agree with the author of the original message, which is in accord with our assumption that forwarding behavior implies people's agreements with the ideas expressed in the information.

With regard to attitude change in response to positive and negative brand information, the results of the first experiment indicated that attitude change was only affected by the message valence not by commitment. These results are inconsistent with some prior research suggesting that brand commitment moderates reactions to negative publicity (e.g., Ahluwalia et al., 2000). Some differences between the two studies are that Ahluwalia et al.'s prior measure (for their study 1) was taken much farther in advance of message exposure than ours, their target brand (Nike) may have been associated with greater levels of commitment than might occur for a fast food, and importantly the negative information concerned the shock absorbing quality of an athletic shoe compared to food safety.

The inconsistency in our findings with Ahluwalia et al.'s (2000) research suggested to us that the nature of the information in the message may have been an important distinction. Specifically, the inconsistency of results might be due to differences in the diagnosticity of the attribute information discussed in the messages. Diagnosticity refers to "the extent to which a given piece of information discriminates between alternative hypotheses, interpretations or categorizations" (Herr et al., 1991). Information is perceived as diagnostic if it helps consumers assign a product to one and only one cognitive category; otherwise, information that implies multiple possible categorizations is nondiagnostic. In Experiment 1, we used messages about food safety that could be considered to be an extremely diagnostic attribute of a fast food brand. As mentioned by Herr et al. (1991), extremely negative information is much more useful for categorizing a product as low in quality than less negative information. Thus, when exposed to the extremely negative message in Experiment 1, most subjects were likely to be influenced by the implications of a safety warning such that they exhibited a great amount of attitude change irrespective of their commitment toward the brand. In contrast, Ahluwalia et al.'s (2000) experiment used the shock absorption of athletic shoes as the target attribute, which is likely to be perceived as less important for categorizing shoes than food safety is for fast food. In order to test the potential effect of message diagnosticity on attitude change and message forwarding, we decided to manipulate the diagnosticity of the attribute in the original brand message in our second experiment.

In addition, we were curious about the unexpected reactions of the high-commitment individuals in their expressed unwillingness to forward negative information even though this information was influential in altering their attitudes toward the affected brand. In our original thinking, we speculated that high-commitment individuals would refrain from forwarding negative information because it might cause others to question their wisdom in committing to a brand that turned out to be associated with a safety problem (albeit only an alleged problem). In other words, their self-presentation concerns might motivate them to withhold potentially useful information from others that participate in their micro blogs.

Much self-presentation research builds on Goffman's (1959) theories of identity and social performance, which proposes that self-presentation is the intentional and tangible component of identity. In any sort of social interaction, people have the desire to control the impressions that others will form of them (i.e., control how others see them). Goffman (1959) refers to this phenomenon as impression management. Several recent studies show that self-presentation is relevant in explaining people's online behavior. For example, Schlosser (2005) found that posters are more likely to have a negative attitude than lurkers. Further, the self-presentational concerns of posters appear to cause the effect as they are inclined to consider critics as more intelligent, competent and expert (cf., Amabile, 1983). Similarly, Kaplan and Haenlein (2010) proposed that the micro blog world is a highly self-presentation-oriented place when compared with other forms of social media. This body of research suggests that the desire to create a positive self-presentation by providing especially useful information to others might overcome one's reluctance to reveal to others that one should not have been so highly committed to a brand that now appears to be associated with a potentially harmful experience. Thus, in our second study, we looked at individuals' forwarding decisions as they might be affected by both the diagnosticity of the brand information that they are exposed to and by their thoughts regarding the importance of letting others know about this information.

In looking at diagnosticity and concern for others, we also considered that their effects might vary with brand commitment. As low-commitment consumers would not be greatly affected by any prior loyalty or identification with the brand, they should be more objective in processing the brand attack message. However, their willingness to forward the message might still depend on the usefulness of the information, that is, its diagnosticity. If the information is seen as not particularly relevant to most consumers' decisions to consume the brand (low diagnosticity), it is less likely to be forwarded than more critical information (high diagnosticity). Further, because low-commitment individuals are unlikely have self- presentation concerns that forwarding such information might cause others to think that their past decisions to use the questioned brand was unwise, they should not need additional motivation to forward the information. Thus, they should not be affected by a reminder of the value of sharing information with others.

Conversely, high-commitment consumers have an attachment toward the brand that may lead to biased processing of negative messages. This may cause them to dismiss negative information that has low diagnosticity as not worth sharing with others (especially as might cause recipients to question the forwarder's brand commitment). On the other hand, negative information of high diagnosticity may create a conflict between their desire to maintain their favored brand's image and an obligation to inform others of an important consideration when deciding to select the brand. Berger (2014) proposed that possessing useful information often motivates individuals to engage in interpersonal communications. However, Experiment 1 revealed that many high-commitment consumers opted not to forward the information even though it was likely to be of interest to others. To increase the salience of the usefulness of the information, in a second study we added to the brand information a notice to individuals that they would enhance their self-image by providing useful information to others.

The second study thus tested the following hypotheses:

H3: Consumer's attitude change will be affected by the diagnosticity of the message, such that attitude change will be greater in response to a brand attack message with high diagnostic information compared to a message with low diagnostic information.

H4: The forwarding decisions of low-commitment consumers will depend on the diagnosticity and the inclusion of a self-enhancing reminder in the following way: (a) when the message contains high diagnostic information, the inclusion of a self-enhancement reminder has no effect; (b) when the message contains low diagnostic information, the inclusion of a self-enhancement reminder will increase willingness to forward the message.

H5: The forwarding decisions of high-commitment consumers will be affected by the inclusion of a self-enhancing reminder in the brand attack message but only when the message includes highly diagnostic information.

Experiment 2

Method

Participants and Experimental Design. One hundred and sixty Chinese undergraduate and graduate students who indicated that they were micro bloggers were recruited for this study. The experimental design used a 2 (consumer commitment toward the target brand: high and low) × 2 (diagnosticity of attribute information: high and low) × 2 (self-presentation: self- enhancing and control) between-subjects design with commitment as a measured variable and diagnosticity and self-enhancement as manipulated variables. The same fast food brand *Little Sheep Hot Pot* used in Experiment 1 was also used as the target brand in this study.

Independent Variables and Stimuli. Brand commitment was used as a measured variable in this experiment. We applied the same three-item brand commitment scale (α = .90) as in Experiment 1. Involvement was also tested by the same three-item scale (α = .88) and used as a control variable to minimize some external influences unrelated to commitment.

Unlike Experiment 1, we only used negative messages as the brand information stimuli. Messages of high and low diagnosticity were carefully developed in pretests. Following procedures used by Skowronski and Carlston (1987), Herr, Kardes and Kim (1991) and Ahluwalia et al. (2000), we measured the perceived diagnosticity of two different attributes in evaluating a fast food brand—food safety and unfair competitive behavior. In the pretest, 176 students were recruited and asked to estimate the percentages of high- and low-level fast food restaurants likely to have a problem with the target attributes of food safety and unfair competitive behavior. The perceived diagnosticity of each attribute was computed by dividing the perceived probability of a low-level fast food restaurant having a problem with food safety or unfair competitive behavior by the same probability of a high-level restaurant having that problem. The result indicated that when evaluating a fast food brand, food safety was perceived as significantly more diagnostic than unfair competitive behavior ($M_{\text{food safety}}$ = .71, $M_{\text{unfair competition}}$ = .63; t = 6.29, $p < .001$). These results support labeling of the message about food safety as being of high diagnosticity and the message of unfair competitive behavior as being of low diagnosticity.

Self-enhancing and control (no self-enhancing information) messages were also developed using pretests. The self-enhancing messages contained a reminder claim that "you are helping people from being hurt by the bad brand by forwarding this message to them," whereas the control message avoided using such a claim. The 176 subjects were randomly assigned to read either the self-enhancing or not self-enhancing message about an unknown brand and asked to respond whether they considered the message to be self-enhancing. Of those who read the self-enhancing message, 93.2% considered it to be self-enhancing, whereas 90.9% of those who read the not self-enhancing message considered it as not self-enhancing.

Dependent Variables. As in Experiment 1, attitude toward the target brand was measured using four nine-point semantic differential scales (good/bad, beneficial/harmful, desirable/undesirable and nice/awful) before and after the message reading with similarly high reliability (α_{previous} = .93; α_{post} = .99). The means for each attitude scale were computed for each subject. Forwarding willingness was measured on the same three-item scale (α = .93) that was used in Experiment 1.

Procedure. All of the 160 subjects in the second study were asked to respond to a questionnaire that had embedded among other questions measures of their commitment, involvement and pre-exposure attitudes toward the target brand or product category as in Experiment 1. Then, the subjects were randomly assigned to read a message representing one of the four different conditions (high or low diagnosticity and self-enhancing or not self-enhancing reminder). To assess the effects of the messages, subjects' post attitudes toward the target brand were measured after they read the messages. Then, subjects' willingness to forward the message, as well as why they would forward it, were also recorded.

Results

Consumers' attitude change. In order to determine the attitudinal effect of the information varying in diagnosticity without the influence of the self-presentation information, we used only the samples exposed to the messages without the self-enhancing reminder (n = 80). Following a procedure used by Tormala et al. (2006), attitudes were submitted to a 2 (measured time of attitudes: previous vs. post) × 2 (diagnosticity: high vs. low) within- and between-subjects mixed ANOVA. A significant measured time of attitudes × diagnosticity effect emerged ($F(1, 70) = 21.0$, $p < .001$). As shown in Figure 10.2, when the diagnosticity of the message was low, the difference between previous and post attitude was not significant ($M_{previous} = 7.50$, $M_{post} = 7.24$; $t = .97$, *ns*). However, when the message included information with high diagnosticity, the attitude difference was large and the post attitude score was significantly lower than the previous one ($M_{previous} = 6.94$, $M_{post} = 4.05$; $t = 5.66$, $p < .001$). The results implied that consumer's attitude change depended on the diagnosticity of the message, with change only occurring when the diagnosticity of the message was high. Thus, Hypothesis 3 was supported.

Consumers' forwarding willingness. A regression analysis was performed with forwarding willingness as the dependent variable, the continuous measure of brand commitment, the diagnosticity of messages (low diagnosticity: 0 and high diagnosticity: 1), the reminder of the self-enhancing value of informing others(no self-enhancing: 0 and self-enhancing: 1) and their interaction as the independent variables, with product involvement measure as a control variable.

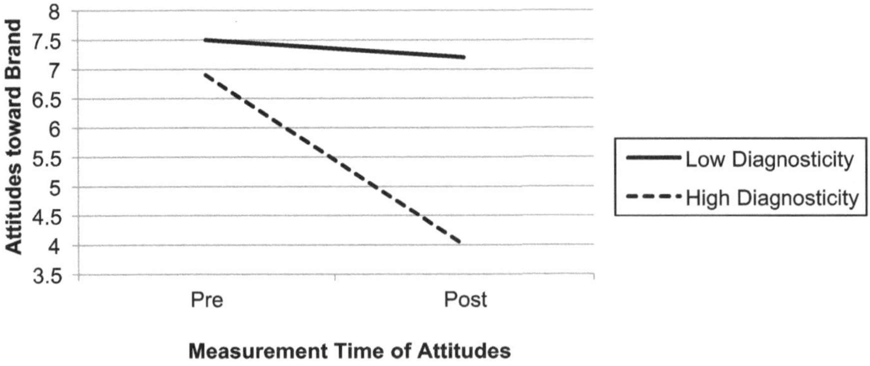

FIGURE 10.2 Interaction of Measurement Time and Diagnosticity on Attitude

The results revealed a significant three-way interaction effect of commitment, diagnosticity and the self-presentation reminder and a significant two-way interaction of diagnosticity and the self-presentation reminder (three-way interaction: *std* $\beta = 1.94$; $t = 3.50$; $p = .001$; two-way interaction: *std* $\beta = -1.69$; $t = -3.08$; $p < .01$). Willingness to forward was also analyzed using dichotomized variable representing high and low commitment based on a split at the mean (5.46) to aid in understanding the effects. This analysis used a 2 (commitment: high vs. low) ×2 (diagnosticity: high vs. low) ×2 (self-presentation: self-enhancing vs. no self-enhancing) ANCOVA while controlling for involvement. In this analysis, the commitment × diagnosticity × self-presentation interaction remained significant ($F(1,148) = 13.59$, $p < .001$).

As shown in Figure 10.3, when the brand attack message is highly diagnostic, whether the consumer is or is not reminded that sharing such information is self-enhancing made no significant difference in the forwarding willingness of low-commitment consumers ($M_{\text{self-enhancing}} = 5.75$, $M_{\text{not-self-enhancing}} = 6.00$; $t = .45$, *ns*). However, when the message was of low diagnosticity, low-commitment consumers were significantly more willing to forward the brand attack message when it include the self-enhancing reminder compared to when it did not ($M_{\text{self-enhancing}} = 5.85$, $M_{\text{not-self-enhancing}} = 4.65$; $t = -2.88$, $p < .01$). This indicates that a reminder of the self-enhancement associated with sharing information can act as an alternative motivation to forward brand attack information when the consumer's objective determination of the usefulness of the information to others may be low. Both Hypothesis 4a and 4b were supported by these results.

Hypothesis 5 predicted that when the brand attack message includes a self-enhancing reminder of the value of sharing information, high-commitment consumers will exhibit a greater willingness to forward the high-diagnostic message. A comparison of the willingness to forward the message with high-diagnostic information revealed that it was greater than that for the low-diagnostic

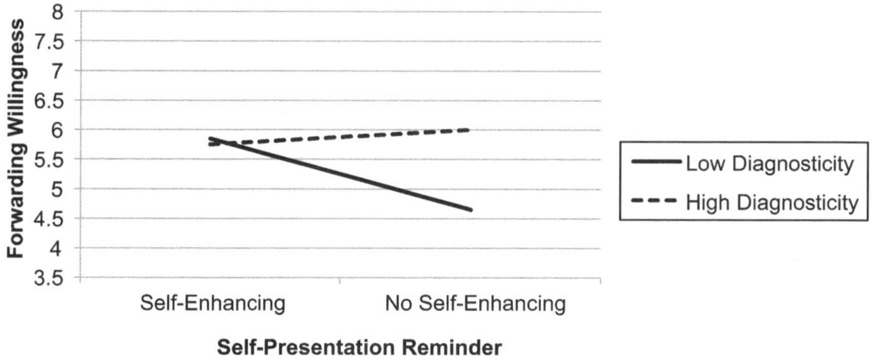

FIGURE 10.3 Interaction of Diagnosticity and Self-Presentation on Forwarding Willingness of Low-Commitment Consumers

information message ($M_{\text{high-diagnosticity}} = 6.60$, $M_{\text{low-diagnosticity}} = 3.83$; $t = -3.96$, $p < .001$) when the message included the self-enhancement reminder. By contrast, when the message did not have a self-enhancing reminder, there was no difference in the willingness to forward the message with high-diagnostic information than the one with low-diagnostic information ($M_{\text{high-diagnosticity}} = 5.37$, $M_{\text{low-diagnosticity}} = 5.18$; $t = .27$, *ns*). These findings support Hypothesis 5 and are shown in Figure 10.4.

Discussion

The results of Experiment 2 demonstrated that the diagnosticity of the information contained in a brand attack message played an important role in changing consumer attitudes and willingness to forward the message to others. A significant difference between pre-exposure and post-exposure attitudes emerged only when the brand attack message included attributes considered to be highly diagnostic in determining the difference between high and low quality brands. When the brand attack message focused on attributes considered to be of low diagnostic value in identifying high and low quality brands, it did not significantly change attitudes.

The critical dependent variable in Experiment 2 was the effect of the messages on the willingness of high and low brand commitment individuals to forward the message to others. This research introduced a new variable for consumers to consider when making their forwarding decision, a reminder of the self-enhancement that comes from helping others by sharing information. However, the experiment demonstrated that the value of such a reminder depended on the diagnosticity of the information contained in the brand attack message and the consumer's stated commitment to the brand.

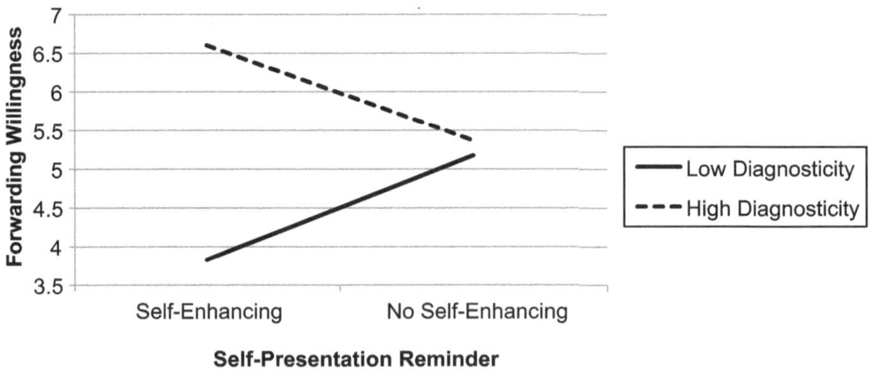

FIGURE 10.4 Interaction of Diagnosticity and Self-Presentation on Forwarding Willingness of High-Commitment Consumers

As predicted in Hypotheses 4a and 4b and shown in Figure 10.3, the willingness to forward the brand attack message was relatively high for low-commitment consumers when the information was considered to be highly diagnostic and therefore likely to be useful to the recipient of the forwarded message. It was also likely to be forwarded when the message was of low diagnostic but the consumer was reminded that it was helpful to share information with others. Otherwise, low commitment seemed to objectively value the message with low diagnostic information as not useful and indicated a low willingness to share it.

As suggested by Hypothesis 5, high brand commitment indicated a reluctance to forward brand attack messages with others, such that there was no difference in their willingness to forward messages containing high and low diagnostic information when there was no reminder that others might be harmed if they were not made aware of the information. Most interestingly, including such a reminder significantly increased their willingness to forward the message with the highly diagnostic, food safety alert. On the other hand, such a reminder actually seemed to reduce their desire to forward the inconsequential, low diagnostic attack related to the effect of the actions of the brand on its competitors. Apparently, when reminded to think about whether others might be harmed by not being aware of this information, the high-brand commitment consumers concluded that the low diagnostic information was not critical. Further, as the information was inconsistent with their loyalty to the brand they apparently decided that it was not desirable to make others aware of it.

The reasons provided by the participants in Experiment 2 for why they would forward the message were similar to those offered by the participants in Experiment 1. That is, 60% of those who expressed a willingness to forward the message presented personal reasons to forward the original message with most stating that they agreed with the author ($n = 60$). An additional 33% of the participants gave no reasons but just said they would forward it ($n = 33$). Interestingly, 7% of them responded that they would forward it even though they did not agree with the author ($n = 7$), perhaps prompted by the self-enhancement reminder. As most consumers responded that they would forward it because they agreed with the author of the original message, it confirms that forwarding usually done to promote one's views rather than counter the views of others.

Conclusions

The two experiments described in this chapter collectively shed light on factors that influence micro blog users' forwarding willingness and demonstrate the relationships between the brand commitment and forwarding willingness. Given the results, we propose that, first, consumer commitment toward the brand plays an important moderating role in the diffusion of brand crisis information. The initial reaction to a brand attack message is to decide whether to accept the information and thereby lowering one's attitude toward the attacked brand or to reject the claims and maintain one's attitude. Contrary to other research (e.g., Ahluwalia et al., 2000), we found that brand commitment did not moderate attitude change in response to positive and negative valenced messages in Experiment 1 or to messages with high or low diagnostic information in Experiment 2. This occurred even though there were significant main effects of message valence in Experiment 1 and diagnosticity in Experiment 2 (i.e., similar attitudinal effects for both high and low brand commitment consumers). Apparently, in the present context, consumers adjusted their attitudes toward the brand without being motivated by their brand commitment to resist the influence.

On the other hand, the results for willingness to forward the brand messages did reveal the expected moderating role of brand commitment. In Experiment 1, low-commitment individuals expressed a greater willingness to forward the negative message than the positive message, ostensibly because they had no reason to disagree with it and considered it useful to inform others of a potential food safety problem. On the other hand, they may not have felt it useful to forward something positive about a brand to which they felt no commitment. In Experiment 2, the low brand commitment consumers indicated a willingness to share the high diagnostic information regarding a potential food safety problem but not the low diagnostic information about the competitive practices of the brand. However, when prompted with a reminder that it was useful to share information with others, their willingness to forward increased significantly for the high but not the low diagnostic information. The behavior of the low brand commitment consumers is consistent with our view that they are objective in their processing of brand information and make forwarding decisions that primarily take into consideration whether or not others will benefit from the information and ignore any effect on the brand.

The message forwarding decisions of the high-commitment consumers differed noticeably from the low-commitment individuals both in what they forwarded and their motivation for doing so. In Experiment 1, the high-commitment consumers expressed a greater willingness to forward positive information about the brand than negative information. This can be attributed to their probably agreeing more the positive than negative information and the tendency of bloggers to share information that supports their behavior and point of view. Thus, they were much more reluctant than the low-commitment consumers to forward information that communicated negative information about one of their favorite brands. This reluctance was also evident in Experiment 2 with no greater willingness to forward potentially critical information (regarding food safety) than less important information (competitive practices). Apparently, high-commitment consumers feel a bond with the brand that causes them to promote it (by forwarding messages with positive information) and protect it (by not forwarding messages with negative information). However, this concern for the welfare of the brand was overcome in Experiment 2 when high brand commitment consumers were primed with a reminder to think about the welfare of other consumers.

Several limitations of this research should be noted. One is that commitment was measured only for a leading brand in a single product category. Consequently, the commitment level for the brand was generally high (M_{exp1} = 5.38; M_{exp2} = 5.46, scale midpoint = 4). Under such circumstances, differences between the low- and high-commitment consumers may have been attenuated. More robust studies should be done using low-share and lesser-known brands. Another limitation is the artificial setting of the research may have limited message credibility, lessening the desire to forward the message. Further, the source was unidentified and therefore may have been considered to have low credibility, which is long been identified as a factor in message evaluation (Hovland & Weiss, 1951). Several subjects indicated doubt that the message was credible when responding to an open-ended question about reasons why they did not forward the message. This potential problem was addressed by using words like "according to reliable sources" in the message design and there were main effects for attitude change attributable to message content. In the future, message credibility should be measured and/or manipulated to assess its influence.

In summary, this research revealed that high and low brand commitment consumers differ in their forwarding decisions primarily because of their underlying motivations. Low-commitment consumers are motivated to provide useful information to others with little consideration of the effect on the brand. High-commitment consumers care primarily about the brand and their relationship with it. Consequently, their forwarding decisions are less driven by objectivity and more by message forwarding's effect on the brand to which they are committed.

References

Ahluwalia, R. (2000). Examination of psychological processes underlying resistance to persuasion. *Journal of Consumer Research*, 27(2), 217–232.

Ahluwalia, R., Burnkrant, R. E., & Unnava, H. R. (2000). Consumer response to negative publicity: The moderating role of commitment. *Journal of Marketing Research*, 37(2), 203–214.

Amabile, T. (1983). Brilliant but cruel: Perceptions of negative evaluators. *Journal of Experimental Social Psychology*, 19(March), 146–156.

Baron, J., & Ritov, I. (2004). Omission bias, individual differences and normality. *Organizational Behavior and Human Decision Making*, 94(2), 64–85.

Beatty, S., Kahle, L., & Homer, P. (1988). The involvement-commitment model: Theory and implications. *Journal of Business Research,* 16(2), 149–167.

Berger, J. (2014). Word of mouth and interpersonal communication: A review and direction for future research. *Journal of Consumer Psychology*, 24(4), 586–607.

Chung, M., & Darke, P. (2006). The consumer as advocate: Self-relevance, culture and word-of-mouth. *Marketing Letters*, 17, 269–279.

Duhachek, A., Zhang, A., & Krishnan, S. (2007). Anticipated group interaction: Coping with valence asymmetries in attitude shift. *Journal of Consumer Research*, 34(3), 395–405.

Fiske, S. (1980). Attention and weight in person perception: The impact of negative and extreme behavior. *Journal of Personality and Social Psychology,* 38(6), 889–906.

Fournier, S. (1998). Consumers and their brands: Developing relationship theory in consumer research. *Journal of Consumer Research,* 24(March), 343–373.

Goffman, E. (1959). *The presentation of self in everyday life.* New York: Doubleday Anchor Books.

Herr, P., Kardes, F., & Kim, J. (1991). Effects of word-of-mouth and product-attribute information on persuasion: An accessibility-diagnosticity perspective. *Journal of Consumer Research,* 17(March), 454–462.

Hovland, C., & Weiss, W. (1951). The influence of source credibility on communication effectiveness. *Public Opinion Quarterly,* 15(4), 635–650.

Kaplan A., & Haenlein M. (2010). Users of the world, unite! The challenges and opportunities of social media. *Business Horizons,* 53, 59–68.

Keller, K. (1993). Conceptualizing, measuring, and managing customer-based brand equity. *Journal of Marketing,* 57(1), 1–22.

Klein, J. (1996). Negativity in impressions of presidential candidates revisited: The 1992 election. *Personality and Social Psychology Bulletin,* 22(March), 289–296.

Krosnick, J., Boninger, D., Chuang, Y., Berent, M., & Carnot, C. (1993). Attitude strength: One construct or many related constructs? *Journal of Personality and Social Psychology,* 65(December), 1132–1151.

Lastovicka, J., & Gardener D. (1978). Low involvement versus high involvement cognitive structures. In Kent Hunt & Ann Abor (Eds.), *Advances in consumer research* (vol. 5). MI: Association for Consumer Research, 87–92.

Petty, R., & Krosnick J. (1995). *Attitude strength: Antecedents and consequences.* Mahwah, NJ: Lawrence Erlbaum Associates.

Pomerantz, E., Chaiken, S., & Tordesillas, R. (1995). Attitude strength and resistance process. *Journal of Personality and Social Psychology,* 69(September), 408–419.

Schlosser, A. (2005). Posting vs. lurking: Communicating in a multiple audience context. *Journal of Consumer Research,* 32(2), 260–265.

Skowronski, J., & Carlston, D. (1989). Negativity and extremity in impression formation: A review of explanations. *Psychological Bulletin,* 105(January), 131–142.

Tormala, Z., Clarkson, J., & Petty, R. (2006). Resisting persuasion by the skin of one's teeth: The hidden success of resisted persuasive messages. *Journal of Personality and Social Psychology,* 91(3), 423–435.

Wojnicki, A.C., & Godes, D. (2011). Signaling success: Strategically positive word of mouth. In *University of Maryland, College Park Working Paper.*

Wood, W., Rhodes, N., & Biek, M. (1995). Working knowledge and attitude strength: An information-processing analysis. In Richard E. Petty & Jon A. Krosnick (Eds.), *Attitude strength: Antecedents and consequences.* Mahwah, NJ: Lawrence Erlbaum Associates, 283–213.

Wright, P. (1974). The harassed decision maker: Time pressures, distractions, and the use of evidence. *Journal of Applied Psychology,* 59(May), 555–561.

11

TO MANIPULATE, OR NOT TO MANIPULATE

The Naïve Beliefs of the Simple Application of Persuasion Techniques

Sascha Langner, Steffen Schmidt, Sebastian Fritz, Nadine Hennigs, and Klaus-Peter Wiedmann

Introduction

The recent development of new media over the past decade has changed the marketing environment dramatically and has provided consumers with multiple new ways to receive, to communicate, and to exchange information about products and services in order to evaluate those via discussion forums, blogs, or social networks (e.g., Goldsmith, 2006; Hennig-Thurau et al., 2010; Schindler & Bickart, 2005). Specifically, consumers are now able to assess products, services, and evaluations of other customers in real-time due to the ubiquitous character of the internet, at least for customers in the developed world. Within the last century, this development has been fostered by improved network technology elements: On a macro level, the implementation of broader infrastructures (e.g., from GSM to LTE), on a meso level the diffusion of more advanced network devices (e.g., from mobile phone to smartphones and tablets), and on a micro level the penetration of social media elements in daily life (e.g., from online chat channels to messaging services like WhatsApp for instant communication). Customers are not just consumers any more, but they are increasingly changing into prosumers, individuals who evaluate their own experience (e.g., by writing a review) as well as the experiences of other consumers (e.g., by rating the written review from others) within their social network.

The best known examples of this trend are the Amazon product reviews (generated by former customers) and product suggestions (generated by analyzing the actual buying behavior of former customers), which serve as primary information sources within the individual buying decision processes of many actual and potential customers. This customer-related information is available near seller-created information partially in order to compensate online consumers for their inability to examine the product and to evaluate products in the real world (Park et al., 2007). In an online context, this limited product examination is of particular importance for experience goods, such as holiday trips, where this is no third party functioning as a salesperson or travel agent acting as an "independent buying consultant."

As a consequence of this limitation, travel portals notably utilize recently established technologies and habits when they present travel offers. For example, providing information such as limited offers (*"Only X rooms left"*), reviews (e.g., by customers and/or third-parties as e.g., Tripadvisor), recent und current customer behaviors (e.g., *"X persons have booked that offer within the last 24 hours"* or *"X persons are watching this offer in this moment"*), and social media applications (e.g. Facebook or Twitter plugins). However, reacting to the subsequent abundance of information and high degree of product homogeneity, consumers often feel no pressure to buy a product or service at a certain website or travel portal. Given this situation, marketers strive to deploy efficient ways of customer persuasion to sell their products and/or services. One method is to encourage positive word of mouth, such as travel recommendations by real customers as they are often major sources of information for those searching for the right travel offer (Miguéns, Baggio, & Costa, 2008).

More than ever, a positive recommendation behavior is highly valued by businesses, especially those engaged in e-commerce, because a single opinion about a product and/or service may be stored in and restored from the internet literally forever. Further, positive recommendations may have an exponential impact due to demand-side economies of scale. In the best case scenario, such network effects may create a bandwagon effect in a positive way (or, in a worst case scenario, quickly kill off demand). The more people connected within a network, the greater is the probability people will get exposed to that opinion, which may result in a positive feedback loop.

In order to deal with a growing "social medialized" network environment, where positive customer opinions and connections are the new gold standard for a successful promotion of products and services, marketers who mainly or totally focus on online business will benefit from understanding and applying classical psychological consumer research findings from the "old marketing world." The more competition exists in that online environment, especially when the provided goods and services are homogeneous and therefore substitutable, facilitating their being presented in an aggregated form with comprehensive overviews provided by numerous price comparison services (e.g., Miguéns et al., 2008), the more the application of psychology knowledge is needed to enhance the customer's perceived value from using a specific e-commerce website. With this perspective, the current study aims to evaluate the effectiveness of well-known persuasion techniques from traditional social psychology research, namely social proof and scarcity, to activate and stimulate, respectively, the intention of potential customers with regard to a positive word of mouth communication (defined here as recommendation behavior).

Theoretical and Conceptual Background

The Power of Persuasion: Cialdini's Principles of Social Influence

Against the backdrop of a highly competitive environment and reasoning the increased importance of recommendations, reviews, and ratings as a source of consumer information, operators of travel portals have identified several methods to persuade their users to book a certain vacation trip—including separated offers for hotels, flights, or rental cars as well as combined packages. From a theoretical viewpoint, falling back on Cialdini (2009), there are six principles of social influence with a powerful impact on individual decision making: (1) reciprocation, (2) commitment and consistency, (3) social proof, (4) liking, (5) authority, and (6) scarcity.

- ***Reciprocation*** refers to the basic societal rule that an individual who received a gift or was given a favor by another person is obligated to future repayment of those gifts or favors—even if they were uninvited.
- ***Commitment and consistency*** as the second principle address the human desire to behave consistently with past choices and after having made a commitment. Being confronted with possible external or personal pressures and the need for consistency, individuals act in accordance to a previous commitment—even if this behavior is against one's own self-interest.
- ***Social proof*** focuses on the tendency to rely on the opinion and the behavior of other people to make decisions and conform to acceptable social behavior.
- ***Liking*** emphasizes the feeling of obligation and the urge to comply with a request by a friend or someone who is likable.
- ***Submission to authority***—e.g., the respect towards and the confidence in a renowned expert—is a principle deeply rooted in early childhood and the desire for a well-ordered human society.
- Finally, the ***scarcity principle*** uses techniques such as limitation, uniqueness, and exclusivity to increase the value of a certain offer that is restricted by amount or time.

In regards of the characteristics of the tourism industry in general and travel portals in particular, there are two principles that companies in this sector often use to influence uncertain consumers in an attempt to persuade them to buy a certain product and/or service: social proof and scarcity.

The Immunizing Potential of Social Proof

Social proof is based on the fundamental insight that people tend to assume that other individuals possess more knowledge about a certain situation (Cialdini & Goldstein, 2004). By orienting one's own behavior to the decisions of others, this principle helps to decide whether something is good or right (Lun et al., 2007). Generally speaking, if many others are doing it, it must be a good decision. People are more likely to engage in a behavior if they realize that many others have already done it (Bearden & Etzel, 1982). It is appropriate and reasonable to act upon this principle: it helps to prevent mistakes and in some situations, these mistakes could even harm one's physical integrity. For example, instead of trying a new fruit for the very first time by oneself, it is reasonable to first observe if and what happens to others after they consume this new fruit. Regarding different other use cases, it becomes obvious that this principle is used by many companies and industries. In advertisements, adjectives like favorite, popular, or top-selling are widely used to demonstrate that many other customers have a positive perception of this product or brand. Besides, sociology has identified the principle of social proof as a powerful method to influence and persuade other individuals. In this context, this principle is e.g., used to treat phobia and anxiety disorders or in the field of algesia. Craig and Prkachin (1978) have shown that patients suffer even more pain if they are present with another patient who is suffering the pain without cognizable reactions. Children are especially likely to respond to the principle of social proof. For example, Bandura, Grusec, and Menlove (1967) conducted an experiment with children who were afraid of dogs. After watching a peer playing with a dog for 20 minutes a day for four days, 67 percent of them agreed to be alone with a dog and even pet and cuddle with him. In sum, following the principle of social proof, individuals will copy the decisions of others because their behavior is assumed to be the right response in a certain situation or because they simply try to conform to group standards (Cialdini, 1984; Cialdini & Goldstein, 2004). Applying this principle to our context of the tourism industry and travel portals, it suggests that consumers will actively search for peer reviews and use the recommendation of others as valid and useful information in a way that influences their individual product choice and consumption behavior.

The Attractive Tonality of Scarcity

Scarcity, the second important persuasive tactic in the context of travel portals, is based on the axiom that something is even more attractive if it's scarce and its availability is limited (e.g., Cialdini & Goldstein, 2004; Brock, 1968). Scarcity includes not only that there is a limitation of the quantity, but also that a certain product and/or service is available for a limited time period. Interestingly, collections of cars, stamps, or baseball cards obtain their value by the principle of scarcity resulting in the "precious mistake" phenomenon. Goods with an alleged mistake, and therefore with a certain extent of uniqueness, become critical in terms of the total value of someone's collection as they convey greater exclusiveness. The scarcity principle is activated if a certain offer is advertised with the claim it has limited availability or is a limited edition. After a certain period of time, the chance to possess this good or to profit from this opportunity is gone.

Consequently, consumers may assign a special, exclusive, and attractive characteristic to such offers increasing their desire to possess that product or service, i.e., it becomes a must-have item for those wanting to belong to a select circle of customers.

The Insinuated Influence of Infecting the Customer's Mind

In sum, theoretical insights as well as empirical evidence based on general heuristic rules support the assumption that the tourism industry and especially travel portals will benefit from the incorporation of the principles of social proof and scarcity. It is suggested that the appropriate application of such persuasive tactics in social media marketing will increase the effectiveness of communication and product offerings to prospective customers. Next, we will evaluate this assumption in an empirical study described below.

Methodology

Overview and Design

An experimental study was conducted to test the two common persuasion techniques of social proof and scarcity on their ability to enhance word of mouth communication (here: the Net Promoter Score) regarding a vacation offer (here: a three-day stay at a hotel in Barcelona, Spain, for 143 EUR). Specifically, we manipulated two factors (offering quality and persuasion technique) between subjects. Offering quality was manipulated by the overall hotel attractiveness based on customer ratings (inferior hotel with 3.0 stars and 70 percent customer recommendation rating, average hotel with 3.8 stars and 80 percent customer recommendation rating, superior hotel with 4.6 stars and 90 percent customer recommendation rating; stars rated on a 1 to 5 stars scale). Persuasion technique was manipulated by using a no-additional-incentive, "intentional motivation" strategy, a social proof technique (*"25 visitors have booked that hotel in the last 24 hours"*), or a scarcity technique (*"Last Chance: Only one room left"*).

The manipulations resulted in a 3 (offering quality: inferior, average, superior) ×3 (persuasion technique: no persuasion, social proof, scarcity) between-subjects factorial design. Word of mouth intention was operationalized using the well-known Net Promoter Score scale (*"How likely is it that you would recommend that hotel offering to a friend or colleague?* Rating: 0 = not at all likely to 10 = extremely likely). Subjects were randomly assigned to one of the nine conditions. First, they received a screenshot of one of the nine hotel offers for the minimum time of 20 seconds, before they answered a questionnaire about the presented offer including the direct Net Promoter question, completed by a socio-demographic survey. In detail, we captured a screenshot of a real existing overnight stay at a hotel in Barcelona, Spain (price: 143 EUR for three days; hotel category: 3 stars), offered by Expedia, a well-known online travel agency. Then, the screenshot was modified according to the targeted nine conditions using GIMP (2013), a professional open source image manipulation program.

A German-language online survey was used for data collection. The recruitment of participants was organized by applying a snowball sampling via email messages and links on selective web pages (e.g., Facebook profile pages) with an invitation to actively contribute to the survey. In total, 540 subjects participated in this specific 3 × 3 factorial design. Seventy-five non-native speaking participants were deleted in order to avoid a language bias. The data of further 28 individuals were removed for not specifying their household income (this socio-demographical information was needed to create three homogenous groups of income). The sample adjustment led to a final pool of 437 subjects. Regarding sample characteristics, the participants encompassed 256 females (i.e., 58.6 percent) and 181 males (i.e., 41.4 percent) who were mainly students: aged 18 to 25 years (89.7 percent, on average 22.01 years old) with higher education background (99.1 percent), single (93.4 percent), and enrolled at a university (92.2 percent).

Eventually, the sample consisted of three main household income groups: low income (47.1 percent, less than 1000 EUR/month), middle income (28.4 percent, 1000 to 3000 EUR/month), and high income (24.5 percent, more than 3000 EUR/month). Because we proposed a varying degree of price sensitivity across income groups, separated analyses were run for each income group. In particular, two-factor ANOVAs were used to determine the effectiveness of offering quality and persuasion technique on word of mouth communication. As emphasized in the introduction, positive word of mouth may result in a boosting bandwagon effect, especially in a social media context, and therefore recommendation behavior was chosen as an indicator for successful persuasion in the current study.

Results

Low Income Group

The empirical assessment based on a factorial 3 ×3 ANOVA as well as the descriptive statistics are shown in Table 11.1. The findings indicate a significant main effect of offering quality ($F(2, 197) = 3.05$, $p < .05$), and a marginal main effect of persuasion technique ($F(2, 197) = 2.62$, $p < .08$) on word of mouth, but no interaction effect ($F(4, 197) = .49$, $p > .70$).

However, a visual inspection of Figure 11.1 suggests the existence of an interaction effect, at least partially. A pairwise comparison including the additional consideration of 95 percent confidence intervals provide support for this assumption. Specifically, one-way univariate ANOVA results provide support for an

TABLE 11.1 Descriptive Statistics, Two Way ANOVA and Pairwise Comparison of the Interaction Term for the Low Income Group

Descriptive Statistics

DV: Net Promoter Scale	*No Persuasion*			*Social Proof*			*Scarcity*		
	n	*M*	*SD*	*n*	*M*	*SD*	*n*	*M*	*SD*
Inferior Product	23	5.739	2.435	20	5.150	2.834	28	4.214	2.200
Average Product	24	6.708	2.805	21	5.714	2.513	23	5.565	2.465
Superior Product	22	6.045	2.627	23	5.957	2.306	22	5.773	2.776

Two Way ANOVA

Source of Variance	*SS (Type III)*	*df1, df2*	*MS*	*F*	*p-Value*
Persuasion Technique	34.016	2, 197	17.008	2.621	.075
Offering Quality	39.563	2, 197	19.781	3.048	.050
Persuasion Technique * Offering Quality	12.590	4, 197	3.148	.485	.747

Pairwise Comparison: Persuasion × Product

Offering Quality	*Persuasion (I)*	*Persuasion (J)*	*ΔM (I-J)*	*p-Value*	*ΔM: 95% CI*
Inferior Product	Social Proof	No Persuasion	−.589	.450	−2.125 : .947
	Scarcity	No Persuasion	−1.525	.035	−2.939 : −.111
	Scarcity	Social Proof	−.936	.211	−2.406 : .535
Average Product	Social Proof	No Persuasion	−.994	.193	−2.495 : .507
	Scarcity	No Persuasion	−1.143	.126	−2.609 : .323
	Scarcity	Social Proof	−.149	.846	−1.665 : 1.367
Superior Product	Social Proof	No Persuasion	−.089	.907	−1.587 : 1.409
	Scarcity	No Persuasion	−.273	.723	−1.787 : 1.242
	Scarcity	Social Proof	−.184	.809	−1.682 : 1.314

effect of applied persuasion technique for the inferior product on WOM ($F(2, 197) = 2.33$, $p < .10$), but not for the average product ($F(2, 197) = 1.39$, $p > .20$) or the superior product ($F(2, 197) = .07$, $p > .90$). Even so, surprisingly the persuasion effect in the inferior product condition is partly negative. In particular, scarcity differs significantly from no persuasion ($\Delta M = -1.525$, $p < .05$, ΔM *95% CI* = −2.939 to −.111), and also from social proof ($\Delta M = -.936$, $p < .30$, ΔM *95% CI* = −2.406 to .535) with regard to the 95 percent confidence interval (CI). Additionally, a relevant WOM reduction compared to a no persuasion situation may be reasonably assumed for the average product condition with reference to persuasion techniques, social proof ($\Delta M = -.994$, $p < .20$, ΔM *95% CI* = −2.495 to .507), and scarcity ($\Delta M = -1.143$, $p < .20$, ΔM *95% CI* = −2.609 to .323).

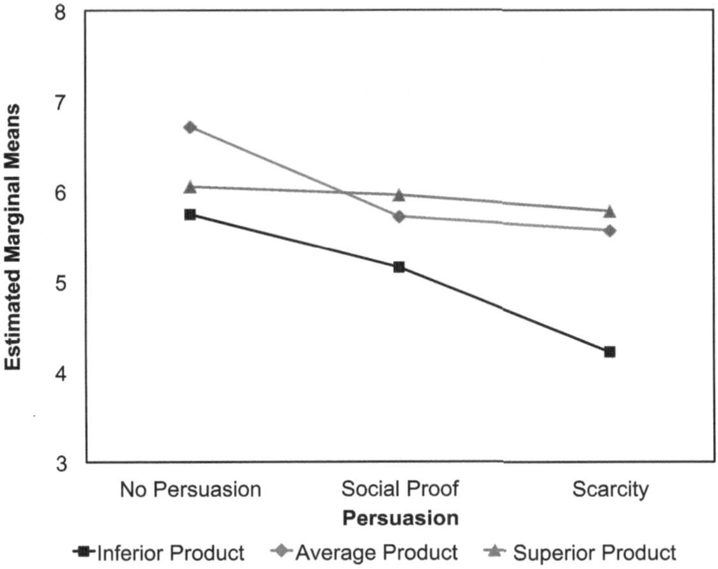

FIGURE 11.1 Mean Net Promoter Scores for Low Income Group

With reference to the superior product category, results suggest no clear WOM difference across all three persuasion conditions.

Middle Income Group

The empirical results are presented in Table 11.2. The overall analysis of variance revealed a significant main effect of offering quality ($F(2, 115) = 3.70$, $p < .05$), a marginal main effect of persuasion technique ($F(2, 115) = 2.42$, $p < .10$), and a non-significant interaction effect ($F(4, 115) = 1.64$, $p < .20$).

Figure 11.2 suggests that a closer look at the interaction effect is warranted. The empirical results of a one-way univariate ANOVA demonstrate the persuasion technique's influence on WOM concerning the inferior.product ($F(2, 115) = 4.64$, $p < .05$), but not with an average product ($F(2, 115) = 1.42$, $p > .20$) or a superior product ($F(2, 115) = .45$, $p > .60$). However, a negative WOM effect of persuasion compared to no persuasion situation is shown for the inferior product regarding scarcity ($\Delta M = -2.482$, $p < .01$, ΔM *95% CI* $= -4.105$ to $-.858$) and social proof ($\Delta M = -1.244$, $p < .20$, ΔM *95% CI* $= -2.940$ to $.451$), here against the additional background of an additional CI interpretation. Also, the 95 percent CI shows a likely lower WOM assessment of scarcity compared to social proof ($\Delta M = -1.237$, $p < .20$, ΔM *95% CI* $= -2.778$ to $.304$). In contrast, within the average product context, a meaningful increase of WOM in comparison to a

TABLE 11.2 Descriptive Statistics, Two Way ANOVA and Pairwise Comparison of the Interaction Term for the Middle Income Group

Descriptive Statistics

DV: Net Promoter Scale	*No Persuasion*			*Social Proof*			*Scarcity*		
	n	*M*	*SD*	*n*	*M*	*SD*	*n*	*M*	*SD*
Inferior Product	15	5.800	2.242	18	4.556	2.229	22	3.318	2.056
Average Product	9	5.111	3.257	11	6.636	2.292	17	5.176	2.604
Superior Product	9	5.556	2.555	13	6.462	2.634	10	5.700	2.669

Two Way ANOVA

Source of Variance	*SS (Type III)*	*df1, df2*	*MS*	*F*	*p-Value*
Persuasion Technique	28.945	2, 115	14.472	2.415	.094
Offering Quality	44.343	2, 115	22.172	3.700	.028
Persuasion Technique × Offering Quality	39.242	4, 115	9.810	1.637	.170

Pairwise Comparison: Persuasion × Product

Offering Quality	*Persuasion (I)*	*Persuasion (J)*	*ΔM (I-J)*	*p-Value*	*ΔM: 95% CI*
Inferior Product	Social Proof	No Persuasion	−1.244	.149	−2.940 : .451
	Scarcity	No Persuasion	−2.482	.003	−4.105 : −.858
	Scarcity	Social Proof	−1.237	.114	−2.778 : .304
Average Product	Social Proof	No Persuasion	1.525	.168	−.654 : 3.705
	Scarcity	No Persuasion	.065	.948	−1.933 : 2.064
	Scarcity	Social Proof	−1.460	.126	−3.336 : .416
Superior Product	Social Proof	No Persuasion	.906	.395	−1.197 : 3.009
	Scarcity	No Persuasion	.144	.898	−2.083 : 2.372
	Scarcity	Social Proof	−.762	.461	−2.801 : 1.278

no persuasion situation is most likely to be expected for social proof ($\Delta M = 1.525$, $p < .20$, ΔM *95% CI* = −.654 to 3.705), but not for scarcity ($\Delta M = .065$, $p > .90$, ΔM *95% CI* = −1.933 to 2.064). Additionally, scarcity seems to be less effective compared to social proof ($\Delta M = -1.460$, $p < .20$, ΔM *95% CI* = –3.336 to .416). Furthermore, no consistent WOM differences emerged for the superior product category across persuasion situations.

High Income Group

Table 11.3 presents the overall empirical findings. The factorial 3 × 3 ANOVA shows a significant main effect of offering quality ($F(2, 107) = 4.24$, $p < .05$), a

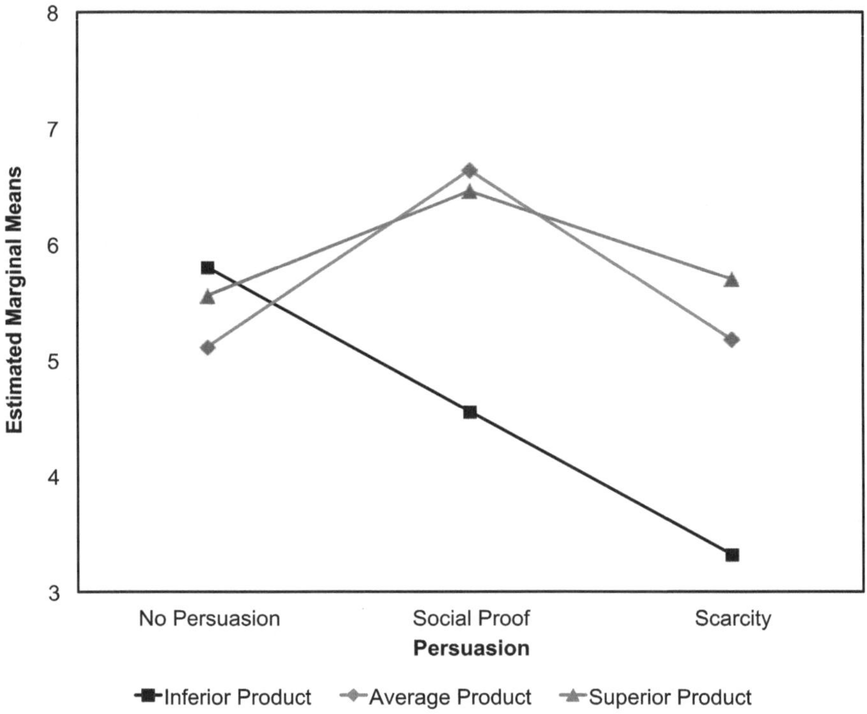

FIGURE 11.2 Mean Net Promoter Scores for Middle Income Group

TABLE 11.3 Descriptive Statistics, Two Way ANOVA and Pairwise Comparison of the Interaction Term for the High Income Group

Descriptive Statistics

DV: Net Promoter Scale	*No Persuasion*			*Social Proof*			*Scarcity*		
	n	*M*	*SD*	*n*	*M*	*SD*	*n*	*M*	*SD*
Inferior Product	13	4.615	2.663	9	4.667	3.202	13	4.462	2.184
Average Product	9	6.556	2.242	11	5.636	2.248	14	4.714	2.400
Superior Product	10	7.700	2.163	12	5.250	2.006	16	5.938	2.205

Two Way ANOVA

Source of Variance	*SS (Type III)*	*df1, df2*	*MS*	*F*	*p-Value*
Persuasion Technique	31.542	2, 107	15.771	2.814	.065
Offering Quality	52.411	2, 107	26.206	4.676	.011
Persuasion Technique * Offering Quality	24.645	4, 107	6.161	1.099	.361

Pairwise Comparison: Persuasion * Product

Offering Quality	*Persuasion (I)*	*Persuasion (J)*	*ΔM (I-J)*	*p-Value*	*ΔM: 95% CI*
Inferior Product	Social Proof	No Persuasion	.051	.960	−1.986 : 2.088
	Scarcity	No Persuasion	−.154	.869	−1.997 : 1.689
	Scarcity	Social Proof	−.205	.842	−2.242 : 1.832
Average Product	Social Proof	No Persuasion	−.919	.390	−3.031 : 1.192
	Scarcity	No Persuasion	−1.841	.072	−3.848 : .166
	Scarcity	Social Proof	−.922	.336	−2.815 : .971
Superior Product	Social Proof	No Persuasion	−2.450	.017	−4.462 : −.438
	Scarcity	No Persuasion	−1.763	.068	−3.656 : .131
	Scarcity	Social Proof	.687	.449	−1.107 : 2.482

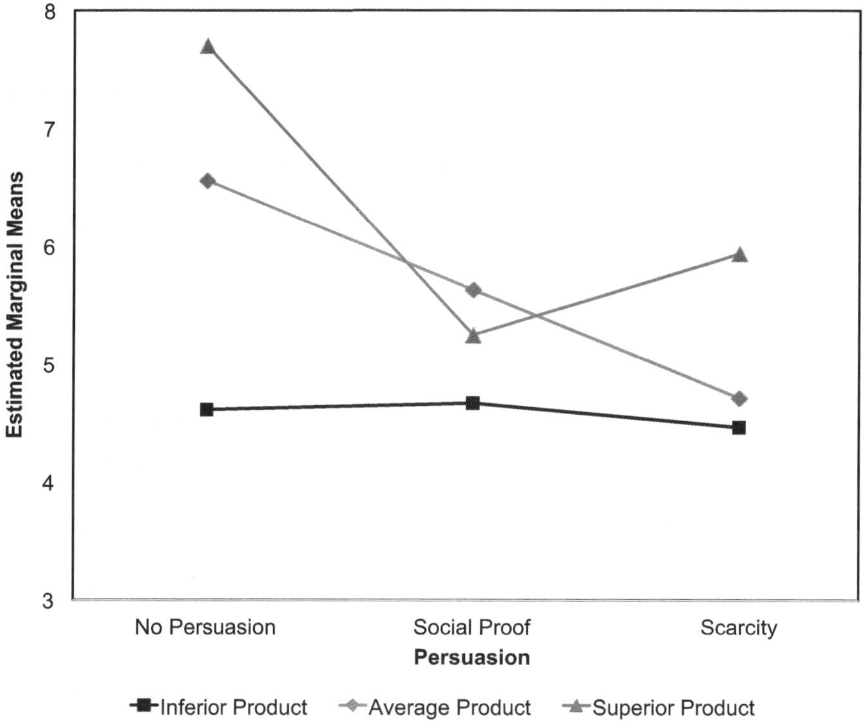

FIGURE 11.3 Mean Net Promoter Scores for High Income Group

marginal main effect of persuasion technique ($F(2, 107) = 2.58$, $p < .10$), and a non-significant offering quality × persuasion technique interaction effect ($F(4, 107) = 1.10$, $p > .30$).

Meanwhile, Figure 11.3 indicates an interaction effect. In fact, the results provide no notable WOM differences between all three persuasion situations for the inferior product category, but a moderate significant decrease of WOM for scarcity in comparison to no persuasion ($\Delta M = -1.841$, $p < .10$, ΔM *95% CI* = −3.848 to .166). Furthermore, persuasion seems to be ineffective within the superior product context. Here, social proof reveals less WOM compared with no persuasion ($\Delta M = -2.450$, $p < .05$, ΔM *95% CI* = −4.462 to −.438) as well as for scarcity against no persuasion ($\Delta M = -1.763$, $p < .10$, ΔM *95% CI* = −3.656 to .131).

Discussion and Conclusion

Implications for Travel Portals and Marketing Researchers

Our results show that two frequently applied persuasion techniques—social proof and scarcity—both have a partial impact on customer behavior. Yet, unlike the primary assumption that persuasion should generally positively influence behavior, our study shows a more differentiated picture. First, social proof seemed to perform better than scarcity. However, several persuasion attempts unexpectedly lead to a decreased outcome regarding recommendation behavior (here: WOM), or at least to an identical WOM intention compared to a no persuasion attempt. Only with regard to an average product context did social proof increase WOM meaningfully higher for the middle income group. Second, (largely negative) persuasion effects highly depend on the analyzed product in combination with the examined target group. In particular, with reference to low and middle income groups, the findings suggest the emergence of persuasion effects within an inferior and average product context, whereas the impact of persuasion on WOM for the high income group can be identified within an average and superior product context. In other words, persuasion does not run like clockwork; it needs to be properly dosed and requires the correct target group to be appropriately addressed in order to work—at least when applied on travel portals.

In our study we analyzed persuasion effects regarding three different product categories combined with three different income groups. In the following, the results of the nine conditions are discussed in more detail regarding the implications for travel portals in specific and marketing research in general.

- **Inferior product:** All attempts using an inferior product as basis for persuasion did not show any positive effects at all. Although the high income group seems to be indifferent (the product category per se may not concern them), medium and low income groups show rather negative WOM reactions regarding both persuasion techniques (social proof and scarcity). Customers probably recognize intuitively a kind of warning signal here that lets them see through the persuasion attempt (i.e., "they smell a rat"). Consequently, travel portals should refrain from using any of the analyzed persuasion elements for this kind of product. The best way to market inferior hotels on travel portals could be to *"let the hotel speak for itself,"* without any surplus added by social proof or scarcity persuasion elements.

- **Average product:** Similar to the inferior product, almost all persuasion techniques applied here show no positive effects. Only the middle income group seems to be receptive to social proof. Assuming that an average hotel could just fit the needs of the target group (middle income meets average hotel => good price-benefit ratio), customers are looking for signals that distinguish one average hotel from another. That only the combination of social proof and middle income had verifiable positive effects on behavior could be explained by exactly this fact. Middle income customers do not generally search for exclusive/expensive places to stay because they are mostly not in line with their budget; still they always look for proven winners. Of course the question arises of why low income customers do not also fall for this persuasion technique. The reason could be that unlike the low income group, middle income customers already have considerable experience regarding overnight stays at a hotel. They know that there can be a big difference between a certain 'good' hotel and another 'good' hotel. Social proof elements as used in our experiments may be a big referring factor here—particularly when someone wants to recommend a hotel without ever having been there. Travel portals should address and assess the integration of social proof elements when focusing on medium up to high hotel prices for a relatively average overnight stay offer, but only when precisely targeting middle income customers (e.g., by using specific advertising depending on landing pages).
- **Superior product:** Regarding this product category, social proof is also the only technique that could positively influence customers on a distinguishable level, even though the identified effect was not significant. And again it is the middle income group that is receptive to this kind of persuasion and shows a relatively higher WOM dissemination. The reasons that social proof may work on the average product seem to also apply to the superior product. Surprisingly, no persuasion technique was able to increase WOM within the low income group. This result could be explained by the fact that low income customers generally recommend fewer superior products as they are almost always expensive and thus not in their relevant choice set; this renders them likely not affordable for the potential receiver of the recommendation (who is probably from the same income group). It is worth mentioning that the high income group as the primary target of such offerings shows noticeable negative effects when social proof or scarcity is applied. Perhaps they see a lack of exclusiveness, which may reduce the genuine premium character of that superior product, so that the demanded status symbol is not available mentally. Against this backdrop, when it comes to superior products, travel portals should again try to only apply social proof elements when they specifically address middle income customers. The same holds for scarcity elements, as they could help increase WOM dissemination.

In summary, although social proof was determined to have at least a positive persuasion effect on the middle income group concerning average and superior products, scarcity almost always shows mostly negative effects over all product categories and income groups. Online travel customers do not seem to be very receptive to "most wanted" (social proof) or "last chance" (scarcity) hotel deals in a positive way—probably because they know that it is too risky to recommend a hotel that has to be booked in a hurry (i.e., a lot of money for a perhaps too quick a decision). Another reason could be that travel customers know that there always is a surplus of hotel space (i.e., overcapacity), so that last chance deals are simply manipulation attempts.

Limitations

Given that our study showed differentiated and unexpected results, both persuasion techniques should be tested and analyzed in more detail. Also, other versions, such as a scarcity technique based on a limited decision time (e.g., "This offer is available for the next X hours") instead of limited capacity ("Only X spots left") and applying them to other products might yield different results. Furthermore, more demographic variable beyond income should be taken into account (e.g., travel experience). It is likely that one's personal category experience could influence persuasion success to a large extent, as customers with high travel expertise would respond faster to the persuasions attempts, leading to even more negative behavioral effects. The opposite might hold for customers with very low travel expertise like young adults.

Another limitation of our study lies in the experimental design itself. On the one hand, all participants saw the respective product offer for at least 20 seconds. As we did not check whether the manipulated elements of the products were seen (e.g., through eye tracking), it is not clear that all participants perceived the whole product offer in the anticipated way. On the other hand, the default time frame of 20 second minimum presentation can be a disturbing issue itself as people do not like to be hurried in their decision behavior (here perhaps producing a decision to skip the offer immediately), with reactance then leading to potential pseudo negative WOM effects (possibly in addition to a perceived persuasion attempt).

Last but not least, our study only analyzed individual persuasion techniques and not a combination of them. In order to explore persuasion in its full complexity, social proof and scarcity should be combined and analyzed in one product offer, possibly including additional social influence techniques like authority or liking.

References

Bearden, W.O. & Etzel, M.J. (1982). Reference group influence on product and brand purchase decisions. *Journal of Consumer Research,* 9(2), 183–194.

Bandura, A., Grusec, J. E., & Menlove, F. L. (1967). Vicarious extinction of avoidance behavior. *Journal of Personality and Social Psychology,* 5, 16–23.

Brock, T. C. (1968). Implications of commodity theory for value change. In Greenwald, A. G., Brock, T. C., & Ostrom, T. M. (Eds.) *Psychological foundations of attitudes.* New York: Academic Press, 243–275.

Cialdini, R. B. (1984). *Influence—The psychology of persuasion.* New York: William Morrow.

Cialdini, R. B. (2009). *Influence: Science and practice,* 5th ed. Boston: Pearson Education.

Cialdini, R. B. & Goldstein, N. J. (2004). Social influence: Compliance and conformity. *Annual Review of Psychology,* 55(1), 591–621.

GIMP (2013): www.gimp.org.

Goldsmith, R. E. (2006). Electronic word-of-mouth. In Khosrow-Pour, Medi (Ed.) *Encyclopedia of e-commerce, e-government, and mobile commerce.* Hershey: Idea Group Reference, 408–412.

Craig, K. D. & Prkachin, K. M. (1978). Social modeling influences on sensory decision theory and psychological indexes of pain. *Journal of Personality and Social Psychology,* 36, 805–815.

Hennig-Thurau, T., Malthouse, E. C., Friege, C., Gensler, S. Lobschat, L., Rangaswamy, A., & Skiera, B. (2010). The impact of new media on customer relationships. *Journal of Service Research,* 13 (3), 311–330.

Lun, J., Sinclair, S., Whitchurch, E. R., & Glenn, C. (2007). (Why) do I think what you think? Epistemic social turning and implicit prejudice. *Journal of Personality and Social Psychology,* 93, 957–972.

Miguéns, J., Baggio, R., & Costa, C. (2008). Social media and tourism destination: Trip Advisor case study, *IASK Advances in Tourism Research 2008,* Aveiro, Portugal, May 26–28, 2008, 1–6.

Park, D-H., Lee, J. & Han, I. (2007). The effect of on-line consumer review on consumer purchasing intention: The moderating role of involvement. *International Journal of Electronic Commerce,* 11 (4), 125–148.

Schindler, R. M. & Bickart, B. (2005). Published word of mouth: Referable, consumer-generated information on the internet. In Haugtvedt, C. P., Machleit, K. A., & Yalch, R. F. (Eds.) *Online consumer psychology—Understanding and influencing consumer behavior in the virtual world.* Mahwah: Erlbaum, 35–61.

PART III

Measurement and Interpretation Issues in Social Media

12

EXPLORING THE MOTIVATIONAL AND CONSUMPTION IMPACT OF PERSONAL ANALYTICS AND INFORMATICS

Heather Honea

The interaction of social, mobile, and cloud-computing combined with recent advances in self-sensing technology are creating new domains of personal monitoring and quantification, reshaping the role of data and analytics in society. Smart technology and sensors (e.g., on wristwatch-like devices, glasses, and cars) that can interconnect opens the possibility for consumers to more accurately or extensively generate personal data stores. These instruments log device interaction; capture real-time experiential and consumption data (e.g., photos, search activity, communications, purchase); employ activity and motion tracking applications (e.g., accelerometers and altimeters) to track motion and exercise; use electroencephalography (EEG) to track brain, nervous system activity, and sleep patterns; use electroencephalogram (ECG) to track electrical activity of the heart; employ global positioning system technology (GPS) to automatically log data about an individual's location. Consumers can leverage the resulting data to manage their lives, remember details, address issues, and pursue opportunities. In many cases, amassed data allows consumers to apply the quantitative methods used in science and business to the personal sphere ("The Quantified Self," 2012), enabling insights about personal context, states, patterns, consumption, performance, and well-being. The adoption of such practices has even been dubbed *The Quantified Self Movement.*

Tracking Health and Wellness

The practice of self-tracking is not a new phenomenon, people have long employed journaling, scales, thermometers, and biofeedback technology in order to monitor and measure personal states. Indeed, the Pew Research Internet Project (Health Fact Sheet, 2014) found that 60 percent of adults track weight, diet, or exercise;

33 percent track health symptoms (e.g., blood sugar and sleep patterns). Technological advances are now offering access to highly informative data streams. University of California in San Diego's Qualcomm Institute has developed an application that alerts users if they have achieved a healthful or blissful state. The user wears monitors that simultaneously transmit real-time data (e.g., heart rate variation) to a tablet; when an optimal state is reached, the tablet triggers a tone or vibration. This process can train the user to become aware of behaviors and thoughts that are beneficial or detrimental. Propeller™ is a small sensor that attaches to the top of an asthma inhaler and automatically records usage trends (e.g., time, date, and location); the device wirelessly syncs to a smartphone, data can be viewed on the phone, and over time, users can begin to determine what locations exacerbate a user's asthma symptoms. The application can even provide prompts when the user is in at-risk situations. Ginger.io analyzes patterns in smartphone usage to predict when people with chronic issues (e.g., diabetes, depression, and cardiovascular disease) are at greater risk for problematic health episodes.

The data automatically collected via sensing and activity recording are commonly augmented with real-time, self-report measures. During specific intervals an individual is prompted by a device to indicate affective state, energy, and motivation levels. TrackYourHappiness.org, for instance, connects with users by email and text messages and asks them to report how they are feeling, what they are doing, and whom they are with; frequency is determined by the users. From this data users can generate reports showing how happiness varies depending on what they are doing, whom they are with, where they are, and times of day.

Although the data measurement has a personal focus, there are a number of platforms enabling individuals to share information, engage in peer-to-peer activities, and compare their outcomes relative to others. Patients Like Me, Smart Patients, myHealth Teams, and CureTogether all provide platforms for individuals, in specific disease categories, to connect and share information. Crohnology (a platform for individuals with Crohn's, colitis, and other inflammatory bowel conditions) allows users to track personal symptomology and then trade information on effective diets and remedies. This type of activity is particularly powerful in categories where medical treatments have with inconsistent efficacies. Most importantly, these platforms allow for data to be pooled for statistical strength whereas findings can be applied individually. The aggregation of outcomes helps individuals identify effective treatments but also the volume of different treatment paths allows them to determine unique treatment paths that are most likely to yield beneficial results based on their specific health profile.

Tracking Behavior and Consumption

The analysis of personal data stores is not limited to wellness, self-tracking has application wherever personal insight, goal pursuit, or performance enhancement is important. With the technology of today we chronicle our lives moment by moment via content downloads, uploads, VOIP calls, emails, texts, tweets, shares, likes, purchases, and search histories. Moreover, platforms such as Facebook, Twitter, Tumblr, and Pinterest represent instrumentation systems as well as self-description engines that encourage us to post data about where we are, what we are doing, and whom we are doing it with (Bersin, 2014). They collect our memories and opinions and provide detailed records of our thoughts and experiences.

Increasingly, sensors are attached to household items (e.g., mattress, shoes, clothing, a toothbrush, watering can, or the collar of a dog) and then data can be sent to a base station to measure and track how often you brush your teeth, water your plants, and walk your dog, among other activities ("The Quantified Self," 2012). These technologies track user related activity (e.g., when and how much someone is sleeping via a mattress) but also environmental conditions (e.g., how far your dog has been walked and what the temperature was during that outing). Home consumption activity can be tracked through products such as Nest or tools such as Wattvision. Wattvision provides an energy sensor that connects a user's electricity meter to a web service. Once connected, the user can view whole-house energy consumption via the web or a smartphone (updated every 10 seconds) and use this information to reduce consumption. In the area of personal finance, Mint automatically organizes and categorizes household spending based on captured bank and credit card data.

Once personal data stores are generated, different data can be blended to empower consumers with descriptive, diagnostic, and prescriptive insights. Wolfram Alpha Personal Analytics, for instance, provides insights on social networking activities allowing users to evaluate peak usage times, characteristics of their social relationships, and construct life stories from personal data (Wolfram, 2012). Tools, such as Daytum and Pachube, can tally statistics for anything of import (e.g., purchase history and transactions). These applications can be configured to notify users when certain conditions are met and users can then view real-time graphs of data. Using these tools consumers can engage in what has been called Vendor Relationship Management (VRM). As they collect information on their purchasing behaviors and service encounters, they can start to understand their buying patterns—relative to vendors, brands, and lifestyle behaviors—and correlate this with satisfaction.

Dimensions of Self-Tracking and Monitoring

Lupton (2014) describes five modes of self-tracking: private, communal, pushed, imposed, and exploited. Two key modes, private versus communal, are differentiated by the degree of personal sharing relative to the tracking activity. *Private self-tracking* refers to practices adopted for self-knowledge and personal optimization that are not shared or shared with only a few individuals. *Communal self-tracking* involves the voluntary sharing of personal data, often through social media, to engage with (and learn from) other self-trackers. In this case, individuals might share how to effectively track data, work toward common goals, and aggregate data to garner richer insights (e.g., Patients Like Me). They might also participate in citizen sensing and community development; in these cases, data (e.g., air quality, traffic conditions, and crime rates) are collected and aggregated on local communities in an effort to improve their local conditions, services, or motivate political action. For instance, SeeClickFix allows anyone to report and track non-emergency issues anywhere in the world; citizens get started by reporting issues, then monitor and participate in generating resolutions to problems.

Lupton's other categories of self-tracking are descriptive of the level of agency an individual has relative to the initiation or on-going pursuit of tracking. *Pushed self-tracking* has some external agency in that the initial incentive (or encouragement to monitor) does not originate from the individual. An example of this could be a life coach or physician encouraging someone to engage in tracking. *Imposed self-tracking* is very externalized and may involve a penalty for non-compliance. Corporate wellness programs, which involve employees being rewarded (pushed) or penalized (imposed) for outcomes, fall along this continuum. *Exploited self-tracking* involves third parties leveraging data that is generated via self-monitoring.

Given that Lipton's different categories of tracking are actually recursive in nature, it is valuable to contemplate additional delineations of tracking when examining the impact of such monitoring. The agency dimension of tracking might best be represented by a continuum anchored by 'elective' (internally motivated) and 'imposed' (externally motivated) with a middle point of 'pushed.' Additionally, categorizing tracking by a beneficiary might represent another dimension and be anchored by 'cooperative' (the third party supports the tracker in finding personal valuable insights, achieving outcomes, or receiving rewards) and 'exploitive' (the third party leverages data for private gain without offering commensurate benefit to tracker). Recently, Mastercard partnered with Shopkick to track consumers' locations and actions. Big name brands such as Best Buy, Target, Old, Navy, Macy's, and Sports Authority used the in-store hardware that emits a signal that is picked up by the shopper's mobile phone, which certainly falls in the category of third party tracking. However, Shopkick tracks store visits and rewards actions like scanning barcodes and trying on clothes so the data store yields benefit for the individual participating in the tracking activity (Perez, 2012). These different dimensions, with respect to personal tracking, are likely important moderators relative to the impact of monitoring on self-regulation and goal pursuit.

Self-Regulation Through Monitoring and Gamification

The accuracy, consistency, and sustainability of self-monitoring—and how the data is represented in order to motivate behavior—is also key. The ability to accurately monitor is critical because self-regulation theory indicates that self-monitoring is an antecedent to the evaluation of progress toward goals and reinforcement of achievements (Kanfer, 1991). Moreover, behavior change depends on attention to action and the impact of the action; both require accurate and consistent monitoring of performance relative to behaviors (Bandura, 1998). Certainly, self-monitoring with respect to health management, sports activity, and academic activity is associated with positive outcomes (Briesch & Chafouleas, 2009; Burke et al., 2011; Martin et al., 2004). In the case of unwanted behaviors, monitoring that changes both implicit and explicit evaluations serves to reduce the behavior; further the mere act of monitoring can lead to more negative implicit evaluations of that behavior even if behavior change does not result (Maas et al., 2013).

Recent efforts in gamification have shown that monitoring (when combined with game dynamics) is incredibly impactful on behavior. Gamification refers to a strategy of applying game design or game-like features to a non-game experience to drive user behavior (Gamification Wiki, 2013). The purpose of gamifying an activity is to trigger engagement in the activity and build meaning around it to sustain it (Gartner Group, 2011). Amy Jo Kim, a researcher and designer of social communities and games, suggests that critical mechanisms to achieve sustained motivation and meaning (via game-like opportunities) involve situations that allow for unique exploration, self-expression, cooperation, and competition. Myriad personal analytics tools have incorporated game mechanics into dashboard displays. They use badges, points, leaderboards, levels, and achievements to cultivate opportunities for competition and self-expression. For instance, BinCam is a tracker installed on users' trashcans to monitor whether any recycling ends up in the waste stream. The application offers visualizations of users' waste (e.g., accumulating trash or a growing tree) that can be shared across Facebook; thus, users can compare their waste relative to others. Online CO_2 emission trackers allow users to evaluate year-over-year emission averages or compare their carbon footprints relative to others. Fuelly.com allows vehicle owners to track the fuel efficiency of their motor vehicles and compare their results with owners of similar vehicles. Stepgreen.org allows users to commit to actions to reduce energy consumption and CO_2 emissions, and then record their reduction achievements; the site displays graphs showing cumulative savings resulting from their actions and allows users to contrast their actions relative to other groups pursuing similar goals.

Using Comparisons to Gamify Self-Monitoring

Self-monitoring theory focuses on expressive control (e.g., Snyder & Gangestad, 1986), an activity that is more related to making comparisons to others' *opinions* (vs. their abilities). However, the term *self-monitoring* has come to refer more generally to the action of observing and recording one's own behavior (Briesch & Chafouleas, 2009) or searching the environment for information to inform changes in one's behavior (Soibel, 2012). Thus, self-monitoring can involve any type of record as well as any form of comparison that can be meaningfully examined.

Research on social and self-comparisons indicates variability in how individuals react to a comparison (depending on whether or not it offers a contrast). When comparisons are made relative to the self, improvement over past self represents a contrast that can generate positive reactions (e.g., Hanko et al., 2010; Wilson & Ross, 2001). In the case of comparisons against others, when another is doing better than oneself, this upward contrast can generate negative reactions; similarly "downward contrast comparisons" (i.e., the other is doing worse than the self) can generate positive reactions (e.g., Kulik & Gump, 1997; Tesser, Miller, & Moore, 1988). However, if individuals perceive they can change their behaviors, there is positive motivation to respond to upward social comparisons (Collins, 1996). For example, a 2005 study by Robert Cialdini found that messages comparing consumers' energy consumption to others were more motivating than environmental, self-interest, or social responsibility messages.

Whereas gamification relies significantly on comparisons (and game triggers are highly effective in suggesting action), very little academic work has explored the mechanism driving consumer response. Even less is understood about how differ types of personal data could activate different responses. Could the monitoring and representation of data via different contrasts elicit different thoughts or feelings that could differentially drive behavior? For instance, *contrasts* or *discrepancies,* highlighted by comparisons, may serve to elicit affective arousal such as surprise (Maguire et al., 2011; Teigen & Keren, 2003). However, this arousal may be positively or negatively valenced depending on the presentation of data in a digital dashboard.

To explore such issues, I conducted a series of experiments utilizing certain types of comparisons and examined whether the positive or negative valence of the arousal associated with these comparisons can trigger certain consumption choices and commitments. In an initial study, participants were provided with information about carbon emissions and carbon footprints. To gamify participants' data, they were presented with digital dashboard information indicating that their carbon footprint was below or above the level from the prior year. Next, they were given information on carbon consuming devices as well as activities that generate carbon emissions in an average person's daily life. Finally, they were asked to commit to a series of activities to reduce their own carbon consumption. Specifically, they were asked if they would commit to turning off lights for the following week when they exited a room and would not be returning (immediately, within five minutes, *or* within 15 minutes). Participants scored a *zero* if they did not commit, *one* if they agreed to turn off the lights when they would be gone for 15 minutes, *two* if they agreed to turn off the lights when they would be gone for five minutes, and *three* if they were going to return immediately but were still willing to turn off the light.

They were also asked if they would be willing to set their computers to go into sleep or stand-by mode when inactive for more than 20 minutes. If they agreed, they were scored a *one*; if they did not, they received a *zero*. Finally, they were asked if they would be willing to turn their computer off after they were done using it for the day. If they agreed, they were scored a *one;* if they did not, they received a *zero*. These points were summed to create a commitment score. Using this measure of commitment, our analysis indicates that participants are more willing to commit to carbon emission reduction strategies when their displayed performances (relative to carbon emissions) were better in the current year than in the previous year.

In a second study, the underlying motivational drivers (related to willingness to make commitments to consumption behavior) were explored. In particular, *surprise* relative to a contrast comparison was examined as a potential mediator of willingness to commit. Participants were again provided with information about carbon emissions and their carbon footprint. They were then presented information through a digital dashboard showing that, on average, their carbon footprint was below or above the level it was in the previous year or that their carbon footprint was below or above the carbon footprint of individuals outside their in-group (social network). Next, they were asked to list any thoughts or feelings they had regarding the information they were presented; these responses were coded in terms of *positive surprise* (e.g., delight) and *negative surprise* (e.g., shock and disappointment). Then, a battery of affective measures were presented (including affect items related to both negative and positively valenced surprise); respondents indicated how the comparison made them feel on a five-item scale anchored by 1 = Not at all to 5 = Very much. Finally, a set of commitment opportunities, similar to the previous study, were provided and participants indicated their willingness to engage in activities on a five-item scale anchored by 1 = Definitely not to 5 = Definitely. Results indicated that when the comparison was related to previous personal behavior (year-to-year), participants were more willing to commit to carbon emission reduction strategies when their current reported performance (relative to carbon emissions) was better than the previous year or better than others outside their personal social network (in-group). Positive *surprise* contributed to their willingness to commit.

In a third study, participants were presented with the same measures as above but instead were presented a digital dashboard showing that, on average, their carbon footprint was below or above the level of individuals inside their personal social networks. When the comparison was against individuals inside their personal network, they were marginally more willing to commit to carbon emission reduction strategies when their reported performances (relative to carbon emissions) were worse than others. In this case, shock/negative surprise contributed to their willingness to commit.

These findings suggest that the positive or negative valence of arousal, associated with different types of comparisons, helps motivate certain desirable consumption choices and commitments. Downward self-comparisons to previous personal consumption activity (and downward social-comparisons to an out-group's consumption activity) motivated commitment to future sustainable consumption behavior. The pleasant surprise generated by the digital display of this downward comparison contributes to this motivation. However, upward social comparison, to an average other in their in-group or personal network, motivates commitment to future sustainable consumption behavior, and it is negative surprise (shock) that contributes to this motivation.

A next step in this vein of research is to begin to explore how degree of social sharing, personal agency, and type of third party participation in the generation of quantified personal data interact with type of comparisons and in turn motivate human behavior. Examining these combined influences and their impact on consumer reactions to the representation of their personal data will provide insights into how self-tracking, the evaluation of personal data stores, and gamification will continue to transform the role of data in consumer behavior and society.

References

Bandura, A. (1998). Health Promotion from the Perspective of Social Cognitive Theory. *Psychological Health,* 13, 623–649.

Bersin, J. (2014). Quantified Self: Meet the Quantified Employee. *Forbes,* Retrieved July 20, 2014 from www.forbes.com/sites/joshbersin/2014/06/25/quantified-self-meet-the-quantified-employee/.

Briesch, A. M. & Chafouleas, S. M. (2009). Review and Analysis of Literature on Self-Management Interventions to Promote Appropriate Classroom Behaviors (1988–2008). *School Psychology Quarterly,* 24 (2), 106–118.

Burke, L. E., Wang, J. & Sevick, M. A. (2011). Self-Monitoring in Weight Loss: A Systematic Review of the Literature. *Journal of American Dietetic Association,* 111 (1), 92–102.

Collins, R. L. (1996). For Better or Worse: The Impact of Upward Social Comparison on Self-Evaluations. *Psychological Bulletin, 119,* 51–69.

Gartner Group. (2011). *Gartner Predicts Over 70 Percent of Global 2000 Organizations Will Have at Least One Gamified Application by 2014.* Retrieved February 6, 2014 from www.gartner.com/newsroom/id/1844115.

Gamification Wiki. (2013). *Gamification.org.* Retrieved August 15, 2013 from www.gamification.org/.

Hanko, K., Crusius, J. & Mussweiler T. (2010). When I and Me Are Different: Assimilation and Contrast in Temporal Self-Comparisons. *European Journal of Social Psychology,* 40, 160–168.

Health Fact Sheet (2014). *Pew Research Internet Project.* Retrieved July 15, 2014 from www.pewinternet.org/fact-sheets/health-fact-sheet/.

Kanfer, F. H. (1991). *Self-Management Methods.* New York, NY: Pergamon Press.

Kulik, J. A. & Gump, B. B. (1997). Affective Reactions to Social Comparison: The Effects of Relative Performance and Related Attributes Information about Another Person. *Personality and Social Psychology Bulletin,* 23 (5), 452–468.

Lupton, D. (2014). Self-tracking Modes: Reflexive Self-Monitoring and Data Practices, Social Sciences Research Network Working Paper Series. Retrieved from http://ssrn.com/abstract=2483549.

Maas, J. Hietbrink, L., Rinck, M. & Kelisers Ger P. J. (2013). Changing Automatic Behavior through Self-Monitoring: Does Overt Change Also Imply Implicit Change? *Journal of Behavior Therapy and Experimental Psychiatry*, 44 (3), 279–284.

Maguire, R., Maguire, P. & Keane, M. T. (2011). Making Sense of Surprise: An Investigation of the Factors Influencing Surprise Judgments. *Journal of Experimental Psychology Learning, Memory, and Cognition,* 37 (1), 176–186.

Martin, G. L., Thompson, K. & Regehr, K. (2004). Studies Using Single-Subject Designs in Sport Psychology: 30 Years of Research. *The Behavior Analyst*, 27, 263–280.

Perez, Sarah (2012). Location-Based Shopping App ShopKick Partners with Mastercard on Rewards Program. *Techcrunch.* Retrieved July 28, 2012 from http://techcrunch.com/2012/06/27location-based-shopping-app-shopkick-partners-with-mastercard-on-rewards-program.

Snyder, M. & Gangestad, S. (1986). On the Nature of Self-Monitoring: Matters of Assessment, Matters of Validity. *Journal of Personality and Social Psychology*, 51, 125–139.

Soibel, A., Fong, K., Mullin, J. B., Jenkins, G. & Mar, R. A. (2012). Is Self-Monitoring Related to Social Comparison? It Depends How You Ask. *Individual Differences Research*, 10 (4), 193–201.

Teigen, K. H. & Keren, G. (2003). Surprises: Low Probabilities or High Contrasts? *Cognition,* 87, 55–71.

Tesser, A., Millar, M. & Moore, J. (1988). Some Affective Consequences of Social Comparison and Reflection Processes: The Pain and Pleasure of Being Close. *Journal of Personality and Social Psychology,* 54, 49–61.

The Quantified Self: Counting Every Moment (2012). *The Economist Technology Quarterly.* Retrieved July 1, 2014 from www.economist.com/node/21548493.

Wilson, A. E. & Ross, M. (2001). From Chump to Champ: People's Appraisals of Their Earlier and Present Selves. *Journal of Personality and Social Psychology*, 80, 572–584.

Wolfram, S. (2012). The Personal Analytics of My Life [Web log comment post]. Retrieved June 20, 2014 from http://blog.stephenwolfram.com/2012/03/the-personal-analytics-of-my-life/.

13

ADVERTISING EFFECTS IN SOCIAL MEDIA

Yogesh Joshi

Since the turn of the 21st century, due to the growth in availability and adoption of many digital social media platforms, interactions between consumers and firms have grown and changed significantly. Consumers are increasingly sharing their thoughts, feelings, opinions, viewpoints, and various kinds of information with one another as well as with firms, leading to a deluge of user generated content. Much of this content is being generated online across multiple channels, such as emails, blogs, user groups and discussion forums, and more recently, various social media platforms. Sites such as Facebook, Google+, and Twitter have provided a medium for quick as well as constant interaction between networks of consumers as well as firms and consumers. Furthermore, numerous tools today allow for cross-posting across platforms, further amplifying the reach and volume of generated content.

The amount of content generated within sites such as Facebook and Twitter is on the rise. For example, Twitter, which started with its first tweet from founder Jack Dorsey in March 2006, has grown to about 340 million tweets per day by 2012, to more than 500 million tweets per day in 2014. Given the tremendous amount of information being exchanged digitally today, not surprisingly, firms as well as researchers have become increasingly interested in understanding what consumers are saying across and within these various digital social media platforms. For instance, understanding the effects of word of mouth generated online and in social media and particularly how it is similar to or different from the effects of traditional offline marketing actions has been of acute interest to marketers for some time now (e.g., Trusov, Bucklin, & Pauwels, 2009). Similarly, understanding how social media and digital technologies shape consumer decisions and consumer journeys is at the top of the list of research priorities for the Marketing Science Institute (MSI, 2014).

Reflecting these trends, a recent survey conducted by McKinsey and Co. reveals that the use of digital social media platforms is no longer a novelty and in fact is now commonplace in firms across a variety of industry sectors (Bughin, Chui, & Harrysson, 2015). In terms of the nature of activities that firms engage in on these platforms, marketing activities rank amongst the top three actions for executives engaging in social media, whereas the other two being public relations and managing customer relationships. A big benefit that firms see from engaging in social media interactions with consumers is a reduction in communication costs, and many firms expect this benefit to further increase, going forward. At the same time, there is strong interest on part of firms towards leveraging social media as an advertising medium for communicating a firm's messages to consumers, as well as in engaging consumers such that they communicate firm related messages proactively with each other. In this context, the McKinsey survey reports that a key challenge faced by firms is being able to measure the impact of their actions on consumer behavior and marketplace outcomes, such as sales.

Early attempts at understanding the impact of consumer generated content as well as the impact of firm actions within social media began with the development of simple metrics related to the volume and frequency of content in these media (e.g., Tumasjan et al., 2010; Asur & Huberman, 2010, among many others; also see Moe & Schweidel, 2014 for an excellent discussion about the history and evolution of such metrics). Examples of such metrics include number of Facebook likes, number of tweets per day, number of re-tweets for a firm's tweet, number of mentions of a brand name, etc. The benefits of volume based metrics are that they are simple to construct, and allow for a quick summary of messy textual data. In that sense, these metrics constitute the low hanging fruit, hence were the first ones to be harvested early work. To some extent, such metrics are also quite useful: for example, all else equal, a firm's post on Facebook that receives more "likes" may be associated with more "engagement" on part of consumers. In traditional advertising parlance, a post with more "likes," "re-tweets," or "mentions" could be more effective for purposes of reach, awareness, etc. than a post that scores lower on these metrics. Indeed, Asur and Huberman (2010) report a strong association between tweet rate and box office success in the context of movies.

However, the main downside to the use of such simple metrics is not being able to capture the richness of information contained in the textual data generated by consumers and firms. To address this downside, one of the first lines of attack from both researchers and practitioners was to understand the valence of textual data generated in an interaction: e.g., whether a given tweet or a Facebook post possesses a positive or negative valence. Building on sentiment analysis approaches developed by computer scientists and linguists, researchers analyze a tweet and assign it a numerical score indicative of its valence. Thus, in addition to volume and frequency, one can use valence as an additional metric for deepening our understanding of consumer as well as firm behavior in digital social media. For instance, O'Connor et al. (2010) showed that tweet sentiment correlated highly with consumer confidence as well as political opinion. Other research (e.g., Bollen et al., 2011) has shown that sentiment as well as mood in Twitter is correlated with outcomes in the stock market.

Whereas valence is an important and complementary step forward from volume based metrics, from a marketer's perspective, there is still vast potential for harnessing knowledge and "social intelligence" (cf. Moe & Schweidel, 2014) from digital social media data. A key challenge in this process of improving our understanding of such data is developing what the right set of metrics should be that capture the nuances that are most relevant to the problem at hand. Popular press often refers to social media as a form of "free" advertising, in that one does not have to spend money "buying" ad time on these media as compared to conventional media such as television and radio. Because surveys also show that one of the top priorities for firms in using social media as a marketing tool is for purposes such as advertising, in our research, we have focused on developing some metrics that would be relevant towards measuring social media data to track advertising related impact. In this chapter, we outline such an approach that combines text analysis methods similar to those used for measuring sentiment with existing advertising theory to define relevant metrics that would help meet the goal of improving our understanding of consumer content in digital social media.

Theory of Advertising Effects

To motivate our metrics, we look at the vast existing research done on advertising and its effects in the past. Doing so reveals that there are many alternative paths one could take towards bringing advertising theory into the digital social age—which is indeed a good problem to have, from a researcher's perspective. Given my past work on advertising and its impact on firm strategy (Chen, Joshi, Raju, & Zhang, 2009), building on advertising theory rooted in economics as a base for constructing such metrics was a natural choice. However, it is important to note that a similar approach can be adopted for alternative theoretical foundations that seek to explain the effects of advertising (for instance, theories rooted in psychology, communications, marketing, etc.); and it is possible that these distinct approaches might find appropriate applications for distinct scenarios.

We now briefly summarize the relevant aspects of existing economic theory in advertising that we build upon subsequently. This theory suggests that advertising has three main effects: *persuasive*, *informative,* and *complementary* (for an excellent and in-depth review of this topic, see Bagwell, 2007; for a recent application in marketing, see Mehta, Chen, & Narasimhan, 2008, among others). Each of these effects impacts consumer preference and hence utility in distinct ways. We describe these mechanisms next.

The *persuasive* effect of advertising suggests that advertising affects consumer tastes by making consumers more brand loyal, and making demand more inelastic (e.g., Kaldor, 1950; Bagwell, 2007). This is akin to shifting consumer tastes towards the firm or product being advertised, by making consumers "like" the product more as a consequence of hearing the advertisement. For instance, upon hearing a persuasive ad about a high performance car, I as a consumer might like the performance attribute more than before seeing the ad, thus shifting my preferences, as well as increasing my utility for a car offering performance as a key benefit or feature.

The *informative* effect of advertising suggests that advertisements provide consumers with direct or indirect information that may earlier not be available to them (e.g., Grossman & Shapiro, 1984; Bagwell, 2007). For instance, a firm might advertise product specifications or availability for its product at certain locations. At a more fundamental level, a firm might simply advertise the existence of a product, and that in itself can lead to increased awareness about the product, and hence subsequent demand for it in the market. A key role for informative advertising then is to reduce imperfection in information available in the marketplace.

Finally, the *complementary* effect of advertising suggests that advertising may or may not change consumer preferences or provide additional information; however it may enter consumer preferences in a way that is complementary to consumption (e.g., Stigler & Becker, 1977, Bagwell, 2007). For example, when consumers value prestige (e.g., for wristwatches), they value consumption (i.e., wearing a Rolex to the opera) more when the product is advertised at the appropriate location (e.g., a Rolex ad in the opera-house lobby). In other words, such advertising may impact consumer expectations for certain product characteristics, such as quality, and hence impact the consumption decision.

The central premise of our argument here is that the persuasive, informative, as well as complementary effects of advertising, which have been documented and researched extensively in the past for traditional forms of advertising, serve as a strong theoretical basis for defining meaningful metrics for improving our understanding of content in digital social media (Joshi, Ma, Rand, & Raschid, 2013; Machedon, Rand, & Joshi, 2013). The intuition behind this premise is that because the underlying mechanisms behind each of these effects are not necessarily tied to the medium or channel of communication, and have been observed to work over alternative channels such as print, audio, and video; they are likely to work in digital channels as well. Once appropriately defined and measured, these metrics could then enable a better assessment of advertising related effects of consumer as well as firm content and interactions in digital social media.

Applying Advertising Theory to Social Media Content

Our approach towards applying advertising theory to social media consists of combining text analysis and classification techniques similar to those used in the context of sentiment analysis to define metrics motivated by advertising theory. We now illustrate this approach below in the context of "tweets," an extremely popular form of short digital online content. However, this approach can be applied in a similar fashion to other social media textual content as well, such as Facebook posts, Google+ comments, and the like.

As discussed earlier, advertising theory proposes three distinct routes via which advertising effects consumers. Hence, we seek to understand to what extent each tweet captures the three proposed effects. Simply put, a basic metric of interest to us in this context is: to what extent is each tweet persuasive, informative, and complementary? One way to answer these questions would be to assess each tweet manually, either using a significant number of experimental subjects, or a small number of expert judges, and have them rate each tweet on a scale that indicates the extent to which it is persuasive, informative, or complementary. The challenge with such approaches is the sheer amount of data involved—given the number of tweets that are generated in most contexts, in any practical application, rating each tweet manually would be time and cost prohibitive.

Consequently, to improve our understanding of advertising effects in social media, it is important to develop an automated approach towards rating each tweet on these dimensions of persuasiveness, informativeness, and complementarity. Such an automated approach can be developed as follows: (a) construct a training dataset of a sample of tweets; (b) run an experiment wherein subjects rate each tweet on dimensions related to persuasiveness, informativeness, as well as complementarity; (c) use these ratings to train a computational algorithm to derive associations between words used and dimensions of advertising effectiveness; and (d) use the trained algorithm to generate advertising effectiveness scores along each dimension for the rest of the tweets not used in the training process. This approach is elaborated on in detail in Machedon, Rand, and Joshi (2013); below we provide a brief discussion that highlights the main considerations during the various steps of this proposed approach.

Automating the Measurement of Advertising Effects in Tweets

We begin with the first step of selecting a sample of tweets for purposes of generating a training dataset. Such a sample could be selected in many ways, with the intent of generating a sample representative of the category or context of research interest. For instance, the focus in Machedon, Rand, and Joshi (2013) was a set of music bands; hence we constructed a set of tweets sent by bands as well as their followers, and sampled tweets from this set for purposes of training.

The second step involves obtaining ratings for each tweet in the selected sample on a host of dimensions related to the advertising effects of interest. Given that this activity would require a large number of subjects, an effective approach towards generating these ratings is using crowdsourcing methods. Our pilots in this context revealed that asking crowdsourcing platforms for straight-out classification of tweets into buckets of informativeness, persuasiveness, and/or complementarity were not as effective; however, questions related to the extent to which users agreed that any given tweet was informative, persuasive, or complementary yielded acceptable levels of consistency in scores across raters (for instance, when asked to rate on a scale of 1–9 their agreement with a statement such as "this tweet provides me with novel information" we observe a higher level of consistency across users, as compared to the consistency observed when users were simply asked whether a specific tweet was informative).

The third step involves developing an algorithm using tweets and ratings from the training sample and crowdsourcing experiment such that it can subsequently automatically classify the remaining tweets along the three advertising measures of interest. The basic intuition behind such an algorithm is to identify a set of commonly used words that are strongly associated with the tweet scoring high on specific advertising effects, and then parsing the remaining tweets to identify such words, as well as related words from a larger corpus of text, so as to determine the nature of these out of sample tweets. Extensive work on such algorithms has been done in computer sciences, linguistics, and other related disciplines; the focus here is to leverage this existing work for purposes of applications of classifications motivated by business theories regarding concepts such as advertising.

In the fourth step, the trained algorithm is then used to assign a score to each tweet on each dimension of advertising effect. Such scores can also be assigned in multiple ways: for instance, one can assign a binary score such that each tweet is classified to either be informative or not, persuasive or not, and complementary or not. Alternatively, one could also generate a score between 0 and 1 that reflects the extent to which a tweet is informative, persuasive, and complementary. The trade-offs in choosing one scoring mechanism versus other involve determining the computational as well as data collection burden imposed.

From our implementation of this above approach in the context of music bands, we observed the procedure to yield excellent results in terms of identifying informative tweets, and good but not excellent results in in terms of identifying persuasive and/or complementary tweets. Put differently, to achieve a similar level of confidence in the classification process as informative tweets would require more training data in the context of persuasive and/or complementary tweets. This reflects the notion that whether or not one learned new information is easier to assess than whether one changed their preferences or felt better being associated with a product or entity. More generally speaking, these observations reveal that current classification techniques using automated procedures might be more accurate/effective for easier to assess and simpler dimensions, and face greater challenges along more complex dimensions. Hence an excellent area for future interdisciplinary research would be to further identify ways such classification can be improved.

Some Applications and Conclusion

The procedure proposed above allows us to assess the content within each digital social interaction in terms of its ability to generate persuasive, informative, and complementary effects akin to the theoretical effects identified in the previous literature. These metrics, along with metrics related to valence (i.e., whether the social interaction is of a positive, neutral, or negative nature), and metrics related to volume and frequency together form a good set of predictor variables that can be utilized for exploring various research questions. For instance, in Joshi et al. (2013), these metrics are used to determine whether specific types of firm actions in social media lead to engagement on part of consumers in social media, and whether such actions and engagement relate to observed sales for these firms.

Metrics such as the ones defined above open up numerous possibilities for future research. For instance, an interesting area for exploration would be whether specific types of actions on part of firms motivate certain specific types of actions on part of consumers—e.g., if firms send positive persuasive tweets, does that in fact motivate consumers to do the same, or otherwise? Do certain types of firm actions increase or decrease the amount and nature of consumer actions in social media? Why? A similar set of questions can be investigated in the context of consumer-to-consumer interactions. Does a particular type of tweet motivate more versus less engagement from fellow consumers, and why? Considering interactions between distinct consumer types—e.g., opinion leaders versus followers, what types of interactions would one anticipate, and do these hypotheses hold in the context of social media data?

Finally, the approach discussed above was applied towards defining metrics that capture specific advertising effects in terms of informativeness, persuasiveness, and complementarity—effects motivated by an established literature on advertising theory in economics. As suggested earlier, one can imagine using a similar approach for defining metrics that capture alternative types of advertising effects—e.g., those motivated by alternative theories from distinct disciplines such as psychology, communications, marketing, etc. For instance, one might be interested in assessing to what extent is a social media interaction novel? Does this interaction increase or decrease involvement? Is the message easy or complex to understand? Does the content provide a specific argument towards a goal/objective? Does the message generate a certain type of emotion? To what extent does the message convey humor, or fear, or warmth? Motivated by specific research questions, the definition, measurement, and testing of such metrics can hopefully lead to novel insights and improved understanding of effective as well as ineffective interactions between consumers and firms in social media.

References

Asur, S., & Huberman, B. A. (2010). Predicting the future with social media. *Proc. IEEE/WIC/ACM Int. Conf. Web Intell. Intell. Agent Technol. (WI-IAT)*, 1, 492–499.

Bagwell, K. (2007). The economic analysis of advertising, in the *Handbook of industrial organization, Volume 3,* Chapter 28, Eds. M. Armstrong and R. Porter, North-Holland, Amsterdam, 1701–1844.

Bollen, J., Huina M.O., & Xiaojun Z. (2011). Twitter mood predicts the stock market. *Journal of Computational Science*, 2(1), 1–8.

Bughin, J., Chui, M., & Harrysson, M. (2015). Transforming the business through social tools. McKinsey & Company. [available at www.mckinsey.com/insights/high_tech_telecoms_internet/transforming_the_business_through_social_tools].

Chen, Y., Joshi, Y. V., Raju, J. S., & Zhang, Z. J. (2009). A theory of combative advertising. *Marketing Science*, 28(1), 1-19.

Grossman, G.M., & Shapiro, C. (1984). Informative advertising with differentiated products. *The Review of Economic Studies*, 51(1), 63–81.

Joshi, Y., Ma, L., Rand, W., & Raschid, L. (2013). Building the b[r]and: Understanding how social media drives consumer engagement and sales, MSI Working Paper Series 2013 Report No. 13–113.

Kaldor, N.V. (1950). The economic aspects of advertising. *The Review of Economic Studies*, 18(2), 1–27.

Machedon, R., Rand, W., & Joshi, Y. (2013). Automatic crowdsourcing-based classification of marketing messaging on twitter. *SocialCom, 2013 International Conference on Social Computing,* 975–978.

Mehta, N., Chen, X., & Narasimhan, O. (2008). Informing, transforming, and persuading: Disentangling the multiple effects of advertising on brand choice decisions. *Marketing Science*, 27(3), 334–355.

Moe, W., & Schweidel, D. (2014). *Social media intelligence.* Cambridge University Press.

MSI (2014). 2014–2016 Research Priorities. Marketing Science Institute.

O'Connor, B., Balasubramanyan, Routledge, B., & Smith, N. (2010). From tweets to polls: Linking text sentiment to public opinion time series. *ICWSM*, 11, 122–129.

Stigler, G., & Becker, G. (1977). De gustibus non est disputandum. *American Economic Review,* 67, 76–90.

Trusov, M., Bucklin, R., & Pauwels, K. (2009). Effects of word-of-mouth versus traditional marketing: Findings from an internet social networking site. *Journal of Marketing*, 73 (September), 90–102.

Tumasjan, A., Timm, O., Sprenger, P., & Welpe, I. (2010). Predicting elections with twitter: What 140 characters reveal about political sentiment. *ICWSM,* 10, 178–185.

14

A WAY WITH WORDS

Using Language for Psychological Science in the Modern Era

Ryan L. Boyd and James W. Pennebaker

The world of human research is changing. Major shifts in technology have created an environment where psychology and the other social sciences are now able to track human thinking and behaviors on a scale that was unimaginable 15 years ago. In the year 2000, if we had an interest in studying thousands of people relatively quickly and cheaply, we would have had to pack up our paper and pencils and head out to the places where people would be willing to work with us—most likely college campuses. Finding more ecologically valid samples was certainly possible (e.g., Barker & Wright, 1954), but was costly, time-consuming, and painstaking.

In the early part of the 21st century, laboratory research expanded outside of the traditional lab to the internet (e.g., Birnbaum, 2004). As with traditional lab studies, many internet studies continued to be highly controlled experiments using paid volunteers. Although these online samples have been larger and more diverse, well-controlled, internet-based experiments have raised the same questions as earlier, in-house lab studies regarding their ecological validity (e.g., Chaytor & Schmitter-Edgecombe, 2003; McNamara & Blumer, 1982).

Revolutionary progress in technology has caused a new model of research to emerge. This new model takes us from the past, where studies were run to generate data from human phenomena, to a place where the data already exists *en masse*. In this chapter, we describe how large data sources based on natural language can be analyzed to reveal central social and psychological principles. We then outline some new ways to think about and analyze natural language using both deductive and inductive methodologies that are fast, automated, and easy to use.

The Rise of Independent Data Generation

Even without any social scientists around, human data is now being generated by virtually everyone on a second-by-second basis on the internet. This new data renaissance has taken the form of online purchase information, logs of internet searches, archived listserv posts, GPS tracking data, forum posts, and social media updates, to name just a fraction of the formats. Additionally, these data sources are often publicly archived or otherwise easily accessible. A major implication of such widespread information generation is that data reflecting many human constructs no longer needs to be created by researchers, only harvested. Indeed, data reflecting the very phenomena in which human researchers are interested—social interactions, information search behaviors, attitudes, cultural movements, and so on—already exist in databases around the world and are ripe for study.

The most common data sources available are made up of the words that people post online. This is most apparent in social media due, in part, to the considerable amount of time that the world spends engaging others online (e.g., Facebook, 2014). The internet, broadly defined, along with websites like Facebook, Twitter, and Reddit, has created a space for people to interact with others while sharing their opinions, recommendations, thoughts, and feelings about practically all subject matter imaginable. What's more, these are inherently *real-world* phenomena that are not solicited by scientists. People are engaging in these behaviors of their volition, in their own idiosyncratic manners, and without any intervention on the part of researchers. Indeed, by perusing social media, it is possible to take a rather candid look into the individual's social and mental worlds.

Despite the appeal of an unimaginably large new source of data, it comes with some significant problems. Principally, social scientists must understand how to begin handling naturally occurring language or, as information scientists refer to it, *unstructured data.* Language data is not inherently quantified, nor does it possess a uniform structure with which to convert it into useable metrics. It is therefore difficult to quantitatively say whether one language sample is meaningfully different from, or the same as, another language sample when adopting an empirical perspective. This raises fundamental questions about how to best work with language as a data source. How do we give structure and meaning to language? How do we grapple with large quantities of it? And, perhaps most importantly, what can we learn from how people use words?

Language in the Psychological Sciences

The sheer quantity of data available via social media outlets has rendered manual coding and qualitative analyses all but obsolete. However, the modern technological boom and widespread generation of large and complex unstructured data has been accompanied by increased interest from researchers and laypeople alike. Within the field of psychology, the past two decades have seen researchers create new tools that help us come to terms with large bodies of language data. Moreover, many of these tools have been designed in an open-ended fashion, allowing researchers to easily quantify language in innovative ways, empowering others to begin their own work within the vast world of words. In order to be useful in the modern era, such tools should 1) provide structure and meaning to language data in a relatively fast, consistent, and automated fashion, and 2) do so in a manner that is easy to use.

In the following sections, we present methods, tools, and research from our lab that span two broad categories of language quantification. The first, and most prevalent method, is a top-down (i.e., dictionary-based) approach to understanding how word use reflects all manner of social and psychological processes. The second method is a bottom-up (i.e., vocabulary-driven) approach that serves a similar purpose, but is more dynamic and flexible and allows greater control over how language is handled. We will discuss these two methods in the context of software that has been explicitly designed to assist with each approach and provide a brief look at research in these areas.

A Top-Down Approach to Language: Linguistic Inquiry and Word Count (LIWC)

Psychologists have long assumed that people's words provide information about their emotions and drives (e.g., Freud, 1891). Following the psychoanalytic movement, a small group of mainstream psychologists continued to explore how basic needs could be reflected in word use. The precursors to the modern approach took hold in the middle of the 20th century. Researchers codified clusters of words into construct-specific "dictionaries" that provided clues people's needs for achievement, power, and affiliation (e.g., Lasswell, Lerner, & de Sola Pool, 1952). For example, people who used words such as *try, succeed, win*, or even *fail* were thought to be concerned with achievement in general. Indeed, multiple studies found that the use of words such as these predicted achievement-related behaviors (e.g., McClelland, Atkinson, Clark, & Lowell, 1953).

With the introduction of mainframe computers in the 1960s, researchers sought to find a way to automate the search for construct-relevant dictionary words inside of books, articles, and other mass media of the day. For example, to determine the degree to which a newspaper article was concerned with war, a computer system could be designed to scan the article for words such as *rifle* and *battle*, among other words belonging to a predefined "military" category. The first major undertaking in this realm was the Harvard General Inquirer (see Stone, Dunphy, Smith, & Ogilvie, 1966). Whereas similar mass media studies were successful in their day, their approach eventually gave way to a return to analyzing the words used by single individuals as a means to better understand their psychological processes (e.g., Martindale, 1975; Mergenthaler, 1996).

A common thread to all of these methods was a top-down, dictionary-based approach to quantifying language. Each subsequent development can be seen as a progressive step towards the goal of automatically extracting some form of consistent, meaningful psychological information from a person's language by looking at their patterns of word use. There were, however, many pitfalls to most of these approaches. First, many researchers' dictionaries contained obscure categories of language that pertained to highly specific theories later demonstrated to be of limited utility. Second, the implementation of these dictionaries was non-transparent and difficult to use. Complicated algorithms and unclear rulesets left many dictionary-based approaches almost exclusively in the hands of those who originally developed them, regardless of their merits.

Linguistic Inquiry and Word Count

By the late 1990s, an important break from the past occurred concerning text analysis. A distinction emerged between linguistic *content* and, for a lack of a better term, linguistic *style*. George Miller (1995), for example, made this distinction when talking about language and brain function. He pointed out that traditional content words, which are made up of nouns, regular verbs, adjectives, and most adverbs, were processed in the temporal lobes such as in Wernicke's area. Style-related words, on the other hand, are made up of function words, which included pronouns, prepositions, articles, conjunctions, auxiliary verbs, and a small number of other words. Function words, it seemed, tended to be processed in more frontal areas such as in Broca's area. (Note that we now know that this is a great oversimplification).

The content-style distinction was important because almost the entire history of language analysis in personality, clinical, and social psychology had focused on content. Interestingly, Miller (1995) noted that it was the function words rather than the content words that often signaled people's psychological states. And it made sense. The ability to use pronouns or prepositions requires well-developed social skills to communicate.

Consider the sentence, "They were here with me and then went back there." On a certain level, the sentence has absolutely no meaning to us because we don't know who "they" or "me" are. The sentence is phrased in the past tense with the verb "were," but there is no corresponding information about when the sentence was written. Similarly, "here," "there," "back," etc. cannot be decoded without knowing more about the broader context of the conversation and participants. Importantly, however, although we might not have any idea about the content of the sentence, we can get a hint of the author's psychology based on this utterance. He or she is likely sociable and knows the message's recipient quite well given that the target *necessarily* must know what the function words refer to for any meaning to be purposefully extracted.

In the late 1990s, the first desktop computer programs were developed that started to look specifically at function words to better understand social and psychological states. Among the first was the dictionary-based program Linguistic Inquiry and Word Count (LIWC; Pennebaker, Francis, & Booth, 2001; Pennebaker, Booth, & Francis, 2007). The two main facets of LIWC are a software package and a dictionary. The software itself is in many ways unique in that it is explicitly single-purpose in nature. That is, it reads text files and counts up dictionary-specified words, tallies them into predefined categories, and then divides them by the total number of words. The simple "word counting" approach allows for the extremely rapid processing of language, bypassing the computational requirements of part-of-speech tagging and opacity of lofty weighting schemes.

The second facet of LIWC is the dictionary. At the highest level, the LIWC dictionary focuses primarily on function words (i.e., closed class) and, to smaller degree, a circumscribed group of content (i.e., open class) words. During their construction, the LIWC dictionaries were built based on standard scale-construction methods, relying on psychometric measures that are well-understood and widely practiced by researchers. Most language categories within the LIWC dictionary involved multiple rounds of human judges making ratings on the appropriateness of specific words assigned to specific word categories. More objective categories of language (e.g., first person singular pronouns) were collected from standard grammar or linguistic texts. In addition to obtaining high inter-judge reliability, we also computed Cronbach internal reliability coefficients based on word uses from a large corpus of texts (see Pennebaker, Chung, Ireland, Gonzales, & Booth, 2007).

As it currently stands, the LIWC dictionary analyzes text by coding for ~80 dimensions of language, including four general descriptor categories (total word count, words per sentence, percentage of words captured by the dictionary, and percent of words longer than six letters), 22 standard linguistic dimensions (e.g., percentage of words in the text that are pronouns, articles, auxiliary verbs, etc.), 32 word categories tapping psychological constructs (e.g., affect, cognition, biological processes), seven personal concern categories (e.g., work, home, leisure activities), three paralinguistic dimensions (assents, fillers, non-fluencies), and 12 punctuation categories (periods, commas, etc.). Each category has been shown to reflect psychologically meaningful information and, depending on the research question, are relatively intuitive and straightforward.

Importantly, the open-ended nature of LIWC allows researchers to create their own dictionaries for specific inquiries—any topic of study can employ the software to convert language into psychologically meaningful metrics. Researchers have used the LIWC software in conjunction with custom-made dictionaries to study topics as diverse as how people perceive their homes (Saxbe & Repetti, 2009), self-talk during problem-solving tasks (Oliver, Markland, Hardy, & Petherick, 2008), moral foundations theory (Graham, Haidt, & Nosek, 2009), mindfulness (Collins et al., 2009), privacy concerns (Vasalou, Gill, Mazanderani, Papoutsi, & Joinson, 2011), and age-related stereotypes (Remedios, Chasteen, & Packer, 2010), among others.

Psychological Research With LIWC

A simple search on Google Scholar for the term "LIWC" returns over 4,900 results, excluding citations and patent information—this figure includes far too many studies for us to review here. Instead, we outline some of the core domains of research that have used the LIWC software and dictionary. For a review of the standard LIWC findings that is written for a social psychological audience, see Tauszik and Pennebaker (2010).

Personality. A major early finding with LIWC was that various facets of people's personalities are reflected in the way that they use function words. For example, Pennebaker and King (1999) found broad dimensions of personality that are expressed in language but only partially captured by traditional self-report questionnaires. This is due in part to the fact that a person's language reflects spontaneous, ongoing processes that occur naturally and bypass problems of introspection and retrospection (Groom & Pennebaker, 2002). Mehl and Pennebaker (2003) extended this line of research into the real world by recording random samples of language from participants using an electronic recording device called the "EAR" (Mehl, Pennebaker, Crow, Dabbs, & Price, 2001). In their work, the researchers found that the language people use in their everyday lives was predictive not only of other psychological measures, but of the behaviors and activities in which people engaged. How people use psychologically meaningful language has been found to covary with changes in personality across the lifespan (e.g., Pennebaker & Stone, 2003), and recent work even suggests that people's use of "filler" words (e.g., "um," "uh-huh") are indicative of gender and personality differences (Laserna, Seih, & Pennebaker, 2014).

Patterns of thought. A second area of research using LIWC that has begun to propel other lines of inquiry addresses the very patterns of thought indicative of the individual across various contexts. Early work with LIWC found consistent markers of severe depression that are reflected in the individual's language, including an acute focus on the self (reflected in first person singular pronouns such as "me" and "I"; Rude, Gortner, & Pennebaker, 2004; Stirman & Pennebaker, 2001). When people talk with others, we can discern truthful statements from deceptive ones with impressive accuracy by simply looking at their words, particularly in how function words are used (e.g., Newman, Pennebaker, Berry, & Richards, 2003; Toma & Hancock, 2012).

Function word use is also a powerful marker of the fundamental ways that people understand and engage the world around them. Using LIWC, researchers have unearthed a core dimension of thinking style called the categorical-dynamic index (CDI; Pennebaker, Chung, Frazee, Lavergne, & Beaver, 2014). Across a wide array of texts, simple factor analyses of eight dimensions of function words (articles, prepositions, personal pronouns, impersonal pronouns, auxiliary verbs, negations, adverbs, and conjunctions) yields a single dimension whereby articles and prepositions are positively loaded and the remaining function word categories are negatively loaded.

Using a simple additive algorithm, any given text can be placed along the CDI's bipolar continuum ranging from categorical thinking (relatively high use of articles and prepositions) to dynamic, or more "here-and-now," thinking (high use of pronouns, auxiliary verbs, etc.). On the categorical end of the CDI, we find individuals who approach the world in a relatively logical, complex, "amateur scientist" manner. On the dynamic end of the spectrum, we find individuals who are more socially engaged, tell stories, and pay more attention to the action of the world around them. This dimension is predictive of academic success, sex, and intelligence (Pennebaker, Chung, et al., 2014) and even serves as a robust measure of personality and author identity (Boyd & Pennebaker, in press).

Social processes. It should come as no surprise that language, a fundamentally social behavior, also tells us a great deal about social processes. Analyzing the relative use of first person singular pronouns, or I-words, of two or more people in ongoing interaction, yields reliable cues to social status. Specifically, people high in social status tend to use I-words much less than people lower in social status (Kacewicz et al., 2013).

By tracking how similarly any two people talk can also reveal how much they are paying attention to each other. Language style matching (LSM; Niederhoffer & Pennebaker, 2002) is a simple measure of the distance between two individual's linguistic styles and is easily calculated using LIWC. LSM has been found to be predictive of relationship longevity (Ireland et al., 2011) and has been used to better understand how two people influence each other in their work (Ireland & Pennebaker, 2010). By monitoring stylistic similarity, researchers have been able to shape the very nature of group interactions (Tausczik & Pennebaker, 2013) and have gained considerable insight into how competing groups negotiate with each other (Ireland & Henderson, 2014).

In sum, simple language analysis methods such as LIWC have been used to great effect in the study of social and psychological processes including personality, cognition, perception, mental health, and others. Its top-down, dictionary driven approach is simple yet powerful, easy to use, and allows researchers to quantify and employ language in their own work with practically no overhead. We now turn to the other side of the coin: the bottom-up approach to psychological research with language.

A Bottom-Up Approach to Language: Topic Modeling and Topic Discovery

The dictionary-based approach adopted by LIWC is one of the fastest and most accessible ways to quantify language in a manner that is theory-driven, simple to apply, and well-suited to studying categories of language that are broad and applicable to virtually all people. In the past two decades, top-down word counting methods have helped us understand how powerful language data can be for addressing questions about human nature. However, in adopting a dictionary-based approach, there is an important missing piece in its applicability and utility. Content coding dictionaries, by definition, rely on predefined categories for various topics such as the self, leisure, and cognitive processes. However, they can fail to recognize content from other topics of interest, limiting the scope of what types of language can be made useful for empirical inquiry.

Should we want to study the common themes of advertising campaigns or examine the most frequent topics found in Facebook status updates, we cannot use a premade dictionary where none exists. Furthermore, if we adopt an exploratory perspective, how are we to know *what* common themes exist in our data in the first place? Issues such as these leave considerable room for language that is not captured by dictionaries, yet remains present in any sample of language data and could potentially reflect hidden psychological processes. A broad set of methods that can address these issue are referred to as various forms of *topic modeling*.

Topic modeling is a computational technique aimed at determining how different words can appear together to form a larger shared meaning. On the surface, most topic modeling can be thought of as a factor analysis of content words. Imagine that we had access to 10,000 legal briefs and we extracted the 500 most common content words used in the briefs. Among the 500 words might be words such as *copyright*, *infringement*, *divorce*, *alimony*, *fraud*, and *embezzlement*. A factor analysis of the rates of the use of the 500 words across the 10,000 documents will yield a coherent group of factors that will reveal the general topics of different documents. For example, one group of legal documents about copyright infringement will likely contain relatively constant rates of some words, such as "copyright" and "trademark," but not others (e.g., "divorce" and "extramarital"). A book chapter on language analysis might be expected to have a particular ratio of the words "language" to "research," and so on. In practice, topic modeling has been used primarily to classify documents into different categories.

The technology-oriented genesis of topic modeling has resulted in a considerable number of approaches to looking for shared meaning in clusters of words. However, popular techniques like Latent Dirichlet Allocation (LDA; Blei, Ng, & Jordan, 2003) and non-negative matrix factorization algorithms (e.g., Arora, Ge, Halpern, Mimno, Moitra, et al., 2012) can, at times, possess rather different assumptions about the nature of word use. As their names may suggest, these methods often employ complex algorithms to achieve the task of understanding, generally speaking, *what* a body of text is trying to convey. However, the power of these algorithms comes at substantial costs to those seeking to use them. The processes by which topics are modeled may be lacking in transparency, resulting in themes that have been extracted from text with no simple way to understand why some words are being clustered together but not others. Additionally, the implementation of these procedures usually requires advanced programming skills and access to appropriate resources for handling such computationally intensive approaches. These factors conspire to create an environment in which popular topic modeling methods can take many days to complete, and sometimes considerably longer, on even modest datasets. Moreover, recent studies suggest that the accuracy of such complicated and popular algorithms has been greatly overestimated in the past (e.g., Lancichinetti et al., 2015).

Currently, psychologists are using topic modeling to explore what different themes can tell us about how groups of people may be similar to, as well as different from, others. Related to topic modeling, *topic discovery* may be thought of as the exploratory uncovering of themes in text. In order to discover new topics in a text, researchers have traditionally relied on having trained experts read through a person's verbal expressions to form qualitative impressions of what core themes are present. The automation of topic discovery process is very desirable and a fast, intuitive method of doing these procedures is in high demand. One of the more promising methods to come from the field of psychology is known as the meaning extraction method.

The Meaning Extraction Method

At its heart, the meaning extraction method (MEM, from Chung & Pennebaker, 2008) operates on the assumption that different words belonging to an overarching theme will tend to be used together. This assumption is meaningful in its own right. By merely observing words that tend to be used together across multiple samples of text, we are able to draw very clear inferences about what is being talked about, by whom, and in what quantities—all in a way that can be applied to virtually any topic in any language. Additionally, these simple assumptions allow for easy application, interpretation, and modification for any line of research, thus bypassing the pitfalls inherent to many more complicated topic modeling approaches.

Like its assumptions, the process by which we perform the MEM is fairly simple and consists of only a few steps after acquiring a body of language. In short, we create a table of all observations in a dataset, noting in a binary fashion which texts used which common content words (1 = used word, 0 = did not use word). This involves the removal of function words (e.g., "the," "if," "did") and uncommon content words to ensure that the most prevalent and meaningful themes can be extracted. Finally, we apply a common factor analytic method known as a Principal Components Analysis (PCA) to the word-by-observation table. The results of the PCA are provided in the form of variable clusters (in this case, words), and these clusters reflect the broader themes that can be found in the sample of text.

As an example, imagine that you have a large sample of text from a social media website wherein people are talking about their favorite beverages. In talking about the *qualities* of their favorite beverage, we may expect some people to use words like "refreshing," "delicious," and "flavorful." On the other hand, individuals describing their *perceived image* of a brand may use words like "exciting," "popular," and "innovative." Across all of the language samples, we remove words irrelevant to thematic content, find the words that most people are using, and then determine who is using which words. The last step, a PCA, will then reveal the word clusters that belong to "qualities" and "brand image" themes, respectively. Importantly, after these themes and others have been uncovered, we can then quantify the degree to which any person invokes these themes in their discussion, later using this data in statistical models. We might find that people who use the "brand image" theme are more extroverted, or perhaps the people using greater amounts of the "beverage qualities" theme are more impulsive. As we will describe shortly, the themes that can be discovered with MEM have indeed been found to be psychologically meaningful, sometimes in surprising ways.

The Meaning Extraction Helper

In its earliest forms, the MEM was both transparent and powerful, but required a considerable amount of manual, hands-on work to complete. Different inflections of words had to be manually converted into the same word (e.g., "running," "ran," and "runs" to their root form, "run"; this process is known as "lemmatization"). The process involved different software packages for each stage, the manual creation of stop lists, and careful attention to word conversions. Two researchers working on the same sample of language may understandably make very different choices at each stage, and these idiosyncrasies would have to be carefully documented in order to be reproducible.

To address these practical considerations, our lab has recently released the Meaning Extraction Helper (MEH; Boyd, 2015), a free program that automates all of the front-end procedures of the MEM, many of which are common to other topic modeling approaches. In its simplest application, users need only to make a few basic selections, point the software to the location of text files, and wait for the analysis procedures to finish. This allows users to easily and efficiently convert large amounts of text into structured data that is ready for analysis, leaving researchers to run PCAs to extract as many themes as they would like at their desired level of molecularity. Major benefits of MEH include its speed, flexibility, and power for analyzing language in different ways. Additionally, it has been designed with scalability and vast amounts of social media data in mind such that it is capable of handling tens of millions of observations in a single run. The software has already seen growing use in the fields of psychology and communication. Additionally, MEH is readily adapted for use in numerous other advanced language analysis procedures, including LDA (Blei et al., 2003) and open vocabulary approaches (Schwartz et al., 2013).

Research Using the Meaning Extraction Method

A growing body of research using the MEM has found that the dimensions of thought revealed through a person's language reflects psychological processes in multiple domains and is predictive of other individual differences factors. In their original introduction of the MEM, Chung and Pennebaker (2008) analyzed over 1,100 open-ended self-descriptions from a student sample. This analysis revealed nine broad dimensions along which people typically described themselves, including sociability (a theme that included words such as "outgoing" and "friendly"), self-evaluation ("attractive," "lazy"), and maturity ("mature," "successful"). The degree to which any person invoked these themes was also found to be predictive of individual differences factors such as the "Big 5" personality traits, sex, prior SAT performance, and subsequent course grades.

A telling follow-up that demonstrated how useful the MEM can be (see Pennebaker, 2011), students were asked to write about a picture of a water bottle (see Figure 14.1) as if they were describing it to someone who had not seen it. Participant's simple responses to this task often included basic descriptions of the bottle's geometry, the images depicted on the label, and the lighting of the image, yet were indicative of deeper psychological phenomena. People who wrote about lighting conditions had a tendency to be more thoughtful and artistic, whereas those focusing on the surface structure of the bottle (i.e., the barrier between the contents of the bottle and the outside world) were more likely to report being disagreeable and having tendencies to avoid sharing feelings with others. The basic contents of a person's water bottle description were predictive of behaviors such as consuming alcohol, regularly cleaning living spaces, and other self-maintenance behaviors.

Students were asked to describe what they saw when looking at a picture of a water bottle. The responses to this task were predictive of various personality and behavioral differences, (e.g., artistic proclivities, agreeableness, and self-maintenance behaviors).

FIGURE 14.1 Water Bottle Exercise

Since its introduction, the MEM has been applied to an increasing number of domains. LeFebvre, LeFebvre, Blackburn, and Boyd (in press) used the MEM to find that students who accurately estimated their ability to deliver speeches described themselves in fundamentally different ways than did students who over- or underestimated their own competence. Boyd and Pennebaker (in press) have found that authors can be uniquely identified by their "thematic signature"—a composite of the MEM-derived themes consistently used across their writings. While researching cultural differences in depression, Ramirez-Esparza, Chung, Kacewicz, and Pennebaker (2008) applied the MEM to the language of internet forum users. By analyzing the natural language of over 800 individuals, the researchers found that depressed individuals who wrote in Spanish were more likely to bring up relational themes than English-speaking individuals, who showed a tendency to invoke themes about medical issues in their lives. Finally, Kramer and Chung (2011) used the MEM on Facebook user updates as a way to explore dimensions of self-expression in social media settings. Their work in this area found three common ways that individuals expressed themselves online—informal speech, description of positive events, and discussion of school—that were largely invariant of culture (US, UK, Australia, and Canada).

Conclusions

In this chapter, we have described two broad methods of taking language data—a dictionary-based approach and a vocabulary-based approach—and deriving metrics that are psychologically meaningful across domains and research interests. By introducing software that corresponds to each method, social scientists can begin to appreciate that the incorporation of language into everyday research is not something for the future, but rather something that anyone can undertake *today*. Real-world, independently generated data has burgeoned in terms of both quality and quantity, and the tools necessary to acquire and make use of this data are already available. Particularly in the case of social media, the data available to curious researchers is of the exact nature that social scientists can best capitalize on.

The future of the social sciences will involve a great deal of venturing outside of the laboratory in order to better understand people in the real world. The form that this research will take is wide open to speculation as the nature of technology and our data is ever changing. However, in the interim, we already have unprecedented access to the thoughts, feelings, and behaviors of people in the form of their words. The prospects for better, faster, and easier methods of studying human nature have already begun to see realization.

References

Arora, S., Ge, R., Halpern, Y., Mimno, D., Moitra, A. Sontag, D., Wu, Y., et al. (2012). A practical algorithm for topic modeling with provable guarantees. *CoRR*, 4777–4803. http://arxiv.org/abs/1212.4777

Barker, R., & Wright, H. (1954). *Midwest and its children: The psychological ecology of an American town*. New York, NY: US: Row, Peterson and Company.

Birnbaum, M.H. (2004). Human research and data collection via the internet. *Annual Review of Psychology, 55*, 803–832.

Blei, D.M., Ng, A.Y., & Jordan, M.I. (2003). Latent dirichlet allocation. *Journal of Machine Learning Research, 3*(2003), 993–1022.

Boyd, R.L. (2015). MEH: Meaning Extraction Helper (Version 1.2.65) [Software]. Available from http://meh.ryanb.cc.

Boyd, R.L., & Pennebaker, J.W. (in press). Did Shakespeare write *Double Falsehood*? Identifying individuals by creating psychological signatures. *Psychological Science.*

Chaytor, N., & Schmitter-Edgecombe, M. (2003). The ecological validity of neuropsychological tests: A review of the literature on everyday cognitive skills. *Neuropsychology Review, 13*(4), 181–197.

Chung, C.K., & Pennebaker, J.W. (2008). Revealing dimensions of thinking in open-ended self-descriptions: An automated meaning extraction method for natural language. *Journal of Research in Personality, 42*(1), 96–132.

Collins, S.E., Chawla, N., Hsu, S.H., Grow, J., Otto, J.M., & Marlatt, G.A. (2009). Language-based measures of mindfulness: Initial validity and clinical utility. *Psychology of Addictive Behaviors, 23*(4), 743–749.

Facebook (2014). *Facebook Q2'14 earnings call transcript*. Available from http://investor.fb.com/eventdetail.cfm?eventid=146445.

Freud, S. (1891). *On aphasia*. E. Stengel (Trans.). International Universities Press, 1953.

Graham, J., Haidt, J., & Nosek, B.A. (2009). Liberals and conservatives rely on different sets of moral foundations. *Journal of Personality and Social Psychology, 96*(5), 1029–1046.

Groom, C.J., & Pennebaker, J.W. (2002). Words. *Journal of Research in Personality, 36*, 615–621.

Ireland, M.E., & Henderson, M.D. (2014). Language style matching, engagement, and impasse in egoistic negotiations. *Negotiations and Conflict Management Research*, 7, 1–16.

Ireland, M.E., & Pennebaker, J.W. (2010). Language style matching in writing: Synchrony in essays, correspondence, and poetry. *Journal of Personality and Social Psychology, 99*, 549–571.

Ireland, M.E., Slatcher, R.B., Eastwick, P.W., Scissors, L.E., Finkel, E.J., & Pennebaker, J.W. (2011). Language style matching predicts relationship initiation and stability. *Psychological Science, 22*, 39–44.

Kacewicz, E., Pennebaker, J.W., Davis, M., Jeon, M., & Graesser, A.C. (2013). Pronoun use reflects standings in social hierarchies. *Journal of Language and Social Psychology, 33*(2), 125–143.

Kramer, A.D.I., & Chung, C.K. (2011). Dimensions of self-expression in Facebook status updates. *Proceedings of the Fifth International AAAI Conference on Weblogs and Social Media*, 169–176.

Lancichinetti, A., Sirer, M.I., Wang, J.X., Acuna, D., Körding, K., & Nunes Amaral, L.A. (2015). High-reproducibility and high-accuracy method for automated topic classification. *Physical Review X, 5*(1). Available from http://link.aps.org/doi/10.1103/PhysRevX.5.011007

Laserna, C.M., Seih, Y., & Pennebaker, J.W. (2014). *Journal of Language and Social Psychology, 33*(3), 328–338.

Lasswell, H.D., Lerner, D., & De Sola Pool, I. (1952). *The comparative study of symbols: An introduction*. Stanford, CA: Stanford University Press.

LeFebvre, L., LeFebvre, L., Blackburn, K., & Boyd, R.L. (in press). Student estimates of public speaking competency: The Meaning Extraction Method and video self-evaluation. *Communication Education.*

Martindale, C. (1975). The grammar of altered states of consciousness: A semiotic reinterpretation of aspects of psychoanalytic theory. *Psychoanalysis and Contemporary Thought, 4,* 331–354.

McClelland, D. C., Atkinson, J. W., Clark, R. A., & Lowell, E. L. (1953). *The achievement motive.* Oxford, England: Irvington.

McNamara, J. R., & Blumer, C. A. (1982). Role playing to assess social competence: Ecological validity considerations. *Behavior Modification, 6*(4), 519–549.

Mehl, M. R., & Pennebaker, J. W. (2003). The sounds of social life: A psychometric analysis of students' daily social environments and natural conversations. *Journal of Personality and Social Psychology, 84,* 857–870.

Mehl, M. R., Pennebaker, J. W., Crow, D. M., Dabbs, J., & Price, J. (2001). The Electronically Activated Recorder (EAR): A device for sampling naturalistic daily activities and conversations. *Behavior Research Methods, Instruments, and Computers, 33,* 517–523.

Mergenthaler, E. (1996). Emotion-abstraction patterns in verbatim protocols: A new way of describing psychotherapeutic processes. *Journal of Consulting and Clinical Psychology, 64*(6), 1306–1315.

Miller, G. A. (1995). *The science of words.* New York, NY: Scientific American Library.

Newman, M. L., Pennebaker, J. W., Berry, D. S., & Richards, J. M. (2003). Lying words: Predicting deception from linguistic styles. *Personality and Social Psychology Bulletin, 29,* 665–675.

Niederhoffer, K.G., & Pennebaker, J.W. (2002). Linguistic style matching in social interaction. *Journal of Language and Social Psychology, 21,* 337–360.

Oliver, E. J., Markland, D., Hardy, J., & Petherick, C. M. (2008). The effects of autonomy-supportive versus controlling environments on self-talk. *Motivation and Emotion, 32,* 200–212.

Pennebaker, J. W. (2011). *The secret life of pronouns: What our words say about us.* New York: Bloomsbury Press.

Pennebaker, J. W., Booth, R. J., & Francis, M. E. (2007). LIWC2007: Linguistic Inquiry and Word Count. Austin, TX: liwc.net

Pennebaker, J. W., Chung, C. K., Frazee, J., Lavergne, G. M., & Beaver, D. I. (2014) When small words foretell academic success: The case of college admissions essays. *PLoS ONE 9*(12): e115844.

Pennebaker, J. W., Chung, C. K., Ireland, M. E., Gonzales, A., & Booth, R. J. (2007). *The development and psychometric properties of LIWC2007.* Austin, TX: liwc.net

Pennebaker, J. W., Francis, M. E., & Booth, R. J. (2001). Linguistic Inquiry and Word Count [computer software]. Mahwah, NJ: Erlbaum Publishers.

Pennebaker, J. W., & King, L. A. (1999). Linguistic styles: Language use as an individual difference. *Journal of Personality and Social Psychology, 77*(6), 1296–1312.

Pennebaker, J. W., & Stone, L. D. (2003). Words of wisdom: Language use over the life span. *Journal of Personality and Social Psychology, 85*(2), 291–301.

Ramirez-Esparza, N., Chung, C. K., Kacewicz, E., & Pennebaker, J. W. (2008). The psychology of word use in depression forums in English and in Spanish: Testing two text analytic approaches. *Proceedings of the 2008 International Conference on Weblogs and Social Media,* 102–108.

Remedios, J. D., Chasteen, A. L., & Packer, D. J. (2010). Sunny side up: The reliance on positive age stereotypes in descriptions of future older selves. *Self and Identity, 9*(3), 257–275.

Rude, S.S., Gortner, E., & Pennebaker, J.W. (2004). Language use of depressed and depression-vulnerable college students. *Cognition and Emotion, 18*(8), 1121–1133.

Saxbe, D.E., & Repetti, R. (2009). No place like home: Home tours correlate with daily patterns of mood and cortisol. *Personality and Social Psychology Bulletin, 36*(1), 71–81.

Schwartz, H.A., Eichstaedt, J.C., Kern, M.L., Dziurzynski, L., Ramones, S.M., et al. (2013). Personality, gender, and age in the language of social media: The open-vocabulary approach. *PLoS ONE, 8*(9): e73791. doi: 10.1371/journal.pone.0073791

Stirman, S.W., & Pennebaker, J.W. (2001). Word use in the poetry of suicidal and non-suicidal poets. *Psychosomatic Medicine, 63*, 517–522.

Stone, P.J., Dunphy, D. C., Smith, M.S., & Ogilvie, D.M. (1966). *The General Inquirer: A computer approach to content analysis.* Cambridge, MA: M.I.T. Press.

Tausczik, Y.R., & Pennebaker, J.W. (2010) The psychological meaning of words: LIWC and computerized text analysis methods. *Journal of Language and Social Psychology, 29*(1), 24–54.

Tausczik, Y.R., & Pennebaker, J.W. (2013). Improving teamwork using real-time language feedback. *CHI*, ACM 978-1-4503-1899-0/13/04.

Toma, C.L., & Hancock, J.T. (2012). What lies beneath: The linguistic traces of deception in online dating profiles. *Journal of Communication, 62*, 78–97.

Vasalou, A., Gill, A., Mazanderani, F., Papoutsi, C., & Joinson, A. (2011). Privacy Dictionary: A new resource for the automated content analysis of privacy. *Journal of the American Society for Information Science and Technology, 62*(11), 2095–2105.

PART IV

Public Policy Issues in Social and Digital Media

15

MARKETING UNHEALTHY FOODS TO CHILDREN ON FACEBOOK

Social Policy and Public Health Concerns

Jennifer L. Harris, Amy Heard, and Dale Kunkel

Low-nutrient, calorie-dense foods and beverages are increasingly advertised and promoted to youth via social media marketing. Older children and adolescents regularly use social networking sites such as Facebook, typically with minimal parental oversight. Marketers of sugary drinks, fast food, candy, and other unhealthy snacks maintain their own brand pages on Facebook and encourage young people to "like" them and share messages with friends. Public health experts also warn that marketing to youth through social media may be unfair and deceptive because this form of marketing is more difficult to recognize as a persuasive attempt and exploits youths' vulnerability to peer influence. What happens when a teenager chooses to "like" a brand such as Coca-Cola or Oreos? How many marketing messages do teens receive from food/beverage companies that they have "liked"? What other types of commercial messages for unhealthy foods and beverages typically appear on teens' Facebook pages? This study provides the first empirical insight towards answering such questions.

Background

In 2004, the American Psychological Association's Task Force on Advertising and Children concluded that advertising to children under age seven–eight is inherently unfair due to their inability to recognize its persuasive intent, and urged companies to stop advertising to this age group (Kunkel, Wilcox, Cantor, et al., 2004). This recommendation was based on research focused almost exclusively on television advertising, yet marketing to youth has changed fundamentally in recent years in ways that concern child health experts. Newer forms of digital marketing have emerged, which often blur the boundaries between entertainment and commercial content (Ali, Blades, Oates, & Blumberg, 2009; Moore &

Rideout, 2007). Disguising advertising as entertainment distracts the viewer from considering the message's persuasive intent, limiting even adult viewers' ability to defend against unwanted advertising influence (Boush, Friestad, & Wright, 2009; Petty & Andrews, 2008). The rise of social media marketing raises additional concerns when targeted to older children and adolescents. Platforms such as Facebook, YouTube, Twitter, and Instagram enable companies to recruit young people as "brand ambassadors" and facilitate the exchange of product endorsement messages between friends. This marketing tactic takes advantage of the developmental importance of peer relationships for these age groups (Montgomery & Chester, 2009), rendering youth particularly vulnerable to messages that imply enhanced peer acceptance through product consumption. Social media platforms on mobile devices now enable companies to target young people virtually anywhere and anytime, bypassing parental knowledge or consent.

The preponderance of unhealthy food products promoted in new media further enhances concerns about digital marketing to youth. The Institute of Medicine (2006) concluded that child-targeted advertising for low-nutrient, calorie-dense foods contributes to childhood obesity and fosters an environment that places children's health at risk. In response, the food industry established the Children's Food and Beverage Advertising Initiative (CFBAI), a self-regulatory program through which participating companies pledge to limit advertising for unhealthy foods and beverages, such as sugary sodas, fast food, candy, and unhealthy snacks, in media primarily directed to children under 12 (Kolish, Hernandez, & Blanchard, 2011). The industry also has reduced food advertising to youth in traditional media (i.e., television, radio, print)—youth-targeted expenditures on food marketing in traditional media declined by 18% from 2006 to 2009—however, expenditures on marketing in digital media (internet, social, and mobile) increased by 66% during the same period (FTC, 2012).

Recent research has documented how companies employ social media to promote unhealthy products to youth. The 12 largest fast food restaurants and 33 sugary drink brands incorporate Facebook, You Tube, and Twitter into their marketing plans (Harris, Schwartz, Brownell, et al., 2010; 2011). Facebook is one of the most popular social media sites for young people. In 2011, two-thirds of 12- to 17-year-olds visited Facebook on average more than once per day (Harris, 2012). When companies establish a Facebook page for a brand, individuals can "like" the page and that brand then becomes part of the individual's social network, allowing the brand to communicate to that individual directly. These marketing communications are referred to as "earned" advertising (Neilsen, 2013) or "organic" reach (Delo, 2014) because companies do not directly pay to distribute these messages. Unhealthy food and beverage brands are extremely popular on social media, comprising eight of the 20 products with the most Facebook fans, including Oreos, Red Bull, Skittles, and Pringles (Top products on Facebook, 2014). Coca-Cola is number three on Facebook (after two Facebook products) with more than 80 million likes (Coca-Cola, 2014). Brands also can purchase advertising directly to appear on Facebook users' pages, known as "sponsored" messages. In 2012, fast food restaurants purchased almost six billion advertisements on Facebook, representing 19% of all fast food advertising on the internet (Harris et al., 2013). If a product is liked by one or more of the ad recipient's Facebook friends, this information can be included in the product's Facebook advertisement.

However, little is known about the volume and content of product messages that appear on young people's social media pages, including on Facebook. There are no publicly available data to document typical exposure to Facebook marketing. Nor does Facebook divulge, even to its advertisers, the algorithm for determining the posts or paid messages that will appear on different individuals' Facebook pages (Lee, 2012). This study documents young people's exposure to marketing messages resulting from "liking" a food or beverage brand on Facebook. Using Facebook accounts set up for two teenage boys for the purpose of this research, we measured the volume and types of messages initiated by food and beverage companies that appeared on the boys' Facebook pages over a two-week period. The boys each liked five food brands. To identify the types of commercial messages that Facebook and advertisers send to young users who like food brands, researchers also controlled the personal information provided to Facebook (including age) and the boys' small network of friends. Such information is important for better understanding media influences on youths' diets, as well as informing efforts to mitigate adverse effects.

Methods

For this study, researchers created a small, controlled social network on Facebook and assessed messages received by two hypothetical 13-year-old boys. Researchers created accounts for the boys, providing only their ages, schools attended, and cities of residence. Each boy liked five different food and beverage brands. To complete the boys' social network, researchers created ten additional Facebook accounts for males and females 13 to 24 years old. The other Facebook accounts liked a total of 70 food and beverage brands in a variety of categories, including both healthy and unhealthy products. They also indicated various other interests on their Facebook accounts. The two hypothetical boys included these ten accounts and the other boy on their Facebook friend lists.

The brands liked by the two boys were selected from foods and beverages that maintained a substantial Facebook marketing presence and were known to target advertising to teens (12–17 years) on television based on previous research (Nielsen, 2012). Researchers accessed the company-sponsored Facebook pages for these brands in February 2013 and identified brands with more than one million Facebook likes that also posted new content approximately once or more per day during the previous month. The final brands were chosen to include examples from a variety of food and beverage categories.

For a two-week period during Feb–Mar 2013, researchers tracked daily activity on the two boys' Facebook accounts. At the end of each day, they viewed the boys' "newsfeed" pages that documented recent Facebook activity by the boys, their friends, and the companies they liked. Posing as the boys, the researchers interacted with posts from liked companies that appeared in the newsfeeds by taking any actions suggested within the posts. An option to "like," "share," or "comment" on the post appeared below all posts from liked companies, and the researchers took one of these endorsement actions for every post received from a liked company. No other activities were initiated by the accounts in this social network during the two-week test period to ensure that all activity on the boys' accounts was either initiated by Facebook or another company or resulted from the other boy's actions. Every day, researchers recorded screen shots of the boys' newsfeed pages, including all activity that had been posted since the previous day and links accessed through company posts.

Researchers also accessed the "see all" link at the top of the "Sponsored" column that appeared to the right of the newsfeed every day. This link connected to a page entitled "Ads and Sponsored Stories You May Like" that included 15 different advertising messages rotated within the "Sponsored" column on the newsfeed page. Researchers recorded a screen shot of this page. On the seventh day of each week, the researchers accessed the "Recommended pages" link that appeared in a column to the left of the newsfeed. This page provided suggestions from Facebook for additional pages the boy could like. Researchers recorded screen shots of the first 50 recommended pages listed on this page.

Researchers used the screen shots to identify all company-initiated activity that appeared within the boys' newsfeeds including: *Posts from liked companies,* placed by one of the liked food and beverage brands on its own page and appearing on the newsfeed of the boy who liked it; *Posts about friends' activities,* notifying the boy that his friend had engaged with a post from a company his friend liked; and *Sponsored messages,* including all paid advertising messages about food and beverage brands that appeared within the boys' newsfeeds or elsewhere on their newsfeed pages.

Content analysis was used to assess company-initiated activity on the boys' newsfeed pages. Sponsored messages were coded only if they referenced food or beverage items. Two researchers were trained in coding. The coding assessed the frequency of five tactics to promote food products on Facebook: *friend references,* when the post indicated that one of the boy's friends liked the company, brand, or post; *engagement devices,* including techniques that Facebook recommends to encourage sharing of posts between users (e.g., pictures, asking questions) and other requests for brand interactions (e.g., to like, comment, or share); *outside links* directing users to a website outside of Facebook for further interaction with the brand; *product messages* that directly encouraged purchases (e.g., discounts, new product announcements); and *celebrity endorsements,* including musicians, athletes, and sports teams/leagues praising the product. For reliability testing, both coders reviewed and coded the same subset of 15% of all posts. Cohen's Kappa values for items ranged from .88 to 1.00, indicating substantial to perfect inter-rater reliability (Viera & Garrett, 2005). After reliability testing, the remaining posts were split evenly between the two coders for final analysis.

One researcher also identified the brand and product category for the "Recommended pages" suggested by Facebook, including foods and beverages (fast food, candy/gum, soda, other drinks, snacks, other foods) and other products and entities (e.g., movies, musicians, entertainers, games).

Results

Table 15.1 presents information used to select the ten Facebook brands liked by the two hypothetical boys. Fanta's Facebook page had the most monthly unique youth visitors 2–17 years old during Oct–Dec 2012 (351,000). Two additional brands averaged more than 100,000 youth visitors per month (Twix and Sonic). Of note, these numbers quantify individuals who visited the brands' Facebook pages but do not indicate how many youth saw messages from the brands on their own Facebook pages. Coca-Cola was the most popular brand in this study with 65 million likes as of Feb 2013, followed by Red Bull and Oreo, each with more than 33 million.

During the two weeks analyzed, a total of 259 messages appeared on the two boys' newsfeed pages that were initiated by food or beverage companies. Approximately three-quarters of these messages were shared posts from companies that one of the boys liked; the remaining messages were paid advertisements

TABLE 15.1 Facebook Statistics for Liked Brands

Brand (company)	*Total likes (million)**	*Monthly unique visitors (2–17 years) (000)***
Coca-Cola	65	55
Red Bull	38	73
Oreo (Mondelez/Nabisco)	33	62
Taco Bell (Yum! Brands)	10	84
Fanta (Coca-Cola)	9	351
Twix (Mars)	8	105
Mountain Dew (PepsiCo)	8	32
Sonic	2	113
Frosty (Wendy's)	3	40
Brisk (PepsiCo)	1	11

*Feb 2013

**Source: comScore Media Builder, unique visitors (ages 2–17) to the brands' Facebook pages from Oct–Dec 2012.

(i.e., sponsored messages). Every day, within the small network created for this research, each boy averaged 5.8 posts from the five companies he liked (n = 162) and 1.6 posts shared by the other boy (n = 44), as well as 1.9 different sponsored messages for foods and beverages (n = 53). Red Bull posts appeared most often on the boys' Facebook pages (averaging 1.9 posts per day). Posts from Brisk and Twix appeared 1.6 times per day, and Sonic, Taco Bell, and Oreo posts averaged more than one post per day. Mountain Dew posts appeared least often (average 0.4 per day).

Figure 15.1 illustrates the different types of messages from food and beverage companies that appeared on the boys' newsfeed pages. In addition to posts from liked companies, two types of sponsored messages (i.e., paid advertisements) appeared on the boys' newsfeeds, interspersed with posts from friends (representing 30% of sponsored messages). *Suggested pages* (n = 9) were placed by unsolicited companies (i.e., those not liked by the boys or their friends), whereas *related posts* (n = 7) were from companies liked by one of the boy's friends. Both types included the word "sponsored" underneath to indicate that they were a form of paid advertising. Sponsored messages also appeared in the "sponsored" column to the right of the boys' newsfeeds. These messages included traditional ads linking to the advertiser's web page and *sponsored stories* inviting the boys to "like" the company's Facebook page. Sponsored stories sometimes included a message listing the boy's friends who liked the product and might include a picture of one of the friends.

Table 15.2 presents the content of company-initiated messages that appeared on the boys' newsfeed pages, including posts from liked companies and sponsored messages. The shared posts from the other boy were removed from the content analysis as they were duplicates of the posts from liked companies. Nearly all posts from liked companies contained one or more engagement devices to encourage users to share the post with a friend or interact with the brand in some other way. Pictures were most popular, included in nine of ten posts, followed by asking a question, requests to like or share the post, and requests to post a comment. All posts from liked companies linked to the brand's Facebook page, but one-quarter also linked to outside websites (e.g., company sites, other social media) encouraging the user to interact with the brand outside of Facebook. Some of these links directed to webpages that requested personal information, such as name or email address. Just 12% of posts from liked companies included any type of direct product message (e.g., discount offer, new product introduction, store visit invitation) that might reveal its persuasive intent.

Table 15.2 also describes the content of sponsored messages for foods and beverages that appeared on the boys' newsfeed pages. These paid advertisements were similar to posts from liked companies. They all included engagement devices, usually a picture and a request to like the brand, whereas just 13% included a direct product message. Contests and sweepstakes appeared more often in these posts, whereas fewer outside links appeared. Approximately

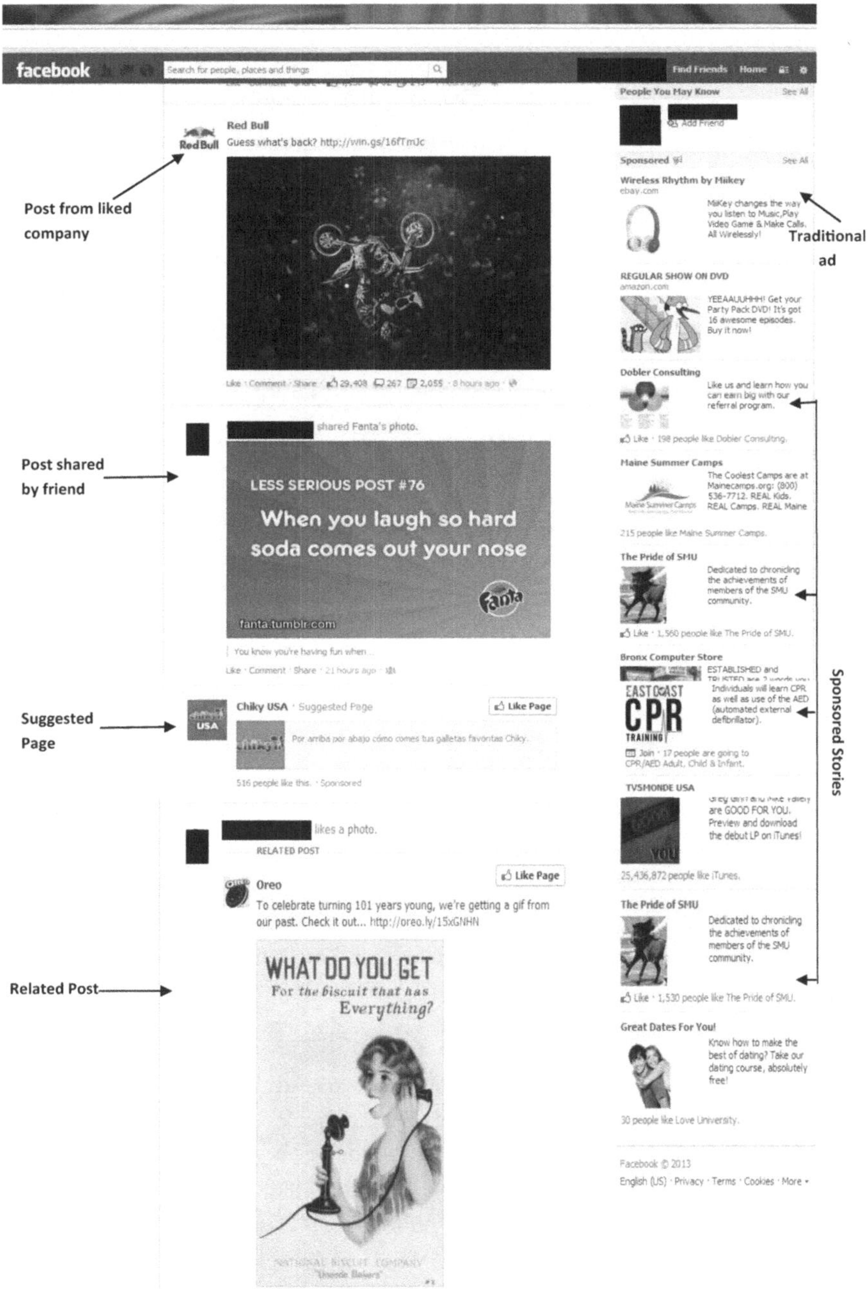

FIGURE 15.1 Examples of Company-Initiated Messages Appearing on Facebook Newsfeed Pages

TABLE 15.2 Company-Initiated Messages for Foods and Beverages on Facebook Newsfeed Pages

	Posts from liked companies		*Sponsored messages*	
	Number	*% of total*	*Number*	*% of total*
Any engagement device	152	93.8	53	100
Show a picture	137	84.6	50	94.3
Ask a question	43	26.4	9	17.0
Request to like or share	13	8.0	47	88.7
Instruct to post a comment	12	7.4	0	0.0
Ask to watch a video	9	5.5	1	1.9
Link to other Facebook content (event or app)	7	4.3	0	0.0
Any link outside Facebook	45	27.6	7	13.2
Instagram, YouTube, or other social media	28	17.3	2	3.8
Company website	15	9.2	4	7.5
Any direct product message	19	11.7	7	13.2
Discount offer	10	6.1	5	9.4
Announce new product	5	3.1	1	1.9
Store visit	3	1.8	0	0.0
Enter contest/sweepstake	2	1.2	5	9.4
Reference famous musician, athlete, or sports team/league	8	4.9	0	0.0
Reference Facebook friend	0	0.0	15	28.3
Total commercial messages	162	100.0	53	100.0
Average per day	5.8		1.9	

*Commercial messages appearing on two accounts during two weeks in Jan–Feb 2013, including posts from liked companies (i.e., "earned" advertising) and sponsored messages (i.e., "paid" advertising).

one-quarter of sponsored messages referenced a friend who liked the brand; the remainder appeared to be targeted based on other personal information about the boys available through Facebook (i.e., age, gender or hometown).

Figure 15.2 provides the categories for additional pages proposed by Facebook for the two boys to like, termed "recommended pages." The majority (58%) of recommendations were for food and beverage products. Soda and other sugary drinks (including energy drinks) were suggested most frequently, followed by candy/gum and fast food. Overall, 42% of Facebook's recommendations were for food/beverage brands that the boys' friends liked. However, 95% of candy/gum and 89% of snack food recommendations *were not* products liked by friends. Facebook does not publish its criteria for recommending pages, but it appears to

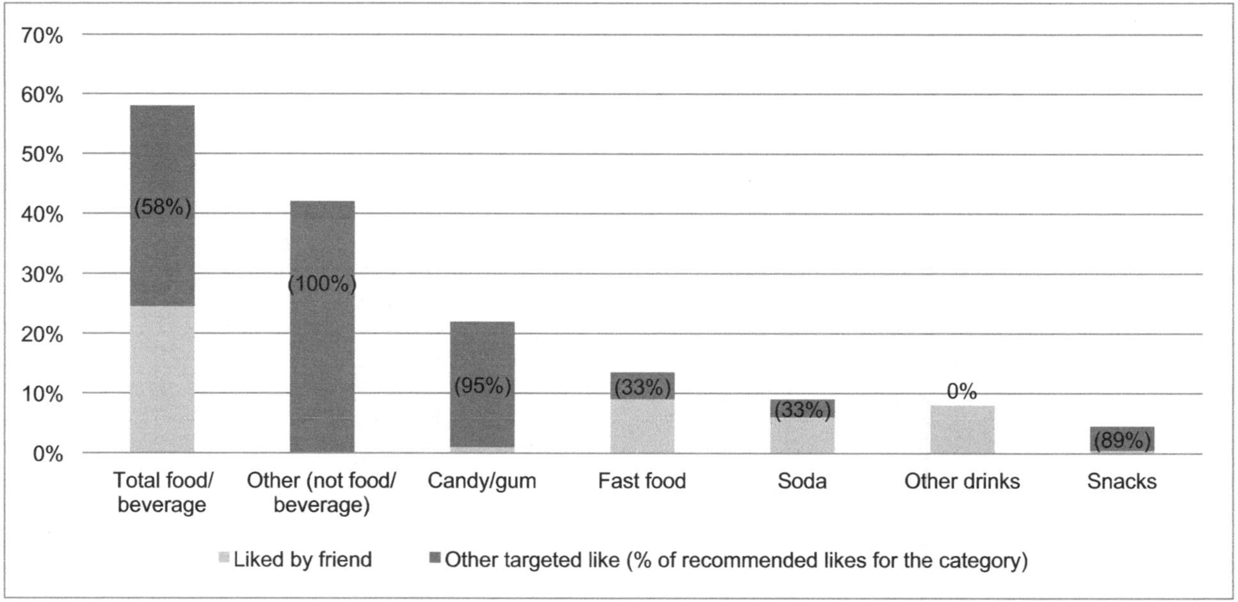

FIGURE 15.2 Additional Pages "Recommended" By Facebook

% of recommended pages for each category indicates potential targeting by Facebook based on demographic information provided (i.e., age, hometown).

have based these recommendations on other information about the boys (e.g., their age, gender, and/or other liked pages). After foods and beverages, Facebook recommended entertainment entities most often to the boys (21% of recommended likes) (e.g., MTV, the rapper 50 Cent). Additional Facebook recommendations included products and interests with youth appeal, such as Being Hyper, Bubblewrap, and PlayStation.

Discussion

These findings suggest that a large volume of unhealthy food marketing messages reach young people via social media such as Facebook. For the purposes of this study, we created Facebook accounts for two typical, albeit fictional, 13-year-old boys. By controlling the messages initiated by other members of the boys' small social network, we were able to identify the likely source of messages from food and beverage companies that appeared on their Facebook pages. Over the two-week period examined, each boy received an average of 5.8 messages daily from the food and beverage brands he liked, or 1.2 marketing messages per day from each of the five liked brands.

Facebook users may share the messages they receive from liked companies with others in their social network, and 94% of these marketing messages contained engagement devices (such as pictures, asking questions, and requests to share the post) designed to encourage sharing. In fact, Facebook recommends that companies use these types of techniques to increase engagement with their brands on Facebook and encourage sharing of their posts ("Facebook Help," 2014). In our protocol, each of the two hypothetical boys shared one of every three posts received. Although norms for typical Facebook behavior by young people are not yet known, we believe this is a realistic level of sharing among teen-aged friends. This sharing yielded another 1.6 messages per day on the boys' Facebook pages.

Commercial messages from food and beverage brands liked by the boys and messages shared by one of their friends appeared in the form of posts directly on the boys' newsfeeds, interspersed with messages from their social network friends. This type of marketing is termed "earned" advertising by the advertising industry, since companies are not charged by media venues such as Facebook for commercial messages spread virally by members of the social network (Nielsen, 2012). Instead, such messages are deemed social interaction accomplished via the network as a result of the user initially reaching out to the company to establish contact, despite the fact that these communications are carefully designed to promote brand recognition, affinity, and product sales. This capacity renders social networks a highly attractive low-cost medium for promoting foods and beverages to American youth.

Actual paid advertising on Facebook, termed "sponsored" messages, represented a much smaller portion of the overall contact from food and beverage brands to the young people in our analysis via their Facebook pages. We observed an average of 1.9 such messages daily for each boy, accounting for roughly one-fifth of all food and beverage marketing communications received. However, overall our two 13-year-olds received a total of 9.3 messages per day promoting foods/beverages. This translates to roughly 280 such prompts per month, or 3,348 per year. This is an impressive volume of media marketing efforts intended to increase the amount of obesogenic products consumed by American youth.

Whereas media effects research has yet to demonstrate the degree of efficacy for such marketing messages in promoting product preferences and sales to youth, the regularity of these prompts is likely to aid in brand recognition and liking as well as serve to prime the receiver to consume the product when messages are received on a daily basis (Harris, Brownell, & Bargh, 2009). A key element likely to enhance the persuasive power of food marketing messages conveyed via social networks is the endorsement effect associated with marketing posts that are shared among friends. Many sponsored posts also note that friends in the same social network "like" the product and may include a picture of the friend. Children and adolescents are uniquely vulnerable to peer status appeals in advertising, given their developmental drive for popularity and acceptance by other youth (Steinberg & Monahan, 2007). It seems ironic that advertising industry guidelines limit this practice on children's television commercials (CARU, 2009),[1] whereas marketing to young people on social networks such as Facebook is fundamentally designed to exploit this same vulnerability through "sharing" of product-based posts, which clearly imply endorsement by the message sender.

Another worrisome aspect of food marketing conveyed on social networks is the likelihood that young people will experience difficulty in recognizing such messages as commercial in nature. In more traditional media such as television and print, clear boundaries are commonly maintained between entertainment and commercial content, but marketing in digital media is more difficult for young people to recognize (Ali et al., 2009). Marketing messages conveyed by food/beverage companies on Facebook are even more disguised, looking much the same as posts received from friends that report on their latest activities. Furthermore, paid advertisements on Facebook are difficult to distinguish from messages sent by liked companies or shared by friends. Only the words "sponsored" and "related post" or "suggested page" subtly indicate that these messages are traditional advertisements. In our analysis, three out of ten of these sponsored messages appeared within the boys' newsfeeds, interspersed with posts from friends and liked companies, making them even more difficult to recognize as advertising. Finally, the messages used in sponsored posts are nearly identical to messages from liked companies. Just one of ten presented any direct information about the product, which could cue the reader to recognize them as traditional commercial messages.

At 13 years of age, young people have only begun to recognize the persuasive intent of advertising messages in a manner that would allow them to defend effectively against commercial persuasion (Carter et al., 2011). To the extent that marketing messages are not clearly recognized as such, the degree to which cognitive defenses can be employed to limit advertising influence is likely to be minimized. In addition, not all Facebook users are 13 years and older; millions of American youth below age 13 use Facebook regularly. Although Facebook's terms of service technically do not permit children under 13 to join, a recent report indicates that 7.5 million children under 13 are on Facebook, and more than five million Facebook members are under the age of ten (Consumer Reports, 2011). The disguised nature of marketing via social media raises even greater concerns for children under age 12 whose less developed ability to recognize advertising intent is well documented (IOM, 2006).

Is the amount of food marketing messages our hypothetical boys received typical for American youth who use social media? It is impossible to know without more clarity about the number of food products most teens choose to like as part of their Facebook activity. Given that incentives are commonly provided by marketers to encourage liking, we felt that liking five of the ten most popular food/beverage brands would be a conservative profile for a teenage user. Another limitation of this research is that the boys only liked food and beverage brands, which likely resulted in a greater proportion of food and beverage products in the mix of company-initiated messages on the boys' Facebook pages. Finally, Facebook recently announced that it was reducing the organic reach of individual company posts (i.e., company posts that appear on the newsfeeds of individuals who like the company) (Delo, 2014). Companies may now have to pay more often to ensure that posts reach a majority of their intended audience, which could result in fewer company posts on users' newsfeeds. Additional research is needed to document actual exposure to food and beverage marketing by children and teens on Facebook, as well as on other social media platforms used regularly by food companies, including Twitter and Instagram. However, this study provides novel insight into the wide variety of marketing practices employed to promote teen-targeted food products to youth via the most popular social media website, Facebook.

Conclusions

In an era of unprecedented childhood obesity, marketing of obesogenic food products to children accomplished via television and other traditional media is recognized as a clear threat to public health, and efforts have already been pursued by both industry and government to limit such practices. Meanwhile, the proliferation in recent years of social media networks such as Facebook now offers an alternative media mechanism to instill desire for unhealthy foods and beverages in young people. Such efforts are less documented by research and less visible in the public eye, though not necessarily any less effective than the food marketing tactics of the past, which often relied on animated commercials featuring iconic characters like Tony the Tiger or Ronald McDonald.

Moreover, social media marketing raises unique implications regarding the fairness of advertising to child audiences. Despite the fact that Facebook does not currently "allow" children age 12 and below to use its services, it is well-documented that millions of young people in this age group are regular users. Furthermore, Facebook has announced that it will consider allowing children on its site in the future (Troianovski & Raice, 2012). Given this context, it is critical to gain precise information about these controversial marketing practices; raise questions for further research regarding children's responses to such advertising; and analyze the propriety of these new marketing tactics considering the policy protections typically employed to avoid children's exploitation by marketers in more traditional media.

Parents, public health officials, and policymakers all should consider the effects of food marketing messages conveyed in social media networks as a potential contributor to youth obesity and poor diets. The data provided by our research make clear that many young people are now being exposed to a high volume of promotional messages for unhealthy food products through venues such as Facebook. It makes little sense to seek reform of unhealthy food marketing practices in one medium of electronic communication, principally television, while ignoring other new media that are rapidly increasing in popularity and afford food companies equivalent opportunities to promote unhealthy products.

Note

1. According to *Self-Regulatory Program for Children's Advertising (9th edition)*, Children's Advertising Review Unit of the National Council of Better Business Bureaus (2009), "Advertisements should not convey to children that possession of a product will result in greater acceptance by peers or that lack of a product will result in less acceptance by peers" (p. 12).

References

Ali, M., Blades, M., Oates, C. & Blumberg, F. (2009). Young children's ability to recognize advertisements in web page designs. *British Journal of Developmental Psychology, 27*(1), 71–83.

Boush, D. M, Friestad, M., & Wright, P. (2009). *Deception in the marketplace: The psychology of deceptive persuasion and consumer self protection.* New York, NY: Routledge.

Carter, O. B., Patterson, L. J., Donovan, R. J., Ewing, M. T., & Roberts, C. M. (2011). Children's understanding of the selling versus persuasive intent of junk food advertising: Implications for regulation. *Social Science & Medicine, 72*, 962–968.

Children's Advertising Review Unit (CARU) of the National Council of Better Business Bureaus (2009). *Self-regulatory program for children's advertising (9th edition)*. Retrieved from www.caru.org/guidelines/guidelines.pdf.

Coca-Cola [ca. 2014]. In *Facebook* [Company page]. Retrieved April 7, 2014 from www.facebook.com/cocacola.

Consumer Reports (2011, June). Online exposure: Social networks, mobile phones, and scams can threaten your security. *Consumer Reports Magazine, 55*, 30.

Delo, C. (2014, March 6). Brands' organic Facebook reach has crashed since October: Study. *Advertising Age*. Retrieved from http://adage.com/article/digital/brands-organic-facebook-reach-crashed-october/292004.

Facebook Help: Best posting practices. (2014). Retrieved April 7, 2014 from www.facebook.com/help/405494409496261.

Federal Trade Commission (FTC) (2012). *Marketing food to children and adolescents: Follow-up report*. Retrieved from www.ftc.gov/os/2012/12/121221foodmarketingreport.pdf

Harris, J. L. (2012). The new hidden persuaders: The digital world of food marketing to children and teens. In P. Pringle (Ed.), *A place at the table: The crisis of 49 million hungry Americans and how to solve it* (pp. 107–122). New York, NY: Participant Media.

Harris, J. L., Brownell, K. D., & Bargh, J. A. (2009). The food marketing defense model: Integrating psychological research to protect youth and inform public policy. *Social Issues Policy Review, 3*(1), 211–271.

Harris, J. L., Schwartz, M. B., Brownell, K. D., Javadizadeh, J., Weinberg, M. et al. (2011). *Sugary drink FACTS 2010: Evaluating sugary drink nutrition and marketing to youth*. Retrieved from http://sugarydrinkfacts.org/resources/SugaryDrinkFACTS_Report.pdf.

Harris, J. L., Schwartz, M. B., Brownell, K. D., Sarda, V., Ustjanauskas, A. et al. (2010). *Fast food FACTS 2010: Evaluating fast food nutrition and marketing to youth*. Retrieved from http://fastfoodmarketing.org/media/FastFoodFACTS_Report_2010.pdf

Harris, J. L., Schwartz, M. B., Munsell, C. M., Dembek, C., Liu, S. et al. (2013). *Fast food FACTS 2013: Measuring progress in nutrition and marketing to children and teens*. Retrieved from fastfoodmarketing.org/media/FastFoodFACTS_Report.pdf.

Institute of Medicine (IOM) (2006). *Food marketing to children and youth: Threat or opportunity?* Washington, DC: The National Academies Press.

Kolish, E. D., Hernandez, M., & Blanchard, K. (2011). *The Children's Food and Beverage Advertising Initiative: A report on compliance and implementation during 2010 and a five year retrospective: 2006–2011*. Retrieved from www.bbb.org/us/storage/16/documents/cfbai/cfbai-2010-progress-report.pdf.

Kunkel, D., Wilcox, B. L., Cantor, J., Palmer, E., Linn, S., & Dowrick, P. (2004). Report of the APA task force on advertising and children. *American Psychological Association, 40*.

Lee, A. (2012, May 9). Edgerank explained in a simple infographic. *iStrategy Digital Marketing Conference*. Retrieved from http://istrategyconference.com/blog/edgerank-explained-in-a-simple-infographic.

Moore, E. S., & Rideout, V. J. (2007). The online marketing of food to children: Is it just fun and games? *Journal of Public Policy and Marketing, 26*(2), 202–220.

Montgomery, K. C., & Chester, J. (2009). Interactive food and beverage marketing: Targeting adolescents in the digital age. *Journal of Adolescent Health, 45*(3), S18–S29.

Nielsen. (2013). Nielsen: Earned advertising remains most credible among consumers; trust in owned advertising on the rise [Press release]. Retrieved from www.nielsen.com/us/en/press-room/2013/nielsen—earned-advertising-remains-most-credible-among-consumer.html.

Nielsen AdViews (2012). Available at http://en-us.nielsen.com/sitelets/cls/adviews.html.

Petty, R. D., & Andrews, J. C. (2008). Covert marketing unmasked: A legal and regulatory guide for practices that mask marketing messages. *Journal of Public Policy & Marketing, 27*(1), 7–18.

Steinberg, L., & Monahan, K. (2007). Age differences in resistance to peer influence. *Developmental Psychology, 43*(6), 1531–1543.

Top Products on Facebook (2014). Retrieved from http://fanpagelist.com/category/products/view/list/sort/fans/page1.

Troianovski, A., & Raice, S. (2012). Facebook explores giving kids access. *Wall Street Journal*. Retrieved from http://online.wsj.com/news/articles/SB10001424052702303506404577444711741019238.

Viera, A. J., & Garrett, J. M. (2005). Understanding the interobserver agreement: The kappa statistic. *Family Medicine, 37*(5), 360–363.

16

ONLINE VIOLENT MEDIA CONSUMPTION IN ADOLESCENTS

An Exploratory Study

Yupin Patarapongsant and Issariya Woraphiphat

Introduction

For decades, researchers and educators have studied the aggressive behavior of children and adolescents in schools. A recent high school shooting in Los Angeles (with a 16-year-old perpetrator) terrified the community not long after a 20-year-old killed 26 children and teachers in Connecticut. These violent incidents raised the alarm regarding issues related to "teen" violent behavior. Recent Asian news reports relate a number of tragedies resulting from the aggressive behavior of adolescents. Past studies have shown a strong link between the consumption of violent social media and violent behavior. This study focuses on factors influencing adolescents' preference for violent media consumption and on ways to mitigate the appeal of such media.

Adolescent Access to Violent Media

Online media has increased in popularity among adolescents because they are growing up with the development of technology, particularly the Internet. Adolescents have higher rates of Internet and e-mail usage as sources of information in comparison to other age groups (World Value Survey, 2007). The Internet has also grown dramatically in the past decade. Therefore, it is not surprising that tech-savvy adolescents have a higher chance of exposure to a wide variety of online sexual and violent content than their parents' generation.

Social learning theory or social cognitive theory (Bandura, 2001) shows that human adaptation and change are rooted in a social system. Social structures embody rules, resources, and social sanctions designed to organize, guide, and regulate human affairs. People can gain an understanding by interpreting symbolic meanings of information derived from personal and vicarious experiences of what they see, hear, and read without direct experience. Because children and adolescents can learn about the world by observing media-based events, exposure to violence in media, movies, and video games could increase the risk of violent behavior in the viewer. It is similar to growing up in an environment filled with real violence (Huesmann, 2007). As most violent video games do not show the negative consequences of violent behavior, adolescents do not receive the negative reinforcement of such behavior (such as going to jail). Consequently, they could learn that this behavior is acceptable. Hence, in the Internet era, the availability of violent media, coupled with the ease of access to such media, could ultimately impact adolescents' behaviors and lead to negative consequences in the lives of children and adolescents. A number of studies examine the effect of violent media consumption. Next, we will discuss these findings in detail.

Effects of Violent Media Consumption

A growing body of literature deals with the impact of violent media consumption on aggressive behavior (Bushman, 1995), particularly in online environments such as gaming websites, Facebook, or chat rooms. Violent media depicts intentional attempts by individuals to inflict harm on others (Anderson & Bushman, 2001). The initial empirical question addresses the impact of violent media exposure on viewers' behavior, compared to those who are not exposed to such materials. Studies show that viewing violent media is an antecedent of aggressive behavior, which is intended to injure or irritate another person. In the short term, violent media could cause an increase in aggression because of priming and arousal processes that lead to mimicry. First, the priming process occurs when an external stimulus can be inherently linked to a cognition, such as that which occurs with the sight of a gun. Then, an arousal process might occur during an exciting media presentation. Together, these processes could cause excitation transfer that motivates the viewer to aggressively respond to a provocation. This response might reflect mimicry, which is an immediate mirroring of a specific behavior (Bushman & Huesmann, 2006).

In the long run, viewers learn how to perceive, interpret, judge, and respond to events in the physical and social environment. Aside from observational learning, in which individuals learn from observing social events, repeated exposure to violent media can also cause psychological-emotional desensitization. Desensitization can lead to feeling less sympathy for victims of violence, having a less negative attitude toward violence, and having less engagement in helping behavior. Bushman and Anderson (2002) found that violent media exposure influences the amount of aggressive expectation, as people tend to interpret ambiguous situations in a relative hostile way. Thus, repeated exposure to violence can also increase adolescents' likelihood of engaging in aggressive behavior by making the hostile expectation chronically accessible.

Adolescence is a period of physical and psychological transition. In comparison to other age groups, adolescents are characterized by heightened sensitivity to salient environmental cues and heightened affective responses to salient emotional expression and reward-salient situations; they lack the ability to exert behavioral control over such stimuli. Thus, the impact of violent media exposure on behavior should be heightened in this particular age group. Despite the potential negative consequences of adolescents' exposure to violent media, many teens seek out and purchase online products with violent media content. Our research investigates factors that could influence the willingness to buy products online that contain violent content, such as violent video games. To answer this question, we first review prior studies that are related to factors influencing the preference for violent media.

Appeal of Violent Social Media

Previous research shows that some people voluntarily expose themselves to, and often seek out, images of violence (Little & Zuckerman, 1986). According to the gratification theory, people actively seek out and make choices from media and other competing information sources in order to gratify a need (Katz et al., 1974). Research on violent video games explains that adolescent gamers play video games to satisfy different needs. They achieve satisfaction through competition, challenge, social connection, and excitement (Jansz, 2005). According to Jansz (2005), a "violent game is a safe, private laboratory where they can experience different emotions, including those that are controversial in ordinary life." Hence, the virtual world becomes a safe place for adolescents to expose themselves to violent media (e.g., playing violent games or watching violent entertainment). The development and availability of violent media such as online games with violent content enable adolescents to select media exposure that matches their needs. Past studies show factors that affect violent media consumption, including personal characteristics such as empathy, sensation seeking, aggressiveness, and demographic characteristics such as gender and age differences.

Empathy is an individual's reaction to the observed experiences of another person. Emphatic concern reflects another oriented focus of concern and caring for others. Evidence suggests that empathy is associated with less enjoyment of horror movies (Hoffner & Levine, 2005). *Sensation seeking* is defined as "the seeking of varied, novel, complex, and intense sensations and experience, and the willingness to take physical, social, legal, and financial risks for the sale of such experience" (Zuckerman, 1996). Sensation seeking is another personal trait that makes people enjoy viewing violent media. High sensation seekers might interpret fear induced by stimuli as a positive emotion, whereas low sensation seekers might regard such fear as unpleasant. High sensation seeking and the need for arousal are associated with a preference for horror.

Aggressiveness refers to the tendency to engage in behavior intended to harm or injure another individual who is motivated to avoid that harm. Bushman

(1995) showed that an aggressive trait correlates with viewing violence. Aggressive thoughts and fantasies were associated with liking violent media as a genre and found to be associated with greater enjoyment of fright and violence (Hoffner & Levine, 2005). According to Bushman's cognitive neoassociation theory, high-trait aggressiveness individuals are more susceptible to the effects of violent media than low-trait aggressiveness individuals are because they possess a relatively large network of aggressive associations that can be activated by violent cues (Bushman, 1995). Hence, we are interested in investigating whether an aggressive trait influences the willingness to purchase violent online media.

Social avoidance distress is a trait-like characteristic that remains relatively stable across temporal and situational variation, often yielding negative interpersonal consequences (Leary & Kowalski, 1995). Individuals with social anxiety are aware of their lack of social skills or are worried about their self, which is consequently inhibited by face-to-face social interactions. Adolescents who are aware of their social disconnectedness might want to gain social interaction and stay connected. Based on the motivation to be included in a peer group, adolescents might play video games containing some sort of violence to engage in social interaction. Although using online communication could lead to social connection, it could also lead to a higher chance of violent media exposure.

Moreover, work on neuroscience examines the interaction of anxiety and the cognitive process, which focuses on the link between emotion and attention to stimuli, found that individuals with social avoidance distress (SAD) traits show hyperamygdale activation in response to fearful facial expressions. Anxious adolescents exhibit amygdale dysfunction when attention is focused on threatening aspects of social cues (McClure et al., 2007). Hence, it is interesting to explore whether adolescents with SAD traits like violent media and if these traits influence their willingness to buy violent online media.

Age and gender differences might also influence violent media preferences. Some researchers argue that interest in violent media peaks during adolescence, especially in male adolescents. However, there is limited support for this curvilinear hypothesis. Other researchers suggested that the appeal of violent media to children of different ages and genders varies by program genre (Cantor, 1998). Further investigation should be made across viewer lifespans to create a more comprehensive understanding about the association between age and violent media consumption. Aside from these individualistic factors, other variables could also facilitate or inhibit the consumption of violent media. One of them is the attitude toward violent media consumption, which will be described next.

Attitude Toward Violent Media Consumption: Effect on Self and Society

Social-cognitive models of aggression distinguish between factors that facilitate the emergence of aggression from those that inhibit it. *Facilitating factors* include aggression cues in a situational context (e.g., violent media) and unpleasant situational events that put people in a bad mood (e.g., provocation, frustration, hot temperatures). *Inhibiting factors* include fear of retaliation, the attitude or moral beliefs opposing violence, and pleasant situational events.

The current study focuses on attitudes toward the impact of violent media exposure on a viewer. Attitude contributes to the process of moral evaluation or the consequences of violent action. The formation of attitudes toward violence is influenced by many factors, such as the amount of exposure to violence and attitudes of peers and parents. If viewers develop the attitude that violence is normative, they may become desensitized to violence and continue to use aggressive behavior in real life. The empirical evidence shows that attitudes about media violence could mitigate the imitation of aggressive behaviors of children (Huesmann et al., 1983). Children who received intervention by writing an argument about the negative aspects of television violence and shared it with others were rated as significantly less aggressive than their peers who were also exposed to violent media. Therefore, a negative attitude toward the consequences of violent media consumption, either among viewers or in society as a whole, might mitigate the likelihood of future violent media consumption.

Current Study

Whereas previous research examines why and how consumers select violent social media and the effects of that exposure on their social media choices, the current study examines which types of people are more likely to make such choices. This study aims to understand which types of people have a greater preference for violent media exposure on the Internet (e.g., they find the violent media interesting and like to see violent pictures) and how their preference links to their willingness to buy online products (e.g., movies, games) that contain violent content and images. We also examined the attitude toward the impact of violent media exposure on oneself and society, which could inhibit violent consumption among adolescents.

This study focuses on adolescents who are eligible to make purchases of certain violence-rated products. With the development of technology and the abundance of violent products online, today's adolescents have a higher chance of being exposed to violent media than previous generations. The online context makes parental supervision difficult. Given the negative consequences of violent media exposure, this study also examines factors that could help adolescents resist the temptation to buy violent online media.

This study proposes that both aggressive traits and SAD increase the preference for violent online media. An aggressive trait is the tendency to engage in behavior intended to harm or injure another individual who is motivated to avoid that harm. Past studies show the association between aggressive traits and violent media enjoyment. SAD is worry about self and is consequently inhibited in face-to-face social interaction. Socially anxious adolescents turn to online

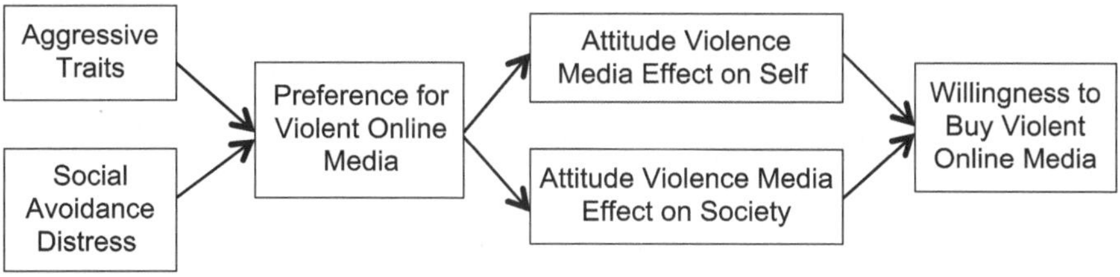

FIGURE 16.1 Conceptualization of the Effects of Online Violent Media Consumption on Adolescents' Willingness to Buy

conversations as a preferred alternative to face-to-face conversation, as it offers them a safer environment than offline settings (Patti & Peter, 2009). Social isolation can have psychological effects, such as anxiety as well as aggression. It is plausible that these traits affect the preference for violent online media.

H1a Aggressive traits increase the preference for violent media among adolescents.

H1b Social avoidance distress (SAD) increases the preference for violent media among adolescents.

This study also proposes that the preference for violent media leads to an increase in the willingness to buy violent online media and correlates with an attitude toward the impact of violent media exposure (see Figure 16.1 for the overall model).

H2a The preference for violent media among adolescents directly increases the willingness to buy violent products online.

H2b The preference for media violent correlates with the attitude toward the impact of violent media on oneself and society.

H2c Attitude toward the impact of violent media on oneself and society correlates with the willingness to buy.

Research Methodology

Samples and Measures. This study employs a research questionnaire, using a seven-point Likert scale (1 = strongly agree to 7 = strongly disagree), which contains five sections with the overall reliability of the scales above .70 (α > .70). The reliability levels of each scale are reported below.

Ten Items Personality Inventories (TIPI). Scales comprise 10 items that measure the traits and characteristics of the individual (e.g., warm, careless, and conventional). Whereas the scale can be divided these into three subscales, the present study focuses on the two bipolar subscales of "Nonaggressive (e.g. sympathetic, warm)" and "Aggressive (e.g. quarrelsome)" with alpha reliabilities of .85 and .86, respectively.

Social avoidance and distress (SAD). Scales comprise eight items measuring in-group and out-group social avoidance, which are divided into two subscales with alpha reliabilities of .85 each.

Preference for violence in social media. Scales comprise three items with an alpha reliability of .90.

Attitude toward violent media. Scale comprises 15 items that measure attitudes toward violence on different issues, including the impact on self and society; these are divided into two subscales: "Impact of violent media exposure on oneself" and "Impact of violent media exposure on society," with alpha reliabilities of .90 and .84, respectively.

Willingness to buy. Scale comprises four items with an alpha reliability of .91 (see Table 16.1 for sample items associated with all employed scales).

TABLE 16.1 Measurement Scales—Sample Items

Measure	*Examples of Items*
10-Item Personality Inventories (TIPI)	
Nonaggressive (5 items)	"I see myself as dependable, self-disciplined." "I see myself as sympathetic, warm."
*Aggressive (3 items)	"I see myself as critical, quarrelsome." "I see myself as anxious, easily upset."
Social avoidance distress (SAD):	
SAD: stranger (4 items)	"I worry about doing something new in front of other kids."
*SAD: in group (4 items)	"It's hard for me to ask other kids to play with me."
Preference for violent social media	
*Preference for violent media (3 items)	"The pictures in violent social media are interesting." "I like violent social media."
Attitude toward Internet violence	
*Impact on oneself (5 items)	"Violence on the Internet orients people to accept violence as normal."
*Impact on society (5 items)	"The violent scenes on the Internet are informative for society."
Willingness to Buy	
*Willingness to buy (4 items)	"I would consider buying violent social media or be a member of social media that has violent content."

*Items we use for the current study

Participants were high school students from two schools located in different parts of Bangkok, Thailand. Participants filled out questionnaires in a classroom under the supervision of a teacher and handed them in to their teacher. They received a gift in compensation for completing the questionnaire.

Data Analysis. The research participants were 376 students: 210 students from a vocational school in a less affluent area of Bangkok, and 166 students from an elite high school in the central business district of Bangkok. Ninety-five percent of the participants were 16–17 years old. Regarding income, 76.8% of the students from the less affluent school had an average household income of less than 30,000 BHT per month (about $1,000), compared to 9.1% of students from the elite school. The frequency of using online communication, such as chat rooms, bulletin boards, blogs, social network sites, and online games, was similar for both types.

Aggressive traits and SAD have a positive correlation with a preference for violence in online media ($\beta_{aggressive} = .32$; $\beta_{SAD} = .22$; $R^2 = .19$; $F(2, 363) = 45.26$; $p < .001$). Adolescents with aggressive traits and SAD have a higher preference for media violence. Results from the regression analysis also show that preference and attitudes toward the impact of violent media on self significantly affect the willingness to buy violent products among adolescents from both schools ($R^2 = .39$, $F(3, 364) = 76.23$, $p < .001$). Preference for violent media has a significant positive correlation with the willingness to buy violent products among adolescents. Attitude toward the impact of violent media on oneself has a significant negative correlation with the willingness to buy. However, the correlation is not significant for the attitude toward impact of violent media on society as a whole.

These findings support the prediction that aggressive and SAD traits increase the preference for violent online media (Hypothesis 1a and 1b) and that the preference increases the willingness to buy violent online media (Hypothesis 2a) (see Table 16.2). However, we only found a correlation between the preference for and willingness to buy violent media and the attitude toward the impact of violent media on oneself. There was no effect on the impact on society (partial support for Hypotheses 2b and 2c).

TABLE 16.2 Regression Models

Dependent variable	*Independent variable*	β	*p-value*	*F-value*	*R2*
Preference for violent media	Aggressive traits	.32	.00	45.26	.19
	Social avoidance distress (SAD)	.22			
Impact on oneself	Preference for violent media	−.25	.00	23.13	.06
Willingness to buy	Preference for violent media	.62	.00	229.42	.38
	Impact on oneself	−.22	.00	17.60	.04

Conclusion and Continuing Research Program

"Virtual venues"—whether technology devices such as smartphone and laptops or PCs in Internet cafés—have made it more difficult for families, neighborhoods, and communities to protect young people than in the past. Common Internet perils, such as pretending and deception, can be carried over to the offline world, including meeting someone from the Internet offline and using the aggressive social language of the Internet in the offline world. A number of studies also show the carryover effect of violent media consumption in real life. In the short run, it could be by means of mimicry, priming effect, and/or eliciting arousal. In the long run, the repeated exposure increases adolescents' likelihood of engaging in aggressive behavior by causing desensitization or a hostile perception bias.

However, not all adolescents are equally at risk. The current study shows that adolescents with aggressive traits and SAD have a higher preference for media violence and that this preference could lead to the "willingness to buy" violent products online. Thus, close attention could be paid to adolescents with aggressive traits and SAD. The current study also shows that the salience of one's attitude toward the negative impact of violent media on oneself might be able to mitigate the willingness to buy violent media. Understanding ways to prevent adolescents from repeated exposure to violent media requires everyone, particularly parents and educators, to inform adolescents of the consequences for themselves and society of repeatedly viewing violent media. However, reinforcing the impact on viewers among adolescents is not an easy task.

Despite accumulating knowledge of the negative effect of violent media consumption, it is hard to change individual attitudes toward the impact of violent media on oneself. Individuals neglect this information to reduce cognitive dissonance and psychological reaction. Anderson et al. (2010) argued that game players who enjoy playing violent video games may feel uncomfortable about the thought that violent games are harmful. To reduce discomfort, they would rationalize their behavior by adjusting their attitude to be in line with their behavior. In addition, as violent games or media are labeled as forbidden media, adolescents might encounter psychological reactance, which is the desire to have freedom of choice—in this case, the choice to expose themselves to violent media. The threatening message might create reactance by provoking negative thoughts and anger, which affects attitude-behavioral intention consequences (Dillard & Shen, 2005). Hence, when adolescents receive a negative message related to violent media, they might want to reclaim their freedom to choose exposure to such media. Therefore, the message fails to cause an attitude change.

Moreover, adolescence is a period of challenge and adjustment, during which young adults experience identity formation. The view of the self as unique can induce a feeling of invulnerability to negative consequences. Hence, adolescents may feel that they are different from others and that they will not experience negative consequences of violent exposure. This is a phenomenon known as the "third person effect." Hence, helping adolescents resist the temptation of violent media exposure requires collaboration from everyone, through the psychological, sociological, and cultural processes that influence the formation of adolescent attitudes toward the negative impact on themselves when viewing violent media.

An area of future study could involve ways to deliver messages that change adolescent attitudes and behaviors. The way the message is framed or presented could be explored. As parents are likely to be those who interact with children and adolescents while playing violent games, dyadic study of adolescents and parents communication is interesting. Talking to adolescents requires different communication strategies than talking to adults. Consequently, this direction of research should be explored further. Moreover, given that aggressive traits and SAD could lead to a higher preference for violent media, future studies could address ways to reduce these risk factors among adolescents.

References

Anderson, C. A. & Bushman, B. J. (2001). Effects of violent video games on aggressive behavior, aggressive cognition, aggressive affect, physiological arousal, and prosocial behavior: A meta-analytic review of the scientific literature. *Psychological Science*, 12, 353–359.

Anderson, C. A., Shibuya, A., Ihori, N., Swing, E. L., Bushman, B. J., Sakamoto, A., Rothstein., H. R., & Saleem, M. (2010). Violent video game effects on aggression, empathy, and prosocial behavior in eastern and western countries: A meta-analytic review. *Psychological Bulletin, American Psychological Association 2010,* 136 (2), 151–173.

Bandura, A. (2001). Social cognitive theory of mass communication. *Media Psychology,* 3, 265–299.

Bushman, B. J. (1995). Moderating role of trait aggressiveness in the effects of violent media on aggression. *Journal of Personality and Social Psychology,* 69 (5), 950–960.

Bushman, B. J. & Anderson, C. A. (2002). Violent video games and hostile expectations: A test of the general aggression model. *Personality and Social Psychology Bulletin,* 28 (12), 1678–1686.

Bushman, B. J. & Huesmann, L. R. (2006). Short-term and long-term effects of violent media on aggression in children and adolescents. *Archives of Pediatrics & Adolescent Medicine*, 160, 348–352.

Cantor, J. (1998). Children's attraction to violent television programming. In J. H. Goldstein (Ed.). *Why we watch: The attractions of violent entertainment* (88–115). New York: Oxford University Press.

Dillard, J. P. & Shen, L. (2005).On the nature of reactance and its role in persuasive health communication. *Communication Monographs,* 72, 144–168.

Hoffner, C. A. & Levine, J. L. (2005). Enjoyment of mediated fright and violence: A meta-analysis. *Media Psychology,* 7, 207–237.

Huesmann, L. R. (2007). The Impact of electronic media violence: Scientific theory and Research. *Journal of Adolescent Health,* 41, S6–S13.

Huesmann, L. R., Eron, L. D., Klein, R., Brice, P., & Fischer, P. (1983). Mitigating the imitation of aggressive behaviors by changing children's attitudes about media violence. *Journal of Personality and Social Psychology*, 44, 899–910.

Jansz, J. (2005). The emotional appeal of violent video games for adolescent males. *Communication Theory,* 15, 219–241.

Katz, E., Bulmler, J. G., Gurevitch, M. (1973–1974). Uses and gratifications research. *The Public Opinion Quarterly,* 37 (4), 509–523.

Leary, M. R. & Kowalski, R. M. (1995). *Social Anxiety.* New York: Guilford.

Litle, P. & Zuckerman, M. (1986). Sensation seeking and music preferences. *Personality and Individual Differences,* 7 (4), 575–578.

McClure, E. B., Monk, C. S., Nelson, E. E., Parrish, J. M., Adleer, A., Blair, R. J., & Pine, D. S. (2007). Abnormal attention modulation of fear circuit functions in pediatric generalized anxiety disorder. *Archived of General Psychiatry,* 64, 97–106.

Zuckerman, M. (1996). Item revisions in the sensation seeking scale form V (SSS-V). *Personality and Individual Differences,* 20 (4), 515.

17

CURRENT ISSUES AND FUTURE CHALLENGES RELATED TO CONSUMER PRIVACY IN SOCIAL MEDIA

Curtis P. Haugtvedt

We all do it whenever the mood strikes us: morning, noon, and night, when bored in a meeting or a class, in a waiting room, or waiting for our food at a restaurant. Our cell phones, pad devices, and computers have become our constant connection to our students, friends, relatives, and sometimes, even total strangers. We post our comments on current events, likes and dislikes, our aspirations for our future homes or lives. It is perhaps an understatement to say that social media now pervades most aspects of the lives a large majority of consumers across the world.

The social media tools we have become so familiar with are provided to us by companies that at the end of the day hope to make profit for their shareholders. The way this works of course is that all of the information we share on social media (and often in our email) provides marketers and advertisers with insights about our lives. They learn about the people we influence as well as the people and groups who influence us. They learn about the products we have or would like to have. They learn which brands we admire and trust. They learn what moves us to action. They know when and where we are using our devices, how much we spend, how quickly we make up our minds, how satisfied we are with our decisions, and what we want to share with our friends and the world about the products or services we pay for.

Whereas many consumers are aware that some of their activities on computer and other devices are tracked and transfer information that is shared with companies, many are surprised to learn just how much data is sometimes collected and with whom it is shared. With location information employed in combination with other knowledge, marketers can now send special coupons and other incentives for products that are highly contextually relevant. The future of such activities promises to be even more precise, perhaps even going so far as predicting our next purchases.

Marketing professors argue that research has always had the potential to help businesses, consumers, and even society at large. In an ideal world, businesses learn about product needs and wants specific to certain market segments and, if deemed feasible and competitively advantageous, create products and services to meet those wants and needs in a way profitable to the companies but also advantageous to consumers. In what some would now call the "early days of marketing," businesses would gain insights about consumer wants and needs by collecting survey data, conducting focus groups, and a using variety of other common marketing research techniques. Products and services would be developed and test marketed, as would various communication messages designed to inform the consumer about these offerings.

With the advent and prevalent use of the internet and social media tools, the processes have changed a bit. Time to do research and to develop new products and services has become much shorter. Ways of testing product concepts and the various kinds of communications have also changed. The ability to track the effectiveness of various efforts has also improved. Various platforms now can easily track the process that evolves from a consumer first seeing a product in a social media environment to their actual purchase as well as their evaluation of the product during or after use.

Popular media reports and recent books highlight the nature and amount of data collected. In a 2014 TV segment on *60 Minutes*, Steve Kroft describes how various "data brokers" collect and sell information about online activities as well as credit card and other financial transactions (see Data Brokers, 2014). Likewise, in her recent book, Dragnet Nation (2014), Pulitzer Prize winning reporter Julia Angwin describes many ways in which data can be collected on consumers and citizens on a routine basis. In a series of quasi experiments she learns how challenging and costly it can be to try to use modern communication technologies without data being collected (Angwin, 2014).

In a review of recent books on the topic of "big data," Scott Berinato of the Harvard Business Review (Berinato, 2014) discusses things like Google's Nest Thermostat ability to track people's movements to optimize comfort and reduce utility costs or Amazon's Fire smartphone's ability to track pupil and head movements and to even use facial recognition software to categorize the gender, age, and ethnicity of the user. Analysis of a wide variety of data offers promises of better service for customers, greater profitability for companies, as well as insights for new products and services. With more and more connectivity and the advent of the "internet of things," the list of data collection possibilities is indeed long.

Many observers note that the collection and use of data from our social media interactions and the use of other devices also leads to important and potentially game changing issues for marketers, consumers, and regulators. There is a general feeling that changes are on the horizon with regard to the transparency of data collection and use, as well as the amount of control consumers should or could have over their own data (e.g., How long should it be stored? Where should it be stored? Who is responsible for data breaches, etc . . . are also important questions to be considered). Details as to how this may play out over time will be interesting for both marketers and consumers. There are also many considerations regarding differences across various countries that are beyond the scope of the current discussion.

The Future of Social Media Data and Marketing

A 2014 issue of the American Marketing Association newsletter, *Marketing News*, included comments from thought leaders and software developers about what marketing in 2024 might look like. Jonathan Becher, CMO of a software company, is quoted saying: "But the real fight for the future is less about the brand and the content, which is where our heads are now, and more about the data. . . . Right now, as a consumer, we hand over our data for free, essentially, so that marketers can better sell us stuff. Frankly, that's how it works and it is a great trade for me, as a marketer, but as a consumer, it's a pretty lousy balance of equity [. . . if] data is the natural resource of the next generation and it is the thing that we should all be competing over, then my data should belong to me . . . I should be compensated in some way for allowing brands to get access to my data" (p. 37).

Right now, most ads and special promotional materials and notifications are simply displayed to consumers. With increasing interest in privacy, consumers may want to know why they were targeted for specific promotions. Indeed, consumers now have access to tools that alert them to tracking and provide ways to stop the tracking (see https://disconnect.me/). Some marketers and policy makers suggest that there should be greater transparency in targeting, so that consumers are told or have the ability to find out why they are receiving certain promotions. Interesting theoretical and empirical questions might focus on the conditions under which transparency in such promotions might induce greater receptivity of messages from marketers and/or greater loyalty to brands and companies.

In her interview with *60 Minutes*' Steve Kroft, Federal Trade Commissioner Julie Brill stated that she feels most consumers are unaware of the amount and kind of data being collected. In a recent series of presentations, Ms. Brill has been a strong advocate of changes she sees as needed regarding privacy and big data (Brill, 2014). Many of the suggested changes involve greater transparency in data collection and data use.

Some marketers seem to be endorsing the idea of greater transparency as well. In considering 2024, Pete Blackshaw of the Nestle's Social Media company Vevey stated that "in 10 years, brand success will be marked more by adding value or 'servicing' consumer needs. Digital, broadly defined, will open up a world of possibility . . . as consumers go 'beyond the label' . . . such transparency will be woven into all parts of the consumer path to purchase."

Gerd Leonhard of the Futures agency suggests that "If we want to live in a world where marketers can reach us and be effective, and be meaningful, then they also have to respect our permissions and the feeling that we want to protect the little bit of privacy we may have left. Otherwise, we (consumers) will disconnect."

As stated from the outset, we do not have definitive answers to the questions raised by the various issues surrounding privacy. We can be confident, however, that there will be a great deal of debate regarding these issues in the coming years. Persons interested in learning more about the complexities of the issues surrounding privacy are encouraged to review the following online sources.

- http://cyber.law.harvard.edu/events/2015/03/Schneier
- www.ftc.gov/system/files/documents/reports/federal-trade-commission-staff-report-november-2013-workshop-entitled-internet-things-privacy/150127iotrpt.pdf
- www.cbsnews.com/videos/the-data-brokers-selling-your-personal-information/
- www.ftc.gov/system/files/commissioner_brill_top_speeches.pdf
- www.ted.com/talks/alessandro_acquisti_why_privacy_matters
- www.npr.org/2014/09/06/345884282/online-dating-stats-reveal-a-dataclysm-of-telling-trends
- www.washingtonpost.com/opinions/book-review-what-stays-in-vegas-about-personal-data-privacy-by-adam-tanner/2014/08/27/916f5016–224f-11e4–8593-da634b334390_story.html
- www.nytimes.com/2014/11/16/books/review/more-awesome-than-money-by-jim-dwyer.html?_r=0
- www3.weforum.org/docs/WEF_GlobalInformationTechnology_Report_2014.pdf

References

Angwin, J. (2014). *Dragnet nation: A quest for privacy, security, and freedom in a world of relentless surveillance.* New York: Holt, Henry, & Company.

Berinato, S. (2014). Privacy's shrinking future. Retrieved October 2, 2014 from https://hbr.org/2014/08/privacys-shrinking-future.

Brill, J. (2014). Sweet sixteen: Commissioner Brill's 16 most popular speeches. Retrieved October 2, 2014 from www.ftc.gov/system/files/commissioner_brill_top_speeches.pdf.

INDEX